CAMBRI]
HISTORY OF

MW00983311

BENJAMIN CONSTANT
Political Writings

CAMBRIDGE TEXTS IN THE
HISTORY OF POLITICAL THOUGHT

Series editors:

RAYMOND GEUSS *Columbia University*
QUENTIN SKINNER *Christ's College, Cambridge*
RICHARD TUCK *Jesus College, Cambridge*

The series is intended to make available to students the most important texts required for an understanding of the history of political thought. The scholarship of the present generation has greatly expanded our sense of the range of authors indispensable for such an understanding, and the series will reflect those developments. It will also include a number of less well-known works, in particular those needed to establish the intellectual contexts that in turn help to make sense of the major texts. The principal aim, however, will be to produce new versions of the major texts themselves, based on the most up-to-date scholarship. The preference will always be for complete texts, and a special feature of the series will be to complement individual texts, within the compass of a single volume, with subsidiary contextual material. Each volume will contain an introduction on the historical identity and contemporary significance of the text concerned.

Among the first titles in the series will be:

Aristorle, *edited by Stephen Everson*
Cicero, *edited by Miriam Griffin*
Seneca, *edited by John Cooper*
Ockham, *edited by A. S. McGrade*
Machiavelli, *edited by Quentin Skinner and Russell Price*
More, *edited by George Logan*
Luther and Calvin, *edited by Harro Hopfl*
Bodin, *edited by Julian H. Franklin*
Hooker, *edited by A. S. McGrade*
Vindiciae contra tyrannos, *edited by George Garnett*
Grotius, *edited by Richard Tuck*
Milton, *edited by Martin Dzelzainis*
Pufendorf, *edited by James Tully*
Leibniz, *edited by Patrick Riley*
Locke, *edited by Peter Laslett*
Kant, *edited by Hans Reiss*
Diderot, *edited by John Hope Mason and Robert Wokler*
Bentham, *introduction by Ross Harrison*
Fourier and Saint-Simon, *edited by Gareth Stedman Jones*
Hegel, *edited by Allen Wood*
Marx, *edited by Terrell Carver and Joseph O'Malley*
Critical Theory, *edited by Raymond Geuss*
Montesquieu, *edited by Anne Cohler et al.*

BENJAMIN CONSTANT

Political Writings

TRANSLATED AND EDITED BY

BIANCAMARIA FONTANA

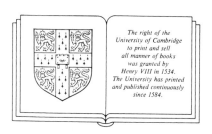

*The right of the
University of Cambridge
to print and sell
all manner of books
was granted by
Henry VIII in 1534.
The University has printed
and published continuously
since 1584.*

CAMBRIDGE UNIVERSITY PRESS

CAMBRIDGE

NEW YORK   NEW ROCHELLE

MELBOURNE   SYDNEY

Published by the Press Syndicate of the University of Cambridge
The Pitt Building, Trumpington Street, Cambridge CB2 1RP
32 East 57th Street, New York, NY 10022, USA
10 Stamford Road, Oakleigh, Melbourne 3166, Australia

First published 1988

Printed in Great Britain by
Redwood Burn Ltd., Trowbridge, Wiltshire

British Library cataloguing in publication data
Constant, Benjamin
The political writings of Benjamin Constant.
1. Political science
I. Title   II. Fontana, Biancamaria
320   JA71

Library of Congress cataloguing in publication data
Constant, Benjamin, 1767–1830
The political writings of Benjamin Constant.
(Cambridge texts in the history of political thought)
Bibliography.
Includes index.
1. Political science – Collected works.
I. Fontana, Biancamaria.   II. Title.   III. Series.
JC179.C6713 1988   320'.092'4   87–24228

ISBN 0 521 303362 (hard covers)
ISBN 0 521 316324 (paper back)

RB

Contents

THE SPIRIT OF CONQUEST AND USURPATION AND THEIR RELATION TO EUROPEAN CIVILIZATION

Part I · The spirit of conquest

Contents

Part II · Usurpation

Contents

Additions to *The spirit of conquest and usurpation*

CHAPTERS ADDED TO THE FOURTH EDITION:

On usurpation

PRINCIPLES OF POLITICS APPLICABLE TO ALL REPRESENTATIVE GOVERNMENTS

Contents

THE LIBERTY OF THE ANCIENTS
COMPARED WITH THAT OF THE MODERNS

Acknowledgements

Etienne Hofmann's work on Constant's early political manuscripts has been of great assistance in preparing the annotation to this volume. My greatest debt, in completing this translation of Constant's political writings, is to John Dunn, who first encouraged me to undertake this project and assisted me throughout its realization; and to George St Andrews, whose patience, literary skill and sensibility have proved invaluable in disentangling the most intricate passages of Constant's prose. I am very grateful to Anthony Pagden, Pasquale Pasquino, Quentin Skinner and Sylvana Tomaselli who read and commented on the Introduction. Finally, I wish to thank Jimmy Burns, John Burrow, Judith Shklar, Gareth Stedman Jones and Salvatore Veca for their help and encouragement during the preparation of this work.

'Pourquoi, je vous prie, m'accuser d'un caractère faible? C'est une accusation à laquelle tous les gens éclairés sont exposés, parce qu'ils voient les deux, ou pour mieux dire, les mille côtés des objets, et qu'ils leur est impossible de se décider, de sorte qu'ils ont l'air de chanceler tantôt d'un côté, tantôt de l'autre.'

Constant to Mme Nassau

x

Introduction

It is surprising that this should be the first English translation of
Benjamin Constant's political writings – indeed of any of his writings
with the exception of the novel *Adolphe*.[a] It is surprising if only because
Constant is one of the few continental thinkers to have gained admission to the eminently Anglo-Saxon sanctuary of the fathers of modern
Western liberalism. It is even more surprising since Constant himself,
who was educated in Scotland and spoke excellent English, was greatly
influenced by, and felt deep affinities with British culture. His friend
Madame de Staël mockingly immortalized this Anglophilia when she
cast him in the role of the admirable, if somewhat splenetic, Lord
Oswald Nevil in her novel *Corinne*.[b]

[a] *Adolphe* was first translated into English during Constant's lifetime by his Edinburgh
friend Alexander Walker: *Adolphe: an anecdote found among the papers of an unknown
person, and published by M. Benjamin de Constant* (London, 1816). For a modern
translation see: *Adolphe*, translated by L. Tancock (Harmondsworth, 1964), repr.
1980.
Some of Constant's pamphlets were translated into English in the early 19th century:

> *The Responsibility of Ministers (De la responsabilité des ministres)*, London, 1815 *(The
> Pamphleteer*, vol. 5)
> *On the Liberty of the Press (De la liberté des brochures)*, London, 1815 *(The Pamphleteer*,
> vol. 6)
> *On the Dissolution of the Chamber of deputies (De la dissolution de la Chambre)*, London,
> 1821 *(The Pamphleteer*, vol. 18)

[b] 'At 25 he despaired of life. His spirit judged everything in advance, and his wounded
sensibility was dead to the illusions of the heart. Nobody was kinder and more
devoted to his friends than he was, whenever he could be of assistance to them. But
nothing caused him any pleasure, not even the good he did to others. He sacrificed
readily and easily his tastes to those of others. Yet generosity was not the only
explanation for his total lack of egoism. This was rather due to a kind of sadness that
prevented him from taking any active interest in his own fate.' A. L. G. de Staël,
Oeuvres complètes (17 vols., Paris, 1820), vol. 8, p. 4. See also the portrait in *Delphine*
of Henri de Lebensei: 'a Protestant gentleman from the Languedoc', who 'had been
educated at Cambridge and had undoubtedly been spoiled by English manners.'
Ibid., vol. 5, p. 287.

We have to turn to the current French editions of Constant's works to realize that being considered a prominent political theorist does not in itself constitute a claim on the reader's attention. During Constant's life, and in the decades following his death, the changing political landscape, combined with his heirs' and survivors' anxieties, kept from the public various segments of his *oeuvre* and correspondence. In the 1950s Constant won a place amongst the classics of the Pléiade. But he was promoted mainly in virtue of his literary gifts, and the political writings in the collection are poorly annotated.[a] More than a hundred and fifty years after his death, there is still no proper French edition of his collected works: a recent move in this direction is due to Swiss scholarship rather than to a French national or celebratory initiative.

The reasons for this unsatisfactory presentation of Constant's writings to the French reading public are apparent enough. They are connected with the highly controversial nature of the historical reflection on the French revolution of 1789 and its impact upon French politics to our day. As François Furet has vividly suggested, throughout the nineteenth and twentieth centuries the revolution has remained the mirror and the constant point of reference for French political debate. It has been impossible at any particular moment in the history of modern France to talk about Jacobins and Girondins, legitimists or Thermidorians, without committing oneself to some current doctrinal cause: revolution or reform, socialism or catholicism, the empire, the Commune or the presidential republic.[b]

In this obsessive re-enactment of the drama of 1789, with its heavily ideological and celebratory atmosphere, Constant could hardly be expected to find a comfortable place. Perhaps his having changed sides in at least one crucial historical circumstance – when he turned from being a vociferous opponent of Napoleon to being his constitutional adviser during the hundred days – may have been forgiven; and even

---

[a] Benjamin Constant, *Oeuvres*, ed. by Alfred Roulin (Paris, 1957). Roulin's edition uses, for the *Principes de politique*, the nineteenth century annotation by Édouard Laboulaye. On the unsatisfactory presentation of Constant's work to the French reading public, see Marcel Gauchet, 'Benjamin Constant: l'illusion lucide du libéralisme', Preface to: *De la liberté chez les modernes* (Paris, 1980), pp. 9–91. There are on the other hand several good editions and translations of Constant's works both in German and Italian. See in particular: Benjamin Constant, *Werke*, ed. by A. Blaeschke and L. Gall, trs. by E. Rechel Mertens (4 vols., Berlin, 1970–2). *Benjamin Constant*, ed. by C. Cordié (Milan, 1946). Benjam Constant, *Conquista e usurpazione*, trs. by Carlo Dionisotti, Preface by Franco Venturi (Turin, 1944), repr. 1983.

[b] François Furet, *Penser la révolution française* (Paris, 1978); English trs., *Interpreting the French Revolution* (Cambridge, 1981).

his consistent political moderation, though somewhat lacking in charm, could have been tolerated, as the distinctive feature of the 'liberal mind'. But the peculiar combination of his sceptical pessimism, mistrust for ideology and genuine cosmopolitanism inevitably placed Constant on the margins of the competition for a French national political identity.

Throughout the nineteenth century the historiography of Constant resembled an ongoing trial, in which his advocates caused at least as much damage as his accusers, withdrawing or manipulating documentary evidence in an attempt to extract from the records either the final proof of his betrayal or some incontrovertible declaration of his faith.[a] Even when the age of the Sainte-Beuves was over, and intellectual historians got out of the habit of constructing political arguments out of people's personal eccentricities or temperament, the literature on Constant retained its accusatory or justificatory tone, while his supporters persevered in their painstaking exercise of ironing out all suspected inconsistencies and contradictions.

Things have considerably improved for Constant since 1945. The experience of the war and the return of despotic and conquering regimes into the heart of Europe revived the significance of his defence of liberty and representative government. More recently, in the last fifteen years or so, the crisis of socialist and liberal ideologies alike has given new meaning to his warnings against the deceptions of revolutionary cant on the one hand and excessive confidence in the resources of market society on the other. Constant's own doubts and oscillations have seemed less the sign of exceptional individual volatility than a reasonable response to the tormented present and uncertain future of modern democracies. As a result of this shift in general political perspective, Constant has been turned into the true representative of 'modern' liberalism, not the simple-minded, crudely utilitarian ideology of triumphant nineteenth-century capitalism, but a

---

[a] Sainte-Beuve, who was close to the de Broglie circle (Mme de Staël's family) and to the *doctrinaires* group, was chiefly responsible for popularizing a damaging private and public image of Constant. See: Charles Augustin Sainte-Beuve, 'Benjamin Constant et Belle de Charrière, Léttres inédites', *Revue des deux mondes*, 14 NS, vol. 6 (15 April 1844), pp. 193–264; 'Benjamin Constant, son *Cours de politique constitutionnelle*' in *Nouveaux lundis* (13 vols., Paris, 1863), vol. 1, pp. 408–34; 'M. Coulmann, Réminiscences', vol. 9, pp. 135–60. See also: Pierre Deguise, *Benjamin Constant méconnu: le livre 'De la religion avec des documents inédits* (Geneva, 1966): 'Comment on crée une légende: Sainte-Beuve et Constant', pp. 3–37.

subtle, sophisticated and sceptical version of that ideology, better suited to the stagnation and gloom of the late twentieth century.[a] This new picture, if more sympathetic to Constant and his work, proves on closer inspection no less artificial, no more historically plausible than that of the pathologically Hamlet-like libertine depicted by Sainte-Beuve. From being the defender of the nebulous and eternal values of 'liberty', 'individual rights' and 'public opinion', Constant has become the symbol of the puzzled and impotent good will of some democrats of our days, unable to understand the world (let alone change it) but determined to uphold their own political respectability. Thus flattened out to a benevolent and ineffective stereotype, prophet by hearsay, Constant's position has considerably improved as far as documentary evidence is concerned. Some losses of course (like his correspondence with Mme de Staël, destroyed by her daughter, Albertine the Duchesse de Broglie, to protect her mother's respectability) will never be repaired. But in the 1970s significant additions have been made by the Constant family to the Lausanne archives. Etienne Hofmann's work on Constant's early political manuscripts offers us a much clearer and more complete picture of his intellectual development and pre-occupations.[b] Moreover, the study and understanding of the French revolution of 1789 and its aftermath has been enriched in the last few years by a series of stimulating new insights and interpretations.

On the whole we are probably better equipped to read Constant than historians have ever been before, with perhaps the sole exception of his own contemporaries: it is a privilege which ought in itself to justify the exercise of our intellectual sympathy.

'I was born on 25 October 1767 at Lausanne, in Switzerland, to Henriette de Chandieu, who was from an old French family that had sought refuge in the region of Vaud for religious reasons and to Juste Constant de Rebeque, colonel in a Swiss regiment in the service of Holland. My mother died in childbed eight days after my birth.'[c] With these words Constant began the account of his life in the famous autobiographical sketch known as the 'Red Notebook'. While Lau-

---

[a] See for example: Larry Siedentop, 'Two liberal traditions' in Alan Ryan (ed.), *The Idea of Freedom, Essays in Honour of Isaiah Berlin* (Oxford, 1979), pp. 153–74; Stephen Holmes, *Benjamin Constant and the Making of Modern Liberalism* (New Haven, 1984).

[b] Etienne Hofmann (ed.), *Les 'Principes de Politique' de Benjamin Constant* (2 vols., Geneva, 1980).

[c] B. Constant, *Le cahier rouge* in *Oeuvres*, pp. 85–133, 87. For a list of biographical studies on Constant see below, pp. 335–6.

sanne was a town with a remarkable intellectual past and some cultural pretensions, the milieu of Constant's family was neither better nor worse than could be expected: a prosperous, solid, unimaginative provincial gentry of old military traditions. Calvinism, to which Constant alludes in relation to his mother's family, was an element of cultural identification, certainly one to which he himself attached great significance.[a]

It was mainly because of his mother's premature death and his father's profession, which forced the latter to reside for prolonged periods abroad, that Benjamin experienced a somewhat eccentric education. After his mother's death he was cared for successively by various female relatives; then by his father's young housekeeper, mistress and later wife, Marianne; subsequently by a series of tutors of whose unedifying habits he left an entertaining, if unreassuring, record. When he was fourteen, his father decided to provide the boy with a more systematic education and in 1782 placed him in the University of Erlangen, in Bavaria. In 1783, after a failed attempt to gain him admission to Oxford (he was still too young to be accepted), Juste sent his son to the University of Edinburgh, where he spent the two most formative years of his education and acquired a number of stimulating intellectual contacts.[b] From Edinburgh Benjamin was then despatched to Paris, where he lived in the house of the worldly intellectual Jean Baptiste Suard, and he finally returned to Switzerland in 1786. These changes of residence were mainly dictated by Juste's increasing inability to exercise any control over his son's life. Guided, or rather led astray, by a careless good nature and a vivid romantic imagination, Benjamin rushed irresponsibly through society life. He soon accumulated an alarming list of unsuccessful or only too successful love affairs, gambling debts, elopements, duels and even one or two soon regretted,

[a] Eugène and Émile Haag, *La France protestante, ou vies des protestants français* (10 vols., Paris, 1847–58), vol. 4; Charles Weiss, *Histoire des refugiés protestants en France* (2 vols., Paris, 1853), vol. 2; William [and Clara de Charrière] de Sévery, *La vie de société dans le Pays de Vaud à la fin du dix-huitième siècle* (2 vols., Lausanne and Paris, 1911–12).

[b] Constant, *Le cahier rouge* in *Oeuvres*, pp. 126–7. Gustave Rudler, *La jeunesse de Benjamin Constant, 1767–1794* (Paris, 1909), p. 163ff.; R. James Mackintosh (ed.), *Memoirs of the Life of the Rt. Hon. Sir James Mackintosh* (2 vols., London, 1835). See also: *History of the Speculative Society of Edinburgh, from its institution in 1764* (Edinburgh, 1845); W. K. Dickson, *The History of the Speculative Society 1764–1904* (Edinburgh, 1905).

[c] On Suard, see: Mme Suard, *Essais de mémoires sur M. Suard* (Paris, 1820); D. J. Garat, *Mémoires historiques sur la vie de M. Suard, sur ses écrits et sur le XVIIIe siècle* (Paris, 1820). For a recent, unflattering portrait see: Robert Darnton, *The Literary Underground of the Old Regime* (Cambridge, Mass., 1982), pp. 3–7.

but luckily very clumsy, attempts at suicide. His correspondence and writings provide an enchantingly candid and ironic record of these adventures.

After his return to Lausanne, he met the first steadying influence in his thus far chaotic life: the novelist Isabelle de Charrière,[a] the author of *Calliste*, a lady from the grand Dutch aristocracy who had married for love her brothers' Swiss tutor. Almost thirty years older than Benjamin, Mme de Charrière took a fancy to him and proved more successful at promoting his intellectual progress than any of the educational institutions patronized by his father. Her house at Colombier, near Neuchâtel, became Benjamin's favourite refuge, and there he began his lifelong, never completed history of religion. In 1787, inspired by Mme de Charrière's eccentric and unconventional views, he attempted to escape from his father's authority by embarking on an adventurous, as well as purposeless, journey through England, which came sadly to an end as soon as his scanty reserves of money were exhausted. Finally, in 1788, Juste, worried about his son's future (and his own position and fortune threatened as the result of a mutiny in his regiment) obtained for him the post of Gentleman of the Chamber at the court of Brunswick, where Benjamin was to remain until 1794.

It is an important and somewhat pardoxical fact about Constant's life that the years of the revolution, with their rapid succession of dramatic experiences, should have been spent by him in this remote and archaic little German court. The muffled echoes of French events did of course reach him there, and like other progressive-minded observers he hesitated between sympathy for the revolutionary cause and horror for the violence it had generated.[b] Oppressed by the boredom of court life, Benjamin married, against the wishes of his father and family, Wilhelmine (Minna) von Cramm, lady-in-waiting to the Duchess of Brunswick. The marriage was very unsuccessful. It ended in a divorce a

---

[a] The correspondence between Constant and Mme de Charrière is at present being published in Mme de Charrière's collected works: Isabelle de Charrière – Belle de Zuylen, *Oeuvres complètes*, ed. by D. Candaux and others (Amsterdam and Geneva, 1979–); for a selection of this correspondence see G. Rudler, *La jeunesse de Benjamin Constant*. See also: Philippe Godet, *Histoire littéraire de la Suisse française* (Geneva, 1890); *Madame de Charrière et ses amis, d'après des nombreaux documents inédits* (1740–1805) (2 vols., Geneva, 1906); Domenico Zampogna, *Benjamin Constant et Belle de Charrière* (Messina, 1969); Roland Mortier, 'Isabelle de Charrière, mentor de Benjamin Constant', Documentieblad, *Werkgroep 18e Eeuw*, 27–9 (1975), pp. 101–40 (Colloque: 'Actualité' d'Isabelle de Charrière', 12–14 September, 1974).

[b] E. Hofmann, *Les 'Principes de Politique' de Benjamin Constant*, ch. 1: 'Benjamin Constant devant le révolution française', vol. 1, pp. 31–77.

few years later, in 1795, not without bitterness and embarrassment, but with little regret on either side. Constant was later to describe the misunderstandings and deceptions of his marital experience in his literary sketch *Cécile*.[b] The divorce, and especially the scandal caused by Benjamin's half-hearted duel with one of his wife's lovers, brought his career at the court of Brunswick to an end, to his great relief. In 1794, harassed and exhausted by the negotiations with his wife's family over the divorce settlement and his attempts to rescue Juste's fortune, he returned to Switzerland and to Colombier. There, at the end of September, he met Anne Louise Germaine de Staël,[b] daughter of the Swiss banker and former minister of France, Jacques Necker.[c]

His encounter with Mme de Staël was probably the most important event in Constant's life. Germaine, the only child of a very rich and famous man, the wife of the Swedish ambassador to Paris and herself a precocious and celebrated authoress, was, at twenty-eight and only a year older than Benjamin, a dazzling and formidable presence. More-over she possessed to the utmost degree those qualities that Benjamin almost pathologically lacked: a very strong will and a great capacity for purposeful activity. She was passionately interested in politics (of which she had acquired early in life an insider's view) and one could hardly imagine her existence away from the centre of the public stage.

[a] B. Constant, *Cécile*, in *Oeuvres*, pp. 135–85. The dating of this work, as well as its relations to *Adolphe*, are controversial, though it was probably written between 1810–12. See: A. Olivier, '*Cécile* et la genèse d'*Adolphe*', *Revue de sciences humaines*, 32 (1967), 5–27; *Benjamin Constant, écriture et conquête du moi* (Paris, 1970); W. Papst, '*Cécile* de Benjamin Constant', *Actes du Congrès de Lausanne*, 1967 (Geneva, 1968), pp. 145–52.

[b] Constant, 'De Mme de Staël et de ses ouvrages' in *Oeuvres*, pp. 825–52; Mme de Staël, *Léttres à Benjamin Constant*, published as *Madame de Staël et Benjamin Constant*, ed. by the Baronne de Nolde (New York and London, 1907); P. Leon (ed.), *Lettres de Mme de Staël à Benjamin Constant* (Paris, 1928); Bengt Hasselrot, *Nouveaux documents sur Benjamin Constant et Mme de Staël* (Copenhagen, 1952). See also: Christopher J. Herold, *Mistress to an Age: a life of Mme de Staël* (Indianapolis, 1958); G. E. Gwynne, *Madame de Staël et la révolution française* (Paris, 1969); Beatrice d'Andlau, *La jeunesse de Mme de Staël* (Geneva, 1970); 'Mme de Staël et l'Europe', *Actes du Colloque de Coppet*, 18–24 July 1966 (Paris, 1970); 'Le Groupe de Coppet', *Actes et documents du deuxième Colloque de Coppet, 1974* (Geneva–Paris, 1977); S. Balayé, *Mme de Staël, lumières et liberté* (Paris, 1979); Ghislain de Diesbach, *Madame de Staël* (Paris, 1983); Renée Winegarten, *Madame de Staël* (Leamington Spa, 1985).

[c] On Necker, see: René Stourm, *Les finances de l'ancien régime et de la révolution* (2 vols., Paris, 1885); Charles Gomel, *Les causes financières de la révolution française* (2 vols., Paris, 1892–93); George Weulersse, *La physiocratie sous les ministères de Turgot et de Necker, 1774–1781* (Paris, 1950); J. F. Bosher, *French Finances, 1770–1795: from business to bureaucracy* (Cambridge, 1970); Henri Grange, *Les idées de Necker* (Lille, 1973); Jean Egret, *Necker Ministre de Louis XVI: 1776–1790* (Paris, 1975); R. D. Harris, *Necker, Reform Statesman of the Ancien Régime* (Berkeley, 1979).

Benjamin succumbed immediately to her brilliant conversation and skilful flatteries. A few days after their first encounter he was ready to follow her to Mézery (her favourite residence at the time, in preference to her parents' château of Coppet, near Geneva) where he spent the winter, as he recalled, boring her to death with protestations of his love.[a] If Mme de Staël was not similarly transported (he had to resort to a theatrical attempt to poison himself to persuade her of his passion) she was sufficiently impressed by his wits and talents to keep him with her when she returned to Paris the following spring. They arrived in the capital on the morning of 25 May 1795, only two days after the repression of the last Jacobin resistance on the part of the Thermidorian Convention.[b]

Constant's arrival in Paris marked the beginning of his public and political career. Thermidorian Parisian society – with its vertiginous social mobility, ostentatious luxury and quick political transformations – was bound to represent a deeply bewildering experience. The majority of Mme de Staël's friends were members of the old aristocracy and belonged to that group of enlightened supporters of the monarchy who, in 1789, had attempted to convert Louis XVI to the cause of constitutional reform. However her *salon* in Rue du Bac brought together royalists and ex-Jacobins, journalists and generals, former *émigrés* and people who had enriched themselves through the purchase of confiscated lands.[c] Constant soon found his way around this confusing environment. He began to write for the press, became one of the founders of the anti-royalist Cercle du Salm, and in the following years produced his first political pamphlets: *De la force du gouvernement actuel*, published in 1796; *Des réactions politiques*, and *De la Terreur* in 1797.[d] In 1798 he undertook the project, soon abandoned, of translating William

---

[a] The circumstances of his first encounter with Mme de Staël are described by Constant in *Cécile*, where she appears as Mme de Malbée: Constant, *Oeuvres*, pp. 150–1.

[b] On the days of Prairial, see: K. D. Tönnesson, *La défaite des sans-culottes: mouvement populaire et réaction bourgeoise en l'an III* (Paris, 1959); see also: I. Woloc, *Jacobin Legacy: the Democratic Movement and the Directory* (Princeton, 1970); Richard Cobb, *The Police and the People: French popular protest, 1780–1820* (Oxford, 1970).

[c] See Constant's witty description of the 'political tribes' who met in Mme de Staël's *salon* in: *Écrits et discours politiques*, ed. O. Pozzo di Borgo (2 vols., Paris 1964), vol. 1, pp. 8–9. On Thermidorian society see: G. Lefebvre, *Les Thermidoriens* (Paris, 1937); F. Furet and D. Richet, *La révolution française* (Paris, 1965), repr. Vervier, 1973, ch. 8: 'Thermidore ou l'impossible oubli', pp. 257–317; M. Lyons, *France under the Directory* (Cambridge, 1975); Denis Woronoff, *La république bourgeoise, de Thermidor à Brumaire, 1794–1799* (*Nouvelle histoire de la France contemporaine*, vol. 3) (Paris, 1972); J. Godechot, *La vie quotidienne en France sous le Directoire* (Paris, 1977).

[d] The last two of these pamphlets are republished in *Écrits et discours politiques*, vol. 1,

Godwin's work on political justice, in which he saw a kind of manifesto for 'moderate' and 'non-violent' Jacobinism.[a] Like most people in Mme de Staël's entourage, Constant foresaw and dreaded the dangers both of a royalist counter-revolution and of a new seizure of power on the part of the Jacobins, and he supported the authority of the Directory as the sole temporary guarantee against the return of factional fury. Unlike his patroness, however, he felt no loyalty towards the fallen monarchy and did not believe in the traditional function of the aristocracy as the custodian of ancient French liberties. He thought that the immediate task of the Directory was to complete and conclude the revolutionary process and promote the transition to a stable representative government with a property-based franchise. For him, as for many of his contemporaries, this belief was associated with the personal ambition to find a place among that newly formed political class which alone could guide this transition to its safe conclusion.[b] Together with most foreigners living in Paris at the time, Constant found his Swiss income greatly boosted by the steep devaluation of the French currency, and he soon joined the ranks of the purchasers of *biens nationaux*. In 1795 he bought the property of Hérivaux, near Luzarches, as a precondition for obtaining French citizenship and qualifying for active political life (this measure was to prove superfluous since Switzerland was annexed in 1798). Constant stood for Geneva in the elections of 11 May 1799, but he was defeated. However, after the coup of 18 Brumaire,[c] Sieyès secured his election to the Tribunate, one of the three chambers created by the constitution of the year VIII. The institution of the Tribunate (originally designed by Rousseau and supported by Cabanis) had not been accompanied by any precise definition of its intended functions. It was a consultative chamber,

---

pp. 20–85 and 93–112. See also: A. L. G. de Staël, *Réflexions sur la paix intérieure* (Paris, 1975); and *Des circonstances actuelles qui peuvent terminer la révolution et des principes qui doivent fonder la république en France*, ed. by Lucia Omacini (Geneva, 1979): this pamphlet, written in 1798 and never published by the author, was drafted with Constant's assistance. On *De la Terreur* see: F. Furet, 'Une polémique thermidorienne sur la terreur', *Passé Présent*, 2 (1983), 44–55.

[a] B. Constant, *De la justice politique: traduction inédite de l'ouvrage de William Godwin*, ed. by Burton R. Pollin (Quebec, 1972). See also: B. Constant, 'De Godwin et de son ouvrage sur la justice politique' in *Mélanges de Littérature et politique* (Paris, 1829), pp. 211–24. Constant abandoned the projected translation when he realized that his views diverged too sharply from Godwin's.

[b] On the formation of the French political class in the early nineteenth century see: Pierre Rosanvallon, *Le moment Guizot* (Paris, 1985).

[c] On Brumaire, see: A. Meynier, *Les coups d'état du Directoire* (3 vols., Paris, 1928), vol. 3: 'Le dix-huit Brumaire et la fin de la République'; A. Ollivier, *Le dix-huit Brumaire* (Paris, 1959).

which discussed the legislative proposals that were subsequently voted on by the Assembly.[a] If it had no real decisional power, the Tribunate put up an extremely brave fight, resisting Bonaparte's pressures to dismantle the representative system. This resistance could hardly last for long. Soon the fragile compromise between the First Consul's personal ambitions and Sieyès' attempts to maintain a functioning constitutional system collapsed. In 1802 Constant was expelled from the Tribunate, together with other leading members of the opposition.[b] He sold his property at Hérivaux to retreat into semi-voluntary exile, which lasted until the arrival of the Coalition troops in Paris in 1814. These twelve years of retreat from public life were particularly troubled and restless ones. They were spent in almost continuous travel, following Mme de Staël's impatient peregrinations, with only short intervals of residence in Paris, at his newly acquired estate of Les Herbages (this too near Luzarches)[c] or at Coppet. Particularly important were two prolonged visits to Germany, at Weimar in 1803–4, and at Göttingen, Brunswick and Hanover in 1812–13. These visits familiarized Constant with German Romantic culture and led him to form personal contacts with its most influential exponents.[d] The years of exile also saw the deterioration of his stormy, if intellectually very fruitful, liaison with Mme de Staël, and his renewed, if feeble attempts to detach himself from her: a task that proved extremely arduous even after his secret marriage to Charlotte von Hardenberg in 1808.[e]

Despite this dense atmosphere of sentimental drama and the disruption caused by a series of personal losses (Necker, to whom he was very close, died in 1804, Mme de Charrière in 1805, Juste Constant in 1812) it is in this period that Constant produced the most significant

---

[a] On the Tribunate, see Jean Jacques Rousseau, *The Social Contract*, ed. by G. D. H. Cole (London, 1903), Book 4, Ch. 5: 'The Tribunate', pp. 106–8; Pierre Jean Georges Cabanis, *Quelques considérations sur l'organisation sociale en général particulièrement sur la nouvelle constitution* (Paris, 1799). See also: J. Godechot (ed.), *Les Constitutions de la France depuis 1789* (Paris, 1979), pp. 143–50; J. Bourdon, *La Constitution de l'an VIII* (Rodez, 1941); Charles Durand, *L'exercice de la fonction législative de 1800 à 1814* (Aix-en Provence, 1955).

[b] With Constant were expelled amongst others: Jean-Baptiste Say, Charles Ganilh, Marie-Joseph Chénier, Pierre Daunou, Pierre-Louis Guinguené.

[c] Constant sold this property in 1810 to pay his gambling debts.

[d] On Constant and German culture the best recent source is: Kurt Kloocke, *Benjamin Constant: une biographie intellectuelle* (Geneva, 1984). See also: A. L. G. de Staël, *De l'Allemagne* in *Oeuvres complètes*, vols. 10–11; repr. ed. by S. Balayé and J. de Pange (Paris, 1958–60); Helene Ullmann, *Benjamin Constant und seine Beziehungen zum deutschen Geistesleben* (Marburg, 1915); Lothar Gall, *Benjamin Constant: seine politische Ideenwelt und der deutsche Vormärz* (Wiesbaden, 1963).

[e] The best source on this tangled sentimental drama is Constant's journal; see: *Journaux intimes* in *Oeuvres*, pp. 223–640.

part of his *oeuvre*. In 1802 he began his outline of a project for a republican constitution in a large state,[a] and in 1806 he completed the first draft of the comprehensive treatise on politics, which was later to evolve into the *Principes de politique* of 1815 published in this collection.[b] During his visits to Germany he continued his researches on religion, which relied quite heavily on German sources.

In 1806 Constant wrote the novel *Adolphe*, probably more inspired by Goethe's work and German Romantic literature than by his own troubled relations with his second wife, Charlotte von Hardenberg, and the Englishwoman Anna Lindsay: yet fear of its real or apparent autobiographical implications led him to delay its publication for several years.[c] Finally in 1807 he produced a French adaptation of Schiller's tragedy *Wallenstein*.[d] In 1813, when Napoleon's power seemed on the point of collapse, Constant published in Hanover the two pamphlets *The Spirit of Conquest* and *Usurpation* collected in this volume, a sweeping attack on the emperor's military regime. In the same period he formed close contacts with the former Bonapartist general, now Prince Royal of Sweden, Charles Bernadotte. Following his somewhat implausible elevation as heir to the Swedish crown, Bernadotte harboured the ambition to put forward his candidature for the French throne, in the eventuality of the deposition of Napoleon by the victorious armies of the Coalition, and he seems to have used Constant as his political adviser. To what extent Constant himself judged Bernadotte's aspirations realistic and what relevance he attached to his own role as counsellor is a matter of contention. It is a fact that he joined Bernadotte in Brussels and followed his troops to Paris, although he denied allegations in the French press that he was doing so as the Prince Royal's private secretary.[e] Bernadotte's hopes were soon shattered by the restoration of the Bourbon monarchy. In Paris, Constant

[a] 'Fragments d'un ouvrage abandonné sur la possibilité d'une constitution républicaine dans un grand pays', Paris, Bibliothèque Nationale, Nouvelles acquisitions françaises, 14363–4.
[b] See footnote *b* p. 4.
[c] *Adolphe* has been the object of many more studies than any other of Constant's works. For a general orientation see: P. Delbouille, *Genèse, structure et destin d'Adolphe'* (Paris, 1971); and also: G. Rudler, *'Adolphe' de Benjamin Constant* (Paris, 1935); Frank P. Bowman, 'Nouvelles lectures d'*Adolphe*', *Annales Benjamin Constant*, I (1980), 27–42.
[d] B. Constant, *Wallstein, tragédie en cinq actes et en vers, précédée de Quelques réflections sur le théâtre allemand* (Geneva and Paris, 1809), repr. ed. by Jean-René Derré (Paris, 1965). Carlo Cordié, 'Il Wallstein di Benjamin Constant nelle testimonianze dell'autore e di alcuni suoi contemporanei' in *Studi in onore di Carlo Pellegrini* (Turin, 1963), pp. 411–54. B. Boschenstein, 'Wallstein et Wallenstein', *Actes du troisième Colloque Coppet, 1980* (Oxford, Voltaire Foundation, 1982), pp. 229–42.
[e] B. Constant, *Lettres à Bernadotte. Sources et origine de 'L'esprit de conquête et de L'usur-*

resumed his journalistic activity. Yet, quite characteristically, at the time when his desire for active political life was close to realization, he became totally absorbed in the last, and probably most theatrical and destructive of all his passions: he fell in love with the beautiful and elusive Juliette Récamier, who received his frantic courtship with prudent detachment. His letters to her are probably as representative a document of Romantic literary taste and sensibility as *Adolphe*.[a] Herself very pious and involved in occult practices, Juliette succeeded in communicating to her disappointed lover some of her spurious mysticism, although the nature of his own beliefs remained to the end of his life somewhat vague and uncertain.

When Napoleon's imminent arrival in Paris was announced after his escape from Elba, Constant, who had just published a series of violent articles in which he compared the exiled emperor to Attila and Genghis Khan, considered the possibility of retreating again into exile, but was held back by his reluctance to be separated from Mme Récamier. On his return to the Tuileries, Napoleon overcame his first impulse to have Constant arrested, and invited him instead to collaborate in drafting the new constitutional foundations of the empire. Constant's willingness to assist him is not very surprising if we consider not only the almost hypnotic force of Napoleon's personality, but, more importantly, the obvious lack of appeal of the existing political alternatives, and Constant's own repugnance for a restoration of the Bourbons effected through the intervention of foreign armies. After Napoleon's final defeat, Constant gave a persuasive account of his personal and political motives in this episode in the *Mémoires sur les Cent-Jours*.[b] In the framework of Napoleon's attempt to rescue his empire through the concession of constitutional guarantees, Constant was charged with the drafting of the *Acte additionnel aux constitutions de l'empire*, the

pation, ed. by B. Hasselrot (Geneva, 1952); Franklin Scott, 'Bernadotte and the throne of France, 1814', *Journal of Modern History*, 5 (1933), 465–78; 'Benjamin Constant's "Project" for France in 1814', *ibid.*, 7 (1935), 41–4; 'Propaganda activities of Bernadotte, 1813–14' in D. Mckay (ed.), *Essays in the History of Modern Europe* (New York, 1936), pp. 16–30; Norman King, 'La candidature de Bernadotte', *Europe*, 467 (March, 1968), 85–92.

[a] B. Constant, *Lettres de Benjamin Constant à Madame Récamier, 1807–1830*, ed. by Louise Colet (Paris, 1864); 'Fragments des mémoires de Mme Récamier' in *Oeuvres*, pp. 931–48. See also: A. L. G. de Staël, *Lettres à Mme Récamier*, ed. by E. Beau de Loménie (Domat, 1952); Edouard Herriot, *Souvenirs et correspondence de Mme Récamier* (2 vols., Paris, 1859); and his *Mme Récamier, les amis de sa jeunesse et sa correspondence intime* (Paris, 1872).

[b] B. Constant, *Mémoires sur les Cent-Jours, en forme de lettres* (Paris, 1820–2). Louis XVIII was amongst those who found Constant's self-defence fully convincing.

constitution also known as the 'Benjamine'. Although it was the product of a compromise between Constant's views and Napoleon's demands, and though it was never implemented, the *Acte additionnel* remains a model legislative design for a constitutional monarchy with a property-based, but comparatively extensive franchise.[a]

In 1815, confident in his newly acquired position as adviser to the emperor, Constant finally published the *Principes de politique*, giving to his previous speculations on political theory the form of a proposal for the further improvement of the existing constitution. With the return of the Bourbons, his collaboration with the fallen government caused him to be exiled once again. In January 1816 he left with Charlotte for London, where he remained until the following summer, when it became clear that Louis XVIII would behave with moderation towards his political opponents. This last visit to England – which he found sadly changed from the fascinating and adventurous land of his youth[b] – marked the beginning of an entirely new period in Constant's life. At the time of his departure, he had finally resigned himself to the failure of his passion for Mme Récamier. On his return he had to face the loss of Mme de Staël, who died in 1817, after rejecting his repeated attempts to bring about a final reconciliation. Significantly it was during this English visit that Constant finally resolved to publish *Adolphe*, thus consigning to literature the heritage of his turbulent and romantic past.

His last years, from 1817 to 1830, were spent in intense writing and the hectic routine of a busy public life (this in spite of his declining health and the permanent injury sustained in a riding accident in 1818). It was in this period, through the relentless fight against the increasingly reactionary Bourbon rule, that Constant made his contribution to the shaping in France of a regular parliamentary opposition of the English type. On his return from exile he resumed his contribution to the *Mercure de France*. Subsequently, when this was closed by the government in 1818, he wrote for the *Minerve Française*, also suppressed after the assassination of the Duke of Berry in 1820.[c] At the same time he

[a] 'Acte Additionnel aux Constitutions de l'Empire du 22 avril 1815' in *Les Constitutions de la France depuis 1789*, ed. J. Godechot, pp. 225–39. On the 'Acte' see: Charles Lajoux, *Les rapports du gouvernement et des Chambres dans l'Acte Additionnel aux Constitutions de l'Empire du 1815* (Paris, 1903); Léon Radiguet, *L'Acte Additionnel aux Constitutions de l'Empire du 22 avril 1815* (Caen, 1911); R. Warlomont, 'La représentation économique dans l'Acte Additionnel aux Constitutions de l'Empire (1815)' in *Revue internationale d'histoire politique et constitutionnelle*, 15 (1954), 244–56 and *Revue du Nord*, Lille, 37, N° 145 (1955), 81–2.

[b] B. Constant, *Journaux intimes* in *Oeuvres*, pp. 773–85.

[c] B. Constant, *Recueil d'articles: 'Le Mercure', 'La Minerve' et 'La Renommée,'* ed. by E.

began the publication of his collected political writings under the title: *Cours de politique constitutionnelle.*[a]
In 1819 he was elected representative for the Sarthe.[b] He lost his seat in 1822, devoted the following years to the publication of a commentary on the work of Filangieri,[c] and of his work on religion,[d] and was re-elected in Strasbourg in 1827.

He died in 1830, during the Orleanist revolution, in which he had played a prominent role as leading representative of the parliamentary opposition and later, member of the Conseil d'État, and which can be described perhaps as his major political success. The socialist leader, Louis Blanc, recalled having been among a crowd of students who, at Constant's state funeral on 12 December, clamoured unsuccessfully to obtain for him the honour of solemn burial in the Panthéon.[e]

The revolution of 1789 – its causes, its implications, its effects – this tangled set of events in which, as we have seen, he had no direct part, was bound to occupy all of Constant's work until the end of his life. In the first instance the revolution was of course a crushing political reality and, like most of his contemporaries, Constant spent his entire life dealing with its practical consequences. But, more importantly, the revolution marked a turning point in the history of social experience and created his pressing need to interpret this change effectively and to adjust to it. This does not mean that revolutionary French society differed beyond recognition from the society of the *ancien régime*. The transition from one to the other was a slow and complex process, hardly concluded in Constant's own lifetime. Moreover it was a transition

Harpaz (2 vols., Geneva, 1972); see also, B. Constant, *Recueil d'articles, 1795–1817*, ed. by E. Harpaz (Geneva, 1978).

[a] *Collection complète des ouvrages publiées sur le Gouvernement representatif et la Constitution actuelle de la France, formant une espèce de Cours de politique constitutionnelle* (4 vols., Paris, 1818–19); the Third edition (2 vols., Paris 1861) is edited and annotated by Edouard Laboulaye, with some significant alterations in the selection of texts.

[b] On Constant's activity in this period see: E. Harpaz (ed.), *Benjamin Constant et Goyet de la Sarthe, correspondence, 1818–1822* (Geneva, 1973).

[c] B. Constant, *Commentaire sur l'ouvrage de Filangieri* (4 vols., Paris, 1822–4). This text contains Constant's most extensive reflection on political economy and economic issues.

[d] *De la religion considérée dans sa source, ses formes et ses développements* (4 vols., Paris, 1824–31). See also the posthumous *Du polythéisme romain considéré dans ses rapports avec la philosophie grecque et la religion chrétienne*, ed. by M. J. Matter (2 vols., Paris, 1833); *De la religion, Livre premier*, ed. by P. Deguise (Lausanne, 1971); *Deux chapitres inédits de "l'Esprit des religions"*, 1803–1804, ed. by Patrice Thompson (Geneva, 1970).

[e] Louis Auguste Blanqui, 'Aux étudiants en médecine et en droit' (Paris, 1830); A. Augustin-Thierry, 'Les funérailles d'Adolphe', *Le Temps*, Paris, 19 December 1830, p. 2; Louis Dumont-Wilden, 'Benjamin Constant et la Révolution française de

which had been anticipated and perceived long before the events of 1789. But with the revolution a complete break with the past, the unmistakable advent (for better or worse) of a new age, became part of people's collective consciousness and decisively shaped their historical identity. The riddle that Constant thus confronted, beneath the surface of political events, was that of modernity, what made his own (and in many respects still our own) age irreparably different from any other, and of the ways in which this difference pervaded all aspects of human experience.

Before the revolution, in the 1780s, Constant had developed an interest in the history of ancient Greece,[a] and had undertaken a comparative study – which he was to pursue throughout his life – on the nature of religious belief in the pre-Christian world and in the culture of modern Europe. This comparative approach to the study of human society and civilization featured very prominently in the contributions of several writers of the Enlightenment such as (to mention those by whom Constant was more directly influenced) Montesquieu, Rousseau, Smith, Hume and Gibbon. In their works Constant found not only an imposing mass of historical and quasi-anthropological information, but, more crucially, some decisive insights into the understanding of modernity.[b] The most influential and articulated of these insights was probably the one offered by the writers in the tradition of Scottish political economy (especially Hume, Smith and Dugald Stewart) to which Constant was exposed during his visit to Edinburgh in the early 1780s.[c] In their approach, the transition to the new age was identified with the growth of free market relations, the development of the international division of labour and, associated with these, the

1830', *Flambeau* (Brussels), 13 (1930), 343–8; David H. Pinkney, *The French Revolution of 1830* (Princeton, 1972), pp. 337–8.

[a] In 1787 Constant published the *Essai sur les moeurs héroïques de la Grèce* (Paris), a translation of part of John Gillies, *The History of Ancient Greece, its colonies and conquests, from the earlier accounts till the division of the Macedonian Empire in the East* (London, 1786). See G. Rudler, *La jeunesse de Benjamin Constant*, pp. 181–3.
[b] Roland Mortier, 'Constant et les lumières', *Europe*, 467 (March 1968), 5–18. See also Constant's judgement on Montesquieu in his journal, 28 January 1804, *Oeuvres*, p. 227.
[c] On the Scottish theories of commercial society, see: Duncan Forbes, *Hume's Philosophical Politics* (Cambridge, 1975); 'Sceptical Whiggism, Commerce and Liberty' in A. S. Skinner, T. Wilson (eds), *Essays on Adam Smith* (Oxford, 1975), pp. 179–201; Nicholas Phillipson, 'The Scottish Enlightenment' in R. Porter, M. Teich (eds), *The Enlightenment in National Context* (Cambridge, 1981); J. G. A. Pocock, *The Machiavellian Moment* (Princeton, 1975); I. Hont, M. Ignatieff, (eds), *Wealth and Virtue: Political Economy in the Scottish Enlightenment* (Cambridge, 1983). See also: J. W. Burrow, *Gibbon* (Oxford, 1985).

emergence of the middling ranks and of free public opinion, which resulted in the subversion of traditional beliefs and social bonds. The political economists were relatively unsentimental about the moral consequences of market society: they expected the new commercial relations to bring about the erosion of those human values normally associated with community life and civic virtue; they also anticipated the growth of luxury and corruption and the development of greater social inequality. Yet they thought that, on balance, modern commercial society was preferable to the ancient ones, where the promotion of public virtue and military values among the citizens was made possible only by slaves, who did the work necessary for the subsistence of the society itself.[a] This view of the modern condition contrasted sharply with that presented by writers such as Rousseau, who saw in the progress of civilization the increasing enslavement of man to artificially created needs.[b] Unlike him, the theorists of commercial society thought the slavery of needs an acceptable and fruitful bondage when compared with other traditional forms of oppression. In Constant's own words, when the *philosophes* claimed that life was more tolerable in the forests of the Orinoco than in the France of the *ancien régime*, they were simply guilty of a rhetorical exaggeration, which betrayed the profound moral uneasiness and *malaise* of their own age.[c]

If the political economists had elaborated a somewhat pessimistic, but fundamentally positive conception of modern society, one by which Constant himself was decisively influenced, they had devoted on the whole little attention to the political implications of their model. They more or less implicitly assumed that, where commercial development was not simply blocked by an oppressive and backward power, the transformation of civil society would in due course bring about the necessary institutional changes. Moreover, an absolute government (such as that of pre-revolutionary France) could prove as favourable to the development of commercial society and to social peace, as a free constitutional government of the English type. When Constant, after his arrival in Paris in the mid-1790s, began to think seriously about politics and picked up the threads of his past reflections on the devel-

---

[a] I. Hont, M. Ignatieff, 'Introduction' to *Wealth and Virtue*.

[b] On Rousseau see: Judith N. Shklar, *Men and Citizens: a Study of Rousseau's Social Theory* (Cambridge, 1969); Robert Derathé, *Jean Jacques Rousseau et la science politique de son temps* (Paris, 1970).

[c] B. Constant, 'De M. Dunoyer et de quelques-uns de ses ouvrages' in *Mélanges*, pp. 128–62, pp. 155–6. This essay is reprinted in M. Gauchet (ed.), *De la liberté chez les modernes*, ed. M. Gauchet (Paris, 1980), pp. 543–62 and in *De la perfectibilité de l'espèce humaine*, ed. by Pierre Deguise (Lausanne, 1967), pp. 66–95.

opment of civilization, he was bound to be struck by the limits of this vision. By contrast with the political economists' faith in the solidity of commercial progress, the revolution had shown only too patently that the entire edifice of modern society could be violently brought down by the failure of its political institutions.

Constant was convinced that the causes of the 1789 revolution were overwhelmingly political. No doubt class conflicts, famine and financial crisis had played their role: yet the economic conditions of France were not especially disastrous. The collapse had been caused only by the combined failure of all the traditional sources of authority: by the 'feeble and corrupt' monarchy, by a clergy 'affecting incredulity while professing traditional cant'; by a magistrature 'of unlimited pretensions'; by a nobility torn between its enlightened aspirations and its attachment to traditional privileges. Modern commercial society was not, in the long run, compatible with even enlightened despotism: the intrinsic weakness of the modern French state lay precisely in its absolutist origins. The real authors of the revolution were not Marat and Robespierre, but Richelieu, Mazarin and Louis XIV. Terror itself was no new barbarism but simply the heritage of the wars of religion, while Louis XVI had paid with his life for the *dragonnades* and the systematic slaughter of the Protestants undertaken by his ancestors.[a] If such were the causes of the revolution, the primary target was to secure the stability of political agency and political institutions by adapting them to the ethos and needs of the new commercial age.

This did not mean simply that modern society must, ideally, respect free trade and the rules of the international market: the political economists were indeed right in believing that any absolute government could do this very effectively if it only had the right advisers and chose to do so. Neither did it mean that some forms of government were in principle more desirable than others. It meant instead that any government, in order to be suited to the new commercial order, must genuinely acknowledge and respect that kind of liberty which is characteristic of and indispensible to the modern condition. Any violation of this liberty (in the form of religious or political persecution, the suppression of freedom of speech, etc.) would in fact undermine, even in an otherwise well-ordered society, the whole edifice of modernity.

---

[a] B. Constant, 'Fragments sur la France du 14 juillet 1789 au 31 mars 1814' in *Mélanges*, pp. 75–92, repr. in *Oeuvres*, pp. 816–25. Constant's judgement on the causes of the revolution was greatly influenced by Jacques Necker, *De la révolution française* (4 vols., Geneva, 1797); and A. L. G. de Staël, *Considérations sur la révolution française* in *Oeuvres complètes*, vols. 12–14; repr. ed. by J. Godechot (Paris, 1983).

But what did the new, 'modern' type of liberty consist of? Constant had been particularly struck by one paradoxical feature of the French revolutionary experience. The Jacobin government had vociferously proposed itself as the instrument of the total renovation of French society, not only through the introduction of a new constitution and new laws, but through the complete transformation of social relations and of the public and private moral beliefs of the French people. Yet the example which inspired this innovatory change was in itself far from new: it was in fact simply borrowed from the tradition of classical antiquity and from the Greek and Roman ideals of courage, patriotism and civic virtue. The rhetoric of the revolutionary movement was saturated with classical imagery and classical models.[a] In Constant's eyes, this revival of Sparta and Rome in late eighteenth-century France appeared not only self-evidently absurd, but, in the light of the Jacobin experience, also an unjustifiable and dangerous folly.[b] Constant's perception of ancient society, chiefly influenced by the views of Montesquieu and Hume,[c] also relied upon his friend Simonde de Sismondi's extensive reconstruction of the development of free political institutions in the West presented in his manuscript work: 'Recherches sur les constitutions des peuples libres' for which, Constant himself had, around 1801–2 unsuccessfully attempted to find a publisher.[d]

In Constant's account, the city-states of classical antiquity were comparatively small communities, with little scope for economic activity, where slaves did the essential work and where the citizens could therefore devote all their time and energies to military life and public service. Moreover in these communities, because of the narrow range of choices and opportunities open to each individual, and the low

---

[a] Harold T. Parker, *The Cult of Antiquity and the French Revolutionaries: a study in the Development of the Revolutionary Spirit* (Chicago, 1937); Luciano Guerchi, *Libertà degli antichi e libertà dei moderni: Sparta, Atene e i 'Philosophes' nella Francia del settecento* (Napoli, 1979).

[b] The Spirit of Conquest and Usurpation, part 2, ch. 7, 'Modern imitators of the republics of antiquity', pp. 105–9 of this edition.

[c] David Hume, *Essays, Literary, Moral, Political* (London, 1903), 'Of Civil Liberty', pp. 89–97; 'Of the Populousness of Ancient Nations', pp. 381–451; Charles Louis de Secondat de Montesquieu, *De l'esprit des lois*, Book 4, ch. 8: 'Explication d'un paradoxe des anciens par rapport aux moeurs', *Oeuvres complètes*, 2 vols., ed. by Roger Caillois (Paris, 1951), vol. 2 pp. 270–3. See also: Norman Hampson, *Will and Circumstance: Montesquieu, Rousseau and the French Revolution* (London, 1983), p. 5.

[d] Marco Minerbi, 'Introduzione' to J. C. L. S. de Sismondi, *Recherches sur les Constitutions des peuples libres* (Geneva, 1965), pp. 7–75.

degree of social mobility, the citizens were subjected to the constant control of the political authority and of the community as a whole. Thus individuals enjoyed a much greater share in public affairs than the citizens of modern states, but they were also much more severely limited in the exercise of their faculties and in their individual choices.[a] In modern European societies this pattern was reversed: communities were much larger, the majority of the citizens, since the abolition of slavery, devoted most of their energies to the production of material wealth and the satisfaction of their collective needs. They had consequently little opportunity to serve the state on a full-time basis and hardly any incentive to engage in military pursuits. For them commerce had replaced war as a means of acquiring material goods.[b] They were, on the other hand, independent of social authority as well as remarkably mobile and flexible in their personal choices.[c]

In sketching this comparison between ancient and modern ideas of liberty – which emerged as a central theme in his political writings – Constant felt profoundly ambivalent as to the respective merits of each. He did not find it difficult to understand why the Jacobins had thought the example of ancient liberty, with its egalitarian and heroic undertones, so utterly invigorating. Nor did he feel unsympathetic towards those critics of the modern condition, such as Rousseau, who depicted contemporary society as dominated by selfishness and greed, enslaved to artificially created needs and ultimately destructive of all spontaneous and generous feelings. Indeed in his writings, especially in *Adolphe*, Constant denounced most forcefully the falsity, sufferings and moral impoverishment of the modern age. Yet he also felt very strongly that living in the present was hardly a matter of choice: as Rousseau himself had only too convincingly shown, modern society was a reality from which there was no viable escape. By the end of the eighteenth century, the old *querelle* of the ancients and the moderns had ceased to be a subject for intellectual and academic dispute and pointed instead to a dramatic historical trauma and a vital political choice. In Constant's view, what remained indefensible, and in the last instance

---

[a] See *The Spirit of Conquest and Usurpation*, Part 2, ch. 6: 'The kind of liberty offered to men at the end of the last century', pp. 102–5 below.

[b] Ibid. Part 1, ch. 2: 'The character of modern nations in relation to war', pp. 52–5 of this edition.

[c] Ibid. Part 2, ch. 18: 'Causes which make despotism particularly impossible at this stage of our civilization', pp. 140–2 of this edition. See also E. Hofmann (ed.), *Les 'Principes de Politique,'* vol. 2, pp. 419–55: 'De l'autorité sociale chez les anciens'.

criminally irresponsible, in the political understanding of the Jacobins was their incapacity to confront the present, their illusion that the advantages of the modern condition might be enjoyed without questioning the most comforting aspects of traditional political imagination. Unsurprisingly violence and terror had proved necessary to enforce the virtues of antiquity upon the reluctant population of a modern commercial state.[a]

In appropriating the heritage of the revolution, Napoleon had carried the anachronism even further: discarding the civic traditions of the ancients he had attempted to emulate instead their military vocation and their appetite for conquest. Thus, after burying an entire generation of Numas and Solons, who had murdered one another in the name of fraternity and justice, France witnessed the exploits of a new Alexander or Caesar, who proceeded to destroy the peaceful commercial *entente* among European nations.[b]

The ideological as well as practical failure of the Jacobins, combined with the equally anachronistic pretensions of the Bourbon monarchy and the Napoleonic empire, betrayed the limitations of traditional political understanding. The revolution had, in other words, exposed the relative poverty of existing political models. The most significant contributions to Western political theory had in fact been elaborated before the full establishment of the new commercial age. Although some insights and principles retained their full validity, there were other respects in which these needed to be adapted to the new socioeconomic conditions of the modern European states. While in England the stability of political institutions suggested the overwhelming continuity of constitutional principles, in the case of France the collapse of the absolute monarchy had reopened the question of the foundations of sovereignty and the social contract. Thus, moving from the experience of post-revolutionary reconstruction, Constant's own reflection focused in particular upon the nature of political representation in modern commercial states.

In his account of modern liberty, Constant had argued that in advanced commercial society the citizens devoted most of their time to the production of wealth, thus leaving little scope for individual participation in public life. Moreover, the large size of these communities

---

[a] E. Hofmann (ed.), *Les 'Principes de Politique,'* pp. 437–44: 'Des imitateurs modernes des républiques de l'antiquité'.

[b] The Spirit of Conquest and Usurpation, Part 1, ch. 15: 'Results of the system of warfare in the present age', pp. 81–3 of this edition.

made contacts between individual citizens and the central authority extremely slight and remote, and the technicalities of government very complex and difficult to master. (The case of the small Swiss city-states, such as Geneva and Lausanne, was the exception which proved the rule.) In such circumstances, the citizens were bound to delegate political decisions to a small minority of the prominent members of the community and to professional politicians.[a] Eighteenth-century reflection upon the nature of this type of representation had, however, already extensively explored the difficulties it involved.[b] Either the delegates had no autonomy and could only carry out the instructions of the social and geographical group which they represented: in this case it proved almost impossible to reach a mediation among the interests of competing groups because the delegates had no power to negotiate. (The States General were an interesting example of this so-called 'imperative' mandate, which in 1789 had resulted in the total paralysis of political decisions.)[c] Alternatively, the representatives were independent of those who had elected them and acted according to their own judgement: in this case their political action could be effective, but

[a] The liberty of the ancients compared with that of the moderns, pp. 307–28 of this edition (*Courts de politique constitutionnelle*, Paris, 1818–19, vol. 4, p. 269).

[b] On the debate on political representation in Britain see: P. A. Gibbons, *Ideas of Political Representation in Parliament 1651–1832* (Oxford, 1914); Edward and Anne Porritt, *The Unreformed House of Commons: Parliamentary Representation before 1832* (Cambridge, 1903); Sir Lewis Namier, *The Structure of Politics at the Accession of George III* (2nd edn, London, 1957); G. S. Veitch, *The Genesis of Parliamentary Reform* (London, 1913); S. H. Beer, 'The representation of interests in British Government', *American Political Science Review*, 51 (September 1957), 619–30; John Cannon, *Parliamentary Reform 1640–1832* (Cambridge, 1973); D. C. Moore, *The Politics of Deference – a Study of the Mid-Nineteenth Century English Political System* (New York, 1976); J. C. D. Clark, *English Society 1688–1832* (Cambridge, 1986). In France: A. Ameline, *L'idée de souveraineté d'après les écrivains français du XVIIIe siècle* (Paris, 1904); Léon Cahen, *Condorcet et la révolution française* (Paris, 1904); Frank Alengry, *Condorcet, guide de la révolution française* (2 vols., Paris, 1904); Henri Sée *L'évolution de la pensée politique en France au XVIIIe siècle* (Paris, 1925); Roland Mousnier, 'Comment les français du XVIIe siècle voyaient la constitution', *XVIIe Siècle*, 256 (1955), 9–36. See also: Furio Diaz, *Filosofia e politica nel 700 francese* (Turin, 1973); John Lough, *The 'Philosophes' and Post-Revolutionary France* (Oxford, 1982).

[c] The literature on the States General of 1789 is immense. For a general orientation see A. Cobban, *A History of Modern France* (2 vols., Harmondsworth, 1981) (First edn, 1957), vol. 1: 1715–1799; see also: P. Renouvin, *Les assemblées provinciales de 1787: origines, développements, résultats* (Paris, 1921); Henri Carré, *La fin des parlements* (Paris, 1912); Jean Egret, *La pre-révolution française, 1787–88* (Paris, 1962); M. Vovelle, *La chute de la monarchie, 1787–92* (Paris, 1972); R. K. Gooch, *Parliamentary Government in France – The Revolutionary Origins 1789–1791* (New York, 1960); W. Doyle, 'Was there an aristocratic reaction in pre-revolutionary France?' *Past and Present*, 57 (November, 1972), 97–122; Bailey Stone, *The 'Parlement' of Paris 1774–1789* (Chapel Hill, NC, 1981); Paolo Alatri, *Parlamenti e lotta politica nella Francia del settecento* (Bari, 1977).

the real control of the electors upon their decisions was necessarily slight and somewhat questionable.

These difficulties in the relationship between society as a whole and its representatives were especially evident in Rousseau's analysis. On the one hand Rousseau defined government as one or several individuals, magistrates or bodies to whom society delegated its power. Government in this sense was legitimately invested with its authority only in so far as it was the expression of the general will of society. The delegates (individuals or bodies) must have, so to speak, no will or opinion of their own: it was only as the chosen instruments of society as a whole that they enjoyed a virtually unlimited power. On the other hand Rousseau described sovereignty as something which could neither be delegated nor divided, since any expression of partial will was bound, sooner or later, to clash with the general interest of the community.[a] Constant acknowledged the full strength of the difficulty that Rousseau stressed. Yet he believed that it was vital to overcome the impasse that the speculations of the *Social Contract* (little as they were intended as a guide for practical action) had so discouragingly reached. What was the point of a sovereignty which could neither be delegated nor exercised? And how could any modern political system function upon premises such as those of Rousseau?[b] Constant had a number of different responses to offer to this problem of the viability of the exercise of popular sovereignty in modern society.

A first set of considerations focused upon the mechanism of political representation as such. Since the delegation of power in large modern states could not be avoided, it was necessary to design, as skilfully as possible, a system of checks and counter-checks to control the representatives without hindering their action. These checks included the balance of constitutional powers, the recognition of the responsibility of the ministers and of their subordinates, the openness of procedure, the decentralization of administrative decisions and liberty of opinion. A system of mutual trust between the citizens and their representatives could be created through a set of well-conceived and explicitly formulated rules, and through the institutionalized practice of denouncing

[a] Rousseau, *The Social Contract*, Book 2, ch. 7, 'The Sovereign' ('Du législateur'), pp. 16–18; Book 3, ch. 15, 'Deputies or Representatives' ('Des deputés ou répresentants'), pp. 82–5. See also: Derathé, *Jean Jacques Rousseau*, p. 297, note 2; and compare with: Maximilien Robespierre, 'Sur la constitution' (Speech of 10 May 1793) in *Discours et rapports à la Convention* (Paris, 1965), pp. 129–57.
[b] For Constant's critique of Rousseau see the 1806 draft, E. Hofmann (ed.), *Les 'Principes de Politique'*, vol. 2, pp. 19–39.

the violation of these rules. In this way legal procedures would protect society against the failures and arbitrariness of human agency.[a] This commitment to the art of legislative engineering betrayed Constant's debt to the work of his political patron of the years of the Tribunate, the former Director and Consul, Emmanuel Joseph Sieyès.[b] To be sure, Constant felt little personal sympathy for the Abbé, of whom he left an unflattering literary portrait, exposing the latter's feelings of hatred and envy towards the aristocracy and his immoderate greed.[c] He also differed from him over a number of technical issues, such as bicameralism and the relevance of the British constitution as a model. Yet he shared with Sieyès the basic insight that modern political representation was the natural outcome of the division of labour in advanced commercial society, and indeed the obvious implication of Smith's analysis in the *Wealth of Nations*.[d] Moreover, like the Abbé (if not with the same feelings of class hatred) he rejected the traditional values of 'aristocratic liberty,' so eloquently defended by Mme de Staël,[e] and instead regarded property as the natural basis for a restricted electoral franchise.[f] Above all Constant saw Sieyès' legislative efforts, retrospectively, as one of the most durable and unambiguous achievements of the revolution.

Unfortunately legislative engineering, no matter how skilful, could hardly overcome the limitations of delegated power. Even in the best of all constitutional worlds, the experience of those who governed was bound to prove significantly different from that of the ordinary citizen.

[a] Principles of Politics, ch. 1, 'On the Sovereignty of the people', pp. 175–82 of this edition.

[b] For a general account of Sieyès' thought and political activity, see: Paul Bastid, *Emmanuel Joseph Sieyès et sa penseé* (Paris, 1970).

[c] B. Constant, 'L'abbé Sieyès' in 'Fragments des Mémoires de Madame Récamier', *Oeuvres*, p. 965.

[d] See E. J. Sieyès, speech of 7 September 1789, *Archives Parlementaires*, VIII, pp. 529–97. On the recurrence of the theme of representation as division of labour in Sieyès unpublished manuscripts and on his interest in Adam Smith's work, see: Pasquale Pasquino, 'Emmanuel Sieyès, Benjamin Constant ed il "governo dei moderni". Contributo alla storia del conćetto di rappresentanza politica', unpublished seminar paper, 1986.

[e] For Constant's critique of Mme de Staël's views on aristocracy see: 'De Madame de Staël et de ses ouvrages' in *Mélanges*, pp. 163–210, repr. in *Oeuvres*, pp. 825–52. Constant's views rely to a large extent on E. J. Sieyès' famous pamphlet, *Qu'est-ce que le Tiers Etat?*, ed. by R. Zapperi (Geneva, 1970). For an influential nineteenth century presentation of the *thème nobiliaire*, see: Robert de Montlosier, *De la monarchie française* (Paris, 1814). On the aristocratic party in revolutionary France see: Jean Egret, *La révolution des notables: Mounier et les monarchiens* (Paris, 1950).

[f] Principles of Politics, ch. 6, 'On the conditions of property' ('Des conditions de proprieté'), pp. 213–21 of this edition. Compare with the 1806 draft: E. Hofmann (ed.), *Les 'Principes de Politique'*, vol. 2, pp. 202–45.

23

Constant was only too conscious of this. There was, indeed, an additional dimension to be taken into account: the main characteristic of modern liberty was precisely that it granted to individuals a wide range of choices and opportunities outside the narrow field of institutionalized political life. Advanced modern society opened to its citizens, through education, the press, public debating, a space for political and cultural self-expression which had been simply unthinkable in other historical ages. Public opinion, the existence of political parties and societies together with a large and independent readership, were the driving force behind modern liberty. The overgrown, somewhat unrestrained and destructive mass of pamphlets and tracts in France at the end of the *ancien régime* had been caused by the absence of adequate political outlets for the self-expression of the middling ranks.[a]

Constant's most keenly pursued target, after 1815 and the return to a relatively normal political life, was precisely to bring the French press to the level of freedom, self-awareness and security which characterized the British one; and, similarly, to see the French political opposition transformed into a proper independent, non-factious party of the British type.[b] Yet this was not enough: the problems of individual identity in modern society could hardly be solved by a well-contrived system of political representation and by the existence of free opinion.

In a society ruled by wealth and material interest, the exercise of political rights may prove merely perfunctory, while their delegation may become a form of complicity in the betrayal of the *res publica*. Similarly, the triumph of public opinion may generate the painless but formidable tyranny of the *idées reçues*, of widely accepted conventions and artificial feelings. (Adolphe's ordinary selfishness and insensitivity, combined with his mistaken and commonplace beliefs about the nature of love, prove much more paralysing than the imposition of any external authority.) Constant's own existential experience was marked by the

---

[a] On the concept of public opinion in the Scottish context the classic reference is: David Hume, *Essays, Moral, Political, and Literary*, Essay 2: 'Of the Liberty of the Press', pp. 8–12; Essay 14: 'Of the Rise and Progress of the Arts and Sciences', pp. 112–38. For contemporary views of the role played by public opinion in the French revolution see: Jean Joseph Mounier, *De l'influence attribuée aux philosophes, aux francs–maçons et aux illuminés sur la révolution de France* (Tübingen, 1802); J. Necker, *De la révolution française*, vol. 1; A. L. G. de Staël, *Des Circonstances Actuelles*, pp. 106–23.

[b] E. Hofmann (ed.), *Les Principes de Politique*, vol. 2, 'De la liberté de la pensée', pp. 127–54; B. Constant, 'Observations sur le discours prononcé par S.E. le ministre de l'intérieur sur la liberté de la presse', *Oeuvres*, pp. 1245–71. See also: E. Harpaz, *'L'école libérale sous la restauration* (Geneva, 1968).

haunting sense of the futility of his public pursuits, of his inability to conform to socially acceptable standards of behaviour, of the rift between private happiness and public expectations.[a] It hardly matters to what extent his temperament and personal circumstances contributed to form his sensibility. It is this alternation between commitment and pessimism, idealism and scepticism, which decisively shaped his intellectual imagination.

However uneasy and ambivalent he might feel about the existential experience of modernity, Constant stressed that, if the values of commercial society flourished in the private rather than the public sphere, they need not be narrowly individualistic and instrumental. Artificiality and alienation may be resisted to some extent. Economically advanced societies must still be able to preserve those 'noble ideas and generous emotions' that the enjoyments of modern life tend to suffocate.[b]

Following Scottish common sense philosophy, Constant rejected utilitarianism, as Jeremy Bentham had formulated it, as a conflation of a rigorous theory of human behaviour and a moral doctrine. In descriptive terms, self-interest was only one feature, though no doubt an important one, of current human behaviour. In moral terms, utility could form no satisfactory foundation for ethical choices, since it might easily lead to the violation of basic individual rights in the name of private or collective interest. It is quite different, Constant argued, to be the member of a society in which any citizen may be put to death for the sake of the public good, and to live in one in which he was sure to enjoy the protection of the law independently of any instrumental considerations. No doubt, in ordinary circumstances, reasons of utility and of justice were likely to overlap. But the experience of the revolution had shown dramatically how they could come to diverge very sharply.[c]

The rejection of utilitarianism, and the aspiration to overcome the

[a] For an accessible and revealing presentation of the biographical evidence see: Georges Poulet, *Benjamin Constant par lui-même* ('Ecrivains de toujours', Paris, 1968), pp. 27–49.

[b] B. Constant, 'De M. Dunoyer et de quelques-uns de ses ouvrages' in *Mélanges*, p. 155. The essay was written as a critique of Charles Dunoyer, *L'industrie et la morale considérées dans leur rapports avec la liberté* (Paris, 1825).

[c] For Constant's assessment of Bentham's thought see: E. Hofmann (ed.), *Les 'Principes de Politique'*, vol. 2, pp. 58–61. Compare with James Mackintosh's position: James Mackintosh, 'Bentham' in *Dissertation on the progress of Ethical Philosophy* in *The Miscellaneous Works of the Rt. Hon. Sir James Mackintosh*, ed. by R. J. Mackintosh (3 vols., London, 1846), vol. 1, pp. 187–209. On Mme de Staël on Bentham, see her *Des circonstances actuelles*, p. 425, note 1.

most crudely individualistic and competitive aspects of human life led Constant to a tentative, but keen exploration of the alternative moral and aesthetic dimensions of the new age. The perfecting of legislative instruments and the instruments of free opinion was merely the scaffolding round the edifice of modern liberty and would remain just that if taken in isolation from the totality of the spiritual and artistic achievements of modernity.

This statement may require some qualification. Constant's thought is currently associated with precisely the reverse of this preoccupation with the promotion of moral values. In his writings, he expressed at great length his condemnation of any interference on the part of political authority, be it absolute or popular, with the private feelings, tastes and beliefs of the citizens. Indeed his passionate denunciation of the Jacobin regime focused precisely upon the violence exercised against individual rights and private freedom in the name of the promotion of allegedly desirable social goals.

In his influential essay on the concept of freedom, Isaiah Berlin characterized Constant's approach as the model for a 'negative' theory of liberty, liberty being simply, in this perspective, the protection of individual experience and choices from external interferences and constraints. Berlin contrasted this kind of freedom with an archetypical 'positive' one, in which liberty was regarded as the product of man's active efforts to bring about some political, social or religious ideal and to realize it in the community or environment in which he happened to live.[a] In recent years, this distinction has come increasingly under attack:[b] and Berlin's typology, designed as it is to highlight a conceptual contrast, proves less illuminating when applied to the interpretation of real historical examples. In any case (and no matter how we view Berlin's classification) to condemn any arbitrary imposition of moral goals by the political authority, or their militant promotion by some political elite, is in no way incompatible with the effort to confront and develop the spiritual features of one's own historical age.

It is important to stress here that for Constant, modern liberty, the protection of the private autonomy of the individual, was no meta-

[a] Isaiah Berlin, *Four Essays on Liberty* (Oxford, 1969).

[b] Gerard MacCallum, 'Negative and Positive Freedom', *The Philosophical Review*, 76 (July 1967), pp. 312–34; Charles Taylor, 'What's wrong with negative liberty' in A. Ryan (ed.), *The Idea of Freedom* (Oxford, 1979), 175–93; John Gray, 'On negative and positive liberty', *Political Studies*, 28 (1980), 507–26; Quentin Skinner, 'The idea of negative liberty: philosophical and historical perspectives' in R. Rorty, J. B. Schneewind, Q. Skinner (eds), *Philosophy in History – Essays on the Historiography of Philosophy* (Cambridge, 1984), pp. 193–221.

physical value, as it clearly was (to use Berlin's own example) for John Stuart Mill.[a] The content of the notion was indeed the same as Mill's: protection of individual life and property; liberty of religion, speech and opinion; autonomy in all those aspects of life that could cause no harm to others or to society as a whole. But, in contrast to Mill, Constant's understanding of the nature of liberty was essentially confined to these practical features. He believed, with Montesquieu and Hume, that any concept of natural right was a fairly useless one in politics: in any given society people had simply those rights which it could afford to give them.[b] Similarly, they observed those principles which were generally accepted and compatible with the conditions of society itself. Thus the protection of private autonomy which he defended was not a natural right, or an essential moral feature of man, but merely the level of security and independence to which citizens of advanced modern communities had become accustomed, and which they consequently found it desirable to preserve. This relativistic nature of the notion of liberty is somewhat blurred by the fact that Constant intermittently expressed in his writings a vague aspiration towards the establishment of a stable system of transcendental values. But he never attempted to develop this line of reflection, and his view of the foundations of society remained firmly grounded in the Humean perspective of systems of shared beliefs. His work on the history of religion, stretching over a period of several decades, offers in itself more than sufficient evidence of his sustained commitment to this kind of approach.

If the ideal of liberty had a sociological foundation, this fact did not in any way diminish the urgency and importance of its realization. As Constant expressed it: 'Il nous faut de la liberté, et nous l'aurons', we must have liberty and we shall have it.[c] Freedom was what was required here and now, the imperative around which revolved the prolonged upheaval of French and European society. The commitment to keep in step with historical development was, no doubt, a rule of political prudence, the necessary precondition for stability. But it was also, in some sense, a moral and even aesthetic duty, namely that of the fulfilment of a collective spiritual potential.

---

[a] On J. S. Mill on liberty, see: C. L. Ten, *Mill on Liberty* (Oxford, 1980); John Gray, *Mill on Liberty: a defence* (London, 1983).
[b] C. de Montesquieu, *De l'esprit des lois, Oeuvres complètes*, vol. 2, Book 11, ch. 2, p. 394: 'Enfin chacun a appelé liberté le gouvernement qui étoit conforme à ses coutumes et à ses inclinations'.
[c] The liberty of the ancients compared with that of the moderns, pp. 307–28 of this edition (*Cours de politique constitutionnelle*, vol. 4, pp. 238–74).

Constant could hardly be described as a builder of philosophical systems, and while his views on legislation were fairly clear and articulated (enough at least to lay the basis of one of France's intellectually most compelling constitutions) his exploration of the aesthetic, moral and religious features of modern civilization remained largely tentative and fragmentary. Although he found inspiration in the writings of the German Romantics, his intellectual sympathy for their aesthetic insights went together with a deep, often contemptuous, disagreement on most political, economic and religious issues.[a] Consequently, he was hardly in a position to take advantage of their overall philosophical vision. The study of religious belief was undoubtedly the area in which Constant's contribution was most substantial. Unfortunately, not only did his ambitious work, *De la religion*, remain incomplete, but the author's intentions in writing it kept fluctuating and changing.[b] We know that he began his work, following Hume's model, as a 'natural history' of religion, exploring the relations between the socio-political conditions of human populations and their myths and cults. Subsequently he abandoned this taxonomy of human social and religious practices, characteristic of most Enlightenment literature on the subject, to stress instead the autonomy and continuity of the religious feeling, only to return intermittently to his original sociological and sceptical approach. The trend that gradually emerged from these oscillations was the search for a universal and interiorized form of religiosity. In this perspective the modern age was characterized precisely by the decline of religion as superstition, empty ritual, fanaticism, priestcraft, the instrument of power, enslavement and manipulation; and the emergence in its stead of religious sentiment as the expression

---

[a] See Constant's harsh judgement on Fichte's *Der geschlossene Handelsstaat* (Johann Gottlieb Fichte, *Der Geschlossene Handelsstaat*, repr. of the original of 1800. Introduction by H. Waentig (Jena, 1920)), where he refers to the 'lunacy' of the views of the German Romantic group on economic policy: *Journal*, 27 May 1804, *Oeuvres*, p. 311; see also his comments on Fichte's pamphlet: *Friedrich Nicolai's 'Leben und sonderbare meinungen'* (Tübingen, 1801), in which he accuses Fichte and Schlegel of displaying at the same time: 'the haughtiness of philosophers and the cunning of inquisitors'; *Journal*, 25 August 1804, *Ibid.*, pp. 325–6. For a general outlook on German Romanticism, see: Friederich Meinecke, *Cosmopolitanism and the National State* (Princeton, 1970); J. L. Talmon, *Romanticism and Revolt: Europe 1814–1848* (New York, 1967); Hans Reiss (ed.), *The Political Thought of the German Romantics, 1793–1815* (Oxford, 1955).

[b] On Constant's work on religion see: Pierre Deguise, *Benjamin Constant méconnu*; Benjamin Constant, *Deux chapitres inédits*; Guy Dodge, *Benjamin Constant's Philosophy of Liberalism: a Study in Politics and Religion* (Chapel Hill, NC, 1980). Also, for the general eighteenth-century background: Frank E. Manuel, *The Eighteenth Century Confronts the Gods* (Harvard, 1959).

of the rational, benevolent and free individual conscience. Protestantism, in its most undogmatic and rationalistic form, lay at the heart of
Constant's view, which was thus much closer to the spirit of Kant's
Religion within the limits of pure reason than to the mystic, neo-classical
or neo-Christian inclinations of the Romantic writers.[a] If his sympathy
for the cause of the Reformation was expressed at length in Constant's
historical writings,[b] the ambiguities and fluctuations of *De la religion*
make it very difficult to establish a precise connection between his
religious and his political views. It seems likely, however, that the
relation between the two was somewhat complementary and that Constant (always disinclined to discuss methodological questions explicitly) used his religious studies as a kind of vast workshop to test and
explore different approaches to the understanding of human communities and the mechanisms of social consensus.

Constant's investigation of the aesthetic of modernity was less extensively, yet suggestively, developed in his literary writings. In his *Réflexions sur la tragédie*,[c] in which he compared the progress of French and
German contemporary drama, he discussed the relationship between
the theatrical representation of human character and the influence
upon it of historical circumstances. Modern tragedy, he argued, tended
to concentrate either upon the description of individual temperaments
and passions, or upon personal responses to external political, social
and historical events. What most contemporary dramatists failed to
grasp was the fact that man's feelings and passions were not merely
interacting with, but actually moulded by the constraints of a given
civilization. In modern drama, as Schiller had admirably shown, history
must play the same determinant role as fate in Greek classical tragedy.
This recognition of the historical dimension of human passions did not
imply that there could not be a free artistic representation of the
individual character. Constant was far from advocating a crude form
of historical determinism.[d] What he meant was rather that most

---

[a] On Constant's knowledge of Kant's work, see K. Kloocke, *Benjamin Constant*, p. 49,
note 120. See also the two influential contemporary works by Charles Villiers: *Philosophie de Kant, ou principes fondamentaux de la philosophie transcendentale* (Metz, 1801);
and *Essai sur l'esprit et l'influence de la Réformation de Luther* (Metz, 1803).
[b] 'De la guerre de trente ans' in *Mélanges*, pp. 255–321, repr. in *Oeuvres*, pp. 860–97.
See also de Sismondi, *Recherches sur les Constitutions des peuples libres*.
[c] 'A l'occasion d'une tragédie allemande, de M. Robert, intitulée du pouvoir des
préjugés', *Oeuvres*, pp. 899–928 (first published as two separate articles in the *Revue
de Paris*, vol. 7, 1829).
[d] For Constant's ideas on historical progress see his 'De la perfectibilité de l'espèce
humaine' in *Mélanges*, pp. 387–415, repr. ed. by P. Deguise (Lausanne, 1967).

traditional representations of human feelings were artificial and out-dated because they failed to take into account the changing role of individuals in modern society.[a]

Love, in the form of exclusive sexual passion, offered a good illustration of the way in which a basic human feature had been characteristically distorted by the literary tradition, which had misrepresented it either as heavenly and sublime sentiment, or as a base and destructive passion. Thus for example Choderlos de Laclos, in his *Liaisons dangereuses* had poignantly depicted sexual desire as the supreme instrument of power and manipulation. Yet, Constant commented, today no-one would any longer be interested in playing the role of Valmont, since very few people indeed, in a busy, commercially active and sexually more permissive society, would find the time, leisure and incentive to pursue idle games of personal domination.[b]

The young *Adolphe*, with whom in this respect Constant identified very deeply, was precisely the victim of this kind of literary delusion. His selfish and inconclusive love for Ellénore – a woman whom it was socially unsuitable for him to marry – became an excuse for failing to exercise more simple and generous virtues and affections. Blinded by his deceptive, and largely self-constructed passion, not only did he fail in his duties towards her, becoming the cause of her ruin and death, but he also failed in his duties towards himself, his family and position in society. Persuaded that Ellénore was the only obstacle in the way of his worldly success, he discovered, after her death, that his incapacity to love her was merely the symptom of his incapacity to perform a useful role in life. In the conclusion of the novel, the author states explicitly that the cause of Adolphe's failure lay in the vices of his character and not in the influence of society and external circumstances.[c] Adolphe's deficiencies make a striking contrast with the successful apprenticeship

---

[a] On the theme of art, literature and historical change, see B. Constant, 'De la littérature dans ses rapports avec la liberté' in *Mélanges*, pp. 225–39; two important contemporary sources are: A. L. G. de Staël, *De la littérature considerée dans ses rapports avec les institutions sociales* in *Oeuvres complètes*, vol. 4, repr. ed. by P. van Tieghen (2 vols., Paris, 1959); J. C. L. S. de Sismondi, *De la littérature dans le Midi de l'Europe* (4 vols., Paris, 1813), English trs. by Thomas Roscoe, *Historical view of the literature of the South of Europe* (4 vols., London, 1823).

[b] B. Constant, 'Réflexions sur la tragédie' in *Oeuvres* p. 905. For Laclos' Rousseauian vindication of the *Liaisons dangereuses* see his 'Des femmes et de leur éducation' in *Oeuvres complètes*, ed. Laurent Versini (Paris, 1979), pp. 387–443. There he argues, in short, that the transformation of sex into a destructive passion is precisely the outcome of the transition to the civilized state.

[c] 'I hate that weakness which is always blaming others for its own impotence and

of Goethe's hero Wilhelm Meister.[a] Wilhelm, like Adolphe, alienated from his family by an unsuitable sentimental attachment, rejected his role as heir to a rich merchant in order to become an actor and playwright. Yet after a series of confusing and frustrating adventures in the world of theatrical make-believe, he learnt that his artistic vocation could develop only through the acceptance of his real circumstances and of his natural place in society. Not until he became fully aware of this was he truly free to pursue his vocation.

Through Adolphe's unsuccessful *Bildung*, Constant indicated some of the moral requirements for the preservation of liberty in modern society. Strength of will, firmness, fidelity to one's commitments, goodness, human sympathy and genuine unwillingness to make others suffer were the ordinary virtues which could help the citizens of modern communities achieve a peaceful and rewarding life. As virtues they were neither heroic, nor aristocratic or indeed revolutionary; they were, on the contrary, domestic, unostentatious and commonplace.[b] In commending them, Constant acknowledged the heavy and often painful constraints that modern life imposed upon the natural inclinations and the traditional beliefs and expectations of men and women. But he stressed that both the utopia of a return to the past, and the paralysing sense of existential impotence (a form of self-indulgence which he reserved largely for himself) were equally unacceptable responses. Above all, the increased artificiality of the modern condition must not be used as an argument either against the practice of freedom of individual and collective choices, or against the acceptance of individual and collective moral responsibility.

A serious difficulty due to the fact that this translation comes so late – both in historical terms and with respect to the progress of the scholarship on Constant – emerges in the choice of texts included in this

which cannot see that the trouble is not in its surroundings but in itself . . . Circumstances are quite unimportant, character is everything; in vain we break with outside things and people; we cannot break with ourselves.' *Adolphe*, trs. by L. Tancock, p. 125. Compare with Meilcour's concluding remarks in: Crébillon fils, *Les égarements du coeur et de l'esprit* (1736–8), ed. by Étiemble (Paris, 1977), pp. 292–5.

[a] W. Goethe, *Wilhelm Meisters Lehrjahre* in *Werke*, ed. by Erich Schmidt (6 vols., Leipzig, 1909), vol. 4. English trs. by Thomas Carlyle: *Wilhelm Meister's apprenticeship and travels* (3 vols., London, 1842).

[b] 'If it has any instructive lesson, that lesson is for men, for it shows that intellect, which they are so proud of, can never find happiness or bestow it; that character, steadfastness, fidelity, and kindness are the gifts we should pray for, . . . The great question in life is the sorrow we cause, and the most ingenious metaphysics cannot justify the man who has broken the heart who loved him.' *Adolphe*, trs. by L. Tancock, p. 125.

volume. On the one hand it seemed obvious, and indeed necessary, to offer to the English reader Constant's major political works such as they appeared during his lifetime, and were generally known throughout the nineteenth and most of the twentieth centuries. On the other hand, recent research on the manuscript sources has fully and convincingly shown that Constant's published works were merely the by-product of a more ambitious project for a comprehensive treatise on political theory which he never completed. It is impossible to reproduce here the body of Constant's notes and unfinished drafts – part of which have only now begun to appear in French. But we must keep in mind the relationship between these and the published works if we are to have a minimally adequate sense of the scale and original character of Constant's intellectual project.

In order to illustrate the function of the unpublished material it may be helpful to describe briefly Constant's method of work. Despite his otherwise disorderly habits and almost incessant travelling, Constant was an extremely well-organized and systematic writer. He collected notes and quotations from his readings in a card-index system (legend claims that he began this practice by writing on the back of a pack of tarot cards) and used the same card or passage over and over again whenever it was convenient to do so. This method (much less common in the eighteenth century than it is now in the age of word processors) had mainly been devised to keep under control the immense mass of bibliographical material connected with his research into the history of religion. Constant's failing eyesight, and the consequent necessity to use a secretary or copyist to transcribe his work, also made it desirable to rely upon a wide selection of ready-made quotations. The creation of texts in the form of lengthy *collages* inevitably resulted in a repetitious and markedly uneven style. Moreover, it meant that the works that Constant hastily published after 1813, with precise political aims and under the pressure of events, were mostly composed by assembling research materials and annotations accumulated for somewhat different purposes over the previous fifteen years or so.[a] Inevitably, some of the old cards did not fit perfectly in their new contexts, thus generating puzzling inconsistencies and obscurities. Between 1800 and 1803, the years of the Tribunate, Constant undertook the composition of a treatise on political theory, probably derived from his commentary on Godwin's *Enquiry on Political Justice*, and known in this early version as:

[a] E. Hofmann (ed.), *Les 'Principes de Politique,'* vol. 1, pp. 243–96.

'Fragments d'un ouvrage abandonné sur la possibilité d'une constitution républicaine dans un grand pays'.[a] This study subsequently became the 'Principes de politique applicables à tous les gouvernements,' an incomplete version of which existed by 1806.[b] The aim of these early drafts was explicitly theoretical: in them Constant stated his ambition to restore the prestige and credibility of political and constitutional reflection, which in his view had been discredited and almost completely abandoned after the revolution.[c] Accordingly, his unfinished treatise showed a central concern with two new factors which, he thought, must be embodied in any modern system of political theory with any hope of achieving some credibility. The first of these was naturally the experience of the revolution itself and its consequences, both for political speculation and for political action. The second was the progress of the study of modern commercial society promoted by the political economists. The 1806 draft in particular can be read as a close commentary on Smith's *Wealth of Nations*.[d] It would be difficult to state precisely why the projected treatise remained unfinished. If we take into account the continuing pressure of the Napoleonic regime, Constant's own personal troubles, the years spent in exile and the growing size and intrinsic intellectual difficulties of the project, one can see his failure to complete it as easily predictable. Between 1806 and 1813, Constant's journal and correspondence contain frequent references to some work in progress, but it is often impossible to establish whether he was in fact referring to the history of religion, to *Adolphe* (also composed in those years), or to some further development of his political thoughts.

In 1813, the disastrous outcome of the Russian campaign and the approaching collapse of the empire pushed Constant to write the first of the texts included in this collection: *The Spirit of Conquest and Usurpation*. Hastily drafted during his visit to Hanover between the end of November and December 1813, it was published there as a single pamphlet, in January 1814. The section on Conquest went through the press first, since Constant was anxious to see it appear, in case he missed the moment of greatest public interest. His haste was

[a] See footnote *a*, p. 11.
[b] This is the text published in E. Hofmann (ed.), *Les 'Principes de Politique'*, vol. 2.
[c] *Ibid.*, pp. 19–20.
[d] See the huge number of references to Smith's work listed in the Index to E. Hofmann (ed.), *Les 'Principes de Politique'*, vol. 2, p. 674.
[e] See 'Notice' in *Oeuvres*, pp. 1569–71.

rewarded, and the work proved a tremendous success: a second edition was published in London in March 1814, and a third in Paris in April of the same year. Written as a rhetorical attack on Napoleon's despotic rule, the *Spirit of Conquest* focused upon one particular feature of the difference between the ancient world and modern market society: the transformation of the role of war and of international relations in the commercially advanced European states. Thus the pamphlet outlined the contrast between the naturally bellicose and conquering tendencies of the ancient and barbarous peoples, and the potentially peaceful and cosmopolitan disposition of the modern trading nations. In Constant's reconstruction, Napoleon's empire was doomed because it attempted to force upon a commercial nation dreams of military conquest which could no longer have any appeal for her population, just as Robespierre had pressed upon her, by means of sheer terror, an impracticable model of ancient republican virtue. Like most of his contemporaries, who had been educated to believe in the miraculous effects of the *doux commerce*, Constant was, underneath the verbal violence of his denunciation, deeply intrigued by the Napoleonic experience. On the one hand he was inclined to see it simply as a nightmarish anachronism, a historical mistake rather than a moral outrage. The system of conquest was a challenge to the spirit of the age, made possible only by the political and moral confusion created by the revolution, which had exposed the people to all sorts of ideological vices and authoritarian temptations.[a] On the other hand the prolonged success of Bonaparte's leadership suggested the possibility of a return of the spirit of conquest in the modern world: a dismal prospect since conquest prompted by rational economic interest and greed would prove infinitely more ruthless than the naturally bellicose disposition of barbarous tribes.[b]

In the *Spirit of Conquest* and *Usurpation* Constant subscribed to the reassuring view that commerce was bound to prevail in the end, in contrast with the opinion of his friend, Sir James Mackintosh, who was more inclined to appreciate the successful economic and social aspects of Napoleon's imperialist policy.[c] Indeed, although his expectations were confirmed by events, Constant proved somewhat obtuse in failing

[a] B. Constant, *The Spirit of Conquest and Usurpation*, part 1, ch. 3, 'The spirit of conquest in the present condition of Europe', pp. 55–6 of this edition.
[b] Ibid., ch. 4, 'Of a military race acting on self-interest alone', pp. 56–9 of this edition.
[c] (James Mackintosh), 'France', *Edinburgh Review*, 24 (November, 1814), 505–37. For a positive judgement on the results of Napoleon's protectionist policy for the French economy see: T. R. Malthus, *The Grounds of an Opinion on the Policy of Restricting the Importation of Foreign Corn* (London, 1815), footnote p. 12.

to perceive both the formidable emotional and nationalistic drive behind the Napoleonic adventure, and the potentially aggressive and conflictual dimensions of the international market. There is however some evidence to suggest that, after the Congress of Vienna, and especially after 1819, with the emergence of movements of national independence such as that of Greece, he came to revise to some extent his optimistic beliefs about the peaceful future of the modern commercial world.[a]

The second part of the work, on usurpation, has often evoked perplexity and disagreement amongst its commentators. The use of the word 'usurpation' to describe Bonaparte's power suggested the recognition of the legitimacy of the Bourbons' dynastic claims; while the chapter on William III (suppressed after the first edition),[b] by presenting the example of a constitutional monarch enthroned by an elective assembly, might be thought to justify Bernadotte's aspirations to the French crown. Thus Constant's somewhat opportunistic coating of the arguments seemed to legitimize incompatible political solutions, which, moreover, patently contradicted his basic republican sympathies.

These inconsistencies, which reflected the tangled events of 1813–1814, were, however, comparatively marginal to the central argument of the essay. What Constant was anxious to expose was not usurpation as such (which he saw simply as an especially offensive and vulnerable kind of despotism),[c] but any form of arbitrary power. His passionate, yet subtle picture of the moral and psychological ravages caused by the systematic violation of political guarantees remains unsurpassed by later writers. It is hardly surprising that the opponents of twentieth century authoritarian regimes should still be struck by its strength and vividness. What makes Constant's analysis especially perceptive and relevant is the fact that he did not represent arbitrary power as the product of a criminal and ruthless will to oppress. He showed instead that tyranny could be the outcome of a series of apparently reasonable measures, instrumental considerations, short-sighted Machiavellianism, ideological fallacies. Similarly, the true horror of tyranny, as he described it, was not in its spectacular excesses and cruelty, but in the

---

[a] B. Constant, *Appel aux nations chrétiennes en faveur des Grecs* (Paris, 1825).

[b] ch. 5: 'Answer to an objection which could be drawn from the example of William III', pp. 165–7 of this edition.

[c] *The Spirit of Conquest and Usurpation*, Part 2, ch. 2, 'Differences between usurpation and monarchy', pp. 87–94 of this edition.

35

daily acceptance of compromises, in the slow erosion of human solidarity and decency, in the general sharing of guilt and complicity.[a]

Another relevant, if somewhat less apparent theme in the *Spirit of Conquest* is that of progress and historical change. In the long chapter 'On uniformity' Constant re-echoed the Burkean critique of hasty and premature reforms, artificially enforced before public opinion was ready for them.[b] In the subsequent editions of the work he found it necessary to add a commentary to this chapter, to correct the impression of excessive (indeed Burkean) conservatism that some readers had derived from his treatment of this topic.[c] Together the two chapters give us a reasonably full picture of Constant's response to Burke, undoubtedly more cautious and balanced than the attack he was planning to write at the time of the publication of the *Reflections*.[d] Like most liberals of his generation, Constant had taken Burke's lesson to heart,[e] and firmly rejected the temptation of political utopias. But he also made a sharp distinction between the desirability of keeping in step with the natural development of civil society, and the mere unwillingness to change. If one was to respect the spirit of the age, then Burke's apology for the *ancien régime* was self-evidently as unrealistic as the utopian reformism of the National Assembly. This judgement is central to Constant's retrospective assessment of the outcome of the revolution. He thought that revolutions ought indeed to be avoided on account of the disproportionate political and human costs they involved. He also believed that the price paid for 1789 was appallingly high, a tragic and terrifying testimony to the failure of political agency. Yet, since it had been paid anyway, it was at least important to consolidate and maximize its advantages. If the previous generation of enlightened politicians had failed to prevent the revolution, it was essential that the present generation should at least succeed in avoiding a counter-revolution which

[a] *Ibid.*, ch. 3, pp. 95–7 of this edition. See also E. Hofmann (ed.), *Les 'Principes de Politique'*, vol. 2, ch. 4: 'De l'effet des mesures arbitraires sous le rapport de la morale, sous celui de l'industrie et sous celui de la duré des gouvernements', pp. 99–101.

[b] *The Spirit of Conquest and Usurpation*, Part 1, ch. 13, 'On Uniformity', pp. 73–8 of this edition.

[c] *Ibid.*, 'On innovation, reform and the uniformity and stability of institutions', chapter 1 added to the Fourth edition, pp. 149–57 below.

[d] E. Burke, *Reflections on the Revolution in France*, ed. by C. Cruise O'Brien (Harmondsworth, 1968). On Constant's project for a critique of Burke see E. Hofmann (ed.), *Les 'Principes de Politique'*, vol. 1, p. 33.

[e] On Burke's impact on early nineteenth-century British liberalism, see B. Fontana, *Rethinking the Politics of Commercial Society: the 'Edinburgh Review', 1802–1832* (Cambridge, 1985), pp. 25–38.

would prove even more destructive. No doubt Constant was right when he identified in this aspiration to secure the stability of the new – beyond all ideological differences and also, to some extent, against the particular interests of some social groups – the main element of cohesion in post-revolutionary French society.[a]

The second text in this collection, the *Principes de politique applicables à tous les gouvernements répresentatifs et particulièrement à la constitution actuelle de la France* (a slight variant on the title of the abandoned 1806 draft) was published in Paris in May 1815, at the time of Constant's collaboration with Napoleon, when he was a member of the Conseil d'État. It was written in the form of a commentary on the *Acte additionel*, illustrating its main features, and indicating possible areas for further improvement. While presenting in some detail Constant's constitutional views (previously sketched out in the *Réflexions sur les constitutions*[b] of 1814), the new *Principes* also retained some of the theoretical insights of the early drafts, such as, the critique of Rousseau's 'general will' in the opening chapter on popular sovereignty. The rigorous division of powers was the central concern of Constant's constitutional design. This was not simply a preoccupation inherited from traditional constitutional reflection. The insufficient delimitation of powers had been one of the most alarming features of the Constituent and later of the National Assemblies. In the years of the revolution, the Assembly, combining legislative with executive and judicial power, had become abnormally strong and totally independent from any other force within French society.[c] It was a new phenomenon which puzzled and worried those observers, like Necker, Sieyès, Mme de Staël and Constant himself, who had not ceased to believe in the old theory of the balance of powers. The coup of Brumaire was Sieyès' last attempt to regain control over the Assembly by legal means through the creation of a strong executive. The failure of this strategy brought the Abbé's political career to an end and haunted Mme de Staël and Constant, who had warmly supported it for the rest of their lives.[d]

---

[a] See his 'De la doctrine politique qui peut réunir les partis en France' of 1816, repr. in *Écrits et discours politiques* vol. 2, pp. 32–56.
[b] *Réflexions sur les constitutions, la distribution et les garanties dans une monarchie constitutionnelle* (Paris, 1814).
[c] This feature of the Constituent and National Assemblies had been stressed by Jacques Necker; see his: *De la révolution française, Oeuvres complètes*, vol. 2, pp. 103–4 and 235–6; and especially: *Du pouvoir exécutif dans les grands états* (Paris, 1792).
[d] The themes of human suffering and individual responsibility in the context of the revolution are central to A. L. G. de Staël, *Des circonstances actuelles*.

The model of representative government outlined in the *Principes* was of course a monarchy, but one in which the powers of the sovereign – of the emperor in this particular instance – were so carefully limited as to justify the description of 'republic in disguise'. The executive power was, however, granted the right of veto and the authority to dissolve the chambers.[a] While the monarch was protected by inviolability, Constant stressed the need to establish the responsibility of ministers as well as of their subordinates, and the openness of all government actions. His discussion of the issue of the responsibility of political agents remains one of the most stimulating and original features of the work.[b]

In this context Constant confronted the problem of the administrative centralization promoted by the revolution and consolidated by the empire, which had predictably resulted either in arbitrary and ill-informed interventions on the part of central government, or, more frequently, in the relapse of the local administrations into the anarchy and chaos of the *ancien régime*. To counteract these effects, Constant favoured what he described as a 'new kind of federalism': meaning by this not the disintegration of the national government into entirely separate political units (an unthinkable development for a country like France), but the decentralization of all those administrative decisions that were obviously of merely local relevance.[c]

As to the legislative power, unlike the leaders of the old Constituent Assembly, and especially Sieyès, Constant opted for the English two chamber system. The hereditary chamber would offer to the aristocracy of blood some real political function: its numbers, however, must not be limited, so as to allow for new promotions and upward social mobility. The acceptance of an upper chamber, (in opposition to the generally Anglophobic tendency of the revolutionary tradition)[d] was not merely a concession to the conservative forces in Napoleon's

---

[a] *Principles of Politics*, ch. 2, 'The nature of royal power in a constitutional monarchy', pp. 183–93: ch. 3, 'On the right to dissolve representative assemblies', pp. 194–8 of this edition. See also J. Necker, *De la révolution française, Oeuvres complètes*, ed. by A. de Staël (15 vols, Paris, 1820), vol. 2, p. 52.

[b] In addition to the *Principles of Politics*, chs. 9 to 11 (pp. 227–50 of this edition), see: B. Constant, *De la responsabilité des ministres*.

[c] *Principles of Politics*, ch. 12, 'On municipal power, local authorities and a new kind of federalism', pp. 251–5 of this edition. On the results of administrative centralization, see J. Godechot, *Les institutions de la France sous la révolution et l'empire* (Paris, 1968).

[d] Frances D. Acomb, *Anglophobia in France, 1763–1789: an essay on the history of constitutionalism and nationalism* (Durham, NC, 1950); H. J. Laski, 'The English Constitution and French public opinion, 1789–1794, *Politica*, 3 (1938), 27–42.

attempted compromise. Although he was no partisan of the merits of the aristocracy, Constant had become convinced that keeping the nobility in active public service was an important condition for social stability. He was later reinforced in his belief by the social and economic tensions that developed in Britain after 1815 and the end of the war, which he was inclined to attribute to the withdrawal of the aristocracy from its traditional function of providing political leadership and patronage for the lower orders.[a] As to the lower chamber, the *Principes* advocated its complete renewal at each election and the inviolability of its members. In his proposal Constant favoured direct popular election, instead of the election in two stages (effected through the local assemblies) which had been practised throughout the revolution. He thought it best for the suffrage to be restricted on the basis of income or taxation, but with a low franchise, so as to allow for a considerably wider electorate than the one existing at the time. He shared the view of most supporters of parliamentary reform in the early nineteenth-century, who thought that the franchise was bound to expand with the growth of general national prosperity and education, and that property must represent the chief instrument of political and social mobility.[b] Finally, the independence of the judicial power was regarded as essential: the introduction of trial by jury, the prevention of any retroactive legislative measure, freedom of the press, freedom of worship and a clear separation between the regular army and the police forces were further guarantees of the protection of individual security.[c]

Needless to say, many features of Constant's constitutional design were dictated by the circumstances of 1815 or, more generally, by the context of nineteenth-century parliamentary reform, and remain in this respect of purely historical interest. Yet beneath the constraints imposed by this constitutional scaffolding, the 1815 *Principes* retained the full theoretical strength of Constant's original design. They contained Constant's painstaking answer to the fallacies of both Jacobin and authoritarian ideologies, together with his attempt to place the revolutionary experience firmly within the tradition of modern constitutional

---

[a] B. Constant, 'De la puissance de l'Angleterre' in *Mélanges*, pp. 28–45.
[b] ch. 6, 'On the conditions of property', pp. 213–21 below.
[c] The last part of the *Principles of Politics* (chapters 15 to 19), is dedicated to the discussion of the various individual rights: property rights (ch. 15); freedom of speech and of the press (ch. 16); of religious belief (ch. 17); individual liberty (ch. 18); and finally judicial guarantees (ch. 19).

theory.[a] If they offered no overall political solution to the problems posed by political representation, they confronted them by defining practical strategies of trust and responsibility for governors and governed alike.

The third and last text in this collection is the famous speech of 1819 'De la liberté des anciens comparée à celle des modernes'. Later published by Constant in his *Cours de politique constitutionelle*,[b] it formed part of a series of lectures on the English constitution given by the author in the Athénée Royal, and inaugurated on 2 December 1818 with the 'Eloge de Sir Samuel Romilly'.[c] The content and implications of the comparison between ancient and modern liberty have already been discussed. The 1819 speech is probably the best known, but also a somewhat belated and idiosyncratic formulation of this topic. Written thirty years after the events of 1789, on the eve of the assassination of the Duke of Berry, when the Bourbon monarchy was embarking on its final ultra-reactionary phase, 'De la liberté' has sometimes been seen as a return of revolutionary nostalgia. Certainly it offered a more sympathetic assessment than ever before of the ideal of ancient liberty, and especially of the attraction that this had exercised upon the participants in the revolution. Yet in this sense the 1819 speech simply made more explicit the ambivalence which had been present throughout in Constant's political reflection. It restated on the one hand the impossibility of turning back from modernity and the constraints of advanced commercial economies. But it insisted on the necessity of keeping alive the need for political participation among the citizens of modern political communities, if these communities were to be protected from the dangers of destructive individualism and authoritarian ambitions. Constant here returned to his early critique of utilitarian ethics by stressing that happiness, though of great importance, could hardly exhaust the moral aspirations of mankind. Institutions, he stated in the last paragraph of the lecture, while respecting the individual rights of the citizens, must achieve their moral education and prevent them from forgetting their stake in the fortunes of the *res publica*.[d] 'De la liberté'

---

[a] On the relevance of the French revolutionary tradition for contemporary constitutional theories see: René Capitant, *Ecrits constitutionnels* (Paris, CNRS, 1982).

[b] B. Constant, *De la liberté des anciens comparée à celle des modernes* (Paris, 1819); repr. in: *Collection complète des ouvrages publiés sur le Gouvernement représentatif et la Constitution actuelle de la France, formant une espèce de Cours de politique constitutionnelle* (4 vols., Paris 1818–19 and Paris and Rouen, 1820), vol. 4, pp. 238–74.

[c] Eloge de Sir Samuel Romilly, prononcé à l'Athénée Royal le 2 decembre (Paris, 1819), repr. in *Cours de Politique Constitutionnelle*, vol. 4, pp. 5–74.

[d] The Liberty of the Ancients, pp. 327–8 below.

40

ultimately left open Rousseau's dilemma as to the nature of democratic participation: yet it left it open not to philosophical despair but to the exercise of political skill and moral prudence. The conflict between ancient and modern liberty must be resolved by combining the two in a new range of social and political practices. If the texts reproduced here, all published since 1814, were deeply embedded in the political events leading up to the collapse of the empire and the restoration, it would be a mistake to exaggerate their distance from the original theoretical design of the early works. Although the author's appraisal of practical political solutions naturally changed over the years, his ambition to define and test the political viability of modern commercial society remained fundamentally unaltered.

In conclusion: what is dead and what is alive in Constant's thought? The reader of these texts is bound to experience alternate feelings of proximity and distance. At times the author's prose loses itself in the depths of nineteenth-century rhetoric, becomes entangled in obsolete technical details, pursues long-forgotten disputes. But at others, it is capable of reminding us of our own unsolved problems, present failings or impending disasters. If we turn to the autobiographical evidence, we are struck again by the same contrast of intimacy and remoteness. At times Constant comes very close to us with the vividness of his wit, the shrewdness of his insights, his adroit and merciless self-irony. But at others he resembles an *ancien régime* aristocrat, a character out of Crébillon and Laclos whom he accused of being so out of date: someone who bursts into tears while reading his novel in the *salons*, takes poison in his mistress' chateau, and keeps scrupulous note in his books of his gambling debts and the cost of the odd *fille* alongside alms and household expenses.[a]

It is generally taken for granted that what links him to us is liberalism, the political doctrine of which he is regarded as a forerunner, and which is still today, for some, perhaps for many, a source of ideological identification. Yet, if we look closely, this word, for Constant as for us, appears to mean either too little or too much. Constant used the terms: *amis de la liberté*, *libéral*, *libéraux*, to indicate those people who were prepared to adopt an open-minded, non-partisan attitude towards post-revolutionary politics.[b] Later on the term was used to designate the members of the parliamentary opposition at large, including groups

[a] Kurt Kloocke and Christian Viredaz, 'Les *livres de dépenses* de Benjamin Constant' in *Annales Benjamin Constant*, 4 (1984), pp. 115–63; 5 (1985), pp. 105–79.
[b] See S. Holmes, *Benjamin Constant*, pp. 10–11 and p. 266, footnote 39.

and writers (the *idéologues*, Guizot, Augustin-Thierry and many others) with whom Constant, intellectually, had very little in common.[a] What to some extent united them, was, of course, a shared aspiration to the democratization of French political life, and the somewhat indeterminate belief in the merits of private property, free trade and economic competition.

None of these beliefs would serve today as a very specific element of political identification. Some of them have become part of a widely, almost universally shared set of political rules and sensibilities; some have become totally obsolete.[b] Indeed, those who propose Constant as a model modern liberal thinker hasten to make the necessary distinctions between the significance that ideals such as those of free trade or of a property-based franchise could have for an enlightened nineteenth-century observer, and that which they have for us. It is probably more helpful when discussing Constant, to think of the definition suggested by Michel Foucault, who wrote that liberalism 'rather than a more or less coherent doctrine, rather than a policy pursuing a given number of more or less defined aims, may be best seen as a form of critical reflection upon the practice of government'.[c]

What does still speak to us in Constant's work today is not the content of his political programme, but the problem he confronted, as well as his conception of the function of political theory. His problem was how to reconstruct a non-dogmatic approach to the interpretation of modern society following the collapse of traditional forms of understanding. His solution was that the world could not be interpreted, let alone governed, by appealing to systems, but rather through the exercise of practical prudence and ordinary human virtues. Thus for political theory he reserved a role which was tentative and critical, unostentatious but relentless in its quest for intellectual clarity and moral decency. All of those who have doubts as to our capacity (the capacity of contemporary political theory) to do much better than that will probably find in his writings a sympathetic voice.

[a] For a general outlook on nineteenth-century French liberal views, see the following recent studies: Cheryl B. Welch, *Liberty and Utility, the French Idéologues and the Transformation of Liberalism* (New York, 1984); Louis Giard, *Les libéraux français, 1814–1875* (Paris, 1985); André Jardin, *Histoire du libéralisme politique, de la crise de l'absolutisme à la Constitution de 1875* (Paris, 1985); and Rosanvallon, *Le moment Guizot*.
[b] John Dunn, 'Liberalism' in *Western Political Theory in the Face of the Future* (Cambridge, 1979), pp. 28–54.
[c] *Annuaire de Collège de France*, 1979, p. 370.

THE SPIRIT OF
CONQUEST AND USURPATION
AND THEIR RELATION TO
EUROPEAN CIVILIZATION

Bibliographical Note

Four editions of *De l'esprit de conquête et de l'usurpation* were published during Constant's lifetime. They all appeared in 1814: the first (Hanover) on 30 January; the second (London) in March; the third (Paris) on 22 April and the fourth (Paris) in July.[a] The second edition (which Constant expected to see translated into English, although the translation never materialized) did not differ from the first. In the third edition Constant suppressed chapter 5 on William III, which he had written in support of Bernadotte, and softened some expressions which might prove offensive to French national feeling. The fourth edition was again revised and two new chapters were added to it. It is this fourth edition, which, as the most complete, we have used for this translation.

The suppressed chapter on William III is given at the end, while variants from the previous editions are signalled in the footnotes. When Constant republished his political writings in 1818–19 in the *Cours de politique constitutionnelle*, he omitted *The Spirit of Conquest and Usurpation* out of sheer political embarrassment. This was only republished over thirty years after Constant's death, in 1861, in the new two-volume version of the *Cours de politique* edited by Edouard Laboulaye.

[a] For further details about the single editions see: C. P. Courtney, *A Bibliography of editions of the writings of Benjamin Constant to 1833* (London, 1981).

Preface to the first edition

The present work is part of a treatise on politics, long since completed, but apparently doomed by the condition of France and of Europe at large never to see the light. At the time when it was written, the continent was merely a vast prison, cut off from all communication with that noble country, England, generous asylum of free thought and illustrious refuge of the dignity of mankind. All of a sudden, from the two extremities of the earth, two great nations answered the call, and the flames of Moscow were the dawn of liberty for the entire world. We may now hope that France itself will be not be excluded from this universal deliverance: the France that commands the respect of the very nations that fight against her; the France whose will is enough by itself both to win and to bestow peace. The moment has therefore come, when each of us, in accordance with his lights and his capacities, can pride himself on being of use.

The author of the present work, until recently one of the representatives of a people reduced to silence, and only illegally deprived of this mandate, believes that his voice, however inconsequential it might otherwise be, will at least have the merit of breaking that appearance of unanimity that so astonishes and offends the rest of Europe, and is in fact simply the effect of the terror experienced by the French people.

[a] Constant refers here to his expulsion from the Tribunate in 1802, when the *sénatus-consulte* of 16 Thermidor, Year X (4 August 1802) reduced the number of the Tribunes from one hundred to fifty. He provocatively signed the work 'Benjamin Constant, membre du Tribunat éliminé en 1802'.

[b] The First edition added after 'believes': 'that although the circumstances were hardly suited to the discussion of a large number of abstract questions . . .' In the same edition this whole passage is not in the Preface, but follows as a separate note (*avertissement*): see footnote *a*, p. 46 below.

The author dares to claim, with deep conviction, that there is not a single line in this book to which almost the whole of the French population, if only it were free, would not be eager to put its signature.

The author has omitted here all purely theoretical discussions, extracting only what seemed to him of immediate interest. He might perhaps have increased the interest of his work by more direct expression of his personal views, but he has preferred scrupulously to retain what profound feeling had dictated to him when the world still lay beneath the yoke of the tyrant. He felt it repugnant to show himself more bitter or more daring against deserved adversity than he had in the face of guilty prosperity. If the present public calamities left any room for the acknowledgement of personal considerations, it would give him pleasure to remember that, when the project of general enslavement brooked no opposition, it was found necessary to stifle his voice.[a]

Hanover, *31 December 1813*[b]

Preface to the third edition

This work was written in Germany[c] in the month of November 1813 and published the following January. It was republished in England at the beginning of March. The present edition has undergone few changes: not because I did not feel that much of it fell far short of perfection, but because a work written for a particular occasion ought, as far as possible, to remain as it was in the circumstances for which it was written.

The reader, I am sure, will not fail to see that, if I had written this work in France or at the present moment, I would have expressed myself differently on more than one subject. To the horror which I felt

---

[a] In the First edition, the following note was added to the Preface: 'Before appending my name to this book I asked myself whether I may not be accused of presumption for discussing interests which are committed to the most powerful and noblest of hands. I concluded, first, that since the general opinion is simply formed by individual ones, today everyone is under a pressing obligation to contribute to the formation of a public spirit which will sustain the noble efforts of sovereigns and peoples.'

[b] In the First edition the Preface was not dated. The work did in fact appear on 30 December.

[c] Constant had arrived in Hanover from Brunswick on 3 November 1813. See his *Journal* in *Oeuvres*, p. 684.

towards the government of Bonaparte was added, I must admit, a degree of impatience against the nation that bore his yoke. No one was more aware how hateful that yoke was to that nation. I suffered to see her courage insulted and her blood spilt to keep her in servitude. I suffered still more that the tributes which she lavished on her tyrant should seem to foreigners a proof that she deserved her fate. It exasperated me to see her acting no only against her own interest, but in conflict both with her own nature and with that delicacy and exquisite feeling for honour and propriety which so peculiarly distinguished her. I felt that France was slandering herself, and that it was useless to attempt to justify her. Whenever we did attempt to do so, we sad refugees in a foreign land, some article in the *Moniteur*[a] would come along to devastate our feeble explanations. Only those who have experienced a comparable misery can fully understand it, and for them it will be easy to forgive the few expressions of bitterness provoked by a grief the vividness of which merely betrayed our jealousy for the honour of the French name.

Paris, *22 April 1814*

---

[a] *Le Moniteur universel*, the main government paper during the first empire.

Foreword to the fourth edition

Men whose opinion I greatly value seem to have misunderstood some of my assertions. Therefore I have added at the end of this edition some thoughts that my fear of losing the reader's attention, amidst the turmoil in which Europe found itself, had previously led me to suppress.

I propose to examine two great scourges in relation to the present condition of mankind and to modern civilization. One of these is the spirit of conquest; the other, usurpation.

There are things that are possible in one age, but that no longer remain so in another. This truth is often neglected, and never without danger.[a]

It is a great evil when the men who hold in their hands the destiny of the world are mistaken about what is actually possible. Experience then, instead of serving them, can only harm and confuse them. They read history and see what was done earlier, and do not stop to consider whether it can still be done now. They try to make use of old, broken tools. Their obstinacy, or, if you like, their genius, may give their efforts an ephemeral success. But since they are at odds with the moods, the interests, the entire moral existence of their contemporaries, these forces react against them. And, within a span of time all too long for their victims, but extremely short if we consider it historically, nothing is left of their enterprises but the crimes they have committed and the sufferings they have caused.

The duration of any power depends on the harmony between its

---

[a] First edition: 'this truth may seem trivial: it is nevertheless often neglected . . .'

48

spirit and the time to which it belongs. Each century, in some sense, waits for a man to represent it. When this man makes his appearance, or seems to do so, all the forces of the moment group themselves around him. If he represents the prevailing spirit faithfully, he cannot but succeed. If he strays from the appointed path, his success becomes at best doubtful, and if he persists in following a wrong path the assent that constituted his power deserts him, and his power collapses.

Woe betide those who, believing themselves invincible, throw down the gauntlet to the human race, and claim to carry out through it, since they have no other instrument, upheavals of which it disapproves and miracles for which it has no wish.

PART I

The spirit of conquest

CHAPTER 1

The virtues compatible with war at given stages of social development

Several writers, led into commendable exaggeration by their love of humanity, have envisaged war only under its baneful aspect. I, however, willingly recognize its advantages.[a]

It is not true that war is always an evil. At certain stages in the history of mankind, war is simply in man's nature. It favours the development of his finest and grandest faculties. It opens up to him a treasury of precious enjoyments. It forms in him that greatness of soul, skill, sang-froid, scorn for death, without which he could never be confident that there was any form of cowardice he might not display, and even crime he might not commit. War teaches him heroic devotion and makes him form sublime friendships. It links him more closely to his country on the one hand and his fellow soldiers on the other. It crowns noble deeds with noble leisure. But all these advantages of war depend on one indispensable condition: that war should be the natural outcome of the situation and the national spirit of the people.

For I am not speaking here of a nation attacked and defending its independence. No doubt such a nation could well combine warlike

---

[a] In the 1806 draft of Constant's political treatise, the discussion of the topic of war in the ancient and modern world was to occupy Book 13: 'De la guerre'. For the surviving fragments of this section of the work, which are re-echoed in Part 1 of the *Spirit of Conquest*, see E. Hofmann (ed.), *Les 'Principes de Politique'*, vol. 2, pp. 333–53.

ardour with the highest virtues; or, rather, its warlike ardour would in itself be the highest of all virtues. In this case, however, we are not talking of war properly, but of legitimate self-defence, that is to say of patriotism, of love of justice, of all the noble and sacred passions.

A people that, without being summoned to defend its own homes, is led by its circumstances or national character towards military expeditions and conquests, may still combine its warlike spirit with simplicity of manners, disdain for luxury, generosity, loyalty, fidelity to agreements, respect for a courageous enemy, even mercy and regard for its defeated enemy. Indeed we find such shining qualities, in ancient history and in the annals of the Middle Ages, in a number of nations, for whom war was a well-nigh habitual occupation.

But does the present condition of European peoples permit one to hope for any such amalgam of virtues? Is love of war really part of their national character? Does it really arise out of their circumstances? If these two questions must be answered in the negative, it follows that in our time, in order to lead nations towards war and conquest, it is necessary to overturn the situation in which they find themselves, which can scarcely be done without inflicting many evils upon them, corrupting their character and endowing them with a multitude of vices.

CHAPTER 2

The character of modern nations in relation to war

The warrior peoples of antiquity owed their bellicose spirit mainly to the situation in which they found themselves. Divided into small tribes, they contended by force of arms for the possession of a narrow territory. Driven by necessity against one another, they fought or threatened each other incessantly. Even those who had no ambition to be conquerors, could still not lay down their sword lest they should themselves be conquered. For all of them the price of their security, their independence, their whole existence was war.

Our world is, in this respect, precisely the opposite of the ancient world. While in the past each nation formed an isolated family, the born enemy of other families, a great mass of human beings now exist that, despite the different names under which they live and their different forms of social organization, are essentially homogeneous in their nature. This mass is strong enough to have nothing to fear from hordes that are still barbarous. It is sufficiently civilized to find war a burden. Its uniform tendency is towards peace. The warlike tradition, a heritage from distant ages, and above all the errors of governments, slow down the effects of this tendency, but every day it makes further progress. The leaders of nations pay tribute to it when they try to avoid an open confession of their ambition for conquest and their hopes for a glory won solely by force of arms. The son of Philip[a] would no longer dare to propose to his subjects the invasion of the universe; and the discourse of Pyrrhus to Cineas[b] would appear today the height of insolence or folly.

A government that spoke of military glory as an aim would betray ignorance of, or contempt for, the spirit of nations and the age. It would be in error by a thousand years. Even if it should initially succeed, it would be interesting to see who in the end would win this odd wager, our own century or the offending government.

We have finally reached the age of commerce, an age which must necessarily replace that of war, as the age of war was bound to precede it. War and commerce are only two different means to achieve the same end, that of possessing what is desired. Commerce is simply a tribute paid to the strength of the possessor by the aspirant to possession. It is an attempt to obtain by mutual agreement what one can no longer hope to obtain through violence. A man who was always the stronger would never conceive the idea of commerce. It is experience, by proving to him that war, that is, the use of his strength against the strength of others, is open to a variety of obstacles and defeats, that leads him to resort to commerce, that is, to a milder and surer means of getting the interests of others to agree with his own.

War then comes before commerce. The former is all savage impulse, the latter civilized calculation. It is clear that the more the commercial tendency prevails, the weaker must the tendency to war become.

---

[a] Alexander of Macedonia.

[b] The original source of this episode is Plutarch, *Lives*, vol. 6 (Pyrrhus-Marius/Lysander-Sylla); but Constant was probably familiar with Boileau's version in the first Épistre: see Nicolas Boileau-Despréaux, *Oeuvres complètes*, ed. by A. Adam and F. Escal (Paris, 1966), 'Épistre I', pp. 103–7.

The sole aim of modern nations is repose, and with repose comfort, and, as source of comfort, industry. War becomes every day a more ineffective means of attaining this aim. Its hazards no longer offer either to individuals or to nations benefits that match the results of peaceful work and regular exchange. Among the ancients, a successful war increased both private and public wealth in the form of slaves, tributes and lands shared out. For the moderns, even a successful war always costs more than it brings in.

The Roman republic, with no commerce, no letters, no arts, no other domestic occupation than agriculture, restricted to a territory too small for its inhabitants, surrounded by barbarous tribes, always threatened or threatening, followed its natural destiny in pursuing uninterrupted military adventures. A government which in our day wished to imitate the Roman republic, would differ from it in that, acting in opposition to its own people, it would make the instruments of its policy at least as unhappy as its victims. A people thus governed would be the Roman republic without its liberty, without that national impulse that makes all sacrifices easy, without the hope that each individual enjoyed of a share in the conquered land, without, in short, all those circumstances which made that hazardous and troubled kind of life attractive to the Romans.

Commerce has modified the very nature of war. In the past commercial nations were always defeated by their bellicose enemies. Today they can successfully resist them. They find support even among their enemies. The infinite and complex ramifications of commerce have placed the interest of societies beyond the frontiers of their own territory; the spirit of the age triumphs over the narrow and hostile spirit that men seek to dignify with the name of patriotism.

Carthage, struggling against Rome in antiquity, was bound to succumb: the force of things was against her. But if the war between Rome and Carthage were fought now, Carthage would have the hopes of the entire world on her side; the customs of today and the spirit of the times would be her allies.[a]

The condition of modern nations thus prevents them from being bellicose by nature: and more detailed reasons for this, which are also connected with the progress of mankind and consequently, with the differences between ages, come to be added to these general causes.

[a] As Edouard Laboulaye observed in his comment on the text (*Cours de politique constitutionnelle*, vol. 2, p. 141, note 2) Carthage and Rome here clearly stand for London and Paris.

The new way of fighting, the changes in weapons, artillery, have deprived military life of what made it most attractive. There is no longer any struggle against danger: there is only fatality. Courage itself must be tinged with resignation or indifference. We no longer enjoy that pleasure of the will, of action, of the development of our physical and moral faculties, that made hand-to-hand fighting so attractive to the heroes of antiquity or to the knights of the Middle Ages.

War has lost its charm as well as its utility. Man is no longer driven to it either by interest or by passion.

CHAPTER 3

The spirit of conquest in the present condition of Europe

Any government that wished today to goad a European people to war and conquest would commit a gross and disastrous anachronism. It would labour to impose upon that nation an impulse contrary to nature. Since none of the motives that induced the men of past ages to brave so many dangers and to endure so many exertions remain for the men of our own day, it would have to offer them motives compatible with the present state of civilization. It would have to stimulate them to combat by means of that same desire for pleasure that, left to itself, could only dispose them to peace. Our century, that values everything according to its utility, and, as soon as one attempts to move out of this sphere, opposes its irony to every real or feigned enthusiasm, could not content itself with a sterile glory, which we are no longer in the habit of preferring to other kinds. It would be necessary to put pleasure in the place of glory, pillage in place of triumph. It makes one shudder to imagine what the military spirit would become if it depended upon these motives alone.

In the picture that I am about to sketch, nothing could be more remote from my intentions than to do injustice to those heroes who, standing with delight between their homeland and danger, have, in all countries, protected the independence of nations; to those heroes who have so gloriously defended our beautiful France.*a* I have no fear of

---

a The First edition had simply: 'defended France'.

being misunderstood by them. There is more than one among them whose soul, in sympathy with mine, shares all my feelings and who, recognizing in these lines his own secret opinion, will regard their author as his own instrument.

CHAPTER 4

Of a military race acting on self-interest alone

The warlike peoples thus far known to us, were all moved by nobler motives than the real and positive profits of war. In some, religion mingled with their bellicose impulses. The turbulent liberty enjoyed by others conferred upon them a superabundant energy, which they needed to exercise outside their own territory. They associated with the idea of victory that of a fame extending well beyond their mortal life, and so fought not to satisfy a base greed for present and material enjoyments, but with a hope which was in some sense ideal, and which exalted their imagination like everything that loses itself in the vagueness of the future.

So it is that, even for those nations that seem to us exclusively preoccupied with pillage and robbery, the acquisition of wealth was by no means the chief aim. Thus we see the Scandinavian heroes having all the treasures they had won during their life burnt on their funeral pyres, to force the generations that succeeded them to win fresh treasures by fresh exploits. Indeed, for them wealth was precious as a dazzling witness to the victories that they had won, rather than as a sign of status or a means to enjoyment.

But, if a purely military race were formed now, since its ardour would not rest upon any conviction, any sentiment, any thought, and since all those reasons for exaltation which formerly could ennoble carnage itself would be strangers to it, its only impulse and motivation would lie in the narrowest and grimmest personality. It would adopt the ferocity of the warlike spirit, but it would retain commercial self-interest. These reborn Vandals would not have that ignorance of luxury, simplicity of manners and contempt for all base actions which characterized their rude predecessors. With the brutality of barbarism they would combine the refinements of luxury, with the excesses of violence, the guile of greed.

Men who were formally told that they were fighting only in order to pillage, men whose bellicose ideas had been reduced to this clear and mathematical result, would be different indeed from the warriors of antiquity.

Four hundred thousand well-trained, well-armed egoists would know that their destiny was either to inflict or to suffer death. They would calculate that it was better to resign themselves to their destiny than to evade it, because the tyranny that condemned them to it was stronger than them. They would turn for consolation to their promised reward, the spoils of those against whom they were being led. Consequently they would march with the determination to make the most of their own strength. They would show neither mercy for the vanquished nor respect for the weak: the vanquished being, to their misfortune, the owners of something, would appear to the conquerors simply as an obstacle between them and their loot. Self-interest would have killed in their souls all natural emotions but those that stem from sensuality. They would still be moved by the sight of a woman, but not by that of an old man or a child. All their practical knowledge would serve them the better to draw up their plans of massacre and despoilment. Their familiarity with legal procedures would give to their acts of injustice the impassiveness of the laws. Their familiarity with social form would give to their cruelties a veneer of unconcern and thoughtlessness, which they would consider elegant. In this way they would travel through the world, turning the progresses of civilization against civilization itself, dedicating themselves entirely to their own self-interest, taking murder as a means, debauchery as a pastime, derision for gaiety, and pillage as their end; separated by a moral gulf from the rest of mankind, and united among themselves only like wild animals that hurl themselves in packs upon the flocks on which they prey.

Such would they be in their triumph. What would they be like in their reverses?

Since they would only have a goal to attain, and not a cause to defend, once they had missed their goal, no conscience would sustain them. They would be bound by no conviction but would stand by one another out of mere physical necessity, and even from that each would seek to struggle free.

For men to unite together in face of their destiny, they need something more than mere self-interest: they need real beliefs; they need morality. Self-interest tends to isolate them, because it offers to each individual the chance to be more successful or more skilful on his own. The same egoism that in times of prosperity would make these conquerors of the earth pitiless towards their enemies, would make them in adversity indifferent and faithless towards their brothers in arms. This spirit would penetrate all ranks, from the highest to the most obscure. In his companion in agony, each of them would see a compensation for the pillage that has become impossible against the enemy. The sick would despoil the dying, the runaway the sick. The weak and the injured would appear to the officer charged with their care a troublesome burden of which he would rid himself at any price. The general, who had led his army into a situation from which there was no escape, would feel no responsibility for the unfortunates whom he has thus led into the abyss; he would not stay with them to save them. Desertion[a] would seem to him a simple means to escape from reverses or to remedy mistakes. Why should he care if he himself has led them there, if they have trusted his word, if they have committed their lives to him, if they defended him to the very last with their dying hands? Useless instruments, must they not be cast aside?

No doubt these consequences of a military spirit founded exclusively upon self-interest could hardly manifest themselves to their full terrible extent among any modern people unless the system of conquest were to last for several generations. Thank heaven,[b] despite all the efforts of their leader, the French have remained and will always remain far from the limit towards which he has been carrying them. Those peaceful virtues that our civilization nourishes and develops still struggle victoriously against the corruption and the vices which the fury of conquest[c] summons up and which are necessary to it. Our armies[d] give proofs of humanity as well as courage, and often win the affection of those populations which today, through the fault of a single man, they are reduced to having to repulse, while formerly they had been

---

[a] The first edition had: 'to abandon them'.
[b] This whole sentence, from 'Thank heaven . . .' to 'carrying them.' is missing in the first edition.
[c] The First edition instead of: 'the fury of conquest' has: 'this system'.
[d] This sentence, from 'Our armies' to 'conquer them' was missing in the First edition.

forced to conquer them. But it is the national spirit, the spirit of the age that is resisting the government. If this government persists, the virtues that survive the efforts of its authority will be a sort of indiscipline. Self-interest being the watchword, any disinterested feeling will smack of insubordination: and the longer this terrible regime[a] lasts, the weaker and rarer these virtues will become.

CHAPTER 5

A further reason for the deterioration of the military class within the system of conquest

It has frequently been observed that gamblers are the most immoral of men. The reason is that every day they risk all that they have. For them there is no secure future: they live and strive under the empire of hazard.[b]

In the system of conquest, the soldier becomes a gambler, with this difference, that his stake is life itself. But this stake cannot be withdrawn. He constantly exposes himself to chance that must sooner or later turn against him. He has no future either. Hazard is his blind and pitiless master too.

Now, morality needs time. It is there that it sets its compensations and rewards. For a man who lives from minute to minute or from battle to battle, time does not exist. The rewards of the future become chimerical. The pleasure of the moment alone has some certainty. To use an expression that is doubly appropriate here, each pleasure is so

---

[a] The First edition instead of: 'terrible regime' had: 'system of conquest'.

[b] It is important, in order to appreciate this analogy fully, to keep in mind that Constant was himself a keen and compulsive gambler. See: René Bourgeois, 'Jeu et politique, le cas de Benjamin Constant' in *Romantisme et politique, 1815–1851*: Colloque de l'École Normale Supérieure de Saint-Cloud, 1966 (Paris, 1969), pp. 55–61 and 129–30.

much won from the enemy. Who could fail to see that the habit of this lottery of pleasure and death must necessarily prove corrupting?

Observe the difference that always distinguishes legitimate defence from the system of conquest; this difference will often reappear. The soldier who fights for his country is only exposed to danger for a while. His more distant view is one of rest, liberty, glory. He has therefore a future; and his morality, far from being depraved, is ennobled and exalted. But the instrument of an insatiable conqueror can see only one war following another, after one devastated country a further country to devastate or, in other words, after danger, yet more danger.

CHAPTER 6

The influence of this military spirit upon the internal condition of nations

It is not sufficient to consider the influence of the system of conquest[a] upon the army and upon the relations it establishes between the army and foreigners. It is also necessary to consider it in the relations that arise from it between the army and its own citizens.

An exclusive and hostile corporate spirit is bound to dominate those associations whose aim is different from that of other men. Notwithstanding the mildness and purity of Christianity, the confederations of its priests have frequently formed separate states within a state. Everywhere the men who compose an army set themselves apart from the rest of the nation. They develop a kind of respect for the use of that force of which they are the holders. Their customs and ideas become subversive of those principles of order and of peaceful and regular liberty that all governments have the interest, as well as the duty, to hold sacred.

Consequently, the creation in a country, through a series of prolonged or incessantly renewed wars, of a large mass imbued exclusively by the military spirit, is not a matter of indifference. For this incon-

---

[a] The First edition has simply 'conquest'.

venience cannot in fact be kept within limits which make its importance less perceptible. The army, marked out from the rest of the people by its spirit, is merged with it in the ordinary administration of affairs.

A government engaged in conquest is more interested than any other in rewarding its immediate instruments with power and honours. It could not keep them in an entrenched encampment. It must on the contrary bedeck them with pomp and civil dignities.

But will those warriors lay down, together with the iron in which they are covered, their spirit, nourished since childhood by familiarity with danger? Will they don, together with civilian dress,[a] that veneration for the laws and respect for protective forms, those tutelary deities of human associations? To them the unarmed class appears vulgar and ignoble, laws are superfluous subtleties, the forms of social life just so many insupportable delays. What they value above all, in social transactions as in military exploits, is the speed of manoeuvre. Unanimity seems to them as necessary as it is for troops to wear the same uniform. Opposition, for them, is disorder; reasoning insubordination, the courts councils of war, the judges soldiers under orders, the accused enemies and the trials battles.[b]

This is no fanciful exaggeration. Have we not witnessed, during the last twenty years, the introduction almost everywhere in Europe of military justice, the first principle of which was to curtail procedure, as if any curtailment of procedure were not in itself the most revolting sophism: since, if procedure is superfluous, all courts ought to abolish it; but if necessary, all courts ought to respect it; and undoubtedly, the more serious the charge, the more important it is to examine it carefully. Have we not more than once seen sitting among the judges men whose very clothing bespoke their sworn obedience and who consequently could not be independent judges?

Our descendants will not believe, if they have some sense of human dignity, that there was a time when men, certainly illustrious for their

---

[a] The First edition has: 'the senatorial toga'.

[b] The organization of justice during the empire was a sort of compromise between the system of the *ancien régime* (in which justice was administered chiefly by the local authorities: *juges de paix, parlements, cours souveraines* and *conseils superieurs*) and the revolutionary one (in which the central government designated the presidents and vice-presidents of tribunals). In attacking the repressive character of Napoleon's justice, Constant had especially in mind the creation of the *magistrats de sureté* (representatives of the government in the local – *départemental* – courts) and the resort to special military courts.

immortal deeds, but bred beneath canvas[a] and ignorant of civil life, interrogated defendants whom they were unable to understand, and condemned without appeal citizens whom they had no right to judge. Indeed our grandchildren will not believe, unless they are the most abject of people, that legislators, writers and people accused of political crimes were called before military tribunals, thus setting up, with ferocious irony, blind courage and thoughtless submission as judges of opinion and thought. They will not believe either that warriors returning from their victories, covered with laurels as yet unwithered, had forced upon them the horrible task of turning themselves into executioners, of pursuing, seizing and slaughtering their fellow citizens, whose names, like their crimes, were unknown to them. No, they will cry, this was never the price of our victories, of our triumphal pomp! No, it is not thus that the champions of France used to reappear in their own country and greet their native land!

Certainly the fault was not theirs. A thousand times I heard them groaning at their unhappy obedience. I am happy to repeat it, their virtues have withstood, more than human nature would allow us to hope, the influence of the system of warfare and the actions of a government which sought to corrupt them. This government alone is guilty, while our armies alone deserve the merit of all the evil that they refrain from doing.[b]

CHAPTER 7

A further drawback of the formation of this military spirit

Finally, by a sad reaction, that part of the population which the government had forced to adopt the military spirit, would for its part constrain the government to persevere with the system for which it had taken so much care to form it.

A large army, proud of its successes and used to pillage, is no easy instrument to handle. We do not speak simply of the dangers it

---

[a] The First edition has simply: 'when men bred beneath canvas . . .'
[b] This last paragraph, from 'Certainly' to 'from doing.' is missing in the First edition.

represents for those peoples that have popular constitutions. History here is only too full of examples which it would be superfluous to mention.

Now the soldiers of a republic, illustrious after six centuries of victories, surrounded by monuments to liberty erected by twenty generations of heroes, trampling upon the ashes of the Cincinnati and the Camilli, march at Caesar's order to profane the graves of their ancestors and to enslave the eternal city. Now the English legions launch themselves, with Cromwell, upon a parliament still struggling against the chains intended for it and against the crimes of which they wished to make it the instrument; and deliver up to a hypocritcal usurpation both the king and the republic.

But absolute governments have no less to fear from this ever-threatening force. If it is terrible against foreigners and against the people itself in the name of its leader, it may, at any moment, become a threat to its own master. In the same way those formidable and colossal beasts[a] which barbarous nations set at the head of their armies to direct them against their enemies, would suddenly recoil, stricken with fear or seized with fury and, not recognizing the voice of their masters, would crush and disperse those same battalions that expected from them their salvation and their triumph.

It is thus necessary to keep that army at work, restless in its fearsome idleness; it is necessary to keep it at a distance; it is necessary to find enemies for it to fight. The system of warfare, independently of the present wars, carries the seeds of future wars. The sovereign who has entered that path, driven by a fatality that he himself has summoned up, cannot at any time revert to peace.

CHAPTER 8

The effect of a conquering government upon the mass of the nation

I have shown, I believe, that a government given up to the spirit of invasion and conquest must corrupt a part of the population to secure

---

[a] In the First edition: 'large animals'.

its active service in its own enterprises. I shall now argue that, while corrupting this chosen portion of the population, it must also act upon the rest of the nation, demanding its passive obedience and sacrifices, in such a way as to disturb its reason, pervert its judgement and overturn all its ideas.

When a people is naturally belligerent, the authority that rules it has no need to deceive it to lead it to war. Attila pointed out to his Huns the part of the world upon which they were to descend, and they fell upon it, because Attila was simply the instrument and the representative of their own impulse. But in our day, since war has no advantages to offer nations and is for them only a source of deprivation and suffering, a defence of the system of conquest can rest only upon sophism and imposture.

Even whilst abandoning itself to its grandiose projects, the government would hardly dare to tell the nation: 'Let us march to conquer the world!' It would reply with one voice: 'We have no wish to conquer the world'.

Instead it would talk of national independence, of national honour, of the rounding off of frontiers, of commercial interests, of precautions dictated by foresight, and what next? The vocabulary of hypocrisy and injustice is inexhaustible.[a]

It would talk of national independence, as if the independence of a nation were in jeopardy because other nations are independent.

It would talk of national honour, as if a nation's honour were injured because other nations retain their own.

It would insist on the necessity of rounding off frontiers, as if this doctrine, once admitted, would not banish all tranquillity and equity from the earth. For it is always outwards that governments wish to round off their frontiers. No government is known to have sacrificed a portion of its territory to give to the rest a greater geometrical regularity. The rounding off of frontiers is a system the basis of which is self-defeating, the elements of which contradict one another and the realization of which only serves to render illegitimate the possession of the strongest since it rests upon the spoliation of the weakest.

The same government would invoke the interests of commerce, as if

---

[a] Compare Constant's illustration of the public rhetoric of military aggression with Marcel Proust's analysis of the language of the French press and French diplomacy during the first world war. See *A la recherche du temps perdu*, ed. by P. Clarac and A. Ferré, 3 vols. (Paris, 1954), vol. 3, pp. 770ff.

it served commerce to deprive a country of its most flourishing youth, to take away from agriculture, from manufacture and from industry[1] the most necessary members of their labour force, to raise barriers drenched in blood between other countries and one's own. Commerce rests upon the good understanding of nations with each other, it can be sustained only by justice; it is founded upon equality; it thrives in peace. Yet it is allegedly in the interests of commerce that a government should incessantly renew fierce wars, that it should call down upon the head of its people universal hatred, that it should march from injustice to injustice, that it should every day weaken its credit by violence, and that it should refuse to tolerate any equals!

Under the pretext of precautions dictated by foresight, this government would attack its most peaceful neighbours and its humblest allies attributing to them hostile intentions, as if anticipating premeditated aggression. If the unhappy objects of its calumnies were easily subjugated, it would then pride itself on having pre-empted them. If they had the time and the strength to resist it, it would cry: 'You see, they did want war, since they are defending themselves!'[2]

One should not think that such conduct is the accidental result of a particular perversity. It is, on the contrary, the necessary outcome of this position. Any authority that wished today to undertake extensive conquests would be condemned to this series of vain pretexts and scandalous lies. It would assuredly be guilty, and we shall not seek to diminish its crime. But this crime would not consist in the means employed, but in the voluntary choice of the situation that imposes such means.

Authority would have to work upon the intellectual faculties of the mass of its subjects in the same way as upon the moral qualities of the

---

[1] War costs more than its expenses, says a judicious writer: it costs all that it prevents a nation from gaining. Say, *Écon. polit.*, v, 8.
[Jean Baptiste Say, *Traité d'économie politique*, 4th edn (2 vols., Paris, 1819), vol. 2, p. 298. Constant probably used the 1803 edition (2 vols., Paris), vol. 2, pp. 408–48.]

[2] The French revolution saw the invention of a pretext for war previously unknown, that of freeing peoples from the yoke of their governments, which were supposed to be illegitimate and tyrannical. On this pretext, death was brought among men, some of whom lived quietly under institutions softened by time and habit while others had enjoyed for several centuries all the benefits of liberty. Forever shameful age, when an infamous government inscribed sacred words on its guilty standards, troubled peace, violated independence, destroyed the prosperity of its innocent neighbours, adding to the scandal of Europe by its lying protestations of respect for the rights of men and zeal for humanity! The worst of all conquests is the hypocritical one, says Machiavelli, as if he had foreseen our history.

military component. It would have to strive to banish all logic from the spirit of the former, as it would have tried to suffocate all humanity in the hearts of the latter. All words would lose their meaning. 'Moderation' would presage violence; 'justice' would announce iniquity. The law of nations would become a code of expropriation and barbarism. All those notions that several centuries of enlightenment have introduced into the relations between societies as in those between individuals, would once again be thrust back. Mankind would regress to that time of devastation that seemed to us the disgrace of history. Hypocrisy alone will distinguish the two: and this hypocrisy will prove still more corrupting since no-one will believe in it. It is not only when they confuse and deceive people that the lies of authority are harmful: they are no less so when they do not deceive them in the least.

Subjects who suspect their masters of duplicity and perfidy, themselves develop a like duplicity and perfidy. He who hears the leader who governs him called a great politician because each line he publishes is an imposture, wishes himself to become a great politician in a more subaltern sphere. Truth seems to him stupidity, deception an index of skilfulness. Before, he lied only out of self-interest; now he will lie from self-interest and from self-regard. He will have all the fatuity of chicanery. If this contagion conquers a people naturally prone to imitation, a people in which everyone fears above all to appear a dupe, how long will it take before private morality becomes engulfed in the wreck of the public?

CHAPTER 9

Means of coercion necessary to supplement the efficacy of falsehood

Supposing, nevertheless, that some shreds of reason should remain afloat, this will prove in other respects yet another evil.

Coercion will have to fill the gap left by sophistry. Because everybody will seek to elude the obligation to shed his blood on expeditions whose utility no-one can prove to him, the authorities will have to bribe a greedy crowd to break the general opposition. We shall see spies and informers, those eternal resources of force when it has created factitious duties and crimes, encouraged and rewarded. We shall see henchmen let loose, like ferocious mastiffs, in the cities and throughout the countryside, to pursue and shackle fugitives who are innocent in the eyes of morality and nature. We shall see a class of the population preparing itself for every crime by accustoming itself to violate the laws; another class familiarizing itself with infamy by living off the misfortunes of its fellows. We shall see fathers punished for the faults of their children; the interests of children thus separated from those of their fathers; families faced only with the alternative of uniting for resistance or dividing for betrayal; fatherly love transformed into conspiracy; filial tenderness treated as sedition. All these troubles will occur not for the sake of legitimate self-defence, but in order to acquire remote countries, the possession of which will add nothing to national prosperity, unless we choose to call national prosperity the vain, nefarious renown of a handful of men!

Let us, however, be just. Some consolations are offered to these victims, doomed to fight and die at the far ends of the earth. Look at them, tottering behind their leaders. They have been plunged into a state of intoxication that inspires in them a gross and forced gaiety. The air rings with their loud cries; the villages resound with their licentious songs. This intoxication, these cries, this licence – who would believe it? – are the crowning achievement of their own magistrates!

What a strange reversal is thus produced by the system of conquest in the action of authority. For twenty years you have preached to these same men sobriety, attachment to their families, regularity in their labours. But now it is time to conquer the world! The same men are seized, trained and incited to despise those virtues that had for so long been inculcated into them. They are numbed by intemperance, they are reanimated by debauchery: this is what they call reviving the public spirit.

CHAPTER 10

Further drawbacks of the system of warfare for enlightenment and the educated class

We have not yet completed our account. The evils that we have described, terrible as they appear to us, would not be alone in weighing upon the wretched nation. Other evils would be added to them, perhaps not as striking at their origin, but more irreparable, since they would wither in the bud all hopes for the future.

In certain periods of life, any interruption in the exercise of our intellectual faculties cannot be repaired. The hazardous, negligent and gross habits of the warrior state, the sudden rupture of all domestic relations, a mechanical dependence when the enemy is not present, total independence in morals at the age when passions are most active in their ferment: these can hardly be irrelevant for either morality or knowledge. The needless condemnation to life in camps or barracks of the youthful offspring of the enlightened class, in whom reside, as in a precious vessel, learning, delicacy, rightness of mind and that tradition of gentleness, nobility and elegance that alone distinguishes us from the barbarians, is to cause to the nation as a whole an evil that can never be compensated either by its vain successes, or by the terror it inspires, a terror that brings it no advantage whatsoever.

To devote to the profession of a soldier the son of the merchant, of the artist, of the magistrate, the young man who consecrates himself to letters, to science, to the exercise of some difficult and complicated skill, is to rob him of all the fruits of his earlier education. That education itself is bound to suffer from the prospect of its inevitable interruption. If the brilliant dreams of military glory intoxicate the imagination of the young, they will disdain every peaceful study, every sedentary occupation and any form of work that requires attention, and is at odds with their inclination and the vitality of their nascent faculties. If it is with grief that they see themselves torn from their homes, if they calculate how much the sacrifice of several years will delay their progress, they will despair of themselves. They will not wish to consume themselves in efforts the fruits of which will be taken from them by an iron hand. They will tell themselves that, since authority is denying them the time necessary for their intellectual development it is pointless to struggle against force. Thus the nation will succumb to moral degradation and evergrowing ignorance. It will become brutalized amidst its victories and, beneath its very laurels, it will be haunted by the sense that it is following the wrong path and that it is missing its true goal.[1]

No doubt all our inferences apply only in the case of gratuitous and useless wars. No such considerations could outweigh the necessity to repel an aggressor. In that case all classes must hasten to respond since all are equally threatened. But since their motive is not an ignoble pillage, they are not in any way corrupted. Because their zeal rests upon conviction, coercion becomes superfluous. The interruption of social occupations, motivated as it is by the most sacred of obligations and the dearest of interests, does not have the same effect as arbitrary interruptions. The people can see its limit; it submits itself to it with joy as the means of recovering a state of repose; and when it does recover this state, it is with renewed youth, with ennobled faculties, with the feeling of a force usefully and worthily employed.

But it is one thing to defend one's fatherland, another to attack people who themselves have a fatherland to defend. The spirit of conquest seeks to confuse these two ideas. Some governments, when they send their armies from one pole to the other, still talk about the defence of their hearths; one would think they call all the places to which they have set fire their hearths.

CHAPTER 11

The point of view from which a conquering nation would today regard its own successes

Let us now consider the external results of the system of conquest.

The very disposition that makes the modern prefer peace to war is

---

[1] In France, under the monarchy, there were sixty thousand men in the militia. They enlisted for six years. Thus every year ten thousand men were called up. Necker called the militia a frightful lottery. What would he have said of conscription?

[For Necker's views on war, population and the economy, see Jacques Necker, *De l'administration des finances de la France* in *Oeuvres complètes*, ed. by A. de Staël (15 vols., Paris, 1820), vols. 4–5, 'De la guerre', vol. 5, pp. 573–610.]

initially likely to grant great advantages to any people forced by its government to become an aggressor. Nations absorbed in their pleasures would be slow to resist. They would readily surrender a part of their rights to save the rest. They would hope to preserve their repose by sacrificing their liberty. By a curious paradox, the more pacific the popular spirit, the easier would be the initial success of a state that sets itself to struggle against it.

But what would be the consequences of such a success even for the conquering nation itself? Since this could hardly expect any increase in its real happiness, would it at least find in it some gratification of its self-esteem? Would it claim its share of glory?

Far from it. Such is the present distaste for conquest, that everybody would feel the imperious need to disclaim responsibility for it. There would be universal protest, no less vigorous because it will be silent. The government would see the mass of its subjects standing aside, glum spectators. In the whole empire there would be only a long monologue of power to be heard. At most this monologue would be interrupted, from time to time, when servile interlocutors repeated to their master the speeches he had dictated to them. But the subjects would soon cease to listen to tiresome harangues that they would never be permitted to interrupt. They would avert their eyes from a vain display of which they would bear only the expense and the danger, while its intention was the very opposite of their wishes.

We marvel that the most wonderful enterprises should fail to cause any sensation in our days. It is because the common sense of the people tells them that such things are not done on their behalf. Since the leaders alone find pleasure in them, they alone are loaded with the reward. The interest in victories is concentrated in the authority of its creatures. A moral barrier is raised between restless power and the inert crowd. Success is only a meteor that enlivens nothing in its passage. We scarcely bother to lift our heads for a moment to look at it. Sometimes indeed we are grieved about it, as an encouragement to madness. We shed tears for the victims, but secretly wish for defeat.

In bellicose ages people admired military genius above all. In our peaceful times, they pray for some moderation and some justice.

When a government lavishes upon us great displays of heroism, of numberless creations and destruction, we are tempted to reply: 'The smallest grain of millet would better suit our business'.[1] The most

[1] La Fontaine.
[Jean de la Fontaine, *Fables choisies, mises en vers*, ed. by G. Couton, Classiques Garnier (Paris, 1962), I, 20: 'Le coq et la perle'.]

brilliant feats and their grandiose celebrations are only funeral ceremonies at which we dance upon the graves.

CHAPTER 12

Effect of these successes upon the conquered peoples

'The law of nations for the Romans' – says Montesquieu – 'consisted in exterminating the citizens of the vanquished nation.' The law of nations that we follow today means that a state, after conquering another one, continues to rule it according to its own laws while reserving for itself only the exercise of political and civil government.[1]

I do not propose to investigate just how correct this statement really is. There are certainly many exceptions to be found in the ancient world.

We often see subjected nations that have continued to enjoy all the forms of their preceding administration and their old laws. The religion of the vanquished was scrupulously respected. Polytheism, which recommended the worship of foreign gods, inspired respect for all cults. The Egyptian priesthood retained their power under the Persians. The example of Cambyses, on account of his madness, is not worth mentioning: but we may cite the case of Darius who, having attempted to place his own statue in front of that of Sesostris in a temple, and meeting the opposition of the head priest, did not dare to do violence to him. The Romans left to the inhabitants of the majority

---

[1] To avoid the accusation of producing a false quotation, I shall transcribe the whole paragraph. 'A state that has conquered another one, will treat it in one of the following four ways: it may continue to govern it according to its own laws, claiming for itself only the exercise of political and civil government; it may give it a new political and civil government; it may destroy its society and disperse it among others; or finally it may exterminate all the citizens. The first way is in accordance with the law of nations that we follow today; the fourth is closer to the law of nations of the Romans.' *Esprit de lois*, Book 10, ch. 3. [C. L. S. de Montesquieu, *L'esprit des lois* in *Oeuvres complètes*, ed. by R. Caillois (2 vols., Paris, 1951), vol. 2, pp. 378–9: 'Du droit de conquête'.]

of the subject regions their own municipal authorities, and they interfered with the religion of the Gauls only to abolish human sacrifices.[a]

We shall, however, agree that the effects of conquest had become relatively mild in the last few centuries, and that they remained so until the end of the eighteenth century. The reason is that the spirit of conquest had come to an end. The conquests of Louis XIV himself were more the consequence of the pretensions and arrogance of a proud monarch than of a genuine spirit of conquest. But the spirit of conquest re-emerged from the storms of the French revolution more imperious than ever. Thus the effects of conquest are no longer what they were in the days of Montesquieu.

It is true that the vanquished are no longer reduced to slavery, that they are not deprived of their lands or forced to cultivate them on someone else's behalf, nor are they declared to be a subject race that belongs to its conquerors.

From the outside their position therefore appears more tolerable than in the past. Once the storm is over, everything seems to return to order. Towns are still standing, markets fill up again with people, shops reopen. Apart from casual pillage, which is a misfortune of circumstance, apart from the habitual insolence which is the privilege of victory, apart from the contributions that, systematically imposed, acquire a mild appearance of regularity, and that cease, or ought to cease, once the conquest is accomplished, one would at first say that all that has changed are the names and a number of formalities. But let us examine this question more closely.

Conquest among the ancients often destroyed entire nations. But when it did not destroy them, it left untouched all the objects of men's strongest attachments: their ways of life, their laws, their customs, their gods. Things are not the same in modern times. The vanity of civilization is more tormenting than the pride of barbarism. The latter sees only the mass; the former examines anxiously and in detail.

The conquerors of antiquity, satisfied with general obedience, did not investigate the domestic life or the local relations of their slaves. The subject populations rediscovered almost intact, in the depth of their remote provinces, all that constitutes the charm of life: the habits of their childhood, the consecrated practices, that cluster of memories that, in spite of political subjection, preserves the feeling of a fatherland in a country.

[a] To illustrate his point, Constant is here using material taken from his research on the history of religions.

The conquerors of our days, whether peoples or princes, wish their empire to present an appearance of uniformity, upon which the proud eye of power may travel without meeting any unevenness that could offend or limit its view. The same code of law, the same measures, the same regulations, and if they could contrive it gradually, the same language, this is what is proclaimed to be the perfect form of social organization. Religion is an exception; perhaps because it is despised, being seen as a worn-out error that should be left to die in peace. But this is the only exception. And it is made up for by separating religion as far as possible from the interests of the country.

In everything else, the key word today is uniformity. It is a pity that one cannot destroy all the towns to rebuild them according to the same plan, and level all the mountains to make the ground even everywhere.[a] I am surprised that all the inhabitants have not been ordered to wear the same costume, so that the master may no longer encounter irregular colours and shocking variety.

It is thus that the vanquished, after the calamities that they have suffered, have to undergo a new kind of evil. They were at first the victims of a chimerical glory. They are next the victims of an equally chimerical uniformity.

CHAPTER 13

On uniformity

It is somewhat remarkable that uniformity should never have encountered greater favour than in a revolution made in the name of the rights and the liberty of men.[b] The spirit of system was first entranced by

---

[a] The obsession with uniformity was indeed a dominant feature of the period. In 1787 the writer Choderlos de Laclos produced a 'Project de numérotage des rues de Paris' in which, to overcome the confusion created by rapid urban growth, he suggested that the roads and houses of Paris should be indicated by the letters of the alphabet and numbers. Later on, after the revolution, he proposed the designation of the main *boulevards* by the dates of memorable revolutionary events. Some aspects of this plan (those concerning the numbering of houses) were adopted in 1800 (*arrête* by the Prefect of the Seine, 15 Brumaire year IX). See C. de Laclos, *Oeuvres complètes*, pp. 595–600 and 797–8.

[b] The overall tone of this chapter is strongly reminiscent of Burke's *Reflections*, where he talks about the new administrative division of France into geometrically shaped *Départements*. See Burke, *Reflections*, pp. 314–15.

symmetry. The love of power soon discovered what immense advantages symmetry could procure for it. While patriotism exists only by a vivid attachment to the interests, the ways of life, the customs of some locality, our so-called patriots have declared war on all of these. They have dried up this natural source of patriotism and have sought to replace it by a factitious passion for an abstract being, a general idea stripped of all that can engage the imagination and speak to the memory. To build their edifice, they began by grinding and reducing to dust the materials that they were to employ. Such was their apparent fear that a moral idea might be attached to their institutions, they came close to using numbers to designate their towns and provinces, as they used these to designate the legions and corps in their army.

Despotism, which has replaced demagogy and has made itself heir to the fruits of all its labours, has continued adroitly in the path thus traced. The two extremes found themselves in agreement on this point, because at the bottom of both there was the will to tyranny. The interests and memories that arise from local customs contain a germ of resistance that authority is reluctant to tolerate and that it is anxious to eradicate. It can deal more successfully with individuals; it rolls its heavy body effortlessly over them as if they were sand.

Today, admiration for uniformity, a genuine admiration in some narrow minds, if affected by many servile ones, is received as a religious dogma, by a crowd of assiduous echoers of any favoured opinion.

Applied to all the parts of an empire, this principle must necessarily apply also to all those countries that this empire may conquer. It is therefore the immediate and inseparable consequence of the spirit of conquest.

'But each generation' – claims one of the foreigners who has from the start best predicted our errors – 'each generation inherits from its ancestors a treasure of moral riches, an invisible and precious legacy that it bequeaths to its descendants.'[1] The loss of this treasure is an incalculable evil for a people. By depriving a nation of it, you deprive it of all sense of its own value and dignity. Even if what you put in its place is of greater value, the fact that the people respected what you are taking away from it, while you impose your own improvement upon it by

---

[1] Rehberg, in his excellent work on the Code Napoléon, p. 8.
[August Wilhelm Rehberg, *Über den Code Napoléon und dessen Einführung in Deutschland* (Hanover, 1813).]

force, the result of your operation is simply to make it commit an act of cowardice that demeans and demoralizes it.

The inherent merit of the laws is, let us dare assert, far less important than the spirit with which a nation subjects itself to its laws and obeys them. If it cherishes them and observes them because they seem to it derived from a sacred source, the legacy of generations whose ghosts it venerates, then they fuse themselves intimately with its morality, they ennoble its character, and even when they are faulty, they produce greater virtue, and consequently greater happiness, than would better laws that rested only upon the orders of authority.

I have, I must confess, a great veneration for the past. Every day, the more instructed I am by experience or the more enlightened by reflection, this veneration increases. I will say, to the great scandal of our modern reformers, whether they call themselves Lycurguses or Charlemagnes, that if I found a people who, having been offered the most perfect of institutions, metaphysically speaking, refused them in order to remain faithful to those of its fathers, I would admire this people, and I would think it happier in its feelings and in its soul under its faulty institutions, than it could be made by all the proposed improvements.

This doctrine, I am aware, is not likely to win much favour. We like to make laws, we believe them to be excellent, we pride ourselves on their merit. The past has made itself without our assistance; nobody can claim the glory for it.[1]

Setting aside these considerations, and taking happiness and morality separately, notice that man adapts himself to those institutions that he finds already established, as he does to the laws of physics. He adjusts, in accordance with the very defects of such institutions, his interests, his speculations and his entire plan of life. These defects[a] become softened, because whenever an institution lasts for a long time, there is some exchange between the institution itself and man's own

---

[1] I exclude from my respect for the past only what is unjust. Time never sanctions injustice. Slavery, for example, cannot be legitimated by any lapse of time. The reason is that, in what is intrinsically unjust there is always an injured party, who cannot adjust to its sufferings and for whom, consequently, the salutary influence of the past does not exist. Those who appeal to habit in order to excuse injustice remind me of that French cook who was reproached for making eels suffer when she skinned them. 'They are used to it', she said, 'I have been doing it for thirty years!'

---

[a] First edition: 'their defects'.

interests. Man's relations and hopes cluster around what is already in existence; to change all this, even for the better, is to do him harm.

Nothing is more absurd than to do violence to customs on the pretext of serving people's interests. The first of all interests is to be happy, and our customs form an essential part of our happiness.

It is evident that peoples placed in different situations, brought up with different customs, living in different places, cannot be subjected to perfectly identical forms, usages, practices and laws without a constraint that costs them much more than it is worth to them. The series of ideas by which their moral being has been gradually formed since birth can hardly be modified by an arrangement that is purely nominal, exterior and independent of their will.

Even in those states that have been in existence for a long time, and whose unification has lost the odium of violence and conquest, we observe the patriotism that springs from local differences, the only genuine patriotism, reborn from its own ashes as soon as the hand of power loosens its grip for a moment. The magistrates of the smallest communes pride themselves on embellishing them. They keep up their ancient monuments with care. There is, in almost every village, some erudite man who likes to retell its rustic annals and who is listened to with respect. The inhabitants enjoy everything that gives them the even if deceptive appearance of forming a nation, and of being united by particular ties. One feels that, were they not hindered in the development of such an innocent and beneficial inclination, they would soon develop amongst themselves a kind of communal honour, the honour, so to speak, of a town or of a province, that would be at the same time a pleasure and a virtue. But the jealousy of authority watches them, takes alarm and destroys the germ that is ready to sprout.

The attachment to local customs touches on all the disinterested, noble and pious feelings. How deplorable is the policy that treats it as rebellion! What happens then? In all those states where local life is thus destroyed, a little state is formed in their centre. All interests are concentrated in the capital. There all ambitions make their way to exert themselves; the rest remains inert. Individuals, lost in an unnatural isolation, strangers in the place of their birth, without contact with the past, living only in a hasty present, cast like atoms upon an immense, flat plain, detach themselves from a fatherland that they can nowhere see. Its entirety becomes a matter of indifference to them since their affection cannot come to rest on any of its parts.

Variety is what constitutes organization; uniformity is mere mechanism. Variety is life; uniformity, death.[1]

Thus conquest in our days has an additional demerit that it lacked in antiquity. It pursues the vanquished into the most intimate aspects of their existence. It mutilates them in order to reduce them to uniform proportions. In the past conquerors expected the deputies of conquered nations to appear on their knees before them. Today it is man's morale that they wish to prostrate.

We are always hearing about the great empire, of the whole nation, abstract notions that have no reality. The great empire is nothing independently of its provinces. The whole nation is nothing separated from the parts that compose it. It is in defending the rights of these parts that one defends the rights of the whole nation; since the nation itself is divided into each of those parts. If they are successively stripped of what they hold dearest, if each of them, isolated so as to be made a victim, reverts, by a strange metamorphosis, to being a portion of the great whole, to serve as the pretext for the sacrifice of another portion, the real beings are sacrificed to the abstract one. The people as individuals are sacrificed for the sake of the people *en masse*.

Let us admit it, large states have great disadvantages. Laws proceed from a place so remote from those places where they must be applied, that frequent and serious errors are the inevitable result. The government mistakes the opinions of its neighbourhood, or at most of its place of residence, for the opinion of the whole empire. A local or momentary circumstance becomes the occasion for a general law. The inhabitants of the most remote provinces are suddenly surprised by unexpected innovations, unmerited rigours, and vexatious regulations that subvert all the bases of their calculations and all the safeguards of their interests, because two hundred leagues away men who are complete strangers to them believe that they have anticipated some danger, have divined some agitation or perceived some advantage.

---

[1] We cannot undertake the refutation of all the arguments that are set forth in favour of uniformity. We must confine ourselves to referring the reader to two imposing authorities, Montesquieu, *Esprit des lois*, Book 29, 18, and the Marquis of Mirabeau in his *Ami des hommes*. The latter proves very convincingly that, even in relation to those objects for which it seems most useful to establish uniformity, for example, in weights and measures, the advantages are far fewer than is generally believed, uniformity carries with them many drawbacks.
[C. L. S. de Montesquieu, 'Des idées d'uniformité', *L'esprit des lois, Oeuvres complètes*, vol. 2, p. 882.; Victor Riqueti, Marquis de Mirabeau, *L'ami des hommes ou traité de la population* (6 vols., La Haye, 1758–62), vol. 1, pp. 78–9.]

One cannot help regretting those times when the earth was covered with numerous and vigorous peoples and mankind could stir and exert itself in every way in a sphere suited to its capacity. Authority had no need to be harsh to be obeyed. Liberty could be stormy without being anarchic. Eloquence dominated spirits and moved souls. Glory lay within the reach of talent which, in its struggle against mediocrity, was not submerged by the waves of a heavy and countless multitude. Morals found support in an immediate public, the spectator and the judge of every action in its minutest detail and most delicate nuance.

Those times are no more, and it is pointless to regret them. At least, since we must renounce all these advantages, we cannot too often insist to the masters of the world: in their vast empires let them allow to persist all the diversities of which these are capable, those diversities that are demanded by nature and consecrated by experience. Rules falsify themselves when they are applied to cases which differ too much from one another. The yoke becomes burdensome when it is kept uniform in circumstances which are too diverse in character.

We may add that, in the system of conquest, this obsession with uniformity recoils from the vanquished upon the conquerors. All lose their national character and original colours. The whole becomes simply an inert mass that, at intervals, comes awake in order to suffer, but which otherwise sinks and grows numb beneath the weight of despotism. For only the excess of despotism can in fact prolong a combination that tends to dissolve itself and retain under the same domination states that everything conspires to separate. The prompt establishment of limitless power, says Montesquieu, is the only remedy that can prevent dissolution in these cases: yet another evil, he adds, on top of that of the state's aggrandizement.[a]

Even this remedy, though worse than the evil itself, is of no lasting efficacy. The natural order of things takes revenge on the outrages that men attempt against it, and the more violent the suppression, the more terrible will be the reaction to it.

[a] *Esprit des lois*, Book 2, ch. 16: D'un état despotique qui conquiert' (*Oeuvres complètes*, vol. 2, p. 392); and Book 9, ch. 6: 'De la force défensive des états en général' (*ibid.*, pp. 373–4).

CHAPTER 14

The inevitable end to the successes
of a conquering nation

The force that a people needs to keep all others in subjection is today, more than ever, a privilege that cannot last. The nation that aimed at such an empire would place itself in a more dangerous position than the weakest of tribes. It would become the object of universal horror. Every opinion, every desire, every hatred, would threaten it, and sooner or later those hatreds, those opinions, and those desires would explode and engulf it.

There would certainly be something unjust in turning such a fury against an entire people. An entire country is never guilty of the excesses that its leader makes it commit. It is the leader that leads his country astray, or even more often who dominates it without even doing so.

But the nations that are the victims of its deplorable obedience, will not be prepared to acknowledge its secret feelings, feelings that its conduct belies. They will reproach the instruments for the crimes of the hand that directs them. All France suffered from the ambition of Louis XIV and detested it; but Europe accused France of harbouring that ambition, while Sweden had to pay the price of Charles XII's folly.

When some day the world has regained its reason and recovered its courage, where on earth will the threatened aggressor turn his gaze to find defenders? To what feelings in them will he seek to appeal? What defence will not be discredited in advance, if it issues from the same mouth that, during his guilty prosperity, had lavished so many insults, uttered so many lies, dictated so many orders of destruction? Will he appeal to justice? He has violated it. To humanity? He has trampled it under foot. To the keeping of pledges? All his enterprises have begun with perjury. To the sanctity of alliances? He has treated his allies like slaves. What people could in good faith have allied themselves with him and voluntarily associated themselves with his gigantic dream? No doubt all bent their heads for a time beneath his dominating yoke; but they considered it as a passing calamity. They waited for the tide to turn, certain that its waves would one day disappear into the arid sands,

79

and that they would then be able to walk dry-shod again over the ground ploughed by its ravages.

Will he be able to count on the support of his new subjects? He has deprived them of all that they cherished and respected. He has disturbed the ashes of their fathers and shed the blood of their sons.

All will unite against him. Peace, independence, justice, will be the general rallying cry; and just because they have been proscribed for so long, these words will have acquired an almost magical power. Men, no longer the playthings of folly, will become enthusiasts for good sense. A cry of deliverance, a cry of unity, will ring out from one end of the earth to the other. The sense of public decency will spread to the most indecisive and will carry along the timidest. Nobody will dare to remain neutral, lest he should betray himself.

The conqueror will then see that he has presumed too much upon the degradation of the world. He will learn that calculations based upon immorality and baseness, those calculations on which he prided himself so recently as a sublime discovery, are as uncertain as they are short-sighted, as deceptive as they are ignoble. He laughed at the stupidity of virtue, at that trust in a disinterestedness that seemed to him a chimera, at that appeal to an exaltation whose motives and duration he could not understand, and which he had been tempted to take as the passing access of a sudden disease. Now he discovers that egoism has its own brand of stupidity: that he is no less ignorant about what is good than honesty is about what is evil, and that, in order to know men, it is not sufficient to despise them. Mankind becomes an enigma to him. All around him people talk of generosity, of sacrifices, of devotion. This unfamiliar language comes as a surprise to his ears. He has no idea how to negotiate in that idiom. He remains paralysed, shocked by his failure to understand, a memorable example of Machiavellianism fallen victim to its own corruption.

But meanwhile, how will the people, whose master has driven it to such extremities, respond? Who could fail to pity it, if it was naturally gentle, enlightened, sociable, susceptible to every delicate feeling and every form of heroic courage, and if a fatality unleashed upon it had in this fashion cast it away from the paths of civilization and morality? How deeply would it feel its own misery! Its intimate confidences, its conversations, its literature, all those expressions that it believed itself able to conceal from surveillance, become a single cry of pain.

It would press its questions now upon its leader, now on its own conscience.

Its conscience will reply to it that to proclaim oneself under constraint is not enough to excuse one, that it is not enough to separate one's opinions from one's actions, to disown one's own conduct, and to mutter about blame while cooperating with atrocities.

Its leader would probably try to blame the uncertainties of war, the inconstancy of fortune, the whims of destiny. Truly a handsome result for so many agonies, so many sufferings, and for twenty generations swept away by a lethal wind and hurled into their tombs!

CHAPTER 15

Results of the system of warfare in the present age

The commercial nations of modern Europe, industrious, civilized, placed on a territory large enough for their needs, linked to other peoples by relations the interruption of which would be a disaster, have nothing to hope for from conquest. A useless war is the greatest offence that a government today can commit. It destroys every social guarantee without compensation; it jeopardizes every form of liberty; it injures every interest; it upsets every security; it weighs upon every fortune. It combines and legitimizes every kind of internal and external tyranny. It introduces into judicial forms a hastiness destructive both of their sanctity and of their purpose. It tends to represent all the men whom the agents of authority view with hostility as accomplices of the foreign enemy. It corrupts the rising generations; it divides the people into two parts, one of which despises the other and passes readily from contempt to injustice. It prepares future destructions by means of the past ones and purchases with the evils of the present the evils that are to come.

These are truths that cannot be repeated too often, since political authority, in its haughty disdain, treats them as paradoxes and despises them as mere commonplaces.

There are, moreover, among us, all too many writers always at the service of the system in power; real mercenaries, save for the daring, to whom recantation costs nothing, they do not shrink from any absurdity, they are always on the lookout for a power whose will they can reduce to principles, they are ready to repeat the most contradictory of doctrines, and their zeal is the more indefatigable because it bears no relation to their convictions. These writers have repeated interminably, whenever they received the sign to do so, that peace was what the world needed. But they say at the same time that military glory is the first of all glories, and that it is by the brilliance of arms that France must make itself illustrious. I find it difficult, myself, to explain how military glory can be won except by war, or indeed how the brilliance of arms could be reconciled with that peace that the world so needs. But why should they care? Their aim is to coin phrases in accordance with the order of the day. From the depths of their murky studies, they praise now demagogy, now despotism, now carnage, launching to the best of their abilities every plague upon mankind, and preaching evil for want of the capacity to commit it.

I have sometimes wondered what one of these men who wish to repeat the deeds of Cambyses, Alexander or Attila would reply if his people spoke to him and told him: nature has given you a quick eye, boundless energy, a consuming need for strong emotion, an inexhaustible thirst for confronting and surmounting danger, for meeting and overcoming obstacles. But why should we pay for these? Do we exist only so that they may be exercised at our expense? Are we here only to build, with our dying bodies, your road to fame? You have a genius for fighting: what good is it to us? You are bored by the inactivity of peace. Why should your boredom concern us? The leopard too, if it were transported to our populous cities, might complain of not finding those thick forests, those immense plains where it delighted in pursuing, seizing and devouring its prey, where its vigour was displayed in the speed and dash of the chase. Like the leopard, you belong to another climate, to another land, to another species from our own. Learn civilization, if you wish to reign in a civilized age. Learn peace, if you wish to rule over peaceful peoples; or look elsewhere for instruments like yourself, who care nothing for rest, for whom life has no charms when it is not risked in the heat of the mêlée, for whom society has created no gentle affections, no stable habits, no ingenious arts, no calm and profound thought, none of those elegant or noble pleasures that memory makes more precious, and that security doubles. Man from another world, stop despoiling this one.

Who could fail to applaud this language? A treaty would soon be concluded between nations that wished simply to be free, and that nation against which the universe would fight only to compel her to be just. We would see her with joy finally abjuring her long patience, making up for her protracted errors, and exerting for her rehabilitation a courage previously only too deplorably employed. Once again, shining with glory, she would resume her place among the civilized peoples, and the system of conquest, that remnant of a state of things that no longer exists, that disorganizing element of all that now exists, will once more be banished from the earth and branded by this last experience with eternal reprobation.

PART II

Usurpation

CHAPTER I

The specific aim of the comparison between usurpation and monarchy

My aim in this work is by no means that of undertaking the examination of the different forms of government. I wish to contrast a regular government with one that is not; I do not propose to compare regular governments among themselves. We are no longer in the days in which monarchy was declared a power against nature; nor do I write in that country where it is obligatory to proclaim the republic an antisocial institution.

Twenty years ago a man of horrible memory, whose name must no longer sully any writing, since death has done justice to this person, on examining the British constitution, declared: 'I see there a king, I step back in horror.'[a] Only ten years ago some anonymous individual pronounced the same anathema against republican governments:[b] so true is it that in certain times it is necessary to run the whole gamut of follies to return to reason.[1]

---

[1] One needs an absurd party spirit and a profound ignorance to wish to reduce to simple terms the choice between republic and monarchy: as if the former were merely the government of many, and the latter simply that of one. Reduced to these terms, the one does not ensure peace, while the other cannot grant liberty. Was there any peace in Rome

---

[a] George Couthon, *Discours prononcé à la séance des Jacobins du 1er pluviôse an II de la République* (20 January 1794) (Paris, Imprimerie des 86 départements) pp. 3–4
'. . . je vois dans cette constitution un *roi*. Un roi! J'en recule d'horreur. Un Roi! C'est un *monstre* que la nature désavoue, c'est un *maître* qu'elle ne reconnaît, c'est un *tyran* qu'elle déteste.'
[b] Louis Matthieu Molé, *Essais de morale et de politique* (Paris, 1806).

85

For my part, I shall not join the detractors of republics. Those of antiquity, where men's faculties could develop over such a wide range, so confident of their own strength, so animated by feelings of energy and dignity, fill all worthy souls with a profound and peculiar emotion. Before those memories the old elements of a nature antecedent, so to speak, to our own, seem to awake in us. The republics of our modern times, less brilliant and more peaceful, have favoured the development of other faculties and created other virtues. The name of Switzerland recalls five centuries of private happiness and public loyalty. The name of Holland evokes three centuries of activity, good sense, fidelity and scrupulous honesty, even amidst civil dissent and indeed even under the foreign yoke; while seemingly insignificant Geneva has given to the annals of the sciences, of philosophy and of morals a far richer harvest than many an empire a hundred times larger and more powerful.

On the other hand, if we consider the monarchies of our days, these monarchies in which peoples and kings are now united in mutual trust and have contracted a genuine alliance,[a] we should be willing to pay them our respect. He who could contemplate coldly the enthusiasm of those peoples at the return of their old sovereigns, and who could

under Nero, under Domitian or Heliogabalus, in Syracuse under Dionysius, in France under Louis XI or Charles IX? Was there any liberty under the decemvirs, the Long Parliament, the Convention or even the Directory? We can imagine a people, governed by men who appear to be of its own choice, yet not enjoying any liberty, if those men form a faction in the state, and if their power is unlimited. Similarly we can imagine a people subjected to a single leader and yet not enjoying any peace, if that leader is not restrained either by the law or by opinion. On the other hand a republic could be so well-organized that the political authority would be strong enough there to maintain order. As to monarchy, to mention only one example, who could deny that in England, for the last 120 years, people have enjoyed greater personal safety and political rights than France ever acquired by its attempt at a republic, whose shapeless and imperfect institutions spread arbitrary power and multiplied the number of tyrants?

Moreover, how many questions of detail that would need to be individually examined! Is monarchy the same thing, when its establishment goes back centuries and when it dates from recent times; when the reigning family has been on the throne from time immemorial, like the descendants of Hugh Capet, or when being of foreign origins, it has been called to the throne by the will of the people, as in England in 1688, or finally, when it is entirely new and has emerged, through lucky circumstances, from a crowd of its equals? and again, when it is accompanied by an ancient hereditary nobility, as it is in almost all the European states, or when a single family alone has elevated itself and is forced to create a nobility without ancestors; when the nobility is feudal, as it is in Germany, or purely honorific, as it was in France, or when it forms a kind of magistrature, like the Chamber of Peers etc.?

---

[a] Allusion to the sixth Coalition of 1813, which included England, Russia, Sweden, Prussia and later Austria.

witness with indifference that passion of loyalty which is also one of man's noblest pleasures, would have little sympathy for human nature.

Finally, when we think that England is a monarchy, and we see that there all the rights of the citizens are safe from attack, notwithstanding some abuses, more apparent than real; that popular elections keep the political body alive, that freedom of the press is respected, while talent is assured of its triumph; when we find, in individuals of all classes, that proud, calm security of the man embraced by the law of his country, a security of which, in our own unhappy continent, we had lost even the memory, how could we fail to do justice to institutions that grant such happiness? Only a few months ago each of us looked around wondering, were England subjugated, in which obscure asylum he would be able to write, talk, think or breathe.

But usurpation cannot offer peoples either the advantages of a monarchy or those of a republic: usurpation is not monarchy; the reason why this truth has been overlooked is that – seeing in one as in the other that power rests on one man – many have failed to distinguish sufficiently between two things which are similar only in that respect.

CHAPTER 2

Differences between usurpation and monarchy

L'habitude qui veille au fond de tous les coeurs
Les frappe de respect, les poursuit de terreurs,
Et sur la foule aveugle un instant égarée,
Exerce une puissance invincible et sacrée,
Héritage des temps, culte du souvenir,
Qui toujours au passé ramène l'avenir

Wallstein, Act 2, scene 4[a]

ἅπας δε τραχὺς ὅστις ἂν νέον κρατῆι.

Aeschylus, *Prometheus*[b]

[a] 'Habit, awake in all men's hearts/fills them with respect and pursues them with terrors;/it exercises an invincible and sacred power/upon the blind crowd, lost for an instant./Heritage of time, cult of memory/which always leads the present back to the past.'

[b] 'A new ruler is always fierce': Aeschylus, *Prometheus*, p. 35.

87

Monarchy, such as it exists in the majority of European states, is an institution modified by time and softened by habit. It is surrounded by intermediary bodies that support and limit it at the same time. Its regular and peaceful transmission makes submission easier, and power itself less suspicious. The monarch is in some respects an abstract being. People do not see in him a single individual, but a whole race of kings, a tradition of several centuries.

Usurpation, on the other hand, is a force that nothing modifies or softens. It is necessarily stamped with the individuality of the usurper, and such individuality, because it is opposed to all preexisting interests, must be in a state of permanent defiance and hostility.

Monarchy is not a preference given to one man at the expense of the rest. It is a supremacy consecrated from the beginning: it discourages ambitions, but does not offend vanities. Usurpation exacts from all an immediate abdication in favour of a single individual. It stirs up all pretensions, it sets all egoisms in a ferment. When the judgement of Pedaretes falls on three hundred men, it is less hard to utter than when it falls on one man alone.[1]

It is not sufficient to declare oneself a hereditary monarch. It is not the throne that one wishes to pass on that makes such a monarch, but the throne one has inherited. One is not a hereditary monarch until after the second generation. Until then, usurpation may well style itself monarchy; but it still retains the turbulence of the revolutions that have founded it. These pretended new dynasties are as tempestuous as factions, or as oppressive as tyranny. It is either the anarchy of Poland, or the despotism of Constantinople; often it is both.

A monarch mounting the throne of his ancestors follows a path on which he has not embarked of his own will. He has no need to make his reputation; he is the only one of his kind; he is not compared with anyone else. A usurper is exposed to all the comparisons that regrets, jealousy or hopes may suggest. He is obliged to justify his elevation. He has contracted the tacit obligation to crown such great fortune with great results. He must fear disappointing the expectations of the public which he has so powerfully aroused. The most reasonable and best

---

[1] Pedaretes [the Spartan general in the Peloponnesian war, who fell in the defence of Chios], leaving an assembly whose votes he had in vain solicited, said: 'I thank the gods that there should be in my country three hundred citizens more deserving than myself.' [Plutarch, *Sayings of Kings and Commanders*, in *Moralia*, trs. by Frank Cole Babbitt, The Loeb Classical Library (15 vols., London and Cambridge, 1968), vol. 3, p. 135.]

motivated inaction becomes a danger to him. 'One must give the French something new every three months', a man who is an expert in the matter used to say,[a] and he acted on his word.

It is undoubtedly an advantage to be fit for great deeds when the general good requires it. But it is an evil to be compelled to them for the sake of one's standing, when the general good does not require it. Much has been said against idle kings. May God give us back their idleness rather than the diligence of a usurper!

To the disadvantages of the position, add the vices of character: since there are vices implied by usurpation, and others which usurpation produces.

How much treachery, violence and perjury usurpation requires! The usurper must invoke principles only to trample upon them, contract engagements only to break them, deceive the good faith of some, take advantage of the weakness of others, awaken greed where it slumbers, embolden injustice where it hides, corruption where it is timid, in a word, he must put all the guilty passions as if in a hothouse, so that they may ripen faster, and yield a more abundant harvest.

A monarch ascends nobly to his throne. A usurper slithers onto it through mud and blood, and when he takes his place on it, his stained robe bears the marks of the career he has followed.

Do we believe that success will come, with its magic wand, to purify him of his past? On the contrary, success would be sufficient to corrupt him, were he not already corrupt.

The education of princes, which may be defective in many respects, has at least this merit: that it does prepare them to fulfil, if not always worthily, the functions of their supreme status, at least not to be dazzled by its brilliance. A king's son, when he comes into power, is not transported to a new sphere. He enjoys calmly what, since his birth, he has been used to consider his own. The height at which he is placed causes him no vertigo. But the head of a usurper is never strong enough to bear his sudden elevation. His reason cannot stand up to such a change in his entire existence. It has been observed that even private individuals, finding themselves suddenly in possession of a great fortune, develop disorderly desires, whims and fantasies. The excess of their wealth intoxicates them, since wealth is as much a force as power. Why should the same not happen to someone who has illegally seized

---

[a] Napoleon.

all power and appropriated all treasures? Illegally, I say, because there is something miraculous in the awareness of legitimacy. Our century, so fertile in experiences of all kinds, gives us remarkable proof of this. Let us look at these two men, one of whom has been called to the throne by the wish of a people and the adoption of a king;*a* the other who has thrown himself upon it relying solely on his own will, and on a consent extracted by terror.*b* The first calm and confident, has the past for his ally. He does not fear the glory of his adoptive ancestors: on the contrary, he enhances it with his own glory. The second, anxious and tormented, does not believe in those rights that he arrogates to himself, though he forces the world to acknowledge them. Illegality haunts him like a ghost. In vain he seeks refuge in splendour and in victory. The ghost accompanies him amidst his pomp and on the fields of battle. He promulgates laws and changes them; establishes constitutions and violates them; founds empires and upturns them. He is never content with his house built on sand, the foundations of which are lost down in the abyss.

If we examine all the details of external and internal administration, we can see everywhere differences in favour of monarchy and to the detriment of usurpation.

A king does not need to command his armies. Others can fight on his behalf, while his peaceful virtues win for him the affection and respect of his people. The usurper must always be at the head of his Praetorian Guard. If he were not their idol, he would be the object of their contempt.

'Those who corrupted the Greek republics' – says Montesquieu – 'did not invariably become tyrants. The reason is that they were more attached to eloquence than to the art of war.'[1] But in our populous societies, eloquence is ineffective, and usurpation has no other support than armed force. Force is necessary to found usurpation, and remains so to preserve it.

Hence under the usurper, there is incessant warfare; this provides

---

[1] *Esprit des lois*, 8, 1.
  [The quotation is in fact in Book 8, ch. 2: 'De la corruption du principe de la démocratie', *Oeuvres complètes*, vol. 2, p. 351.]

---

a Bernadotte, general of the Republic and later Marshal of the Empire, in 1810 was adopted by the king of Sweden Charles XIII as Crown Prince, and in 1818 became King of Sweden with the name of Charles XIV.
b Napoleon.

the pretext to surround himself with guards; it offers him the opportunity to mould those guards into obedience. It enables him to dazzle people's minds and, for lack of the prestige of antiquity, to win that of conquest. Usurpation returns us to the system of war, and thus brings with it all the drawbacks that we have already seen in that system. The glory of a legitimate monarch is enhanced by the glory of those around him. He gains from the consideration that he bestows upon his ministers. He has no competition to fear. The usurper, previously the equal, or even the inferior, of his instruments, is compelled to abase them, so that they may not become his rivals. He insults them, in order to use them. Thus, if you look closely, you will see all the proud spirits remove themselves, and when proud spirits remove themselves, who are left? Men who know how to crawl, but not how to fight; men who would be the first to insult, after his fall, the master whom they had flattered.

This makes usurpation more expensive than monarchy. It is first necessary to pay the agents so as to corrupt them; it is then necessary to pay these corrupted agents again to make them useful. Money must take the place of both opinion and honour. But those agents, while corrupt and zealous, are not used to government. Neither they nor their master, new to it as they are, know how to get round obstacles. Whenever they are faced with some difficulty, violence has become so easy to them, that they think it is always necessary. Were they not tyrants by intention, they would be such out of mere ignorance. Under monarchy you see the same institutions lasting for centuries. You see, on the other hand, no usurper who has not twenty times repealed his own laws and suppressed the forms he has just instituted, as an inexperienced and impatient workman breaks his own tools.

A hereditary monarch may subsist alongside, or rather at the head of, an ancient and brilliant aristocracy. He, like them, is rich in memories. But where the monarch sees supporters, the usurper sees enemies. All nobility, whose existence precedes his, is bound to overshadow him. To support his new dynasty, he must create a new*a* nobility.[1]

---

a The First edition added: 'But do you wish to know what this new nobility will be like? During the war of the peasants of the Schwaben against their lords, the former often wore the arms of their masters whom they had killed. What happened? Under the guilded helmet of the noble, one could recognize the peasant, and the knightly armour was a disguise rather than an apparel.'

---

[1] What I wrote here applies only to the system which I examined then; that is, to the

91

There is confusion in the minds of those who move from[a] the advantages of an already acknowledged heredity to conclude from these the possibility of creating a new one. Nobility bestows on a man and his descendants the respect not only of future generations, but of the present ones. This last point is indeed the most difficult. It is possible to accept this convention if one finds it already sanctioned at one's birth. But to witness such a contract and to be reconciled to it is virtually impossible, unless one is the beneficiary.

Heredity is introduced either in the centuries of simplicity, or in those of conquest; but it cannot be instituted in the midst of civilization. It may then be preserved, but not established. No institutions carrying prestige are ever the product of will: they are the work of circumstances. Any piece of land can be given geometrical form, but nature alone creates picturesque sites and effects. A heredity established without the support of a respectable and quasi-mysterious tradition, would fail to rule the imagination. Passions would not be disarmed. On the contrary, they would be excited even more against an inequality suddenly set up in their presence and at their expense. When Cromwell sought to institute an upper chamber, there was general revolt by English public opinion: the former peers refused to be members of it; while the nation for its part refused to acknowledge as peers those who accepted his invitation.[1]

It will be objected that nobles are nonetheless created. But then the glory of the entire order is reflected on to them. But if you create the body and its limbs at the same time, where will the glory come from?

hypothesis of a usurper who was to destroy all ancient institutions to replace them by institutions created by a single man. The revolution which has been effected answers many of my objections. In relation to the nobility, for example, the combination of the old and the new one is a happy and liberal idea. The first will confer upon the second the glory of antiquity; the latter, fortunately formed in large part by men covered with glory, will bring as its endowment the brilliance of its military triumphs. In this case, as in that of almost all the difficulties which it confronted, the present constitution has adroitly overcome them, and has preserved all that was good in a regime that, as a whole, was otherwise hateful. To judge my work one must not forget that it was written and published four months ago: at the time I could see the evil but I could not foresee the good.

[1] A pamphlet published against the so-called High Chamber of the time of Cromwell is a remarkable proof of the impotence of the political authority in institutions of this kind. See *A reasonable speech made by a worthy Member of Parliament in the House of Commons, concerning the other House*, March 1659.

---

[a] The First edition has *partent* (move from) instead of *parlent* (talk). Of the two verbs the first makes better sense, and the alteration was probably simply a misprint.

Similar considerations may be applied to those assemblies that, in some monarchies, defend or represent the people. The King of England is venerable in the midst of his parliament. But this is because he is not, we repeat, a simple individual. He represents also the long line of kings who have preceded him. He is not eclipsed by the representatives of the nation. But a single man, emerged from the crowd, is of too diminutive a stature, and to sustain the parallel that stature must become fearsome. Under a usurper the representatives of the people must be his slaves, lest they should be his masters. Of all political curses the most terrible is an assembly that is but the instrument of a single man. Nobody would dare to wish, in his own name, what he can order his agents to wish when they claim to be the free interpreters of the national will. Think of the senate of Tiberius, think of the parliament of Henry VIII.

What I argued about the nobility applies equally to property. The old proprietors are the natural support of a legitimate monarch; they are the born enemies of the usurper. I think it is agreed that, for a government to be pacific, power and property must be in accord. If you divide them, there will be a struggle and, at the end of the struggle, either property will be invaded, or the government will be overturned.

It would certainly seem easier to create new proprietors than new nobles. But this is to suppose that to enrich men who have become powerful is the same thing as to give power to men who were born rich. Wealth does not have a retroactive effect. Suddenly bestowed upon some individuals it can give them neither that confidence in their own situation, nor that absence of narrow interests, nor that careful education, that constitute its main advantages. One does not acquire the spirit of a proprietor as easily as one acquires property. God forbid that I should suggest here that wealth must constitute a privilege! All natural faculties, as all social advantages, must find their place in the political organization, and certainly talent is no less a treasure than wealth. But in a well-organized society, talent leads to property. Thus the body of the old property holders recruits new members, and this is the only way in which a progressive, imperceptible and always partial change should be effected. The slow and gradual acquisition of legitimate property is different from the violent conquest of property taken away from others. The man enriched by his industry or his faculties learns to deserve what he acquires; the one enriched by spoliation can only become more undeserving of what he has appropriated.

93

More than once, during our recent troubles, our masters of a day, hearing us hark back to the government of the property holders, have been tempted to become property holders to make themselves more worthy to govern.[a] But if they were to bestow substantial properties upon themselves, within a few hours, by virtue of an act of will that they called 'law', the people and they too would think that what the law had given, the law could take away. Property, instead of protecting the institution, would need constantly to be protected by it. With wealth, as with other things, nothing can make up for time.

Besides, to enrich some, one has to impoverish others: to create new property-holders, one has to dispossess the old ones. The general usurpation must surround itself with partial usurpations in the way of outworks, to defend it. For every interest that it manages to conciliate, ten take up arms against it.

Thus, despite the deceptive resemblance that there appears to be between usurpation and monarchy, both regarded as forms of government in which power is in the hands of one man, nothing could be more different. Everything which strengthens the latter threatens the former; everything which in a monarchy is a cause of union, harmony and peace, is in usurpation a cause of resistance, hatred and upheavals.

These arguments do not lose any of their strength when applied to those republics that have been in existence for a long time. In this case they acquire, like monarchies, a heritage of traditions, usages and habits. Usurpation alone, bare and stripped of all those things, wanders around haphazardly, sword in hand, seeking on all sides, to cover its shame, its rags, which it tears and bloodies in snatching.

[a] First edition: 'worthy to govern us'.

CHAPTER 3

One respect in which usurpation is more hateful than absolute despotism

I am certainly no partisan of despotism. Yet if I had to choose between usurpation and a consolidated despotism, I wonder whether I would not prefer the latter.

Despotism banishes all forms of liberty; usurpation needs these forms in order to justify the overturning of what it replaces; but in appropriating them it profanes them.[a] Because the existence of public spirit is a danger for it, while the appearance of one is a necessity, usurpation strikes the people with one hand to stifle their true opinion, and subsequently strikes them again with the other to force them to simulate the appropriate opinion.

When the Grand Turk sends the rope to one of his disgraced ministers, the executioners are as silent as their victim. When a usurper proscribes an innocent, he orders his calumniation, so that, repeated often enough, it may seem the judgement of the nation. The despot prohibits discussion and exacts only obedience; the usurper insists on a mock trial as a prelude to public approval.

This counterfeiting of liberty combines all the evils of anarchy with all those of slavery. There is no limit to the tyranny that seeks to exact the signs of consent. The quiet are persecuted as indifferent, the energetic as dangerous; servitude has no rest, agitation no pleasure. This agitation no more resembles moral life than the hideous convulsions, which an art, more frightful than useful, inflicts upon corpses without reanimating them, resembles physical life.

It is usurpation which has invented those pretended sanctions,[b] those monotonous congratulations, customary tribute that in all ages the same men lavish, in almost the same words,[c] upon the most opposite measures. Fear apes all the appearances of courage to congratulate itself on its shame, and to give thanks for its misfortune. A singular kind

---

[a] The First and Fourth editions have 'elle le profane' instead of 'elle les profane': the singular makes no sense and is obviously a misprint.

[b] The First edition has: 'that pretended sanction of the people, those addresses of support, monotonous tribute that in all ages . . .'

[c] 'in almost the same words' is missing in the First edition.

of artifice, which fools nobody! Contrived comedy, which impresses nobody, and should have long since succumbed to ridicule. Yet ridicule attacks everything and destroys nothing. Everyone thinks to regain through mockery the honour of independence and, satisfied with disavowing his actions by his words, is at ease in belying his words by his actions.

Who can fail to see that, the more oppressive a government, the more the terrorized citizens will rush to pay it the homage of their enthusiasm? Do you not see, beside the registers that everyone signs with a trembling hand, these informers and these soldiers? Do you not read these proclamations denouncing as factious or seditious anyone voting against the government? What is it to interrogate a people, in the midst of prisons and under the empire of the arbitrary, if it is not to demand of the opponents of the regime a list to enable them to be recognized and struck down at leisure?

The usurper, however, registers these acclamations and these harangues: the future will judge him by the monuments he has erected.[a] Where the people were so base, it will be said, the government had to be tyrannical. Rome did not prostrate itself before Marcus Aurelius, but before Tiberius and Caracalla.

Despotism stifles freedom of the press; usurpation parodies it. When freedom of the press is entirely crushed, public opinion slumbers, but it is not fooled. When, on the contrary, suborned writers get their hands on it, they are carried away as if there were some opposition; they insult, as if anyone could answer back. Their absurd defamations are the prelude to barbarous sentences; their ferocious pleasantries are the prelude to illegal condemnations; their demonstrations would make us believe that their victims put up a resistance; in the same way as, when watching from a distance the frenetic dance of savages around the prisoners they are tormenting, one would think they were fighting the unfortunate they are about to devour.

Despotism, in a word, rules by means of silence, and leaves man the right to be silent; usurpation condemns him to speak, it pursues him into the most intimate sanctuary of his thoughts, and, by forcing him to

---

[a] Similarly, Mme de Staël wrote: 'Despots must never be judged from the temporary successes that the very dynamics of power grant them. It is the conditions in which they leave the country on their death or fall, it is what remains of their reign after them, that reveals what they have been.' *Considérations sur la révolution française*, part I, ch. 2 in *Oeuvres complètes*, vol. 12, p. 45.

lie to his own conscience, deprives the oppressed of his last remaining consolation.

When a people is but enslaved without being abased, there is still the possibility of an improvement in its situation; if some fortunate circumstance presents itself, it will prove worthy of it: despotism leaves at least this chance to the human race. The yoke of Philip II and the scaffolds of the Duke of Alba did not degrade the valiant Dutch; but usurpation abases a people at the same time as oppressing it. It makes it accustomed to trample under foot what it used to respect, to court what it despised, to despise itself and, no matter how short its duration, even after its fall it makes all liberty and all amelioration impossible. Commodus is overthrown; but the Praetorians put the empire up for auction and the people obey the buyer.

In thinking of the famous usurpers who are celebrated over the centuries, only one thing seems wonderful to me, and that is the admiration that people have for them. Caesar and Octavius, called Augustus, are models of this type: they began by proscribing all that was eminent in Rome; they continued by degrading everything that remained noble; they ended by bequeathing to the world Vitellius, Domitian, Heliogabalus and finally the Goths and the Vandals.

CHAPTER 4

Usurpation cannot survive in this period of our civilization

After this picture[a] of usurpation, it will be a consolation to show that it is today an anachronism no less gross than the system of conquest.

Republics live through that deep sense which each citizen has of his rights, and the happiness, reason, calm, and energy that the enjoyment of liberty procures for man; monarchies, through time, habits and the sanctity of past generations. Usurpation can establish itself only through the individual supremacy of the usurper.

---

[a] The First edition has: 'faithful picture'.

97

There are periods in the history of the human race when that supremacy, necessary to make usurpation possible, could not exist. In Greece such a period was that from the expulsion of the Pisistratids to the reign of Philip of Macedonia; in Rome, the first five centuries from the fall of the Tarquins to the civil wars.

In Greece, single individuals distinguished and elevated themselves, and guided the people; their empire was that of talent: a brilliant but transient empire, soon contested and taken away from them. Pericles more than once saw his power on the point of slipping away from him, and only owed his death at the helm of power to the plague which struck him. Miltiades, Aristides, Themistocles and Alcibiades all seized power and lost it again almost without any upheavals.

In Rome, the absence of any individual supremacy was even more noticeable. For five centuries, one cannot find in the immense throng of the great men of the republic the name of a single one who governed it for a substantial amount of time.

In other periods, on the other hand, it seems that the government of peoples belonged to the first individual who came forward. Ten ambitious men, full of talent and audacity, had attempted in vain to enslave the Roman republic. It took Caesar twenty years of dangers, travails and triumphs to arrive at the steps of the throne, and he was assassinated before he could mount it. Claudius hid behind a tapestry, where he was discovered by soldiers: he became emperor and reigned for fourteen years.

This difference is not just to be ascribed to that lassitude that comes over men after prolonged agitations: it is also to be ascribed to the progress of civilization.

When the human race is still in a condition of deep ignorance and degradation, almost totally lacking in moral faculties, and also almost devoid of knowledge, and consequently of physical instruments, nations follow, like herds, not only anyone distinguished by some brilliant quality, but also anyone thrown by some chance to the head of the crowd. To the extent that enlightenment makes progress, reason calls in doubt the legitimacy of chance, while comparative reflection discerns among individuals an equality opposed to any exclusive supremacy.

It was this that made Aristotle say that there was hardly any true royalty in his day. 'Merit', he went on, 'today always finds its equals, and no-one has virtues so superior to the rest of men, that he can claim for himself alone the prerogative of command.'¹ This passage is all the more remarkable in that the philosopher of Stagyra was writing under Alexander.

Cyrus perhaps needed less effort and less genius to subjugate the barbarous Persians than the pettiest tyrant of Italy in the sixteenth century needed to maintain the power he usurped. The very advice of Machiavelli proves this growing difficulty.

It is not exactly the extent, but the equal distribution of enlightenment that sets an obstacle to the supremacy of individuals. This in no way contradicts what we have previously affirmed, namely that each century awaits a man to represent it. This is not to say that every century finds one: the more advanced a civilization, the more difficult it is to represent it.

Twenty years ago, in this respect, the situation of France and of Europe approached that of Greece and Rome in the periods mentioned. There was such a multitude of equally enlightened men, that no single individual could derive from his personal superiority the exclusive right to govern. Thus no-one, in the first ten years of our troubles, succeeded in marking out a special place for himself.

Unfortunately in any such period, a danger hangs over the human race. In the same way as, when a cold liquid is poured into a boiling one, the heat of the latter is diminished, similarly, when a civilized nation is invaded by barbarians, or when an ignorant mass penetrates to its heart and takes over its destiny, its progress is arrested, and it takes steps backwards.

Such was, for Greece, the introduction of Macedonian influence; for Rome, the successive annexation of the conquered peoples; and finally, for the entire Roman empire, the irruption of the northern hordes. The supremacy of individuals, and consequently usurpation, became possible again. It was almost always barbarian legions which created emperors.

In France, when the troubles of the revolution introduced into the government an uneducated class and discouraged the enlightened, this new irruption of barbarians produced a similar but less lasting effect, because the disproportion was less marked. The man who amongst us aspired to usurpation was forced for a time to leave the paths of

---

¹ Aristot., *Polit.*, v, 10.
    [Aristotle, *The Politics*, with an English trs. by H. Rackham, The Loeb Classical Library (London, 1932), 5, 10.]

civilization: he turned to more ignorant nations as towards another century; it was there that he laid the foundations of his pre-eminence. Since he could not bring ignorance and barbarism to the heart of Europe, he took some Europeans to Africa, to see if he could succeed in forming them in barbarism and ignorance; and then, to maintain his authority, he worked to make Europe go backwards.[a]

In the past people were ready to sacrifice themselves for individuals, and gloried in it. In our days, individuals are forced to pretend that they are acting solely for the advantage and the good of the people. One sometimes hears them trying to talk of themselves, of the duties of the world towards their persons, and to revive a style fallen into desuetude since Cambyses and Xerxes. But nobody replies to them in this way and, disowned by the silence even of their flatterers, they fall back, in spite of themselves, upon a hypocrisy which is a tribute to equality.

If one could scrutinize the obscure ranks of a people apparently subject to the usurper who is oppressing them, one would see them as by some confused instinct fixing their eyes in advance on the moment when this usurper should fall. Their enthusiasm contains a bizarre mixture of analysis and mockery. They seem, lacking much faith in their own convictions, to be trying at the same time to stupefy themselves with acclamations and relieve themselves by raillery, and to anticipate the moment when the glory will be past.

Do you wish to see how far the facts show the double impossibility of conquest and usurpation in the present age? Reflect on the events which have mounted up under our own eyes during the past six months. Conquest had established usurpation in much of Europe; and that usurpation, sanctioned, recognized as legitimate even by those in whose interest it was never to recognize it, had adopted all the forms appropriate to its consolidation. It had now threatened, now flattered the peoples; it had succeeded in assembling vast forces to inspire fear, sophisms to dazzle people's minds, treaties to reassure their consciences; it had gained several years that were beginning to veil its origins. The governments, be they republican, be they monarchical, which it had destroyed, were without apparent hope or visible resources: yet they survived in the hearts of their peoples. Twenty lost

---

[a] Constant is talking here, in strongly negative terms, of Bonaparte's military expedition in Egypt in 1798–9. For an assessment of the Egyptian campaign see: Christopher J. Herald, *Bonaparte in Egypt* (New York, 1962).

battles could not dislodge them from there: one single battle was won[a] and usurpation was seen to be put to flight on all sides. In several countries where it ruled without opposition the traveller would be hard put to find any trace of it today.

CHAPTER 5[b]

Can usurpation not be maintained by force?

Could usurpation not perpetuate itself by force? Does it not have in its service, like all governments, jailers, chains and soldiers? What more is needed to ensure its duration?

This reasoning, since usurpation sitting on the throne holds gold in one hand and an axe in the other, has been reproduced in wonderfully varied forms. Experience itself seems to speak in its favour; yet I dare to call this experience into doubt.

These soldiers, jailers and chains, which are the last resort of regular governments, must be the norm to usurpers, given the obstacles that it encounters on all sides. Despotism, which regular governments only make their subjects experience at intervals, and in time of crisis, is for usurpation a permanent condition and a daily practice.

The theory of despotism can be defended speculatively by writers or orators because words lend themselves docilely to the expression of any error; but the prolonged practice of despotism is impossible today. Despotism is a third anachronism, like conquest and usurpation.

Let us develop this assertion,[c] let us first say how it could have been believed that our generation would be ready to resign itself to despotism. It is because it was offered, with ignorance, obstinacy and rudeness, forms of liberty to which it was no longer susceptible, and subsequently, in the name of liberty, was presented with a tyranny more frightful than any of those whose memory has been passed down to us

---

[a] Napoleon's defeat at Leipzig on 16–19 October 1813.
[b] The First edition contained a fifth chapter on William of Orange which Constant suppressed in the following editions, because of its transparent allusion to Bernadotte. The text of this suppressed chapter is given below, pp. 165–7.
[c] First edition: 'this assertion will perhaps surprise a large number of readers. Consequently, I shall try to expand on it. Let me say, first . . .'

by history. It is not surprising that it should conceive a blind terror of liberty, which plunged it into the most abject slavery.

Fortunately despotism, and let us be truly grateful for this, has done its best to cure us of this shameful error. It has proved that under its true colours, without disguises and palliatives, it caused at least as many evils as what had been so-called liberty. The moment has then come when some reasonable views on this matter might be given consideration.

CHAPTER 6

The kind of liberty
offered to men at the end of
the last century

The liberty which was offered to men at the end of the last century was borrowed from the ancient republics. Several of the circumstances shown in the first part of this work as the cause of the bellicose disposition of the ancients, contributed also to rendering them capable of a kind of liberty for which we are no longer fitted.[a]

That liberty consisted in active participation in collective power rather than in the peaceful enjoyment of individual independence. And to ensure that participation, it was even necessary for the citizens to sacrifice a large part of this enjoyment; but this sacrifice is absurd to ask, and impossible to exact, at the stage the people have reached.

In the republics of antiquity, the exiguous scale of the territory meant that each citizen had, politically speaking, a great personal importance. The exercise of the rights of citizenship represented the occupation and, so to speak, the amusement of all. The whole people contributed to the making of the laws, pronounced judgements, decided on war and peace. The share of the individual in national sovereignty was by no means, as it is now, an abstract supposition. The will of each individual had a real influence; the exercise of that will was a vivid and repeated

---

[a] Compare the arguments developed in this chapter and in the two following ones with the 1806 draft of the *Principes*; E. Hofmann (ed.), *Les 'Principes de Politique'*, vol. 2, pp. 417–55: 'De l'autorité sociale chez les anciens.'

pleasure. It followed from this that the ancients were prepared for the conservation of their political importance, and of their share in the administration of the state, to renounce their private independence.

This renunciation was indeed necessary; since to enable a people to enjoy the widest possible political rights, that is that each citizen may have his share in sovereignty, it is necessary to have institutions which maintain equality, prevent the increase of fortunes, proscribe distinctions, and are set in opposition to the influence of wealth, talents even virtue.[1] Clearly all these institutions limit liberty and endanger individual security.

Thus what we now call civil liberty was unknown[a] to the majority of the ancient peoples.[2] All the Greek republics, with the exception of Athens,[3] subjected individuals to an almost unlimited social jurisdiction. The same subjection of the individual characterized the great centuries of Rome; the citizen had in a way made himself the slave of the nation of which he formed part. He submitted himself entirely to the decisions of the sovereign, of the legislator; he acknowledged the latter's right to watch over his actions and to constrain his will. But the reason was that he was himself, in his turn, that legislator and that sovereign; and he felt with pride all that his suffrage was worth in a nation small enough for each citizen to be a power; and this consciousness of his own worth was for him an ample reward.

It is quite a different matter in modern states. Because their territory is much larger than that of the ancient republics, the mass of their

---

[1] Hence ostracism, petalism [banishment by voting with olive leaves], the agrarian laws, censorship etc.

[2] See the more elaborate proof in the memoirs on public education by Condorcet, and the history of Italian republics by Simonde Sismondi, IV, 370. I quote with pleasure this last work, the product of a character as noble and distinguished as the talent of the author.
[J. A. N. Caritat de Condorcet, *Sur l'instruction publique* (abstract from the Bibliothèque de l'homme public, seconde année, vol. I) (Paris, 1791); J. C. L. S. de Sismondi, *Histoire des républiques italiennes du moyenâge* (16 vols. Paris, 1807–24).]

[3] It is rather odd that it should be precisely Athens that our modern reformers have avoided taking as a model. The reason is that Athens was too similar to us, and they wanted greater difference to have greater merit. The reader eager to convince himself of the utterly modern character of the Athenians may consult Xenophon and Isocrates.
[Xenophon, *La Constitution d'Athènes attribuée à Xénophon*, Annales de l'Université de Besançon (Paris, 1976); *La république des Lacedemoniens*, ed. by F. Ollier, Annales de l'Université de Lyon (Lyon, 1934); English trs. J. M. Moore (ed.), *Aristotle and Xenophon on democracy and oligarchy* (London, 1975); Isocrates, *Works*, with an English trs. by G. Norlin (London, 1928); repr. 3 vols., 1966–8.]

---

[a] First edition: 'almost unknown'.

inhabitants, whatever form of government they adopt, have no active part in it. They are called at most to exercise sovereignty through representation, that is to say in a fictitious manner.

The advantage that liberty, as the ancients conceived it, brought people, was actually to belong to the ranks of the rulers; this was a real advantage, a pleasure at the same time flattering and solid. The advantage that liberty brings people amongst the moderns is that of being represented, and of contributing to that representation by one's choice. It is undoubtedly an advantage because it is a safeguard; but the immediate pleasure is less vivid; it does not include any of the enjoyments of power; it is a pleasure of reflection, while that of the ancients was one of action. It is clear that the former is less attractive; one could not exact from men as many sacrifices to win and maintain it.

At the same time, these sacrifices would be much more painful: the progress of civilization, the commercial tendency of the age, the communication among the peoples, have infinitely multiplied and varied the means of individual happiness. To be happy, men need only to be left in perfect independence in all that concerns their occupations, their undertakings, their sphere of activity, their fantasies.

The ancients found greater satisfactions in their public existence, and fewer in their private life; consequently, when they sacrificed individual to political liberty, they sacrificed less to gain more. Almost all the pleasures of the moderns lie in their private life. The immense majority, always excluded from power, necessarily take only a very passing interest in their public existence. Consequently, in imitating the ancients, the moderns would sacrifice more to obtain less.

Social ramifications are more complicated and more extended than in the past; even those classes which seem enemies, are bound by imperceptible but indissoluble ties. Property is more intimately identified with man's existence: all the shocks that it is made to experience are more painful.[a]

We have lost in imagination what we have gained in knowledge; as a result, we are even incapable of lasting emotion; the ancients were in the full youth of their moral life, we are in its maturity, perhaps in its old age; we are always dragging behind us some sort of afterthought, which

---

[a] In the 1806 draft, Constant observed: 'Credit did not have the same influence amongst the ancients. A deficit of 60 million caused the French revolution. A deficit of 600 did not cause, under Vespasian, the slightest sign of collapse of the empire.' E. Hofmann (ed.), *Les 'Principes de Politique'*, vol. 2, p. 426. The example is taken from Charles Ganilh, *Essai sur le revenu public* (2 vols., Paris, 1806), vol. 1, pp. 64–5.

is born from experience, and which defeats enthusiasm. The first condition for enthusiasm is not to observe oneself too acutely. Yet we are so afraid of being fools, and above all of looking like fools, that we are always watching ourselves even in our most violent thoughts. The ancients had complete conviction in all matters; we have only a weak and fluctuating conviction about almost everything, to the inadequacy of which we seek in vain to make ourselves blind.

The word illusion is to be found in no ancient language, because the word only comes into being when the thing has ceased to exist.[a]

Legislators must renounce all disturbance of habits, all experiment,[1] in order to act forcefully upon opinion. No more Lycurguses, no more Numas.

It would be easier today to make Spartans out of an enslaved people, than to turn free men into Spartans. In the past, where there was liberty, people could endure hardship; now, wherever there is hardship, they need slavery so as to be resigned to it.

The people most attached to its liberty in modern times is also that most attached to its pleasures. It holds to its liberty above all because it is enlightened enough to see in it the guarantee of its pleasures.

CHAPTER 7

The modern imitators of the republics of antiquity

These truths were entirely overlooked by the men who, towards the end of the last century, believed themselves charged with the regener-

---

[1] 'The Greek politicians, who lived under a popular government', says Montesquieu, 'did not recognize any power other than virtue; those of today talk only of manufactures, of commerce, of finances, of riches and even of luxury', *Esprit des lois*, 3, 3. ['Du principe de la démocratie', *Oeuvres complètes*, vol. 2, p. 252]. He attributes this difference to republic and monarchy respectively: we must attribute it to the contrasting spirit of ancient and modern times. Citizens of republics, subjects of monarchies, all wish for pleasures and comfort, and indeed no-one can, in the present condition of societies, fail to wish for them.

---

[a] For a development of these themes, see Mme de Staël, *De la littérature*, Part 1: 'De la littérature chez les anciens et chez les modernes' in *Oeuvres*, vol. 4, pp. 71–187.

ation of the human race. I am not casting aspersions on their intentions: their movement was noble, their aim generous. Who among us did not feel his heart beating with hope on entering the path which they seemed to open up? Woe betide even today whoever does not feel the need to declare that to recognize errors is not to abandon those principles that the friends of humanity have professed from age to age. But these men had taken as their guides writers who had not themselves suspected that two thousand years could have brought some alteration in the disposition and the needs of peoples.

Perhaps one day I will examine the theory of the most illustrious of those writers and I shall bring out what is false and inapplicable in it. It will be apparent, I believe, that the subtle metaphysics of the *Social Contract* can only serve today to supply weapons and pretexts to all kinds of tyranny, that of one man, that of several and that of all, to oppression either organized under legal forms or exercised through popular violence.[1]

Another philosopher, less eloquent but no less austere in his principles than Rousseau, indeed, even more extreme in applying them,

---

[1] I do not wish to join Rousseau's detractors. At present they are numerous enough. A crowd of servile spirits, who find their ephemeral success in questioning all courageous truths, clamour to blacken his glory: this in itself is an additional reason to be prudent in criticizing him. He was the first to make a sense of our own rights popular; his voice has awakened generous hearts and independent minds. But what he felt so passionately, he failed to define clearly. Several chapters of the *Social Contract* remind one of the scholastic writers of the 15th century. What is the meaning of rights which we enjoy more, the more completely we alienate them? What is that liberty in virtue of which one is so much the freer the more wholeheartedly one does what is against one's own will? The supporters of despotism can derive immense advantages from Rousseau's principles. I know one of them[(1)] who, like Rousseau, believing that unlimited political authority resided in society as a whole, supposes it is transferred to the representative of that society, a man whom he defines as the species personified, the union individualized. In the same way as Rousseau maintains that the social body could not harm either the whole of its members or any of them in particular, this writer claims that the holder of power, the man constituted as society, cannot harm society itself, because any injury he caused to it he would suffer fully himself, since he himself *is* society. Similarly, where Rousseau says that the individual cannot resist society because he has alienated his rights to it without reservation, the other claims that authority entrusted with power is absolute, because no member of a society can fight against the entire association; that the holder of power cannot be in any way responsible because no individual can demand an explanation from the whole of which he forms part, while the latter can answer him only by returning him to that order which he should never have violated.

And in order to dissipate our fears he adds: 'This is why his authority (that of the holder of power) was not arbitrary: he was no longer a single man, he was a whole people.' What a wonderful guarantee this change of words affords! Is it not odd that all the writers of this kind should reproach Rousseau with losing himself in abstractions? When they talk to us of had an almost equal influence on the reformers of France: this was the Abbé de Mably. We can regard him as the representative of that numerous class of well- or ill-intentioned demagogues who, from the height of the tribune, in the clubs and in pamphlets, spoke of the sovereign nation so that the citizens might be even more subjected, and of the freedom of the people, so that each individual might be totally enslaved.

The Abbé de Mably,[1] like Rousseau and many others, had mistaken authority for liberty, and to him any means seemed good if it extended the action of this authority upon that recalcitrant part of human existence, whose independence he deplored. The regret he expresses everywhere in his works is that the law can only cover man's actions; he would like it to cover the most fleeting thoughts and impressions; to pursue man relentlessly, leaving him no refuge in which he might escape from his power. No sooner did he learn of any oppressive measure, no matter by whom it was practised, than he thought he had made a discovery, and proposed it as a model. He detested individual liberty like a personal enemy; and whenever he came across a nation deprived of it, even if it had no political freedom, he could not help admiring it. He went into ecstasies over the Egyptians, because, he said, among them everything was prescribed by the law. Down to every relaxation, every need, everything was subjected to the empire of the legislator. Every moment of the day was filled with some duty; even love was submitted to this accepted intervention. It was the law that, in turn, opened and closed the curtains round the nuptial bed.[2]

the individualized society and of the sovereign being no longer a man but a people, are they by any chance avoiding abstractions?

[(1) Variant to footnote 19:
The First edition has: 'Do you wish to judge the advantage that the partisans of despotism can derive from Rousseau's principles? Read a work already cited above [Louis Matthieu Molé, *Essais de morale et politique*.] In the same way as Rousseau had supposed . . .']

The work of Mably on legislation is the most complete code of despotism which one can possibly imagine. Combine his three principles: 1. The legislative authority is unlimited. It must be extended to all and all must be subjected to it. 2. Individual liberty is a curse: if you cannot stamp it out, at least limit it as much as possible. 3. Property is an evil. If you cannot destroy it, weaken its influence by all possible means. From these conditions you will have in one the constitution of Constantinople and that of Robespierre.
[Gabriel Bonnot de Mably, *De la législation, ou principes des lois* (Paris, 1776); see also, by the same author, *Parallèle des romains et des français par rapport au gouvernement* (2 vols., Paris, 1740); *Entretiens de Phocion, sur le rapport de la morale avec la politique*, translated from the Greek of Nicocles (Amsterdam, 1763).]

[2] For some time we have heard the same absurdities about the Egyptians repeated in France. We have been invited to imitate a people, victim of a double servitude, kept back

Sparta, which combined republican forms with the same enslavement of the individuals, aroused in the spirit of that philosopher an even more vivid enthusiasm. That monastic barracks appeared to him as the ideal of a free republic. He had a profound contempt for Athens, and would gladly have said of this first nation of Greece what an academic and great nobleman[a] said of the Academy: 'What appalling despotism! Everyone does what he likes there.'

During the French revolution, when the tide of events brought to the head of the state men who had adopted philosophy as a prejudice, and democracy as fanaticism, these men were seized by a boundless admiration for Rousseau, Mably and all the writers of that school.

The subtlety of the former, the austerity of the latter, the latter's intolerance, hatred of all human passions, eagerness to enslave them all, his extreme principles about the competence of the law, the difference between what he recommended and what had existed before, his declamations against wealth and even against property, all of these things were bound to charm men excited by their recent victory, who, having conquered a power which was called law, were only too eager to extend that power to all possible objects. It was for them a precious authority that writers who, disinterested on this matter, and declaring royalty to be anathema, had, long before the overturning of the throne, made axiomatic all the maxims necessary to organize the most absolute despotism under the name of republic.

Our reformers wanted to exercise public power as their guides had told them it had been exercised in the free states of antiquity. They believed that everything should give way before collective authority, and that all restrictions of individual rights would be compensated by participation in the social power. They attempted to subject the French to a multitude of despotic laws which grievously offended all that they held most dear. They proposed to a people grown old in pleasure, to

by its priests from the sanctuary of every form of knowledge; divided into castes, the lowest of which was deprived of all the rights of the social state; kept in an eternal infancy; an immobile mass, equally incapable of enlightening and of defending itself, a constant prey to the first conqueror who invaded its territory. But we must admit that these new apologists of Egypt are more consistent than the philosophers who showered upon it the same praises; they attach no value to liberty, to the dignity of our nature, to the activity of the mind, to the development of intellectual faculties. They write panegyrics for despotism in order to become its instruments.

[a] The Duke of Richelieu.

sacrifice all these pleasures. They made a duty out of what ought to have been voluntary. They even put constraints on the celebrations of liberty, and were surprised to find that the memory of several centuries did not vanish instantaneously in the face of the decrees of a day. The law, being the expression of the general will, must in their eyes prevail over every other power, even those of memory and time. The slow and gradual effect of the impressions of childhood, the direction taken by the imagination over long years, appeared to them acts of rebellion. They gave to habits the name of ill will. One would have thought that ill will was a magic power that, by some inexplicable miracle, constantly forced the people to do what was against their own will. They attributed to the opposition the troubles of the struggle, as if it were ever legitimate for authority to make changes which provoked such an opposition, as if the difficulties met by these changes were not in themselves a verdict on their authors.

Nevertheless all their efforts collapsed constantly under the weight of their own extravagance. The most insignificant saint, in the most obscure of villages, successfully resisted the entire national authority arrayed in battle order against him.[a] The social power harmed individual independence in all sorts of ways, without suppressing the need for it. The nation did not feel that ideal participation in an abstract sovereignty was worth what they were suffering. It was vainly repeated to them, following Rousseau, that 'the laws of liberty are a thousand times more austere than the yoke of tyrants'. The result was that the nation did not want these austere laws, and as it only knew the yoke of tyrants by hearsay, it thought it would indeed prefer that yoke.[1]

---

[1] The disharmony between these measures and France's disposition was felt from the beginning, and long before it reached its climax, by all enlightened men. But, by a curious misunderstanding, these men came to the conclusion that what must be changed is the nation, and not the laws imposed upon it. 'The national assembly', wrote Chamfort in 1789 'has given to the people a constitution which is stronger than the people themselves. It must hasten to raise the nation to the same height. Legislators must be like those skilful physicians who, in treating an exhausted patient, administer restoratives with the help of stomachic medicines [i.e. emetics].' What is unfortunate in this comparison is that our legislators were themselves sick men who claimed to be doctors. You cannot sustain a nation at a height to which its own disposition fails to raise it. In order to keep it at that level, you must exercise violence upon it, and by the very fact that violence is exercised, it will collapse and in the end sink lower than ever before.
[Nicolas-Sébastien Roch (dit de Chamfort), *Maximes, pensées, caractères, et anecdotes* in

---

[a] Constant himself, as president of the Commune of Luzarches, scrupulously observed the revolutionary calendar and festivals. See Ernest Tambour, *Etudes sur la Révolution dans le Département de Seine-et-Oise* (Paris, 1913), pp. 276–399.

CHAPTER 8

The means employed to give to the moderns the liberty of the ancients

The mistakes of men in authority, of whatever degree, cannot be as innocent as those of private individuals.[a] Force always waits behind these errors, ready to lend them its terrible resources.

The partisans of ancient liberty were furious to see that the moderns did not wish to be free according to their method. They redoubled their demands, the people redoubled their resistance, and crimes soon followed their mistakes.

For the sake of tyranny, says Machiavelli, everything must be changed.[b] Similarly one could say that, in order to change everything, you need tyranny. Our legislators understood this, and declared that despotism was indispensable as the foundation of liberty.

There are axioms that seem clear because they are short. Cunning men throw them out like food to the crowd, fools take them up, because they spare them the trouble of thinking, and they repeat them to give the impression that they understand them. In this way, propositions whose absurdity amazes us, when analysed, insinuate themselves into a thousand heads, are repeated by a thousand mouths, and one is constantly compelled to demonstrate what is obvious.

The axiom which we have just cited is of this kind. For ten years it has resounded from all the tribunes of France. Nonetheless, what does it mean? Liberty is of inestimable price only because it gives soundness to our mind, strength to our character, elevation to our soul. But do not these benefits all depend on the existence of liberty? If, in order to introduce it, you resort to despotism, what will you have established in the end? Only vain forms: the substance will always escape you.

Oeuvres complètes, ed. by P. R. Auguis (5 vols., Paris, 1824), vol. 1, p. 447; for an English translation see W. G. Hutchison (ed.), *The Cynic's Breviary: Maxims and Anecdotes from Nicolas de Chamfort* (London, 1902).]

---

[a] In the 1806 draft Constant wrote:
  'If private individuals follow the wrong path, the laws are there to repress them. But if the authorities are mistaken, their errors are re-enforced by the strength of the laws.'
  E. Hofmann (ed.), *Les 'Principes de Politique'*, vol. 2, p. 75.
[b] Niccolò Machiavelli, *Discorsi sopra la prima Deca di Tito Livio* in *Tutte le opere*, ed. by M. Martelli (Firenze, 1971), pp. 73–254, Book 1, chs. 25 and 26 (Per il dipostismo bisogna cambiare tutto'), p. 109.

What should one say to a nation to make it see the advantages of liberty? You were oppressed by a privileged minority; the great number were sacrificed to the ambition of a few; unequal laws supported the strong against the weak; you enjoyed only precarious pleasures, which arbitrary power threatened to take away from you at any moment; you contributed neither to the making of your laws, nor to the election of your magistrates. All these abuses will disappear, all your rights will be restored.

But what can they say, those who claim to establish liberty through despotism? No privilege will weigh upon the citizens, but every day suspected men will be struck down without being heard. Virtue will be the first, indeed the only distinction, but those who are most active in persecution and violence will form a patriciate of tyranny maintained through terror. The laws will protect properties, but expropriation will be the lot of suspected individuals or classes. The people will elect their magistrates, but if they fail to elect them in the way prescribed in advance, their choices will be declared null. Opinions will be free, but any opinion in opposition not only to the general system, but even to trifling circumstantial measures, will be punished as treasonable.

Such was the language, such was the practice of the reformers of France for long years.

They won apparent victories, but those victories were contrary to the spirit of the institution which they wished to establish. And as they failed to convince the conquered, so they failed to reassure the conquerors. In order to prepare men for liberty, they surrounded them with the horrors of executions. The attacks made by the deposed authority on freedom of thought were remembered and exaggerated, while enslavement of thought was precisely the distinctive character of the new regime. They declaimed against tyrannical governments, while setting up the most tyrannical of all.

Liberty, they argued, had to be postponed until factions died down; but factions only die down when liberty is no longer postponed. Violent measures, adopted dictatorially in advance of a public spirit, prevent that spirit from coming into being. It is a vicious circle. People look ahead to a time which is certain never to be reached, because the means chosen militates against its being reached. Force increasingly necessitates more force. Anger is fed by anger. Laws are forged like weapons, codes become declarations of war, and the blind partisans of liberty, who thought that they could impose it through despotism, stir up all the spirits against themselves, and are left only with the support of the vile flatterers of power.

In the first rank of the enemies that our demagogues had to fight, were all those classes that had benefited from the fallen social organization, and whose privileges, abusive perhaps, had nevertheless been the means of leisure, improvement and enlightenment. A great independence of fortune is a guarantee against many sorts of baseness and vice. The certainty of being respected preserves against that restless and touchy vanity, which imagines insults and suspects disdain everywhere: implacable passion, which takes revenge for its present sufferings by the evils it commits. The usage of gentle forms and the habit of subtle nuances give the spirit a delicate susceptibility, and the mind a swift and quick flexibility.

Advantage should have been taken of these precious qualities.[a] The spirit of chivalry[b] [the aristocracy] should not have been allowed any privileges which it could abuse but left free to display its good qualities. The Greeks spared the prisoners who recited verses of Euripides. The faintest glimmering of intelligence, the slightest germ of thought, the least gentle sentiment or elegant form, must be carefully protected. They are indispensable elements of social happiness. They must be saved from the storm: it is necessary both for the sake of justice and for that of liberty: for those things lead to liberty by a more or less direct path.

In order to revive and fuel hatred, our fanatical reformers mixed up different eras. Just as their predecessors had turned to the Franks and the Goths to sanction oppressive distinctions, they too turned to them to find pretexts for an inverted oppression. Vanity had searched the archives and the chronicles for titles of honour. A more bitter and vindictive vanity drew on them for acts of indictment. They refused to take account of the times, to distinguish nuances, to reassure anxieties, to forgive passing social ambitions, to let vain murmurings die down, or puerile threats evaporate. They noted all the engagements of pride. A new distinction – persecution – was added to those which they wanted to abolish, and, their abolition being accompanied by such unjust

---

[a] Compare with Burke, *Reflections*, p. 139: 'Woe to the country which would madly and impiously reject the service of the talents and virtues, civil, military, or religious, that are given to grace and to serve it; and would condemn to obscurity everything formed to diffuse lustre and glory around the state.'

[b] Another Burkean theme; see: *Reflections*, p. 170.

rigours, were furnished with the certain hope of being revived along with justice.

In all violent struggles, interests follow closely upon the steps of exalted opinions, as birds of prey follow armies before a battle. Hatred, revenge, greed, ingratitude, shamelessly parodied the most noble examples, because their imitation had been blindly recommended. The unfaithful friend, the untrustworthy debtor, the obscure informer, the prevaricating judge, all found their justification already written in the language of the day. Patriotism became the banal excuse for all crimes. The great sacrifices, the acts of devotion, the victories won by the austere republicanism of antiquity over natural inclinations, became the pretext for the unrestrained eruption of selfish passions. Because at one time inexorable but just fathers had condemned their guilty children, their modern imitators delivered their innocent enemies to the executioners. The most obscure of lives, the least active existence, the least known of names, were ineffective protections. Inaction appeared a crime, domestic affections neglect of the fatherland, happiness a suspicious desire. The crowd, corrupted at the same time by danger and by example, repeated, trembling, the prescribed formulae, and took fright at the sound of their own voice. Each one formed part of the mass and was terrified by the mass which he contributed to swell. Thus was spread throughout France that inexplicable fever which has been called the Reign of Terror.[a] Who can be surprised that the people turned away from the goal towards which their rulers wanted to lead them by such a terrible path?

Not only do the extremes touch, they also follow upon one another. One exaggeration always produces the contrary exaggeration.[1] When certain ideas have become associated with certain words, it is in vain to demonstrate that this association is false: these words, when repeated, will for a long time recall the same ideas. It is in the name of liberty that we were given prisons, scaffolds, countless persecutions; this name, in

---

[1] 'Everything that aims at restricting the power of kings', said M. de Clermont-Tonnerre in 1790, 'is accepted with enthusiasm because people remember the abuses of royalty. A time will come, perhaps, in which everything that tends to limit the rights of the people will be received with the same fanaticism because they will have experienced with equal intensity the dangers of anarchy.'

[Stanislas-Marie de Clermont-Tonnerre, *Recueil des opinions de Stanislas de Clermont-Tonnerre* (4 vols., Paris 1791), vol. 2, p. 232.]

---

[a] See Constant's pamphlet *Des Effets de la Terreur* (1797) in *Ecrits et discours politiques*, vol. 1, pp. 93–112.

which a thousand odious and tyrannical measures were taken, was bound to arouse hatred and fear.

Yet would it be right to conclude from this that the moderns are disposed to resign themselves to despotism? What was the cause of their obstinate resistance to what was offered to them as liberty? Their firm determination to sacrifice neither their peace, nor their habits, nor their pleasures. If despotism is the most irreconcilable enemy of all peace and all pleasures, does it not follow from this that the moderns while thinking they abhorred liberty, in fact only abhorred despotism?

CHAPTER 9

Does the aversion of the moderns for this pretended liberty imply that they love despotism?

I certainly do not mean by despotism those governments in which the powers are not explicitly limited, but where there are nevertheless intermediaries; where a tradition of liberty and justice restrains the agents of the administration; where the authority handles customs with tact; where the independence of the courts is respected. Such governments may be imperfect: they are the more so accordingly as the guarantees which they establish are less assured. But they are not purely despotic.

I mean by despotism a government in which the will of the master is the only law; where political bodies, if they exist, are simply his instruments; where the master regards himself as the exclusive owner of his empire and considers his subjects merely as usufructuaries; where liberty can be taken away from the citizens without the authorities deigning to explain their motives, and without the citizens having any right to know them; where the courts are subjected to the whims of power; where their sentences can be annulled; where those who are acquitted are dragged in front of new judges, instructed, by the example of their predecessors, that they are there only to condemn.

Only twenty years ago no such government existed in Europe. There now exists one, the government of France. I set aside here everything concerning its practical consequences; I will discuss them later. For the moment I only speak of the principle, and I affirm that the principle is the same as that of the government detested by the moderns when it displayed the colours of liberty. This principle is arbitrary power. The only difference is that, instead of being exercised in the name of all, it is exercised in the name of only one. Is this a reason for it to be more tolerable, and for men to be more readily reconciled to it?

CHAPTER 10

A sophism in favour of arbitrary power exercised by one man

Yes, say its apologists, arbitrary power concentrated in the hands of a single individual, is not as dangerous as it is when contended for by factions. The interests of one man invested with immense power, are always the same as that of the people.[1] Let us set aside for the moment the evidence offered by experience. Let us simply analyse this assertion in itself.

Is the interest of the holder of a limitless authority necessarily in accord with that of his subjects? I can well see that these two interests meet at the extremities of the line which they follow, but do they not perhaps diverge in the middle? In the matter of taxes, wars and police measures, there is a wide gap between what is just, that is to say indispensable, and what would clearly be dangerous for the master himself. When power is unlimited, he who exercises it, assuming him to be reasonable, will not overstep this latter term, but he will frequently exceed the former. To exceed it, though, is already an evil.

Secondly, let us assume these interests are identical: would this provide us with an infallible guarantee? Every day we are told that when men understand their interests properly, these lead them to a respect for the rules of justice. Yet laws are made against those who violate

---

[1] 'The sovereign justice of God', says a French writer, 'is embodied in his sovereign power', and he concludes that sovereign power is always sovereign justice. To complete the reasoning, he should have stated that the depository of such power will always be like God.
[Antoine François Claude de Ferrand, *L'esprit de l'histoire* (4 vols., Paris, 1802).]

them: so well-known is it that men frequently deviate from their own interests, properly understood or not.[1]

Finally, does the government, whatever its form, reside in practice in the possessor of supreme authority? Is not power subdivided? Is it not shared among thousands of subordinate agents? Is the interest of those innumerable rulers still the same as that of the ruled? Undoubtedly not! Each of them has, near him, some equal or inferior whose losses would enrich him, whose humiliation would flatter his vanity, whose removal would deliver him from a rival, from an inconvenient supervisor.

To defend the system one wishes to establish, what must be proved is not identity of interests, but universality of disinterestedness.

At the top of the political hierarchy, a man without passions or whims, invulnerable to seduction, to hatred, to favour, to anger, to jealousy; active, vigilant, tolerant of all opinions; not obstinately repeating the mistakes he makes, consumed by a desire for good and yet knowing how to contain his impatience and await the right moment; lower down the scale of power, ministers endowed with the same virtues, dependent without being servile, in the midst of arbitrary power, but neither tempted to lend themselves to it out of fear, or to abuse it out of egoism; and finally, everywhere, in the subordinate posts, the same combination of rare qualities, the same love of justice, the same self-denial: such are what one would have to assume: do you think it likely?

If just one link in this chain of supernatural virtues is broken, everything is in peril. The two halves thus separated would in vain remain irreproachable: truth would no longer descend, whole and pure, down to the obscure ranks of the people. One single unfaithful transmission would be sufficient to deceive the authority and to arm it against innocence.

Those who vaunt despotism always see it in terms of the despot alone; whereas in fact one inevitably has as much to do with all his subordinates. It is no longer enough to attribute to one man superior faculties and an unswerving equity. It is necessary to suppose the

---

[1] 'It is absurd to believe', says Spinoza,' that the only man not to be led astray by his passions will be precisely the one whose situation is such that he is surrounded by the strongest temptations, and for whom it is easier and less dangerous to succumb to them.'

[Benedict de Spinoza, *The Political Works – The Tractatus Theologico-politicus in part, and the Tractatus politicus in full*, ed. by A. G. Wernham (Oxford, 1958), chs. 6 and 7 of the *Tractatus politicus* contain the substance of Constant's argument, but I have been unable to find a passage which corresponds precisely to the quotation.]

existence of one or two hundred thousand angelic creatures, raised above all the weaknesses and vices of mankind.

Thus people mislead the French when they tell them: the interest of your master is in accord with your own; do not worry: arbitrary power will not affect you. It only strikes those who are imprudent enough to provoke it. Those who are resigned and silent will be safe anywhere.

Reassured by this vain sophism, people do not rise against the oppressors, but find fault with the oppressed. No-one is capable of courage, even when prudence would dictate it. People open the way for tyranny, flattering themselves that they are being well-treated. Everyone marches, his eyes lowered, on the narrow path which is to lead him safely towards his grave. But when arbitrary power is tolerated, it spreads in such a way that the most obscure citizen can suddenly find it in arms against him.

Whatever the hopes of pusillanimous spirits, it is not, fortunately for the morality of mankind, sufficient to stand aside and let others be struck down. A thousand ties bind us to our fellows, and the most anxious egoism cannot sever all of them. You believe yourself invulnerable, in your voluntary obscurity. But you have a son, youth makes him rash; a brother less prudent than yourself lets slip some murmur of dissent; an old enemy, whom you have offended in the past, has succeeded in acquiring some influence; your country villa catches the eye of a Praetorian. What will you do then? After having bitterly censured all protests, and rejected all complaints, will you in turn complain? You are condemned in advance both by your own conscience and by that debased public opinion which you have yourself contributed to form. Will you give in without resistance? But then will you be allowed to do so? Will you not be pushed aside and pursued as a troublesome object and a monument to injustice? Some innocent people disappeared; you judged them guilty; thus you opened up the path where you in turn now walk.

CHAPTER 11

The effects of arbitrary power upon the different aspects of human existence

Arbitrary power, whether exercised in the name of one man or of all, will not let man be, even in his moments of rest and joy.

It destroys morality, because there can be no morality in the absence of security, no gentle affections in the absence of the certainty that the objects of these affections are safe and sheltered, protected by their innocence. When arbitrary power strikes without scruples those men who have awakened its suspicions, it is not simply one individual who is persecuted, it is the entire nation which is first insulted, and subsequently degraded. Men always seek to free themselves from pain. When what they love is threatened, they either detach themselves from it or defend it. Morals, says de Pauw,[a] undergo sudden deterioration in towns attacked by the plague: the dying rob the dying. Arbitrary power is to morality what plague is to the body. Everybody rejects the fellow sufferer who clings on to him. Everyone abjures the bonds of their past life. He isolates himself in defence and sees in the supplications of weakness and friendship only an obstacle to his security. Only one thing keeps its value: it is not public opinion, since there is no longer either glory for the powerful or respect for the victims; it is not justice, since its laws are ignored and its forms violated; it is wealth. Wealth can disarm tyranny; it can corrupt some of its agents, appease proscription, make escape easy, spread a little temporary pleasure in a life permanently under threat. People accumulate wealth for the sake of enjoyment, they enjoy in order to forget inevitable dangers; they react harshly to the misfortunes of others, and with insouciance to their own; they see blood flowing next to feasts; they stifle their sympathy like fierce stoics, or plunge themselves into pleasure like voluptuous sybarites.

When a people look coldly upon a succession of tyrannical acts, when

---

[a] Probably Constant refers to: Cornelius Johannes de Pauw, *Recherches philosophiques sur les Grecs* (2 vols., Berlin, 1788). In this work (vol. 1, pp. 174–5), de Pauw talks about the effects of an epidemic of plague in Athens under Pericles; but I have been unable to find a passage which corresponds precisely to Constant's argument in this or in any other of de Pauw's works.

they observe without a murmur the prisons filling up, the letters of exile multiplying, can one believe that, in the face of this detestable example, a few banal phrases will be sufficient to revive honest and generous feelings? The need for paternal power is always being asserted: but the first duty of a son is to defend his oppressed father; if you take a father away from his children, if you force these to keep a cowardly silence, what is the effect of your maxims and your codes, your declamations and your laws? People pay homage to the sanctity of marriage; yet on an obscure denunciation, on a simple suspicion, by what is called a police measure, a husband is separated from his wife, a wife from her husband. Is it thought that conjugal love can die or revive as it suits the authorities? People praise domestic ties; but the sanction of domestic ties is individual liberty, the hope that has been created of living together, of living free, in that shelter which justice grants to citizens. If such domestic ties really existed, would the fathers, the children, the husbands, the wives, the friends, the relations of those who are oppressed by arbitrary power submit to it? People talk of credit, of commerce, of industry. But an arrested man has creditors whose fortune rests on his own, associates with a stake in his enterprises. The effect of his arrest is not simply the temporary loss of his liberty, but the interruption of his speculations, perhaps his ruin. This ruin extends to all who have a share in his interests. It extends even further: it strikes at all opinions and shatters all security. When an individual suffers without having been found guilty, anyone who has some intelligence believes, with good reason, that he is threatened too, because all guarantees have been destroyed. People keep silent, because they are afraid; but all transactions are affected. The earth trembles and no-one walks without dread.[1]

---

[1] One of the greatest errors of the French nation is never to have attached sufficient importance to individual liberty. We complain of arbitrary power when we are its victims, but more as a mistake than as an injustice. Few men, in the long series of our various oppressions, have acquired the easy merit to protest in favour of individuals belonging to a party other than their own. One writer, whose name I do not know, has already observed that M. de Montesquieu, who energetically defends the rights of private property against the very interest of the State, treats with much less vigour the question of the freedom of individuals, as if people were not as sacred as goods. There is a very simple reason why, among a negligent and selfish people, the rights of individual liberty are less protected than those of property. The man who is deprived of his liberty is disarmed by this very fact, while the one who is despoiled of his property preserves his liberty to claim it back. Thus liberty is defended only by the friends of the oppressed; property by the oppressed person himself. It is easy to see that the intensity of the defences will be different in the two cases.

In our large societies, in the midst of relations which are so complicated, everything hangs together. Those injustices which are called
partial are inexhaustible sources of public misfortune. Power cannot
circumscribe them within a limited sphere. One can never entirely get
the measure of iniquity. A single barbarous law determines the character of the entire legislation. No just law can remain inviolable beside
one single illegal measure. One cannot refuse liberty to some and
accord it to others. Imagine a single punitive measure against men who
have not been convicted of a crime, and all liberty becomes impossible.
The freedom of the press? It could be used to move the people in favour
of victims who are perhaps innocent. Individual liberty? Those whom
you pursue could take advantage of it to escape you. The freedom of
industry? It could offer resources to the proscribed. It will thus be
necessary to hinder them all, to destroy them altogether. Men would
like to compromise with justice, to go beyond its bounds for one day, to
tackle one obstacle, and afterwards to return to order. They would like
both the guarantee of the rule and the success of the exception. Nature
is opposed to this: its system is complete and regular. One single
deviation destroys it, in the same way as, in an arithmetical calculation,
an error of one or of a thousand falsifies the result equally.

CHAPTER 12

The effects of arbitrary power upon intellectual progress

Man does not only need rest, industry, domestic happiness, private
virtues. Nature has also given him other faculties, if not nobler, at least
more brilliant. These faculties are threatened more than all the others
by arbitrary power: after attempting to bend them to its service, irritated
by their resistance it finally stifles them.

'There are', says Condillac, 'two sorts of barbarism: one that precedes, and the other that follows the enlightened centuries.'[a] The
former is a desirable condition compared with the latter. But it is only

---

[a] Etienne Bonnot de Condillac, *Introduction à l'étude de l'histoire* in *Cours d'études pour
l'instruction du Prince de Parme* (12 vols., Geneva, 1775), vol. 4, p. 2.

towards the latter that arbitrary power can reduce peoples today. In this way their degradation is even more rapid: what debases men in fact is not the lack of some faculty, but the abdication of it.

Let us imagine an enlightened nation, enriched by the works of many studious generations, and having made immense progress in the sciences and the arts. If the authorities were to place obstacles in the way of the expression of thought and the activity of the mind, that nation might live for some time on its old capital, on, so to speak, its inherited enlightenment. But there would be no renewal of its ideas; the principle of their reproduction would have dried up. For a few years vanity would replace the love of knowledge. Sophists, recalling the glory and consideration formerly won by literary works, would devote themselves to works apparently of the same kind. They would combat with their writings the good done by other writings; and as long as there remained some trace of liberal principles there would be some kind of movement in literature, a sort of struggle against these writings and these principles. But this movement would itself be a heritage of the liberty that had been destroyed. As the last vestiges of this liberty and the last traditions disappeared, the fight would come to an end because the combatants would no longer see any enemies, and victors and vanquished alike would keep silent. Indeed, who knows whether the authorities would not judge it useful to impose silence? After all, they would not like to see dead memories revived, abandoned questions stirred up again. They would press upon their too zealous acolytes as they had once on their enemies. They would forbid all writing, even in accordance with their own views, on the subject of the human race, in the same way as a certain devout government forbade anyone to speak either ill or well of God. They would declare on which questions the human mind might exercise itself: it would be allowed to disport itself, though under supervision, within the space allowed it. But a curse upon it if it should attempt to stray beyond its limits; if, refusing to abjure its divine origins, it should pursue prohibited speculations, if it should have the temerity to think that its most noble end is not the ingenious adornment of frivolous subjects, adroit flattery, sonorous declamation upon indifferent objects, but that heaven and its own nature have made it an eternal tribunal, where everything is analysed, examined and ultimately judged. Thus the career of genuine thought would be definitively closed. The enlightened generation would gradually disappear; the following generation, seeing no advantage in intellectual pursuits, and even seeing dangers in them, would turn irrevocably away from them.

It is in vain for you to say that the human mind could still shine in light literature, that it could engage itself in the exact and natural sciences, that it could devote itself to the arts. Nature, when creating man, did not consult the authorities; it ordained that all our faculties should be intimately bound together, and that none of them could be constrained without affecting the others. Independence of thought is as necessary, even to light literature, the sciences and the arts, as air is to physical life. One might just as well make men work under a pneumatic pump, arguing that they are not compelled to breathe, but only to move their arms and legs, as keep the mind active on a given subject, while preventing it from exercising itself on those important objects which give it its energy because they remind it of its dignity. Writers, thus stifled, begin by writing panegyrics; but they become little by little incapable even of flattery, and literature in the end loses itself in anagrams and acrostics. Learned men cease to be anything but the depositories of ancient discoveries, which deteriorate and are debased in hands shackled with irons. The source of talent dries up in artists together with that hope for glory which feeds on liberty alone; and, by some mysterious but undeniable connection between things which they thought could be kept isolated, they no longer possess the faculty to represent the human face nobly, once the human soul has been abased.

Yet this is not all. Soon commerce, together with the most necessary professions and vocations, would suffer from this apathy. Commerce is not in itself a sufficient motive for action; the influence of personal interest is generally exaggerated; personal interest needs opinion in order to act; the man whose stifled opinion languishes, is not excited for very long, even by his own interests; a kind of stupor comes over him. As paralysis spreads from one part of the body to another, so it spreads from one to another of our faculties.

Interest, when separated from opinion, is limited in its needs, and easy to satisfy in its enjoyments: it labours just as much as is necessary for the present, but does not prepare anything for the future. Thus the governments that wish to kill opinion and think to encourage interest, find themselves having killed both by a twofold and clumsy operation.

There is undoubtedly one kind of interest which is not crushed under arbitrary power, but it is not the one which stimulates man to labour, it is that which leads him to beg, to pillage, to enrich himself through the favours of power and the spoils of weakness. This interest has nothing in common with the motive necessary to the labouring classes; it encourages great activity in the entourage of the despots, but it cannot stimulate either the efforts of industry or the speculations of commerce.

Intellectual independence has an influence even upon military successes; one does not at first see the relation that exists between the public spirit of a nation and the discipline or valour of an army; yet this relation is both constant and necessary. Nowadays we like to think of soldiers as nothing but docile instruments whom it is sufficient to employ skilfully, and, in some respects, this is only too true. Nonetheless these soldiers need the awareness that at least part of public opinion is behind them; they are animated by it almost without knowing it; it resembles that music, the sound of which accompanies them when they march against the enemy. Nobody pays close attention to it; but all are stirred, encouraged, elated by it. It was thanks to Prussia's public spirit, as much as its legions, that Frederick the Great drove off the European coalition. This public spirit has taken shape from the independence that this monarch had always allowed to the development of intellectual faculties. During the Seven Years War, he experienced frequent reverses; his capital city was taken, his armies dispersed, but there was a kind of buoyancy which he communicated to his people, and his people to him. The wishes of his subjects reacted upon his defenders; they supported them through a kind climate of opinion which sustained them and doubled their strength.[1]

In writing these lines I am quite aware that a certain class of writers will see in them nothing but a subject for mockery. They wish with all their strength that there should be no morality in the government of mankind; they employ what faculties they have to prove the uselessness and impotence of such faculties. They construct the social state out of a small number of very simple elements: prejudices to deceive men, torments to frighten them, greed to corrupt them, frivolity to degrade

---

[1] These considerations, written eight years ago [1806], have since provided me with striking proof of the sure triumph of true principles. Prussia, which I presented as an example of the moral force of an enlightened nation, seemed to have lost its energy and all its warlike virtues altogether. The friends to whom I had shown my work asked me, after the battle of Jena, what had become of the relation between public spirit and victories. A few years elapsed, and Prussia has recovered from its fall. It has assumed a position amongst the first rank of nations; it has conquered the right to the gratitude of future generations, to the respect and enthusiasm of all the friends of humanity.

them, arbitrary power to guide them and, since it is necessary, positive knowledge and exact sciences to serve this arbitrary power more adroitly. I cannot believe that this should be the end of forty centuries of travails.

Thought is the basis of everything: it is applied in industry, in military art, in all the sciences and the arts. It is the cause of their progress and subsequently, by analysing this progress, it extends its own horizon. If arbitrary power seeks to restrict it, morality will be less healthy,[1] factual knowledge less exact, sciences less active in their development, military art less advanced, industry less enriched by discoveries.

Human existence, attacked in its noblest parts, soon feels the poison gradually spreading to the remotest. You think you have only deprived it of some superfluous liberty or cut back on some useless pomp, while your poisoned weapon has wounded it right to the heart.

I know we often hear of a circle which the human spirit supposedly follows and which, it is said, brings back by inevitable fatality, ignorance after enlightenment and barbarism after civilization. Unfortunately for this system, despotism has always insinuated itself between these periods so that it is difficult not to accuse it of having some part in this revolution.

The real cause of these vicissitudes in the history of peoples is that man's intelligence cannot remain stationary; if you do not stop it, it will advance; if you stop it, it will go backwards; if you cause it to lose confidence it will no longer exercise itself on any object without languor. One would almost say that, indignant at seeing itself excluded from its proper sphere, it wants to take revenge, by a noble suicide, for the humiliation inflicted on it.

It is not in the power of any authority either to quieten or to arouse peoples according to its own convenience or momentary fancy. Life is not something one can take away, and then give back.

Even if the government wished to substitute its own activity for the natural activity of enslaved opinion, in the same way as, in besieged fortresses, the imprisoned horses are made to stamp the ground between columns, it would be taking a difficult task upon itself.

---

[1] Barrow's voyage to China may serve to illustrate what happens to the morals, as to the rest of the lives of a people reduced to immobility by the authority which governs it.
  [Sir John Barrow, *Travels to China* (London, 1804). Constant may have used the French translation: *Voyage en Chine, formant le complément du voyage de Lord Macartney*, ed. by J. Castère (3 vols., Paris, 1805).]

In the first place, an entirely artificial activity is expensive to keep up. When everybody is free, every individual is interested and amused by what he does, what he says and what he writes. But when the great mass of the nation is reduced to the role of spectators forced into silence, in order to induce these spectators to applaud, or even simply to look, the impresarios of the show must stimulate their curiosity by *coups de théâtre* and scene changes.

This factitious agitation is at the same time more apparent than real. Everything is in motion, but only by order and threat; everything is less easy, because nothing is voluntary. The government is obeyed rather than followed. At the least interruption all the wheels would cease to turn. It is like a game of chess: the hand of power directs it; no piece makes any resistance; but if the arm stops moving, they would all stay motionless.

Finally, the lethargy of a nation in which there is no public opinion spreads to its government, whatever it does. Having failed to keep the nation awake, it ends by falling asleep with it. Thus in a nation in which thought is enslaved, everything is silent, everything sinks, everything degenerates and is degraded. Sooner or later such an empire offers a spectacle like those plains of Egypt, where one sees an immense pyramid resting upon arid dust and reigning over silent deserts. The evolution that we are sketching here is by no means theory, it is history. It is the history of the Greek empire, of that empire, the heir of that of Rome, invested with a great portion of its strength and with all its enlightenment, in which arbitrary power established itself with all the conditions most favourable to its stability, and which nevertheless declined and fell, because arbitrary power in all its forms is bound to decline and fall. This history will be that of France, of this country privileged by nature and by chance, if despotism perseveres in the silent oppression which it has for a long time disguised under the vain brilliance of external triumphs.[1]

---

[1] Had I wished to multiply the proofs, I would have talked once again of China. The government of that country has succeeded in enslaving thought and reducing it to a mere instrument. Sciences are cultivated only on its orders, under its direction and empire. No-one dares to open a new course, or to stray in any way from the prescribed opinions. Thus China has been repeatedly conquered by foreigners, less numerous than the Chinese themselves. To arrest the development of the spirit it has been necessary to break in the people those resources which would have helped them to defend themselves and their government. The leaders of ignorant peoples, says Bentham (*Principles of Legislation*, III, 2), have always in the end become the victims of their narrow and cowardly policy.

We must add a last consideration of some importance. Arbitrary power, when it touches thought, closes its finest career to talent; but it could not prevent the birth of men of talent, and their ability must find exercise. What will happen then? They will divide themselves in two classes. Some, faithful to their original vocation, will attack authority; the others will plunge into selfishness, and they will use their superior faculties for the accumulation of all possible means of enjoyment, the sole reward which would be left to them. Thus despotism*a* will have divided the men of superior intelligence into two groups: the former will be seditious, the latter corrupt; they will be punished, but for an inevitable crime. If their ambition had found free scope for its honourable hopes and efforts, the former would still be peaceful, the latter still virtuous. They only took a culpable path after they were driven back from the more natural paths which they had the right to follow. I say they had the right because reputation, fame, glory belong to the human race. No-one can legitimately rob his equals of them, nor wither their life by stripping it of everything that makes it brilliant.

It was a fine idea of nature's to have placed man's reward outside himself, lighting in his heart that indefinable flame of glory which, feeding upon hopes, is the source of all great actions, a protection against all vices, a bond between generations and between man and the universe, rejecting gross desires and disdaining sordid pleasures. Woe betide he who extinguishes this sacred flame! He performs in this world the role of the evil principle. He bends our brow to the ground with his iron hand, while heaven created us to walk with our heads held high, so as to contemplate the stars.

These nations, who have grown old in their infancy, under tutors who prolong their stupidity to govern them more easily, have always proved an easy prey to the first aggressor. [Jeremy Bentham, *Traité de législation civile et pénale, précédé de principes généraux de législation et d'une vue d'un corps complet de droit*, ed. by E. Dumont (Paris, Year x, 1802).]

---

a First edition: 'thus arbitrary power'.

CHAPTER 13

Religion under arbitrary power[a]

It might be thought that, under the most tyrannical governments, one refuge remains open to man: religion. Here he can lay down his secret burdens; here he can place his last hope, and no authority appears deft and nimble enough to pursue him into this asylum. Yet despotism does pursue him there. Everything that is independent infuriates it, because everything that is free threatens it. In the past it sought to dictate religious beliefs, and thought it could make of them, at its pleasure, a duty or a crime. Nowadays, having learned from experience, it no longer persecutes religion directly, but it looks out for whatever may humiliate it.

Sometimes it recommends religion as only necessary for the people, knowing perfectly well that the people, led by an unfailing instinct for what takes place over their heads, will never respect what their superiors disdain, and that everybody, through imitation or through self-esteem, will push religion a step lower. Sometimes, bending it to its whims, tyranny makes it its slave; religion is no longer that divine power that descends from heaven to astonish or to reform the earth; humble, dependent, timid instrument, religion now prostrates itself at the feet of power, whose every move it watches, and whose orders it awaits; it flatters those who despise it and only teaches the nations its eternal truths with the permission of the authorities. Its ministers stammer broken words at the feet of its enslaved altars. They do not dare to make the ancient vaults sound with the accents of courage and conscience, and far from addressing the great of this world, like Bossuet, about that severe God who judges kings, they search with terror for the words to speak of their God before the haughty gaze of their master. Yet they would still be fortunate were they not forced to bestow the sanction of religion upon inhuman laws and decrees of spoliation. Oh shame! We have seen them ordering invasions and massacres in the name of a religion of peace, soiling the sublimity of holy books with the sophisms of politics, disguising their sermons as

---

[a] On the First Consul's religious policy, see A. L. G. de Staël, *Considérations sur la révolution française*, part 4, ch. 6: 'De l'inauguration du Concordat' in *Oeuvres complètes*, vol. 13, pp. 268–76.

manifestos, blessing heaven for the triumphs of crime and blaspheming against the will of God by accusing it of complicity.

Yet do not think that such servility can spare them from insults: the man who will stop at nothing is sometimes seized by a sudden delirium, for the simple reason that no resistance recalls him to reason. Commodus, carrying the statue of Anubis in a ceremony, had the sudden inspiration of using that image as a club and to knock the Egyptian priest who accompanied him senseless.[1] This is a close enough symbol of what happens under our very eyes, of that haughty and capricious patronage that takes a secret pleasure in ill-treating what it protects, and in dealing out humiliating orders.

Religion cannot withstand so many degradations and insults. Weary eyes turn away from its pomp; the withered souls detach themselves from its hopes.

It must be admitted that for an enlightened people, despotism is the strongest argument against the existence of Providence. I say for an enlightened people, because peoples who are still ignorant may be oppressed without their religious conviction being diminished. However, once the human spirit has entered the path of reason, once incredulity has arisen, the spectacle of tyranny seems to support with horrible evidence the claims of that incredulity.

Incredulity suggests to man that no just being watches over his destiny, and his destiny has in fact been abandoned to the whims of the most ferocious and the most vile of humans. It says that the rewards of virtue, the punishments of crime, the promises of a fallen faith, are the vain illusions of weak and timid imaginations, while it is crime that is rewarded, and virtue that is punished. It says that the best thing to do, during this ephemeral life, during this bizarre apparition without past and without future, so short that it barely seems real, is to take advantage of every moment, so as to shut our eyes to the abyss which waits to swallow us. Despotism preaches the same doctrine by all its acts. It invites man to voluptuousness through the dangers with which it surrounds him; he should seize each minute, being uncertain of what the next may bring. A truly strong faith would be necessary to hope

---

[1] Lamprid., in *Commodo*, cap. 9.
  [Scriptores Historiae Augustae, *Lives of the later Caesars*, the first part of the Augustan History trans. by A. Birley (Harmondsworth, 1976), Aelius Lampridius, 'Commodus Antoninus', pp. 161–78.]

under the visible reign of folly and cruelty, for the invisible reign of wisdom and goodness.

Such a vivid and unshakable faith could hardly be the lot of an ancient people. The enlightened classes, for their part, seek in impiety a paltry compensation for their servitude. By defying, with apparent courage, a power which they no longer fear, they feel themselves less contemptible in their baseness towards that power which they dread. One might say that the certainty that no other world exists is a consolation to them for the infamy of the present one.

We pride ourselves on the enlightenment of the age, and the destruction of spiritual power and on the cessation of the struggle between the church and the state. For my part, I confess, if I had to choose, I would prefer the religious yoke to political despotism. Under the former, there is at least genuine conviction amongst the slaves, and only the tyrants are corrupt; but when oppression is separated from any religious idea, the slaves are as depraved and as abject as their masters.

We must pity, though we may respect, a nation bent under the burden of superstition and ignorance: such a nation preserves some good faith in the midst of its errors; it is still guided by some duty; it can still possess virtues, even if those virtues are misguided. But incredulous lackeys docilely crawling, bustling zealously about, denying God and trembling before a man, moved by nothing but fear, having no motive other than the salary which their oppressor throws to them from the height of his throne; a race that, in its voluntary degeneration, has no illusions to raise it up, no errors to excuse it, such a race has fallen from the rank which Providence had assigned to mankind; while the faculties which remain to them and the intelligence which they display are for them and for the world merely an additional evil and shame.

CHAPTER 14

Men's inability to resign themselves voluntarily to arbitrary power in any form

If such are the effects of arbitrary power, whatever form it may put on, men cannot resign themselves to it voluntarily. They cannot therefore resign themselves voluntarily to despotism, which is a form of arbitrary power, as that which was called liberty in France was another. And even by saying that this pretended liberty was a form of arbitrary power different from despotism, I am conceding more than I ought to. It was simply despotism under a different name.

It was a great mistake on the part of those who described the revolutionary government of France to call it anarchy, that is, the absence of government.[a] Certainly in the revolutionary government, in the revolutionary tribunal, in the law of suspects, there was no absence of government, but rather the continuous and universal presence of an atrocious government.

So true is it that this pretended anarchy was nothing but despotism, that the present master of the French imitates all those measures of which it gives him examples, and has preserved all the laws which it promulgated. He has always evaded the repeal of these laws, which he had often promised. He has sometimes claimed the merit of having suspended their execution, but he has reserved for himself their use. While denying his authorship of them, he has become their legatee. It is an arsenal of poisoned weapons, which he discards and takes up at his pleasure. These laws hang over everyone's head, as if shrouded in a cloud, and lurk in ambush to reappear at the first sign.

While writing these words, I receive the decree of 27 December 1813 where I read these three articles: '4. Our special commissioners are authorized to order any measure of strict policing required by the circumstances and the maintenance of public order. 5. Similarly, they are authorized to form military commissions and bring before them, or before the special courts, any person charged with favouring the enemy, with being in intelligence with them, or with attempting to disturb the peace. 6. They have the authority to make proclamations and to issue orders. Such orders will be compulsory for all the citizens. The judicial, civil and military authorities will be bound to comply with them and carry them out.' Are these commissioners not the proconsuls of the Convention? Do we not find in this decree, once again, unlimited powers and the revolutionary tribunals? If Robespierre's government was anarchy, then Napoleon's government is anarchy too. But no: Napoleon's government is despotism, and we must acknowledge that Robespierre's was also nothing but despotism.

Anarchy and despotism have this in common, that they both destroy

---

[a] On the usage of the term 'anarchy' in Thermidorian political debate, see E. Hofmann (ed.), *Les 'Principes de Politique'*, vol. 2, p. 23, footnote 14.

security and trample legal guarantees under foot. But, of the two, despotism appropriates the very forms it violates, and puts in chains the victims it means to sacrifice. Both anarchy and despotism introduce barbarism into civilization, but while anarchy returns all men to it, despotism reserves it exclusively for itself, and strikes its slaves bound with the irons of which it has freed itself.

It is therefore by no means true that today, more than in the past, men are ready to resign themselves to despotism. A nation exhausted by twelve years of convulsions may indeed have fallen through weariness and slumbered for a while under an oppressive tyranny, just as an exhausted traveller may fall asleep in a forest notwithstanding the brigands who infest it: this passing stupor cannot be taken for a stable condition.

Those who claim that they want despotism are in fact saying either that they want to be oppressed, or that they want to be oppressors. In the first case, they do not understand what they are saying; in the second, they do not wish others to understand them.

Do you want to judge despotism from the viewpoint of the different classes? For the enlightened think of Traseas and Seneca; for the people, think of the fire of Rome and the devastation of the provinces; for the master himself, remember Nero's or Vitellius' death.

I thought it necessary to develop these points before examining whether usurpation can be maintained through despotism. Those who today point to this means as assured, talk endlessly of the desire, of the wish of peoples, of their love for an absolute power which oppresses them, puts them in chains, protects them from their own mistakes and prevents them from doing harm to themselves by reserving this privilege for itself alone. One could say that it is sufficient to proclaim quite openly that it is not in the name of liberty that we are being trampled under foot, to let ourselves be trampled with joy. It was my intention to refute these absurd and treacherous claims and to expose the abuse of words that underlies them.

Since we must all be convinced that mankind, despite its last unhappy experience of a false liberty, is not in fact more favourably disposed towards despotism, I shall investigate whether usurpation, by mustering all the instruments of tyranny, may possibly escape from its many enemies and avert the innumerable dangers by which it is surrounded.

CHAPTER 15

Despotism as a means of preserving usurpation[1]

To preserve usurpation through despotism it is necessary that despotism should be capable of lasting. I would like to ask among which civilized people of modern Europe despotism has ever been known to last. I have already explained what I meant by despotism. Turning to history, I see that all the governments which have approached it have opened under their own feet an abyss into which they always fell in the end. Absolute power has always collapsed at the very moment when long efforts, crowned by success, had delivered it of all obstacles and seemed to promise it a peaceful continuance.

In England such power was established under Henry VIII and consolidated by Elizabeth. The boundless power of this queen is generally admired; the more so since she only used it with moderation. Yet her successor was condemned to struggle ceaselessly with the nation which had been thought to be enslaved; while the son of that successor, illustrious victim, imprinted by his death on the British revolution a stain of blood for which a century and a half of liberty and glory can barely console us.

Louis XIV in his memoirs[a] complacently lists all that he had done to destroy the authority of the parliaments, of the clergy, of all the intermediary bodies. He congratulates himself on it before the kings

---

[1] In publishing the following considerations on despotism, I believe I pay to the present governments of Europe, that of France always excepted, the tribute which they most deserve. Our age, still marked by many sufferings, and during which humanity has received wounds which will be long to heal, is fortunate in at least one important respect. The kings and the peoples are so closely united by interest, by reason, by morality, I would almost say by a mutual recognition of the services which they rendered to one another, that it is impossible for perverse men to separate them. The former find a magnanimous glory in recognizing the rights of the latter, and in granting them their enjoyments. These on the other hand know that they have nothing to gain from violent shocks, and that institutions consecrated by time are to be preferred to any others, precisely because the time by which they have been consecrated modifies them. If we take advantage adroitly, that is with loyalty and justice (for to do so is the true political skill) of this double persuasion, we shall have no need to fear either revolutions or despotism for a long time, and the evils which we have suffered will be amply compensated.

---

[a] *Mémoires de Louis XIV, écrits par lui-même, composés pour le Grand Dauphin, son fils et addressés à ce Prince*, ed. by J. L. M. de Gain-Montagnac (2 vols., Paris, 1806). On Constant's impressions of this work, see: Constant and Mme de Staël, *Lettres à un ami; Cent onze lettres inédites à Claude Hochet* (Neuchâtel, 1949), pp. 116–17.

who would take his place upon the throne. He was writing around the year 1666: a hundred and twenty three years later the French monarchy was overthrown.[1] The reason for this inevitable progression of things is simple and manifest. Those institutions which act as barriers against power simultaneously support it. They guide it in its progress; they sustain its efforts; they moderate its excesses of violence and stimulate it in its moments of apathy. They rally around it the interests of the various classes. Even when it fights against them, they impose upon it certain considerations which make its mistakes less dangerous. But[a] when these institutions are destroyed, power, lacking anything to guide it, anything to contain it, begins to march haphazardly; its step becomes uneven and erratic. As it no longer follows a fixed rule, it now advances, now recoils, now becomes agitated, now restless; it never knows whether it is doing enough, or too much. Sometimes it is carried away and nothing can stop it; sometimes it subsides and nothing can revive it. It rids itself of its allies while thinking to be rid of its enemies. The arbitrary power it exercises is a sort of responsibility mixed with the remorse which troubles and torments it.

It has often been said that the prosperity of free states is transitory; yet that of absolute power is much more so. No despotic state, with all its might, has ever lasted as long as English liberty.

Despotism faces three possibilities: it may cause the people to revolt, and in this case the people will overthrow it; it may exasperate the people and then, if it is attacked by foreigners, it will be overthrown by them;[2] or, if no foreigners attack it, it will decline, more slowly but in a more shameful and no less certain manner.

We find a pleasant oblivion of facts in one of the most zealous partisans of absolute power, who however at least has the merit of having been a courageous enemy of usurpation. 'The Kingdom of France', he says [The First edition has: 'The Kingdom of France', says M. Ferrand (Esprit de l'hist. III, 448), 'united . . .'] 'united under the single authority of Louis XIV all the means of force and prosperity . . . Its greatness was delayed for a long time by all the vices with which a moment of barbarism had burdened it and from which it took almost seven centuries wholly to remove the rust. But the rust had been removed; all its mechanisms had been newly tempered. Their action was made freer, their play prompter and safer; they were no longer impeded by a multitude of foreign movements. One alone among them gave impulse to the rest.' And yet what came of all this? Of this unique and powerful mechanism, of this unlimited authority? A brilliant reign, then a shameful one, subsequently a weak one and finally a revolution.
[Antoine François Claude de Ferrand, *L'esprit de l'histoire*, vol. 3, p. 448.]

2 The conquest of the Gauls, says Filangieri, cost Caesar ten years of exertions, of labours

---

a First edition: 'when such institutions'.

Everything confirms that maxim of Montesquieu, that as power grows, so security diminishes.[1]

No, say the friends of despotism, when governments collapse it is always on account of their weakness. What they must do is to watch, to punish, to put in chains, to strike, without allowing themselves to be held back by vain forms.

To support this doctrine, two or three examples of violent and illegal measures are cited which appear to have saved the governments that resorted to them. However, in order to make use of these examples, one has to restrict oneself adroitly to a small number of years. If one were to look further, one would see that, through these measures, the governments in question, far from being strengthened, were lost.

This point is extremely important, because even regular governments are sometimes seduced by this theory. I hope to be forgiven if in a short digression, I expose their danger and their falsity.

CHAPTER 16

The effect of illegal and despotic measures on regular governments themselves

When a regular government resorts to arbitrary measures, it sacrifices the very aim of its existence to the means which it adopts to preserve this. Why do we wish authority to repress those who attack our properties, our liberty and our life? Because we want to be assured of their enjoyment. But if our fortune may be destroyed, our liberty threatened, our life disturbed by arbitrary power, what good shall we derive from

and negotiations, while it cost Clovis, one could say, only a single day. Yet the Gauls who resisted Caesar were certainly less disciplined than those who fought against Clovis, and who had been trained in the Roman tactics. Clovis, who was between 15 and 16, was certainly no greater captain than Caesar. But Caesar was fighting against a free people, Clovis against an enslaved one.

[Gaetano Filangieri, *Scienza della legislazione* (8 vols., Napoli, 1780–8); French trs. by J. A. G. Gallois, *La science de la législation* (5 vols., Paris, 1786–8), vol. 2, p. 105.]

[1] *Esprit des lois*, book 8, ch. 7.
['De la corruption du principe de la monarchie. Continuation', *Oeuvres complètes*, vol. 2, p. 356.]

the protection of authority? Why do we wish it to punish those who plot against the constitution of the state? Because we fear that these conspirators might replace a legal and moderate organization by an oppressive power. But if authority itself exercises this oppressive power, what advantage can it possibly offer? Perhaps for a while an advantage of fact. The arbitrary measures of an established government are always less numerous than those of factions which still have to establish their power. Yet even this advantage is lost because of arbitrary power. Once its methods have been admitted at all, they are found so economical and convenient, that it no longer seems worthwhile to use any others. Presented initially as a last resort, to be used only in infinitely rare circumstances, arbitrary power becomes the solution to all problems and an everyday expedient. At that point, not only does the number of the enemies of the authority increase along with that of its victims, but its distrust also grows out of all proportion to the number of its enemies. Any encroachment made upon liberty calls for other encroachments of the same kind, and any power that has entered upon that course ends up putting itself on a par with the factions.

It is easy to talk about the usefulness of illegal measures, and of that extrajudicial expedition which, by leaving no time for the seditious to rally, re-establishes order and maintains peace. Let us look instead at the facts, since it is facts that are being cited to us, and let us judge the system by the very elements adduced in its favour.

The Gracchi, we are told, put the Roman republic in jeopardy. All legal procedures were impotent against them. The senate resorted twice to the terrible law of necessity and the republic was saved! That is to say: it is from that time that we can date its fall.[a] All rights were disregarded, every form of constitution subverted. The people had merely demanded equal rights: it swore to punish the murderers of its defenders, and the ferocious Marius came to preside over its revenge.

The ambition of the Guises disrupted the reign of Henry III. It seemed impossible to bring the Guises to justice. Henry III had one of them assassinated. Did this make his reign more peaceful? On the contrary: twenty years of civil wars tore the French empire apart, and it is likely that, forty years later, the good Henry IV paid the penalty for the last of the Valois.[b]

---

[a] First edition: 'its loss'.
[b] Henri IV was assassinated in 1610 by Ravaillac.

During crises of this nature the culprits who are punished are always a small number. Others remain silent, conceal themselves, and wait. They take advantage of the indignation that violence has aroused in men's spirits. They take advantage of the consternation that the appearance of injustice arouses in the minds of men of scruples. Power, by emancipating itself from the laws, has lost its distinctive character and its happy pre-eminence. When the factions attack it, with weapons like its own, the mass of the citizens may be divided, since it seems to them that they only have a choice between two factions.

We will be challenged by citing the interest of the state, the danger of tardy procedures, public safety. Have we not heard these expressions often enough under the most execrable of regimes? Will they never be exhausted? If you admit these imposing pretexts, these specious words, every party will identify the interest of the state with the destruction of its enemies, see the dangers of delay in an hour's work of inquiry, and public safety in a condemnation pronounced without judgement and without proofs.

There are, no doubt, for political societies, moments of danger that human prudence can hardly conjure away. But it is not by means of violence, through the suppression of justice, that such dangers may be averted. It is on the contrary by adhering, more scrupulously than ever, to the established laws, to tutelary procedures, to preserving safeguards. Two advantages result from such courageous persistence in the path of legality: governments leave to their enemies the odium of violating the most sacred of laws; and the more they win by the calm and assurance that they display, the trust of that timid mass that would remain at least uncertain, if extraordinary measures were to betray, in the custodians of authority, a pressing sense of danger.

Any moderate government, any government resting upon regularity and justice, is ruined by every interruption of justice, by every deviation from regularity. As it is in its nature to soften sooner or later, its enemies wait until then, to take advantage of memories armed against it. Violence seemed for a moment to come to its rescue, instead it has made its fall the more inevitable, since, by delivering it from some of its opponents, it has generalized the hatred that those opponents felt for it.

Be just, I would always recommend to the men in power. Be just whatever happens, because, if you cannot govern with justice, even with injustice you would not govern for long.

During our long and sad revolution, many persisted in finding the cause of the events of the day in the acts of the day before. Whenever violence, having caused a momentary surprise, was followed by a reaction which destroyed this effect, they attributed this reaction to the suppression of violent measures, to an excessive parsimony in the proscriptions, to the relaxation of authority.[1] Yet it is in the nature of authority to soften, even unwittingly. Precautions become odious and are neglected; opinions exert their weight even in silence; power yields; but as it yields out of weakness, it fails to reconcile men's hearts. Intrigues are renewed; hatreds grow. The innocent who have been stricken by arbitrary power reappear with new strength; the guilty who have been condemned without being heard appear innocent, while the evil which has been postponed for a few hours returns more terrible, aggravated by the evil which has now been committed.

There are no justifications for those means that serve equally for all intentions and all aims and that, advocated by honest men against brigands, reappear in the mouths of brigands with the authority of honest men, with the same apology of necessity, the same pretext of public safety. The law of Valerius Publicola which permitted killing without formalities whoever should aspire to tyranny, served alternatively the purposes of aristocratic and popular fury, and led to the ruin of the Roman republic.

The obsession of almost all men is to show themselves to be above their real condition. The favourite obsession of writers is to present themselves as statesmen. Consequently, all the great development of extrajudicial force, all the examples of recourse to illegal measures in dangerous circumstances, have from century to century been re-counted with respect and described with complacency. The author, sitting comfortably at his desk, hurls arbitrary measures in every direc-tion, seeks to incorporate into his own style the same brevity that he recommends in the measures themselves. For a moment, he believes himself invested with power just because he is preaching its abuse. He

---

[1] The authors of the dragonnades under Louis XIV followed the same reasoning. At the time of the insurrection of the Cévennes, says Rhulières (*Eclaircissements sur la Révocation de l'Édit de Nantes*, II, 278) the party that had solicited the persecution of the followers of the reformed religion claimed that the revolt of the Camisards had no other cause than the relaxation of harsh measures. Had the oppression continued, they said, there would have been no insurrection. Had the oppression not begun, said those who had opposed those acts of violence, there would have been no discontent.
[Claude Carloman de Rhulières, *Eclaircissements historiques sur les causes de la Révocation de l'Édit de Nantes, et sur l'état des protestants en France depuis le commencement du règne de Louis XIV* (2 vols., Paris, 1788), vol. 2, pp. 278–9.]

revivifies his speculative life with all the demonstrations of force and power with which he embellishes his phrases, and in this way he gives himself something of the pleasure of authority; he repeats as loud as he can the great words of public safety, supreme law, public interest; he is full of admiration for his own profundity and marvels at his own energy. Poor imbecile! He talks to those who are only too glad to listen to him and who, at the first opportunity, will test out his own theories upon him.

This vanity, which has misled the judgement of so many writers, has, during our civil dissensions, caused more trouble than is generally thought. All the mediocre minds, ephemeral conquerors of a fragment of authority, were full of all these maxims, the more agreeable to stupidity in that they enable it to cut those knots it cannot untie. They dreamt of nothing else but measures of public safety, great measures, masterstrokes of state; they thought themselves extraordinary geniuses because at every step they departed from ordinary means. They proclaimed themselves great minds because justice seemed to them a narrow preoccupation. With each political crime which they committed, you could hear them proclaiming: 'Once again we have saved the country!' Certainly, we should have been adequately convinced by this, that a country saved every day in this manner must be a country that will soon be ruined.

CHAPTER 17

Implications of the preceding considerations in relation to despotism

If even in regular governments that, unlike despotism, do not unite all human interests against themselves, illegal measures, far from favouring their duration, compromise and threaten it, it is clear that a despotic government which relies entirely upon such measures cannot carry within itself any germ of stability. It lives from day to day, striking with its axe the innocent and the guilty alike, trembling in front of the accomplices whom it organizes, flatters and enriches, and maintaining itself through arbitrary power, until the same arbitrary power, seized by someone else, overthrows it with the assistance of its henchmen.[1]

To stifle discontented public opinion in blood is the favourite means of some shrewd politicians. But public opinion cannot be stifled: blood flows but public opinion remains afloat, charges once more and triumphs. The more it is repressed, the more terrible it becomes; it penetrates minds with the air they breathe; it becomes everyone's habitual sentiment, everyone's obsessive conviction. People do not assemble to plot, yet all those who meet one another become conspirators.

No matter how debased a nation might appear from the outside, generous affections will always find refuge inside a few isolated spirits, and there, outraged, they will slowly ferment. The vault of the assemblies can resound with furious declamations, the walls of the palaces with expressions of contempt for the human race; the flatterers of tyrants denounce courage to them. But no century will ever be so disinherited by heaven as to present the whole of mankind as despotism[a] would need to have it. The hatred of oppression, either in the name of a single individual or in the name of all, is transmitted from age to age. The future will not betray this good cause. There will always remain some of those men for whom justice is a passion, the defence of

---

[1] It is interesting to observe the sequence of the main arbitrary acts that marked the first four years of Napoleon's government, after his usurpation at Saint-Cloud; a usurpation which Europe excused because it believed it to be necessary but which came only when the internal troubles that it claimed to have set to rest had already ceased by the simple means of constitutional power. See how, immediately after that usurpation there was the deportation without trial of thirty or forty citizens, subsequently another deportation of 130 who were sent to perish on the shores of Africa; then the establishment of the special courts, together with the maintenance of the military commissions; then the elimination of the Tribunate and the destruction of all that was left of the representative system; finally the proscription of Moreau, the assassination of the duke of Enghien, the assassination of Pichegru, etc. I leave aside the individual instances which are innumerable. Notice that these years may be regarded as the most peaceful of this government, and that the government itself had the most pressing interest in displaying an appearance of regularity. It must be true that despotism and usurpation are condemned by their own nature to such measures, if this patent interest could not restrain from them a very calm and cunning usurper, in spite of his rages which are only instrumental; not lacking in intelligence, if we can call intelligence knowledge of the ignoble part of the human heart; indifferent to good and evil, and who, in his impartiality would perhaps have preferred the first as the most effective; and, finally, who had studied all the principles of tyranny, and whose self-regard would have been flattered by displaying a kind of moderation as proof of his dexterity.

---

[a] First edition: 'as arbitrary power . . .'

the weak a need. Nature has willed this continuity: no-one has ever been able to break it; no-one will ever be able to do so. These men will always give way to their magnanimous impulse; many will suffer, many perhaps will die; but the earth with which their ashes will mingle will be uplifted by them and sooner or later will open once again.

CHAPTER 18

Causes which make despotism particularly impossible at this stage of our civilization

These reasonings are of a general character and apply to all civilized nations and to all ages; but several other causes, which are specific to modern civilization, set new obstacles to despotism in our own time.

These causes are, to a large extent, the same as those which have supplanted the warlike by the peaceful tendency, the same which have made it impossible to transplant the liberty of the ancients amongst the moderns.

Being unshakably attached to their own quiet and enjoyment, men will always react, individually and collectively, against all authority which chooses to trouble them. From the fact that we are, as I have said, much less passionately committed to political liberty than the ancients, it might follow that we neglected those guarantees which reside only in forms; but from the fact that we are much more attached than they were to individual liberty it also follows that, when the basis of liberty itself is attacked, we shall defend it by all the means open to us. Moreover, we possess for its defence means of which the ancients could not avail themselves.

I have already shown that commerce makes the interference of arbitrary power in our existence more vexatious than it was in the past, and this because, our speculations being more diversified, arbitrary power must multiply itself to reach them; but at the same time commerce makes it easier to evade the influence of arbitrary power because it changes the very nature of property, and thereby makes it virtually impossible to seize.

Commerce confers on property a new quality: the circulation of money; without it property is merely a usufruct; authority can always affect usufruct, because it can prevent its enjoyment; but the circulation of money creates an invisible and invincible obstacle to this exercise of social power.

The effects of commerce extend even further; not only does commerce emancipate individuals; by creating credit it also makes authority itself dependent.

Money, says a French writer, is despotism's most dangerous weapon, but it is also its most powerful restraint.[a] Credit is subject to opinion: against it, force is useless; money hides or takes flight. All the operations of the state are suspended. Credit had no such influence among the ancients; their governments were stronger than private citizens, while in our own time private citizens are stronger than political powers. Wealth is a power more readily available at every instant, more applicable to all interests, and consequently far more real and better obeyed. Power threatens, while wealth rewards: one may elude power by deceiving it, but in order to obtain the favours of wealth one must serve it; it is wealth which is bound to prevail.

Through a series of similar causes, individual existence today is less submerged in political existence; individuals can take their treasures far away; they can carry with them all the enjoyments of private life. Commerce has brought nations closer together and has given them virtually identical customs and habits; monarchs may still be enemies, but peoples are compatriots. Expatriation, which for the ancients was a punishment, is easy for the moderns; and far from being painful to them, it is often quite agreeable.[1]

It remains open to despotism to prohibit expatriation; but to prevent

---

[1] When Cicero said: *pro qua patria mori, et cui nos totos dedere, et in qua nostra omnia ponere, et quasi consecrare debemus* (the fatherland for which we must be prepared to die, to which we must dedicate ourselves, give all we have and almost consecrate ourselves) it is because the fatherland embodied at the time all that was dearest to a man. To lose one's country was to lose one's wife, children, friends, all affections, and nearly all communication and social enjoyment. The age of that sort of patriotism is over; what we love now in our country, as in our liberty, is the property of whatever we possess, our security, the possibility of rest, activity, glory, a thousand sorts of happiness. The word fatherland reminds us more of the whole of these goods than of the topographical notion of a specific country. When we are deprived of them at home, we go and seek them beyond it.

[Marcus Tullius Cicero, *De Re Publica. De legibus* with an English trs. by C. W. Keyes, The Loeb Classical Library (London, 1928), II, 2, 5.]

[a] C. L. S. de Montesquieu, *Esprit des lois*, Book 20, ch. 10 in *Oeuvres complètes*, vol. 2, p. 592.

it, it is not enough merely to prohibit it. One only leaves with even greater eagerness those countries from which it is forbidden to emigrate. It is therefore necessary to pursue those who have abandoned their country, to force first neighbouring states, and then remote ones, to expel them. Thus despotism returns to the system of enslavement, conquest and universal monarchy. It is a matter of seeking to try to remedy one impossibility by another.

What I am claiming here has just occurred under our very eyes. French despotism has pursued liberty from climate to climate; it has succeeded for a time in suppressing it in every region into into which it has penetrated. But since liberty always sought refuge from one region in another, despotism has been compelled to follow it so far that in the end it has met its own doom. The genius of mankind was waiting for it at the furthest boundaries of the world to make its retreat more shameful and its punishment more memorable.[1]

CHAPTER 19

As usurpation cannot be maintained through despotism, since in our days despotism itself cannot last, usurpation has no chance of enduring

If despotism is impossible in our time, to support usurpation by despotism is to sustain something that is bound to collapse with a support that is itself bound to collapse also.

A regular government places itself in a dangerous position when it aspires to despotism; and yet it still has habit on its side. Consider how long it took the Long Parliament to emancipate itself from that veneration that accompanies all ancient and sacred power, be it republican or monarchical. Do you think that the corporations existing under a

---

[1] I wish to acknowledge the courage and intelligence of one of my colleagues [in the Tribunate] who published a few years ago, under the tyranny, the truth which I develop here, sustaining it with a different kind of evidence from the one I offer, which could not have been published at the time. 'In the present condition of civilization, and in the commercial system under which we live, all public power must be limited, and no absolute power can survive.' Ganilh, *Hist. du Revenu public*, I, 419.
[Charles Ganilh, *Essai politique*.]

usurper would feel, in breaking his yoke, the same moral obstacle, the same conscientious scruple? Those corporations may well be enslaved; the more enslaved they are, the more fierce they become when some contingency arises to set them free. They want to expiate their long servitude. The senators who had voted for public festivities to celebrate Agrippina's death, and congratulated Nero on his mother's assassination, sentenced him to be beaten with rods and thrown into the Tiber.

The difficulties that a regular government encounters in becoming tyrannical derive precisely from its regularity. They impede its success but they also reduce the dangers which such attempts draw down upon it. Usurpation does not meet these systematic resistances. Its immediate triumph is more complete; but the resistance that is aroused in the end is more tumultuous: it is chaos against chaos.

Whenever a regular government, after having attempted abuses, returns to the practice of moderation and justice, all are grateful to it. It returns in fact to a position which is already known, which reassures people because of the memories it recalls. A usurper who renounced his enterprises would only prove his weakness. The point at which he chose to stop would be as ill-defined as the point which he had hoped to reach. He would be despised more without being hated less.

Usurpation then is unable to subsist either without despotism, as all interests would rise up against it, or through despotism, as despotism itself cannot last. Consequently it is impossible for usurpation to endure.

No doubt the sight that France presents to us is such as to discourage any hope. We see there usurpation triumphant, armed with every frightful memory, the heir of all criminal theories, thinking itself justified by all that has been done before it, strong through all the outrages, all the errors of the past, displaying its contempt for mankind, its disdain of reason. Around it are grouped all ignoble desires, all adroit calculations, all refined degradations. Those passions that in the violence of revolutions have proved so destructive, are reproduced in other forms. In the past, fear and vanity parodied the spirit of party in its most implacable furies. Now they surpass in their senseless demonstrations the most abject servility. Self-regard, which survives everything, sees success in the very baseness in which terror seeks refuge. Cupidity comes into the open, offering its own shame as a guarantee to tyranny. Sophism throws itself at its feet, astounds it by its zeal, overcomes it with its clamour, obscuring all ideas, and calling seditious any voice that attempts to confound it. Intelligence itself comes to offer its services, that intelligence which, when it is separated from conscience, is the vilest of instruments. The apostates of all opinions flock together, having retained from their past doctrines only their propensity for unsavoury means. Astute renegades, grown illustrious through the tradition of vice, slither from the prosperity of yesterday to the prosperity of today. Religion is the mouthpiece of authority, reason a mere gloss upon force. The prejudices of all ages, the injustices of every land, come together as the materials of the new social order. By returning to past centuries, by travelling through remote countries, they form, from a thousand sparse elements, a servitude complete enough to serve as a model. A dishonoured word goes from mouth to mouth, setting out from no real source and carrying conviction nowhere; a tiresome noise, idle and ridiculous, which leaves to truth and justice no unsullied expression.

Such a condition is more disastrous than the stormiest of revolutions. We may sometimes detest the seditious tribunes of Rome; but we are oppressed by the contempt we feel for the senate under Caesar. We may find harsh and culpable the enemies of Charles I, but we are overcome by a profound disgust for the creatures of Cromwell.

When the ignorant sections of society commit crimes, the enlightened classes remain intact. Their misfortune preserves them from the contagion. Since the force of things will sooner of later restore power to their hands, they can easily repair the damage to public opinion, which is more disoriented than corrupt. But when those classes themselves, repudiating their ancient principles, set aside their accustomed modesty and lend themselves to execrable examples, what hope is left? Where can we find a germ of honour, a trace of virtue? All is dirt, blood and dust.

How cruel, in every age, the destiny of the friends of humanity! Unrecognized, suspected, surrounded by men incapable of believing in courage or in disinterested convictions, tormented alternately by a feeling of indignation, when the oppressors are the stronger, and by one of pity when the same oppressors have become victims, they have always wandered upon this earth, exposed to all parties, alone in the midst of generations that are at times raging, and at others depraved.

Yet it is in them that hope for the human race always lies. We owe to them that great correspondence across the ages which bears witness in indelible letters against all the sophisms that every tyrant revives. It was thanks to it that Socrates survived the persecutions of a blind populace, and Cicero did not wholly die beneath the proscriptions of the infamous Octavius. May their successors never be discouraged! Let them raise their voices once again. They have done nothing for which to be forgiven. They have no need for atonements or disavowals. They possess intact the treasure of an unstained reputation. Let them dare to express the love of generous ideas. These would never bring upon them the accusing light of day. The times when despotism, disdaining what it regards as a useless hypocrisy, parades its own colours and insolently displays banners which have long been well-known, have their compensations. How much better it is to suffer the oppression of one's enemies than to blush for the excesses of one's allies! It is on those occasions that one meets the approval of all that is virtuous upon earth. One pleads a noble cause in the face of the world, seconded by the wishes of all well-meaning men.

A people can never detach itself from what is true liberty. To say that it does detach itself from this means to say that it welcomes humiliation, suffering, destitution and misery. It is to claim that it resigns itself without pain to being separated from the objects of its love, interrupted in its activities, deprived of its possessions, tormented in its opinions, and in its most secret thoughts, dragged into dungeons and to the scaffold. It is precisely against these evils that the guarantees of liberty were created. It is to be preserved from scourges such as these that we appeal to liberty. These are the scourges that the people fears, curses and detests. Wherever and under whatever denomination it encounters them, it will take fright and recoil from them. It was slavery that the people loathed in what its oppressors called liberty. Today slavery has shown itself under its own name, in its own true form. Should we believe that the people loathe it any less?

Missionaries of truth, if the road is obstructed, redouble your zeal; redouble your efforts. Let the light shine through from every side. If it is obscured, let it reappear again; if it is suppressed, let it return. Let it reproduce, multiply, transform itself. Let it be as indefatigable as persecution. Let some march with courage, while others cleverly insinuate themselves. Let truth itself spread and penetrate, sometimes resoundingly, sometimes in a mere whisper. Let all reasons coalesce together, let all hopes revive, let everyone work and serve and wait.

Tyranny, immorality and injustice are so much against nature that one single effort, one courageous voice is sufficient to rescue man from this abyss. He returns to morality through the unhappiness which results from forgetting it. He returns to liberty through the misery caused by neglecting it. No nation's cause is ever truly hopeless. England during her civil wars, offered examples of inhumanity. That same England appeared to have recovered from her delirium only to fall into servitude. And yet she has resumed her place amongst the countries that are wise, virtuous and free, and in our own day we have seen it as both their model and their hope.

———————

During the printing of this work, which began in November of last year,[a] the events which have succeeded one another so rapidly have supported with such patent proofs the truths I intended to establish, that I could not prevent myself from making use of the examples they have offered me, notwithstanding my original desire to confine myself as far as possible to general principles.

He who for twelve years proclaimed himself destined to conquer the world, has made honourable amends for his pretensions. His speeches, his initiatives, all his actions are more victorious arguments against the system of conquest than anything I have been able to assemble. At the same time his behaviour, so little reminiscent of that of those legitimate sovereigns who have been exposed to similar adversities, adds a very poignant difference to all of those I had emphasized as distinguishing usurpation both from monarchy and from republic. Look at Venice at the time of the League of Cambrai or at Holland threatened by Louis XIV. What confidence in the people, what calm intrepidness in the magistrates. The fact is that these governments were legitimate. Look at Louis XIV himself in his old age. He had to fight against the whole of Europe. He was weakened by the outrages of time. His pride acknowledged the need to yield to fortune. Yet his language was full of dignity. Despite the dangers, he established the limit beyond which he would not retreat. His nobility in misfortune almost excuses the faults that his good fortune had led him to commit. And, as is always the case, just as his errors had been punished, his magnanimity of soul was rewarded. An honourable peace saved both his throne and his people. In our time the King of Prussia loses a portion of his domains. He cannot sustain an unequal struggle. He resigns himself to his fate, but he preserves,

———

[a] 1813. According to Constant's journal, the work did not go to press until 18 December.

amidst his reverses, the firmness of a man and the attitude of a true king. Europe respects him; his subjects pity and cherish him. From all sides secret wishes join themselves to his own, and as soon as he gives the signal, a generous nation hastens to revenge him. What shall we say of that even greater example, unique in the annals of peoples? This time we are no longer talking of a few peripheral provinces occupied by the enemy: it is instead the enemy penetrating to the heart of a vast empire. Do you hear a single cry of discouragement? Can you detect a single sign of weakness? The aggressor advances, all is silent. He threatens, nothing yields. He plants his flags on the towers of the capital and the answer he receives is that same capital reduced to ashes.[a]

He, on the contrary, even before his territory is invaded, is stricken by an anxiety he cannot conceal. No sooner are his frontiers reached, than he throws away all his conquests. He exacts the abdication of one of his brothers and sanctions the expulsion of another.[b] Without being asked, he declares that he will give up everything.

How can we account for this difference? If kings, even when vanquished, do not abjure their dignity, why should the conqueror of the entire earth yield at the first setback? It is because these kings knew that the foundation of their throne rested upon the hearts of their subjects. But a usurper sits with fear on an illegitimate throne, as on a solitary pyramid. No assent supports him. He has reduced everything to dust, and that loose dust lets the wild winds blow at him. His family's cries, he tells us, rend his heart. Were they not members of the same family, then, those who died in Russia of the triple agony of wounds, cold and famine? But while they perished, deserted by their chief, that chief believed himself in safety. Now the dangers he has come to share have suddenly restored his sensibility.

Fear is a bad counsellor, especially for those without a conscience. In adversity, as in good fortune, there is measure only in morality. Where morality does not rule, good fortune is lost by folly, adversity by degradation.

Which effect upon a courageous nation must they cause – this blind fright, this sudden cowardice, still unparalleled amidst all our storms? Those revolutionaries who were justly condemned for their great excesses felt at least that their life belonged to their cause, and that one must not provoke Europe without being prepared to resist it. No doubt,

---

[a] Constant is referring to Napoleon's Russian campaign of 1812.
[b] Jérôme, King of Westphalia and Joseph, King of Spain.

France has been suffering for twelve years under a heavy and cruel tyranny. The holiest of rights had been violated, every liberty had been encroached upon. Yet there was a kind of glory. National pride found (albeit wrongly) a certain reward in being oppressed only by an invincible chief. Today what is left? No more prestige, no more triumphs, a mutilated empire, the world's execration, a throne whose pomp is tarnished, whose trophies have been cast down, a throne which has for its entire entourage only the wandering shades of the Duke of Enghien,*[a]* of Pichegru,*[b]* of so many others who were butchered in order to establish it. Proud defenders of the monarchy, will you suffer the oriflamme of St Louis to be replaced by a standard bloody with crimes, and stripped of all success? And you, who would wish for a republic, what can you say of a master who has deceived your hopes and blighted those laurels, whose shade veiled your civil dissensions and caused one to admire even your errors?

[a] The Bourbon Duke of Enghien was sentenced to death in 1804 on a fabricated accusation of conspiracy, as an act of intimidation to the Royalist party.

[b] Jean-Charles Pichegru (1761–1804). A general in the French revolutionary army, he defected to the royalists. In 1797 he became a member of the Council of the Five Hundred and, after 18 *Fructidor*, was deported to Guyana. He escaped, reached London and in 1804 returned to France to take part in the royalist conspiracy against Bonaparte organized by Cadoudal. Arrested, he was found strangled in his cell on 6 April 1804.

Additions to *The Spirit of Conquest and Usurpation*

CHAPTERS ADDED TO THE FOURTH EDITION

CHAPTER I

On innovation, reform and the uniformity and stability of institutions

[a]Some seem to have believed that, in recommending respect for the past, I blamed all innovations, making no allowances for the progress of ideas, and failing to recognize the necessity for those inevitable changes that time introduces in opinions and that must consequently be introduced also in human institutions. Yet I had excepted from my respect for the past all unjust institutions. I had recognized that no prescription could legitimate injustice. But it is certainly true that when it is simply a matter of imperfections, when the desired changes are not exacted by rigorous equity, but merely motivated by their supposed utility, I think that one ought to proceed to those innovations only slowly and with reserve.

When authority tells public opinion, like Seide to Mahomet,

'I have anticipated your order.'

public opinion answers, like Mahomet to Seide:

'You should have waited for it.'[b]

and if authority refuses to wait, public opinion takes its revenge.

---

[a] Compare the rest of this chapter with the 1806 draft, Book 15, ch. 7: 'Des améliorations prématurées', E. Hoffmann (ed.), *Les 'Principes de Politique'*, vol. 2, pp. 406–12.

[b] François Marie Arouet de Voltaire, *Fanatisme, ou Mahomet le prophète, tragédie* (Brussels, 1742), Act II, Scene 3. In 1806 Constant acted in the role of Zopire in an amateur performance of *Mahomet* at Coppet.

Those men who wish to anticipate it fall, perhaps without realizing it, into a strange contradiction. In order to justify their premature attempts, they tell themselves that one must not rob the present generation of the benefits of their new system. And when the present generation complains of being the victim of this system, they excuse this sacrifice in the name of the interest of future races.

Any amelioration, any reform, the abolition of any abuse, all these are beneficial only when they second the wish of the nation. When they precede it they become nefarious. They are no longer improvements, but acts of tyranny. What it is reasonable to regard as important is not how fast improvements are implemented, but if the institutions are in accord with the ideas. If you neglect this rule, you will never know where to stop. All abuses are connected and several of them are intimately related to essential parts of the social edifice. Unless public opinion has marked them out already, you will, by attacking them, destroy the entire edifice.

It may be objected that it is difficult to know precisely the state of public opinion and what it wants; that it would be impossible to count the votes; that it is often after the adoption of a measure which had seemed popular, that opposition manifests itself, when it is too late to go back.

I shall answer, first, that if you allow public opinion free expression you will have no difficulty in knowings its feelings. Do not provoke it; do not excite it with hopes by prompting those views which you would like it to express. If you do, flattery, in order to please power, will then assume the form of opinion. Place an irreligious monarch at the head of a devout people, and the most pliable of courtiers will be the most sceptical. Replace a bigoted court at the head of an enlightened people and the atheists of that court will revert to hair-shirts and discipline. But if authority will only remain silent, the individuals will speak up, the clash of ideas will generate enlightenment, and it will soon be impossible to mistake the general feeling. You have here an infallible as well as easy means, freedom of the press; that freedom to which we must always return; that freedom which is as necessary to governments as it is to the people; that freedom, the violation of which, in this respect, is a crime against the state.

Secondly, in practice, public opinion imperceptibly modifies those laws and institutions which hinder it. Let it do its work. Time, says

Bacon, is the great reformer.[a] Do not refuse its assistance. Let it march in front of you; it will smooth your path. If what you establish has not been prepared by it, you will command in vain. It will be no more difficult for your successors to abolish your laws than it was for you to abolish those of others, and all that will be left of the laws which you have abolished will be the evil that they have caused.

I look back at Europe in the eighteenth century. I take facts haphazardly as they present themselves: they all confirm my claim.

With the death of John V, I see Portugal steeped in ignorance and bent under the yoke of priesthood. A man of genius came to the head of the state.[b] He failed to calculate that, in order to break that yoke and to dissipate that ignorance, it was necessary to find some support in national feeling. By a mistake common to the holders of power, he sought that support in authority. By striking the rock, he expected to make the vivifying source gush out from it.[c] His imprudent haste turned against him the spirits most inclined to support him. Persecution of the priests only increased their influence. The nobility rose up; frightful punishments created general dismay. The minister was exposed to the hatred of all classes. After twenty years of tyrannical administration the death of the king deprived him of his protector; he barely escaped the scaffold, and the nation blessed the moment when, delivered from a government which pretended to enlighten it in spite of itself, it could rest again in superstition and apathy.[1]

In Austria, Joseph II succeeded Maria Theresa. He found that the degree of enlightenment of his subjects was inferior to that of the neighbouring countries. Impatient to overcome an inequality which offended him, he called to his assistance all the means which his power granted him, without neglecting those promised to him by liberty. He lent to those writers who exposed abuses the support of force. But

[1] I do not claim to make any statement on the present condition of the Portuguese nation; I am only talking of the revolution that the Marquis of Pombal attempted to carry through fifty years ago.

---

[a] 'Novator maximum tempus, quidni igitur tempus imitemur?' Francis Bacon, *De augmentis scientiarum*, Book 6, *Exempla antithetorum*, XL. In *The Works of Francis Bacon*, ed. by J. Spedding, R. L. Ellis, D. D. Heath (London, 1857–74), 14 vols., vol. I, p. 704.

[b] See: Sebastien Joseph de Carvalho e Mello, Marquês de Pombal, *Mémoires de S. J. de Carvalho et Mélo, Comte d'Oeyras, Marquis de Pombal* (4 vols., Lyons, 1784).

[c] Like Moses on Mount Horeb: *Exodus*, 17, 1–7.

public opinion, seeing itself bypassed, remained immobile and indifferent. Obscure monks and privileged egoists resisted the projects of the emperor–philosopher. His administration became odious because, in the name of the people's interests, it went against their habits and prejudices.

The regrets accompanying his disappointed good intentions, the pain of being misunderstood, brought Joseph prematurely to his grave, and his last words were a confession of his impotence and an expression of his misery.[1]

The history of our Constituent Assembly is even more instructive. Public opinion appeared to have long demanded several of the improvements which that assembly attempted to enact. Too eager to please it, that gathering of enlightened but impatient men did not think that they could go too far or too fast. Yet public opinion was infuriated by the haste of its own interpreters. It drew back, because those interpreters wanted to rush it into change. Delicate to the point of capriciousness, it is irritated when its vague aspirations are mistaken for orders. Because it attacks something, it does not necessarily mean that it wants that thing to be destroyed. Often, just as kings would be angry if every word they uttered were immediately enacted by the zeal of their entourage, so that it may talk freely, it often wants to talk without its words necessarily having any consequences. The Constituent Assembly's most popular decrees were disowned by a large proportion of the people. Among the voices which were raised against those decrees there were, no doubt, many who had previously contributed to bringing them about. It is only when the discontented faced the threat of being deprived of the benefits of those reforms which they had censured so bitterly, that public opinion, its independence no longer wounded, again committed itself to those reforms which an immoderate enthusiasm had discredited and condemned.

Look instead at Russia since the beginning of the reign of Alexander. The improvements there are slow and gradual; the people are fully and freely enlightened; the laws are perfected in detail, and no-one thinks of subverting the entire system. By preceding theory, practice prepares the spirit to accept it, and the moment arrives when that theory, which is merely the exposition of what must be, will be received even better because it will simply be the explanation of what already is. Honour to

---

[1] Joseph II asked to have engraved on his tomb that he had been unfortunate in all his undertakings.

that prince who, in his prudent and generous march, favours all natural progress, respects all necessary adjournments, and knows how to protect himself equally from the suspicion that wishes to stop him, and from the impatience which seeks to precede him.

In order to remedy abuses, let the people free themselves from them: let them, do not force them. By letting them, you call all progressive forces to your aid; by forcing them, you arm many interests against you.

Let us take an example: there are two ways of suppressing convents: you may open their doors; or you may drive out their occupants. If you adopt the first solution, you do something good without causing any harm; you break chains without violating refuges. If you adopt the second, you upset calculations based upon public faith; you insult old age, which you drag languishing and unarmed into an unknown world; you violate an incontestable right of all individuals in the social state, the right to choose their way of life, to hold their property in common, to gather in order to profess the same doctrine, to enjoy the same leisure, to savour the same rest. These injustices so enrage public opinion that they rebel against the reform you now order despite the fact that they called for and sanctioned it by vote.

I apply these principles to that uniformity, which I have been accused of censuring too severely. I do not wish to deny that in some respects uniformity, whose defects I have exposed, also has some advantages. All social institutions are simply forms, adopted for the same aim, for the greatest happiness, and especially for the greatest improvement of the human race. There is always one of these forms which is worth more than all the others. If it can be introduced peacefully, and win for itself a general and voluntary consent, no-one can doubt that this will be a real gain. But if, in order to introduce it, you need constraint, laws to prohibit it, and their inseparable companions, penal laws, the evil will outweigh the good.

To go from one village to another, the straightest line is unquestionably the shortest. The inhabitants of the two villages would spare themselves time and effort if they followed this route. But if you can trace this only by demolishing houses and devastating fields; if, after having traced it, you need police measures to prevent the passers-by from returning to their old paths; if you need guards to arrest the trespassers, prisons to receive them, gaolers to detain them, will this not cost more time and more effort? If the authorities can, without violating private property and the rights of individuals, open a direct route, they do well. But let them confine themselves to opening that route without forbidding those which usage has consecrated, even if they are longer and more inconvenient. Let them leave interest to fight against habit; sooner or later interest will prevail, and the desired change, gained at a smaller cost, will prove more complete and irrevocable.

This applies also to names, means of calculation, weights and measures, in short, to all those methods which simplify daily operations and the transactions between individuals. These methods are in themselves improvements. Let the authorities adopt them, proclaim them and use them. But let them refrain from investigating whether private citizens still make use of the old faulty methods. Let them ignore deviations. If the improvement is real, that is to say, if the method is in fact clearer and easier, it will soon be adopted; and even if it were to be a little delayed, the evil would be trifling. By using force, you distort the question. The man who feels offended by your violent measures no longer examines what you propose to him. He revolts against the injury which you do to him. He averts his eyes from your aim, which may be good, in order to fix it on your means, which are bad, and what you wish to establish becomes hateful to him.

The question of the uniformity of the laws is even more delicate. You cannot give uniform laws to a country whose provinces have ancient laws, which are different from one another, except by changing the latter. To overcome the shock of change it is not sufficient to declare that the new laws will have no retroactive effect. Their change does nevertheless place the transgressors of yesterday and those of tomorrow in a different position; and because the transactions of yesterday are the basis of those of today, and since the former have often taken place only because people assumed that the latter would be based on the same premises, it is clear that your innovation frustrates hopes and destroys security.

When I see the indignation that Voltaire and so many other writers affect to feel in the face of those numerous and opposed customs which coexisted in France, I wonder at the errors to which they were led by their love of symmetry. 'What', they cry out, 'two portions of the same empire are subjected to different laws because they are separated by a hill or a stream of water! Is justice not the same on the two sides of a hill, or on the two banks of a stream of water?' But laws are not justice: they are merely forms to administer it; if two tribes which, although close to one another, have for a long time enjoyed a separate existence, find after their union, that they have preserved different forms, this difference must not be judged in terms of a geographical proximity or common denomination, but in the light of the moral attachment to the hereditary laws on which all their calculations are based.

The freest country in our old world, Great Britain,[1] is governed by very diversified laws. There is no county which does not have some customs which are different from those observed in the neighbouring one.[2] Nowhere else, however, is property more protected, or the rights of individuals more respected, or justice more impartial.[3]

This variety could hardly serve as a model in theory. It would be absurd to give at random different laws to the different parts of a totally new country, inhabited entirely by new men (though if those men arrived in that country with memories and habits, the laws given to them should not offend either their habits or their memories). But when we employ elements already in existence we must respect all interests created and guaranteed by the old institutions.[4]

Moral beings cannot be subjected to the rules of arithmetic and of mechanism. The past puts down deep roots in them, which cannot be pulled up without pain. By uprooting them, you subject them to

[1] In expressing myself in these terms I do not wish to deny that Sweden also enjoys great liberty. I am glad to pay a just tribute to this generous nation which we have seen, guided by a great man, appear in the first rank of our liberators when other peoples, or their governments, seemed still to hesitate. I know that in Sweden individuals are protected from all arbitrary acts by equitable laws, by an independent representation and a noble national spirit. But I see, among the last decrees of the Diet, restrictions on freedom of the press; I see a kind of censorship, entrusted, it is true, to the judgement of a very enlightened man. Before numbering Sweden amongst the truly free nations, I wait to see the decree limiting the freedom of the press removed, as it ought to be, from amongst her laws.

[2] See Blackstone.
[William Blackstone, *Commentaries on the Laws of England* (4 vols., Oxford, 1765–9); French trs. *Commentaires sur les lois anglaises* (6 vols., Paris, 1822–3).]

[3] England's persistence in preserving the ancient usages of each province proves, I may observe *en passant*, how much true liberty is slandered when it is represented as dangerous and disorganizing. Slaves only cause mischief when they break their chains: then, no doubt, they cause a great deal, and, to their great misfortune and shame, that mischief is often gratuitous, so that, exhausted by their excesses, they tend always to return to their servitude.

[4] Notice that this applies only to what is to be done, and not to what has been done already. To destroy has often proved a mistake, but to restore would also be a mistake. It would cause a double inconvenience: instead of one innovation, there would be two. From the fact that the local customs of the provinces of France have been abolished too thoughtlessly, in order to subject the country to a uniform code, it does not follow that we must now abolish that code to revive local customs. The change which took place, even if it was introduced imprudently, nevertheless belongs to the past; it must be respected, because after twenty-five years habits have become attached to it.

Polydor's torment.[a] There is not a single one which would not put up resistance and, uprooted, shed some drops of blood.

By reflecting even briefly upon this doctrine, we shall be convinced that it does not favour those exaggerated ideas of stability which men neither less systematic, nor less obstinate, wish to oppose to necessary improvements. It is another extreme, or rather it is the same error, differently applied. It is always the rights of public opinion which are in question: some do not wish to wait for it; others do not wish to march in step with it.

At the time when some institutions were established, because they were in accord with the degree of knowledge and the current customs, they had some utility, some relative good. With the progress of the human mind, these advantages have diminished; institutions have been modified. To wish to re-establish those institutions in what is called their original purity would be in this case a great error, as that purity would be found to be precisely the most opposed to contemporary ideas, and the most apt to cause evil.

This error is that of the majority of governments and of many pamphleteers. They see that, in a certain age, certain laws, certain practices were useful, and that now they are hateful. They imagine that it is because they have degenerated; it is, on the contrary, because the institution has remained the same while ideas have changed. The cause of the evil for which they would like to find a remedy is by no means the degeneration of the former, but the disharmony which has grown up between it and the other institutions. Consequently the remedy which they employ can only aggravate the evil.

Because the march of the human race is gradual, any innovation which gives it a violent shock is dangerous; but because that march is also progressive, all that opposes its progress is equally dangerous. If the opposition is effective, there is stagnation and soon degeneration in men's faculties. If the opposition is impotent, the consequences are struggle, conflict, convulsions and calamities.

We are afraid of upheavals, and with reason; but sometimes we provoke these upheavals by a blind and obstinate attachment to exaggerated ideas of stability as much as by imprudent innovations. The

---

[a] Reference to Virgil (*Aeneid*, III, 45ff.) where the youngest of Priam's sons, assassinated, is transformed into a bush.
   [Maro Publius Virgil, *Eclogues, Georgics, Aeneid*, English trs. H. R. Fairclough, Loeb Classical Library (2 vols., London, 1916–18).]

only way of avoiding them is to favour those imperceptible changes which take place in moral as well as in physical nature. Unfortunately, we allow ourselves to be seduced by certain words, especially we who, because we have in general more intelligence than imagination, study with our minds what ought to strike the imagination that we lack, and then make it a duty for ourselves to appear enthusiasts for it. The word regeneration has led us to destroy everything. The word stability would lead us to restore everything. But to restore, in this case, is only another way of innovating. Authorities wishing today to re-establish feudalism, servitude, religious intolerance, inquisition, and torture would claim in vain that they were merely rebuilding ancient institutions. Those ancient institutions would be for us only absurd and nefarious novelties.

They would not even offer the advantage which they may have had in the past, that of maintaining, through stupor, a kind of oppressive and heavy slumber. As all the moral forces of the century would react against them, their re-establishment could not last long. If their re-establishment had caused harm, their overthrow would cause even greater harm; and yet it would be inevitable. To renew such institutions is to give encouragement to all those who wish to overturn all institutions.

Obey time; do every day what that day calls for; do not be obstinate in keeping up what is collapsing, or too hasty in establishing what seems to announce itself. Remain faithful to justice, which belongs to all ages; respect liberty, which prepares every sort of good; let many things develop without you, and leave to the past its own defence, to the future its own accomplishment.

CHAPTER 2

Further reflections on usurpation

The ideas which I presented on usurpation have met with two kinds of opponents. Some have accused me of considering as usurpers all those governments which were not founded upon heredity. Others have refused to consider the consequences which I attribute to usurpation as being truly inevitable.

I could have anticipated the objections of the former had I not left in my work a lacuna, which I believed I had justified, by declaring that I did not wish to go back to the origins of governments. Had I treated this question, I could hardly have failed to acknowledge that no authority which is established by national will can be suspected of usurpation. Washington was certainly no usurper. The Prince of Orange of the time of Philip II was no usurper. William III was no usurper. A usurper is one who, without the sanction of the national will, seizes power, or who, having been invested with a limited power, exceeds the limits prescribed.

I do not wish to deny that for the spectator it is difficult to decide when a national will exists and when it does not exist. This is why I always mistrust those men who, during a revolution, rise at the head of peoples. Again, this is why new dynasties inspire in me an unfavourable and almost invincible prejudice. But the difficulty of uncovering the truth does not change truth itself. When a nation is forced to simulate a will which is not her own, it knows perfectly well that this wish is not genuine. When a man compels a people to express a sentiment opposed to the one they feel, that man cannot have many illusions as to the sincerity of the feeling which he commands. People know perfectly well when they are governed by a usurper. It is precisely this knowledge which usurpation has of itself, and which is betrayed by those who obey it; it is this knowledge, I claim, which gives it its character and leads it to the consequences I described and to which I shall return in answering the second group of my opponents.

Those to whom I am now replying must acknowledge that, in the end, we are of the same opinion. I admit two sorts of legitimacy: one positive, which derives from free election, the other tacit, which rests upon heredity; and I shall add that heredity is legitimate because the habits it generates and the advantages it grants render it the national will. For the rest, I do not like to discuss these questions: as I said elsewhere, they are dangerous when they are superfluous, but they become clear enough when it is necessary to raise them.[1] But on the other hand it is somewhat imprudent to reproduce systems that the progress of enlightenment has rendered null.[2]

---

[1] *Réflexions sur les constitutions*, Preface, p. IX.
[2] In order to persuade himself of the dangers that this system represents for sovereigns, even more than for peoples, the reader may consult the work of M. de Lévis on England in the nineteenth century, pp. 259–62, and especially p. 259.
    [Pierre Marc Gaston, duc de Lévis, *L'Angleterre au commencement du dix-neuvième siècle* (Paris, 1814).]

Pamphleteers should learn from the example of Bonaparte himself, whose history is too recent for the lessons it offers us to have been already forgotten. No-one has worked harder than that man to revive the dogma of divine right. He has had himself consecrated by the head of the Church; every focus of religious pomp has surrounded his throne. His elevation itself seemed to be something supernatural. All the sophisms of the mind were at his service, from the catechism to academic harangues. The works of a thousand writers have been filled with dissertations of naive baseness, on the duty of implicit obedience and the mystery of authority. Yet what has been the result of all these efforts? The moment of truth has arrived: and in that nation, sworn to obedience and indoctrinated for twelve years, not a single voice was raised to recall a profession of political faith commented on and amplified by so many indefatigable rhetoricians, inculcated into a docile youth and subscribed to a thousand times by an immense nation with every appearance of enthusiasm. True, the arguments upon which that profession rests prove too much or they prove nothing. They prove too much if they are established in all their rigour, because they invalidate the legitimacy of any family which has elevated itself at expense of another one. They prove nothing if they are bent to serve the circumstances, because in that case the source of legitimacy is merely power, and power belongs to whoever seizes it. Finally, what need do we have of such arguments in a nation in which there is no-one who does not sincerely wish to enjoy a wise liberty under an august dynasty, guarantee of repose and cherished protection against all new agitation?

Of the two kinds of legitimacy which I admit, the one which derives from election is more seductive in theory, but it has the inconvenience that it can be counterfeited: as it was in England by Cromwell and in France by Bonaparte.

History offers us only two examples in which the election of a single man, substituted for heredity, has had favourable results.[1] The first example is that of the English in 1688; the second that of the Swedes today. But, in these two cases, legitimacy, consecrated by heredity, has come to the aid of election. The prince whom the Swedes have summoned[a] has been adopted by the royal family; while the English

---

[1] I am not talking of America, where the power entrusted to the president is republican and removable.

---

[a] Bernadotte.

sought in William III the closest relative of the king whom they had resolved to depose. In one case as in the other the result of this combination has been that the prince freely elected by the nation, has found himself to be as strong in his ancient dignity as in his new title. He has satisfied imagination by memories which captivated it, and reason by the national suffrage by which he was supported. He has not been condemned to employ only the elements of a recent creation. He has been able to dispose confidently of all the forces of the nation, because he was not robbing it of any part of its political heritage. The pre-existing institutions were in no way adverse to him; he associated himself with them, and they joined together to sustain him.

Add to this that the circumstances gave to William III an interest other than the one which usually animates princes and leads them to work only to increase their power. Having to preserve his power against a competitor who contested it, he made common cause with those friends of liberty who, while preserving for him his entitlements, did not wish these to be enlarged. Those who wished to extend the royal prerogative aimed at the same time to entrust it to someone else. Hence it followed that, during the three reigns of William III, Queen Anne and George I, these monarchs were on the defensive against a theory of despotism which would have turned against them. They saw themselves obliged to stress the dangers of that theory. If the principles of obedience were favourable to the power of the king as king, the principles of liberty were favourable to the security of the king as individual. Queen Anne thought it in her interests to prosecute Sacheverel[a] who had preached the doctrine of passive obedience and divine right. Thus the crown was influential in preparing the public spirit for liberty.

Yet note, even in that important part of English history which includes its most recent revolution since 1625, the tendency of the people to prefer hereditary legitimacy. No sooner was Cromwell dead than the English recalled the Stuarts with a great show of rejoicing. They wanted to give them some proof of their attachment, to show them their repentance, to surround them with their boundless trust. It was only after a second terrible experience, after having seen acts of arbitrariness renewed and multiplied, properties invaded, judgements annulled, citizens stricken by illegal sentences, freedom of the press

---

[a] Henry Sacheverell (1674?–1724), political preacher, tried and silenced in 1710.

trampled under foot, in short all promises broken, all social guarantees violated, that the British nation decided to move away from the direct line and to be contented with the legitimacy which her choice conferred upon a new sovereign. This is certainly a proof that heredity has a charm for people, and that they are happy when they can, without too much inconvenience, remain faithful to it!

Finding myself, with this explanation, in accord with those who have censured my opinions simply because I had developed them only in part, I must still answer those who reproach me for having transformed particular facts into general rules, and for having taken the conqueror and usurper who oppresses us as the model of all conquerors and all usurpers. But a detailed comparison between Bonaparte and all these curses of the human race would be necessary, and this comparison, which would require a mass of historical discussions, cannot be placed at the end of this work.

I shall not be accused of trying to justify someone whom I never wished to acknowledge. But I believe that those who attribute his enterprises, his crimes and his fall to a perversity or folly peculiar to him, are in the wrong. On the contrary, he seems to me to have been powerfully affected both by his position as usurper and by the spirit of his century. Indeed, it was in his nature to be more affected by these causes than any other man would have been. What characterized him was the absence of all moral sense, that is of all sympathy, all human emotion. He was self-interest personified; if that self-interest produced results which were disastrously odd, it is because it rested upon two opposed and irreconcilable terms, usurpation, which made despotism necessary, and a degree of civilization which made it impossible. From this there resulted contradictions, incoherences, a violent double reaction which have been wrongly taken for individual eccentricities.

No doubt, a character like Philopoemen, Washington, Kosciusko would not have followed the same course, or committed the same errors. The reason is that Philopoemen, Washington and Kosciusko were no usurpers. But they were also very rare characters; they were exceptions.

Surely, Bonaparte is a thousand times more guilty than those barbarous conquerors who, ruling over barbarians, were by no means at odds with their age. Unlike them, he has chosen barbarism; he has preferred it. In the midst of enlightenment, he has sought to bring back the night. He has chosen to transform into greedy and bloodthirsty nomads a mild and polite people: his crime lies in this premeditated intention, in his obstinate effort to rob us of the heritage of all the enlightened generations who have preceded us on this earth. But why have we given him the right to conceive such project?

When he first arrived here, alone, out of poverty and obscurity, and until he was twenty-four, his greedy gaze wandering over the country around him, why did we show him a country in which any religious idea was the object of irony? When he listened to what was professed in our circles, why did serious thinkers tell him that man had no other motivation than his own interest? If he discovered easily enough that all the subtle interpretations through which, once the principle had been stated, we sought to elude its implications, were illusory, it was because his instinct was sound and his judgement quick. As I never attributed to him virtues which he did not possess, I am not obliged to deny him the faculties which he did. If in the heart of man there is nothing but interest, tyranny has only to frighten or to seduce him in order to dominate him. If in the heart of man there is nothing but self-interest, it is not true that morality – that is, elevation, nobility, resistance to injustice – is in accord with real self-interest. Properly understood, self-interest, in this case, given the certainty of death, is nothing but enjoyment, combined, since life can be more or less long, with that prudence which grants to enjoyment a certain duration. Finally, when in a France torn apart, tired of suffering and lamenting, and demanding only a ruler, he offered to become that ruler, why did the multitude hasten to solicit from him their enslavement? When the crowd is pleased to show its love for servitude, it would be too much for it to expect its master to insist on giving it liberty instead.

I know, the nation slandered herself, or let herself be slandered by unfaithful interpreters. Despite the wretched affectation which mimicked incredulity, not all religious sentiment had been destroyed. Despite the fatuity which proclaimed itself selfish, egoism did not reign alone; and whatever acclamations may sound in the air, the national desire was not for servitude. But Bonaparte must have deceived himself over this, he whose reason was not enlightened by sentiment, whose soul was incapable of being exalted by a generous whim. He judged France by her own words, and the world by France as he imagined her to be. Because immediate usurpation was easy, he believed it could be durable, and once he became a usurper, he did all that usurpation condemns a usurper to do in our century.

It was necessary to stifle inside the country all intellectual life: he banished discussion and proscribed the freedom of the press.

The nation might have been stunned by that silence: he provided, extorted or paid for acclamation which sounded like the national voice. Had France remained at peace, her peaceful citizens, her idle warriors would have observed the despot, would have judged him, and would have communicated their judgements to him. Truth would have passed through the ranks of the people. Usurpation would not have long withstood the influence of truth. Thus Bonaparte was compelled to distract public attention by bellicose enterprises. War flung onto distant shores that part of the French nation that still had some real energy. It prompted the police harassment of the timid, whom it could not force abroad. It struck terror into men's hearts, and left there a certain hope that chance would take responsibility for their deliverance: a hope agreeable to fear and convenient to inertia. How many times have I heard men who were pressed to resist tyranny postponing this, during wartime till the coming of peace, and in peacetime until war commences!

I am right therefore in claiming that a usurper's sole resource is uninterrupted war. Some object: what if Bonaparte had been pacific? Had he been pacific, he would never have lasted for twelve years. Peace would have re-established communication among the different countries of Europe. These communications would have restored to thought its means of expression. Works published abroad would have been smuggled into the country. The French would have seen that they did not enjoy the approval of the majority of Europe: their prestige could not have been sustained. Bonaparte perceived this truth so well that he broke with England in order to escape the British newspapers. Yet even this was not enough. While a single country remained free, Bonaparte was never safe. Commerce, active, adroit, invisible, indefatigable, capable of overcoming any distance and of insinuating itself through a thousand roundabout means, would sooner or later have reintroduced into the empire those enemies whom it was so important to exile from it. Hence the Continental blockade[a] and the war with Russia.

Notice how true it is that the need for war to maintain usurpation is characteristic of our age. A century and a half ago, Cromwell had no

---

[a] The embargo on British goods established by Napoleon between 1806 and 1813.

need for it. Communications between peoples were neither as frequent nor as easy. Continental literature was almost unknown to the English. The writings directed against their usurper were composed in Latin. There were no newspapers which, coming from the outside, might deal him blows whose constant repetition would render each day more dangerous. Cromwell was not forced to war to prevent the hatred of the English from being reinforced by foreign sympathy, as would have happened to the French under Bonaparte had he not isolated them from the rest of the world. The latter needed war everywhere, to make of his slaves: 'Semotos penitus orbe Gallos'.[a]

I could offer on all these points a similar demonstration if I wished to analyse all of Bonaparte's actions. Many of his cruelties seem futile to us: but challenge is an inseparable component of usurpation, and those crimes which may be useless in themselves, become part of its nature. Bonaparte could take no reassurance either from tumultuous assent or from silent submission, and the most horrible of his actions was committed because he believed he could find a monstrous security in imposing on his agents complicity in a great crime.[b]

What I assert about the means of usurpation, I assert also about its fall. I claimed that it must fall by the inevitable effect of the wars which it requires. Some have objected that, had Bonaparte not made such and such a military error, he would not have been overthrown. Not this time but some other time; not today but tomorrow. It is only too natural that a gambler, who every day takes a new risk, should some day meet with the one which must ruin him.

Some reproached me for having claimed that conquests were impossible at a time when the whole of Europe was the prey of one vast conquest, and that usurpation could not establish itself in our century while usurpation was triumphant. While this objection was being set forth, all the conquered territories were taken back, and usurpation collapsed.

I had claimed that peace was in accord with the spirit of our present civilization, and all peoples were at war. But it was in the name of peace that they rose. No constraint, no threat, was necessary to unite and to lead them, while in France, where the nation had to fight not for peace

---

[a] Constant is quoting somewhat freely from Virgil, *Eclogues*, I, 67: 'Et penitus toto divisos orbe Britannos' 'the Britons, shut away from the whole world.'
    [Maro Publius Virgil, *Eclogues, Georgics, Aeneid*. English trs. H. R. Fairclough, Loeb Classical Library (2 vols., London, 1916–18).]
[b] The assassination of the Duke of Enghien.

but for conquest, henchmen, gendarmes, executioners, barely succeeded in forcing the citizens to take arms.

It seems to me, therefore, that I have not generalized from a particular idea. I have simply refused to adopt a logic in virtue of which all general ideas would be banished, since it is always possible to imagine circumstances other than those which existed already, and disguise as accidents the laws of nature. I confess that I believe it is more important to show that the evils inflicted by Bonaparte on France derived from the fact that his power had degenerated into usurpation, and thus put the blame on usurpation itself, rather than on some individual as a unique being, made for evil, and committing crimes out of neither necessity nor self-interest. The first perspective teaches us great lessons for the future; the second transforms history into a sterile study of isolated phenomena, and into the mere enumeration of effects without causes.

On usurpation

CHAPTER 5[a]

Answer to an objection which could be drawn from the example of William III

The example of William III seems at first glance a very strong objection to all the assertions which we have just read. Should we not consider William III the usurper of the throne of England from the Stuarts? Yet his reign was glorious and peaceful, and it is from this reign that England's prosperity and liberty date. Is this not a proof that usurpation is not always impossible in modern times, and that its effects are not always nefarious?

---

[a] Of the original edition, suppressed in the following ones.

Yet the name of usurper in no way fits William III. He was called by a nation which wished to enjoy a peaceful liberty, to the exercise of an authority for which he had already been trained, and, already invested with power in another country, he did not obtain the crown through the usual means of usurpation: guile or violence.

To understand better what was distinctive and advantageous in his position, compare him with Cromwell. The latter really was a usurper. To support him he did not have the lustre of a glorious rank which he had already held. Thus, despite his personal superiority, he could only win contested and ephemeral success. His reign had all the characteristics of usurpation. Like it, it was of brief duration; and death came very opportunely to preserve him from an imminent and inevitable fall.

The intervention of William III in the revolution of 1688, far from being a usurpation, probably preserved England from the yoke of a new usurper, and delivered her at the same time from a dynasty against which too many national interests had pronounced themselves.

Whenever stormy circumstances interrupt the regular transmission of power, and this interruption lasts long enough for all interests to detach themselves from the dispossessed authority, we do not need to examine whether the preservation of that authority would have been good: it is certain that its re-establishment would be an evil.

In this situation a people is exposed to different chances, two of which are good and two bad.

Either power returns to the hands that lost it, and this is the occasion for a violent reaction, for revenge and upheavals. The counter-revolution which is thus effected is only a new revolution. This is what happened in England under the two sons of Charles I, and the injustices which filled these two reigns are a memorable lesson from which it is to be hoped nations will benefit.

Or, alternatively, some individual with no legitimate claim seizes power and all the horrors of usurpation bear down upon that people. This is what happened in England under Cromwell, and has occurred once in our own day, in an even more terrible form, in France.

Or, again, the nation succeeds in giving itself a republican constitution, sufficiently wise to grant her repose as well as liberty. We must not be told that this is impossible because the Swiss, the Dutch and the Americans have all succeeded in doing so.

Or, finally, that nation calls to the throne a man who is already eminent elsewhere, and who received the crown subject to certain restrictions. This is what the English did in 1688. This is also what the Swedes have done in our own day. Each of them will be well-satisfied with their choice. For, in this case, the depository of power has an interest besides that of enlarging and increasing his own power. He has an interest in securing the triumph of those principles which are the guarantee of that power, and these principles are those of liberty. A revolution of this kind has nothing in common with usurpation. The prince, freely elected by the nation, is as strong in his ancient dignity as in his new title. He pleases the imagination by memories which captivate it, while he satisfies reason by the national choice on which his power rests. He is by no means reduced to employing only instruments of recent creation. He disposes with confidence of all the forces of the nation because he does not despoil her of any part of her political heritage. The former institutions are not hostile to him: he associates them with himself, and they contribute to his support.

Let us add that the English had the good fortune to find in William III precisely what a people needs in similar circumstances, a man not only familiar with power, but also used to liberty, the first magistrate of a republic. His character matured amidst the storms and experience taught him not to fear the agitation which always accompanies a free constitution.

Viewed in this perspective the example of William III, far from being against my argument is, on the contrary, rather favourable to it. Because his advent was not usurpation, it does not prove that usurpation is possible today. The happiness and liberty which England enjoyed under his reign do not at all imply that usurpation can be beneficial. Finally, the duration and tranquillity of that reign do not prove anything in favour of the duration and tranquillity of usurpation.

PRINCIPLES OF
POLITICS APPLICABLE
TO ALL REPRESENTATIVE
GOVERNMENTS

Bibliographical Note

We translate here the text of the first and only edition of the *Principes de politique* published by Constant in his lifetime, which appeared in Paris in May 1815, during the hundred days.

Like *De l'esprit de conquête et de l'usurpation*, it was not included by Constant in his *Cours de politique constitutionnelle* of 1818–20 out of political embarrassment at its Bonapartist implications. It was republished in the new edition of the *Cours* by Édouard Laboulaye in 1861.

Foreword

It seems generally acknowledged that the present constitution,[a] even after its acceptance by the French people, is still open to improvement in several of its provisions. I believe that, on studying this constitution closely, it will be found that very few of its articles are incompatible with those principles which preserve human associations and favour liberty. It is nonetheless useful and reasonable to leave to the constituted powers the authority to improve the act which determines their competence and establishes their reciprocal relations.

I argued long ago that, as the constitution is the guarantee of people's liberty, anything to do with liberty is constitutional, while anything bearing no relation to it cannot be; that to subject everything to the constitution means to transform everything into a danger for it, to create traps all around it; that there are broad principles which no single national authority could touch; but that national authorities jointly can do anything which is not incompatible with those principles.[1]

I think therefore that it is not superfluous to examine our consti-

---

[1] *Réactions Politiques*, Paris, 1797, [Repr. *Ecrits et discours politiques*, ed. by O. Pozzo di Borgo, vol. 1, p. 80]: I professed the same opinion seventeen years later: 'The unhappiness of societies and the security of individuals rest upon certain positive and immutable principles. These principles are true in all climates and latitudes. They never vary, whatever the size of the country, its mores, its beliefs, its usages. It is as unquestionable in a village of twenty huts as it is in a nation of thirty million that no-one must be arrested arbitrarily, punished without being tried, tried outside the pre-existing laws and the prescribed procedure, or prevented from exercising his physical and moral rights and his right of work

[a] The *Acte additionnel aux constitutions de l'empire* of 22 April 1815, to the drafting of which Constant contributed. References to the *Acte* in this text are quoted from: J. Godechot (ed.), *Les Constitutions de la France*.

tution both in general and in detail, because, although it has been sanctioned by the suffrage of the nation, it is still possible to improve it.

In the researches which I publish here the reader will frequently find not only the same ideas, but also the same words as in my previous writings. It will soon be twenty years since I first became interested in political considerations, and I have always professed the same opinions, expressed the same wishes. What I demanded then was individual liberty, freedom of the press, absence of arbitrary power, respect for the rights of all. This is what I still advocate now with undiminished zeal and with greater hope.

No doubt, when we examine the condition of France superficially, we are tempted to believe in the dangers which threaten her. Numerous armies gather against us. Peoples, like their leaders, seem blinded by their memories. The remnants of that national movement which animated them two years ago still confer on the efforts demanded of them the appearance of being national. But, if we observe them more closely, those alarming symptoms lose most of their gravity. Today it is no longer their own country that these peoples are defending: they are attacking a nation which remains within her own frontiers and does not intend to cross them; a nation which claims simply her domestic independence, and the right to choose her own government, in the same way as Germany laid claims to it when it chose Rudolph of Habsburg, England when it summoned the House of Brunswick, Portugal when it gave the crown to the Duke of Braganza, Sweden when it elected Gustavus Vasa: in a word, as every European tribe has exercised at some time, generally the most glorious of its history.

in innocent and peaceful ways. These fundamental rights of individuals must not be open to violation by the combined power of all the authorities. But the union of these authorities must be competent to dictate on all that is not contrary to those inviolable and imprescriptible rights. Thus in England the conjunction of the king and the two chambers can effect all the changes which they think necessary to the government and the administration's legitimate field of intervention . . . The axiom of the English barons: 'we do not wish to change the laws of England', is much more reasonable than if they had said: 'we cannot change them'. The refusal to change the laws because one does not wish to do so could be explained by their intrinsic goodness or by the inconvenience of an immediate change. But the same refusal motivated by I do not know what mysterious impossibility becomes unintelligible.

Constitutions are seldom made by the will of men. Time makes them. They are introduced gradually and in an almost imperceptible way. Yet there are circumstances in which it becomes indispensable to make a constitution. But then do only what is indispensable. Leave room for time and experience, so that these two reforming powers may direct your already constituted powers in the improvement of what has been done and the completion of what is still to be done.' *Réflexions sur les constitutions*, pp. 159–66.

There is in men's spirits a natural reason which always recognizes evidence in the end, and the people will soon tire of shedding their blood for a cause which is not their own. As for us, two feelings are shared by the immense majority of the French: the desire for liberty, and the hatred of foreign rule. We all know that liberty cannot come to us from abroad. We all know that a government which reappeared beneath foreign banners would be opposed to our interests as well as to our rights.

To this persuasion, which fills all hearts, are linked all those memories that arouse national pride: our eclipsed glory, our invaded provinces, barbarians guarding the gates of Paris and the ill-disguised insolence of the victors which revolted every Frenchman, when he saw foreign colours flying over our towers, and when, to cross our streets, to enter our theatres, to return to our homes, it was necessary to beg for the indulgence of a Russian or the moderation of a Prussian. Today even this very indulgence and moderation would be abjured. No-one now mentions either the constitution or liberty. It is the nation which is being accused: it is the atrocities of the army which they wish to punish.

Certainly, our enemies have short memories. Twenty-three years ago[a] the language to which they now returned shattered their thrones. Then, like now, they attacked us because we wanted our own government, because we had liberated the peasant from the tithe, the protestant from intolerance, thought from censorship, the citizen from arbitrary detention and exile, the plebeian from the insults of the privileged. However, there is a difference between these two periods, that then our enemies fought only against our principles, while now they fight against our interests which time, habit and innumerable transactions have identified with our principles. What in us was then only presentiment is now experience. We have tried counter-revolution. We have attempted to reconcile it with the guarantees which we demanded. We have obstinately believed (in my own case longer than some others), in a good faith the need for which was obvious. The last days have proved that the hatred of liberty was stronger even than the instinct for self-preservation. We do not wish to insult misery: we respect age and misfortune. But the test has been made, the principles are opposed, the interests are at odds, the ties are broken.

[a] In 1792.

CHAPTER I

On the sovereignty of the people

Our present constitution formally recognizes the principle of the sovereignty of the people,[a] that is the supremacy of the general will over any particular will. Indeed this principle cannot be contested. In our days many have attempted to obscure it; the evils which were caused and the crimes which were committed on the pretext of enforcing the general will lend apparent strength to the reasonings of those who would like to assign a different source to the authority of governments. Nevertheless those reasonings cannot stand against the simple definition of the words which they use. The law must be either the expression of the will of all, or that of the will of some. What would be the origin of exclusive privilege if you should grant it to that small number? If it is power, then power belongs to whoever takes it. It does not constitute a right, and if you acknowledge it as legitimate, it will be equally legitimate whoever sets his hands on it, and everyone will want to conquer it in his turn. If you suppose that the power of a small number is sanctioned by the assent of all, then that power becomes the general will.

This principle applies to all institutions. Theocracy, royalty, aristocracy, whenever they rule men's minds, are simply the general will. When, on the other hand, they fail to rule them, they are nothing but force. In short there are only two sorts of power in the world: one, illegitimate, is force; the other, legitimate, is the general will. But while we recognize the rights of that will, that is the sovereignty of the people, it is necessary, indeed imperative, to understand its exact nature and to determine its precise extent.

Without a precise and exact definition, the triumph of the theory could become a calamity in its application. The abstract recognition of the sovereignty of the people does not in the least increase the amount of liberty given to individuals. If we attribute to that sovereignty an amplitude which it must not have, liberty may be lost notwithstanding that principle, or even through it.

The precaution which we recommend, and which we shall take

[a] '. . . En conséquence les articles suivants, formant un acte supplémentaire aux constitutions de l'Empire, seront soumis à l'acceptation libre et solennelle de tous les citoyens, dans toute l'étendue de la France.' J. Godechot (ed.), *Les Constitutions de la France*, p. 232.

ourselves, is the most indispensable in so far as men of party, no matter how pure their intentions, are always reluctant to limit sovereignty. They regard themselves as its presumptive heirs, and they administer their future property, even when it is in the hands of their enemies. They mistrust such and such a kind of government, such and such a class of rulers; but let them organize authority in their own way, let them commit it to delegates of their choosing and they will come to believe there is no limit to it.

When you establish that the sovereignty of the people is unlimited, you create and toss at random into human society a degree of power which is too large in itself, and which is bound to constitute an evil, in whatever hands it is placed. Entrust it to one man, to several, to all, you will still find that it is equally an evil. You will think that it is the fault of the holders of such power and, according to the circumstances, you will accuse in turn monarchy, aristocracy, democracy, mixed governments or the representative system. You will be wrong: it is in fact the degree of force, not its holders, which must be denounced. It is against the weapon, not against the arm holding it, that it is necessary to strike ruthlessly. There are weights too heavy for the hand of man.

The error of those who, in good faith, in their love of liberty, have granted boundless power to the sovereignty of the people, derives from the way in which their political ideas were formed. In history they have observed a small number or men, or even a single individual, in possession of an immense power which caused much harm. But their wrath has been directed against the holders of the power rather than against the power itself. Instead of destroying it, they have simply thought of replacing it. It was a curse, yet they have regarded it as a conquest. They have bestowed it upon the entire society. It has necessarily passed from society at large to the majority, from the majority to the hands of a few men, often to a single man. It has caused as much evil as before; while the examples, the objections, the arguments and the evidence have multiplied themselves against all political institutions.

In a society founded upon the sovereignty of the people, it is certain that no individual, no class, are entitled to subject the rest to their particular will. But it is not true that society as a whole has unlimited authority over its members.

The universality of the citizens is sovereign in the sense that no individual, no faction, no partial association can arrogate sovereignty to itself, unless it has been delegated to it. But it does not follow from this that the universality of the citizens, or those who are invested with the sovereignty by them, can dispose sovereignly of the existence of individuals. There is, on the contrary, a part of human existence which by necessity remains individual and independent, and which is, by right, outside any social competence. Sovereignty has only a limited and relative existence. At the point where independence and individual existence begin, the jurisdiction of sovereignty ends. If society oversteps this line, it is as guilty as the despot who has, as his only title, his exterminating sword. Society cannot exceed its competence without usurpation, nor bypass the majority without being factious. The assent of the majority is not enough, in any case, to legitimate its acts: there are acts that nothing could possibly sanction. Whenever some authority commits any such acts, it hardly matters from which source it emanates. It is irrelevant whether it calls itself an individual or a nation. Were it the whole of the nation, save the citizen whom it oppresses, it would be none the more legitimate.

Rousseau[a] overlooked this truth, and his error made of his *Social Contract*, so often invoked in favour of liberty, the most formidable support for all kinds of despotism. He defined the contract struck between society and its members as the complete alienation of each individual with all his rights, without any reservations, to the community. In order to reassure us about the consequences of such an absolute renunciation of all the parts of our existence for the benefit of an abstract being, he tells us that the sovereign, that is the social body, can neither harm the totality of its members, nor any of them in particular. Since everyone gives himself entirely, all share the same condition, and nobody is interested in making that condition onerous to the others. Because every individual gives himself to all, he does not give himself to anyone in particular. Everybody acquires over his associates the same rights as he surrenders in their favour. Thus he gains the equivalent of all that he loses together with greater strength to preserve what he has. However, Rousseau forgets that all those preserving attributes which he confers on the abstract being he calls the sovereign, derive from the fact that it is formed by all individuals without exception. But as soon as the sovereign must make use of the power which he possesses, or in other words, as soon as it is necessary to proceed to the practical organization of authority, as the sovereign

---

[a] See the discussion of Rousseau's position in the 1806 draft: E. Hofmann (ed.), *Les 'Principes de Politique'*, vol. 2, pp. 22–39.

cannot exercise it himself, he must delegate it, and all those attributes disappear. Because the action performed in the name of all is necessarily, whether we like it or not, at the disposal of a single individual or of a few, it happens that, in giving oneself to all, one does not give oneself to nobody, on the contrary, one submits oneself to those who act in the name of all. Hence it follows that, by giving ourselves entirely, we do not enter a condition equal for all, because some derive exclusive advantage from the sacrifice of the rest. It is not true that nobody has an interest in making the condition of the others more onerous, because there are associates who are above the common condition. It is not true that all associates gain the same rights as those they renounce. Not all of them gain the equivalent of what they lose, and the result of what they sacrifice is, or can be, the establishment of a power which takes away from them whatever they have.

Rousseau himself was appalled by these consequences. Horror-struck at the immense social power which he had thus created, he did not know into whose hands to commit such monstrous force, and he could find no other protection against the danger inseparable from such sovereignty, than an expedient which made its exercise impossible. He declared that sovereignty could not be alienated, delegated or represented. This was equivalent to declaring, in other words, that it could not be exercised. It meant in practice destroying the principle which he had just proclaimed.

Observe instead how much franker the partisans of despotism are in their course when they set out from the same axiom, since it is an axiom which supports and favours them. Hobbes, the man who has most intelligently reduced despotism to a system,[a] hastened to acknowledge sovereignty as unlimited, in order to infer from this the legitimacy of the absolute government of a single individual. Sovereignty, he says, is absolute; this truth has been recognized in all times, even by those who have excited sedition or provoked civil wars: their aim was not to annihilate sovereignty, but rather to transfer its exercise elsewhere. Democracy is absolute sovereignty in the hands of all; aristocracy absolute sovereignty in the hands of some; monarchy absolute sovereignty in the hands of one man. The people have relinquished that absolute sovereignty in favour of a monarch, who has become its absolute possessor.

[a] See the 1806 draft, Book 1, ch. 7: 'De Hobbes', *ibid.* pp. 39–43.

It is clear that the absolute character which Hobbes attributes to the sovereignty of the people is the basis of his entire system. The word *absolute* distorts the whole question, and leads us in to a series of fresh implications. It is the point where the writer abandons the path of truth to proceed by sophism, towards the aim which he proposed to himself when he set out. He proves that, since the conventions established by men are not sufficient to ensure that they will be observed, a coercive power is necessary to force men to observe them. Because society must protect itself from external aggression, it needs a common force armed for common defence. Because men are divided by their pretensions, they need laws to regulate their rights. He concludes from the first point that the sovereign has the absolute right to punish; from the second, that he has the absolute right to make war; from the third, that he is the absolute legislator. Nothing could be more false than these conclusions. The sovereign has indeed the right to punish, but only in the case of guilty actions. He has the right to make war, but only when society is attacked. He has the right to make laws, but only when these laws are necessary and when they are in accord with justice. Consequently, nothing is absolute or arbitrary in these attributions. Democracy is indeed authority entrusted to the hands of all, but it is only the measure of authority necessary for the safety of the association. Aristocracy is the same authority entrusted to a few. Monarchy, the same authority conferred on a single person. The people can renounce that authority in favour of a single individual or of a few. But their power is still as limited as that of the people who have invested them with it. By the suppression of a single word, gratuitously introduced into the construction of a sentence, Hobbes' whole dreadful system collapses. On the contrary, with the word *absolute*, neither liberty nor, as we shall see below, peace nor happiness are possible under any institutions. Popular government is simply a violent tyranny, monarchical government only a more concentrated despotism.

When sovereignty is unlimited, there is no means of sheltering individuals from governments. It is in vain that you pretend to submit governments to the general will. It is always they who dictate the content of this will, and all your precautions become illusory.

The people, Rousseau says, are sovereign in one respect and subject in another. But in practice, these two relations are always confused. It is easy for the authority to oppress the people as subject, in order to force it to express, as sovereign, the will which the authority prescribes for it.

No political organization can escape from this danger. You may divide powers as much as you like: if the total of those powers is unlimited, those divided powers need only form a coalition, and there will be no remedy for despotism. What matters to us is not that our rights should not be violated by one power without the approval of another, but rather that any violation should be equally forbidden to all powers alike. It is not sufficient that the agents of the executive should have to appeal to the authority of the legislator; the legislator must be unable to authorize their action outside their legitimate sphere. It is of little account that the executive power should have no right to act without the support of the law, unless there are limits to that support, unless it is established that there are objects on which the legislator has no right to make a law, or, in other words, that sovereignty is limited, and that there are wills which neither the people, nor its delegates, have the right to have.

This is what we must declare; this is the important truth, the eternal principle which we must establish.

No authority upon earth is unlimited, neither that of the people, nor that of the men who declare themselves their representatives, nor that of the kings, by whatever title they reign, nor, finally, that of the law, which, being merely the expression of the will of the people or of the prince, according to the form of government, must be circumscribed within the same limits as the authority from which it emanates.

The citizens possess individual rights independently of all social and political authority, and any authority which violates these rights becomes illegitimate. The rights of the citizens are individual freedom, religious freedom, freedom of opinion, which includes the freedom to express oneself openly, the enjoyment of property, a guarantee against all arbitrary power. No authority can call these rights into question without destroying its own credentials.[a]

The sovereignty of the people is not unlimited, and since its will is not sufficient to legitimate whatever it happens to wish, the authority of

---

[a] In the 1806 draft Constant wrote: 'The rights of society could not be helpfully distinguished from those of the government, because it is impossible to indicate a way in which society could exercise its rights without the interference of the government. But the rights of individuals can usefully be distinguished from those of the government and of society, because it is possible to indicate the objects on which the government and society must abstain from dictating and must leave individuals perfectly free.' *Ibid.* p. 58. For a discussion of the concept of natural right see also the chapter on Bentham, *ibid.* pp. 58–61.

the law, which is nothing but the true or supposed expression of that will, is not unlimited either.

We must be prepared to make many sacrifices for public peace; we would be guilty in the eyes of morality if, out of a too inflexible attachment to our duties, we should resist all those laws which seem to encroach upon them. But no duty binds us to those pretended laws, whose corrupting influence threatens the most noble parts of our existence, to those laws which not only restrain our legitimate liberties, but demand from us actions contrary to those eternal principles of justice and mercy that man cannot cease to observe without debasing and betraying his nature.

As long as the law, be it good or bad, does not tend to deprave us, as long as the encroachments of the authority exact from us sacrifices which do not make us either cowardly or ferocious, we may subscribe to them. We make a compromise only with ourselves. But if the law should order us to trample under f.ot either our affections or our duties; if, on the pretext of a gigantic and factitious devotion for what would be called in turn, now monarchy, now republic, the law should prevent us from being faithful to our unfortunate friends; if it pre-scribed treachery towards our allies, or even the persecution of our vanquished enemies, let a curse fall upon the list of injustices and crimes thus covered by the name of the law.

A positive, general, unrestricted duty, every time a law seems unjust, is to avoid becoming its executor. This passive resistance does not carry with it any upheavals, revolutions or disorders.

Nothing justifies the man who lends his assistance to a law which he believes iniquitous.

Terror is by no means a more valid excuse than any other infamous passion. Woe betide those zealous and docile instruments, eternally oppressed, according to them, indefatigable agents of all existing tyran-nies, posthumous accusers of all tyrannies that have been overthrown.

In one terrible era we were told that one became the agent of unjust laws in order to mitigate their rigour, that the power of which one agreed to become the depository would have caused even greater evil had it fallen into less pure hands. Deceitful transaction, which opened a limitless career to every sort of crime. Everyone bargained with his own conscience, and every degree of injustice found its worthy executors. I cannot see why, in such a system, one should not volunteer to become the executioner of the innocent, on the pretext that one would strangle him more gently.

Let us now sum up the consequences of our principles. The sovereignty of the people is not unlimited: it is, on the contrary, circumscribed within the limits traced by justice and by the rights of individuals. The will of an entire people cannot make just what is unjust. The representatives of the nation have no right to do what the nation itself has no right to do. No monarch, whatever title he may claim, whether that title rests upon divine right, the right of conquest or the assent of the people, possesses a power without limits. God, if he intervenes in human affairs, can only sanction justice. The right of conquest is simply force, which is not a right, since it passes to whomever seizes it. The assent of the people cannot legitimate what is illegitimate, because the people cannot delegate to anyone authority which they do not themselves possess.

An objection presents itself against the limitation of sovereignty. Is it really possible to limit it? Can any force effectively prevent it from crossing the barriers prescribed to it? It is possible, some will argue, through ingenious combinations, to restrain power by dividing it. We may set its different parts in opposition and balance them against one another. Yet by what means can we ensure that the total sum will not be unlimited? How is it possible to limit power other than through power itself?

No doubt, the abstract limitation of sovereignty is not sufficient. We must find for political institutions foundations which combine the interest of the different holders of power so that their most apparent, most durable and most certain advantage would be to remain within the limits of their respective attributions. Yet the first question is still that of the competence and limitation of sovereignty. Before we organize something, we must have determined its nature and extension.

Second, without exaggerating, as philosophers have done only too often, the influence of truth, we may affirm that when certain principles are clearly and completely demonstrated, they tend to become their own guarantee. A universal opinion is formed on the basis of evidence which is soon victorious. If it is recognized that there is on earth no unlimited power, no-one, in any age, will dare to claim such a power. Experience has already proved this. We no longer attribute, for example, to society as a whole the right of life and death without judgement. Thus no modern government claims to exercise any such right. If the tyrants of the ancient republics appear to us far more unrestrained than the governors of modern history, it is partly for this particular reason. The most monstrous acts of the despotism of a single individual were often based on the doctrine of the boundless power of all.

Thus the limitation of sovereignty is real, and it is also possible. It will be ensured firstly by the same force which legitimates all acknowledged truths: by public opinion. Subsequently it will be guaranteed more precisely by the distribution and balance of powers.

But you must begin by acknowledging this salutary limitation. Without this preliminary precaution, all is useless.

In encompassing the sovereignty of the people within its just limits, you have nothing to fear. You take away from despotism, either by individuals or by assemblies, the apparent sanction it draws from the assent it commands, because you can prove that such assent, were it genuine, would still lack the power to sanction anything whatever.

The people have no right to strike a single innocent, nor to treat as guilty a single accused, without legal evidence. Consequently, it cannot delegate such a right to anyone. The people have no right to violate the freedom of opinion, religious freedom, judicial safeguards, protective forms. Therefore no despot, no assembly, can exercise such a right claiming that the people have invested them with it. Thus all despotism is illegal. Nothing can sanction it, not even the popular will to which it appeals. It claims in fact, in the name of the sovereignty of the people, a power which is no part of that sovereignty, and which is not only the illegal displacement of an existing power, but the creation of a power which should not exist in the first place.

CHAPTER 2

The nature of royal power in a constitutional monarchy

Our constitution, in establishing the responsibility of the ministers, clearly separates ministerial from royal power. The simple fact that the monarch is inviolable and that the ministers are responsible indicates this separation. It cannot be denied that in this way ministers do have, up to a point, a power which properly belongs to them. If they were considered merely as passive and blind agents, their responsibility would be absurd and unjust, or at least they ought to be responsible only towards the monarch and for the strict execution of his orders. Instead, the constitution makes them responsible towards the nation, and establishes that in some case the monarch's orders cannot constitute an excuse for them. Therefore it is clear that they are not passive agents. Ministerial power, though emanating from royal power, nevertheless has an existence which is genuinely separated from the latter. There is an essential and fundamental difference between responsible authority and authority invested with inviolability.

Since this distinction is thus sanctioned by our constitution, I think I must put it in the context of a number of other considerations. Outlined in a work I published before the promulgation of the Charter in 1814,[a] it was found clear and helpful by men whose opinion is to me of great importance. Indeed it is, I believe, the key to all political organization.

Royal power (I mean the power of the head of the state, whatever title he happens to bear) is a neutral power. That of the ministers instead is an active power. In order to explain this difference, let us define political powers as they have been known thus far.

The executive, legislative and judicial powers are three competences which must cooperate, each in their own sphere, in the general movement. When these competences, disturbed in their functions, cross, clash with and hinder one another, you need a power which can restore them to their proper place. This force cannot reside within one of these three competences, lest it should assist it in destroying the others. It must be external to it, and it must be in some sense neutral, so that its action might be necessarily applied whenever it is genuinely needed, and so that it may preserve and restore without being hostile.

Constitutional monarchy creates this neutral power in the person of the head of state. The true interest of the head of state is not that any of these powers should overthrow the others, but that all of them should support and understand one another and act in concert.

Until now, three powers only have been identified in political organizations.

In a constitutional monarchy I believe I can distinguish five distinct powers: (1) royal power (2) executive power (3) representative power of

---

[a] *Réflections sur les constitutions*, Ch. 3: 'De la responsabilité des ministres'.

long duration (4) representative power of public opinion (5) judicial power.

The representative power of long duration resides in the hereditary assembly; the representative power of public opinion in the elective assembly; the executive power is entrusted to the ministers; the judicial power to the tribunals. The two first powers make the laws, the third proceeds to their general execution, the fourth applies them to particular cases. The royal power is in the middle, yet above the four others, a superior and at the same time intermediate authority, with no interest in disturbing the balance, but on the contrary, with a strong interest in maintaining it.

Because men do not always act according to their well-conceived interest, it is necessary to take the precaution that the head of state should not be able to act in the place of the other powers. It is precisely in this precaution that the difference between absolute and constitutional monarchy lies.

Since it is always helpful to move away from abstractions and turn to facts, we shall refer to the English constitution.

No law can be made without the participation of the hereditary and elective chambers; no act can be executed without the signature of a minister; no judgement pronounced other than by independent tribunals. Having taken this precaution, observe the way in which the English constitution employs the royal power to end any dangerous conflict, and to re-establish harmony among the other powers. Should the action of the executive power be dangerous, the king will dismiss his ministers. Should the hereditary chamber prove harmful, the king will impress a new direction upon it by creating new peers. Should the action of the elective chamber prove threatening, the king will make use of his power of veto by dissolving the elective chamber. Finally, if the action of judicial power is damaging because it applies excessively severe general punishments to individual actions, the king will temper its action through his right of pardon.

The vice of almost all constitutions has been to fail to create a neutral power, and to place instead the total sum of power with which such a power ought to be invested in one of the active powers.[a] Whenever that amount of authority has been combined with legislative power, the law, which ought only to extend to determinate objects, has been instead

---

[a] This particular problem is the object of Necker's work: *Du pouvoir exécutif*, by which Constant's own reflections were greatly influenced.

extended to everything. There has been arbitrariness and tyranny without limits. Hence the excesses of the Long Parliament, those of the popular assemblies in the Italian republics, and those of the Convention at various stages of its existence. Whenever the same amount of authority has been combined with the executive power, there has been despotism. Hence the usurpation that resulted in the dictatorship in Rome.

Roman history is generally a good example of the necessity for a neutral power to mediate between active powers. We see in this republic, in the midst of the frictions between the people and the senate, that each party was looking for guarantees. But since it invariably placed them in itself, each guarantee became a weapon against the opposition. As the people's uprisings threatened the state with destruction, they created the dictators, magistrates devoted to the patrician class. Although the oppression exercised by that class reduced the plebeians to despair, the dictatorship was not abolished. They resorted instead to the institution of the tribunes, a wholly popular authority. Thus the enemies confronted one another again: except that each of them had strengthened its position. The Centuriae were an aristocracy, the Tribes a democracy. The plebiscites, decreed without the support of the senate, were nonetheless compulsory for the patricians. The senatus-consulta, though emanating only from the patricians, were nonetheless binding for the plebeians. Thus each party appropriated in turn the power which ought to have been entrusted to neutral hands, and abused it, an outcome which could hardly fail to occur, for as long as the active powers refused to renounce it and make it into a separate power.

The same consideration applies to the Carthaginians: you see them creating successively the suffetes [Carthaginian magistrates] to set a limit to the aristocracy of the senate; the tribunal of the hundred to restrain the suffetes; the tribunal of the five to control the hundred. They wanted, says Condillac,[a] to impose a limit on one authority, and they created another which needed equally to be restrained, thus leaving unaffected the abuse which they thought they were curing.

Constitutional monarchy offers us, as I said, that neutral power so indispensable for all regular liberty. In a free country the king is a being apart, superior to differences of opinion, having no other interest than the maintenance of order and liberty. He can never return to the

---

[a] de Condillac, *Histoire ancienne*, Book 7, ch. 7 in *Cours d'études pour l'instruction du Prince de Parme*, vol. 5, pp. 473–4.

common condition, and is consequently inaccessible to all the passions that such a condition generates, and to all those that the perspective of finding oneself once again within it, necessarily creates in those agents who are invested with temporary power. This august prerogative of royalty must infuse calm into the spirit of the monarch, repose into his soul, such as can hardly be experienced by any individual in any subordinate position. He floats, so to speak, above human anxieties. It is indeed the masterpiece of political organization, to have created, amidst those dissensions, without which no liberty is possible, an inviolable sphere of security, majesty, impartiality, which leaves those dissensions to develop without danger, provided they do not exceed certain limits, and which, as soon as some danger becomes evident, terminates it by legal constitutional means, without any trace of arbitrariness. Yet we can lose this immense advantage either by lowering the power of the monarch to the level of the executive powers, or by elevating the executive power to the level of the monarch.

If you confuse these powers, two great questions became insoluble: the first is the dismissal of the executive power itself, the second is responsibility.

The executive power rests as a matter of fact in the ministers; but the authority which could dismiss it has under an absolute monarchy the defect of being its ally, and, under a republic, that of being its enemy. It is only under constitutional monarchy that this authority rises to the level of being its judge.

We see for example that, under absolute monarchy, there is no other means of deposing the executive power than subversion, a remedy which is often more terrible than the evil. Even if republics have attempted to organize more acceptable means, those means have often produced the same violent and disorderly outcome.

The Cretans had invented a sort of legal insurrection, through which all the magistrates were deposed, and several writers praise them for it.[1] In Athens, the law gave every citizen permission to kill anyone invested with a magistracy who should make an attempt on the freedom of the republic.[2] In Rome the law of Publius Valerius Publicola served the same purpose. The Florentines had their Ballia, or extraordinary

---

[1] Filangieri, 1, 10; Montesquieu, *Esp. des lois*, 8, 11.
   [Gaetano Filangieri, *La science de la législation*, trs. J. A. G. Gallois, C. L. S. de Montesquieu, *Oeuvres complètes*, pp. 357–8: 'Effets naturels de la bonté et de la corruption des principes'.]
[2] Petit, *de Leg. Att.*, 3, 2.
   [Samuel Petit, *Leges Atticae* (Ludun, 1742).]

council created in emergency, which, invested with all powers, had the right of universal dismissal.[1] However, in all these constitutions, the right to dismiss the executive power somewhat drifted at the mercy of whoever seized it, and whoever actually seized it, used it not to destroy, but to exercise tyranny. The consequence of this was that the winning party was not satisfied with the dismissal, it also resorted to violence, and since it did so without judgement, what resulted was murder rather than an act of justice.

In Florence the Ballia, born of the storm, stayed only too true to its origins. It sentenced to death, imprisoned, dispossessed, because it had no other means of depriving of their authority, the men who were entrusted with it. Thus, after plunging Florence into anarchy, it became the chief instrument of the Medici's power.

What is needed is a constitutional power which can always offer what is useful in the Ballia without any of its dangers: that is to say a power which cannot condemn, imprison, despoil or proscribe, but limits itself to depriving of their authority those members of the assemblies who can no longer retain it without danger.

Constitutional monarchy resolves this great problem. In order to establish these ideas more definitely, I must ask the reader to confront my assertions with reality. This reality can be found in the English monarchy. The English monarchy has created this neutral and inter-mediate power: a royal power separated from the executive power. The executive power can be dismissed without being persecuted. The king does not need to accuse his ministers of an error, a crime or a plot in order to dismiss them. He can dismiss them without punishing them. Thus all that is necessary can be done without any injustice. Moreover, as is always the case, this method, because it is just, is also useful in another respect.

It is a great vice for any constitution to leave to powerful men no alternative between their own power and the scaffold.

Between the dismissal of the executive power and its punishment, there is the same difference as between the dissolution of the repre-sentative assemblies and the indictment of their members. If the first of these measures were replaced by the second, we have no reason to doubt that assemblies threatened not only in their political, but also in their individual existence, would be maddened by the sense of danger, and the state would be exposed to the greatest evils. The same is true of

[1] Machiavelli, *passim*.

executive power. If you replace the power of deposing it without any prosecution with that of indicting it, you excite its fear and its rage. The representatives after the dissolution of their assemblies, the ministers after their dismissal, return to the condition of ordinary citizens, and the results of these two great protective measures against these abuses are as effective as they are peaceful.

Similar considerations present themselves over the issue of responsibility.

A hereditary monarch can and must be answerable to no-one. He is a being apart at the summit of the pyramid. His entitlements, which belong to him as an individual, also belong in perpetuity to his entire lineage, from his ancestors to his descendants, and thus set him apart from all his subjects. It is hardly extraordinary to declare a man inviolable when a family is invested with the right to govern a large nation, to the exclusion of all other families and at the risk of all the hazards of succession.

The monarch himself accepts without reluctance the responsibility of his ministers. He has more precious goods to defend than such and such a detail of administration, such and such a partial exercise of authority. His dignity is a family patrimony, which he withdraws from the struggle by deserting his ministry. But it is only when power is in this way sacred that you can separate responsibility from power.

A republican power periodically renewed is by no means a being apart. It in no way strikes the imagination. It has no right to indulgence for its errors, since it has canvassed to obtain the post which it occupies, and has nothing more precious to defend than its own authority, which is compromised as soon as its ministry, formed by men like itself, to whom it has always shown solidarity, comes under attack.

To make the supreme power inviolable is to make its ministers the judges of the obedience which they owe to it. It is true that they can refuse their obedience only by resigning. But in this case public opinion becomes in its turn the arbiter between the superior authority and the ministers, and its favour is naturally on the side of those men who seem to have sacrificed their interests to their conscience. In a hereditary monarchy this would present no difficulty. The things that make up the veneration by which the monarch is surrounded prevent any comparison between him and his ministers, while the permanent character of his dignity turns all the efforts of their partisans against the new ministry. In a republic, on the other hand, a comparison would be made between the supreme power and the former ministers. This comparison would lead to the desire that these latter should become the supreme power, and nothing, either in its composition or in its forms, would appear to oppose this project.

Between a republican power with no responsibility and a responsible ministry, the second would be everything, while the first would soon be deemed useless. The fact that it is not responsible, forces the government to do nothing except through its ministers. But what then is the point of a power superior to the ministry? In a monarchy, it is to prevent others from appropriating it, and to establish a fixed, unassailable point which passions cannot reach. Nothing of the kind happens in a republic, where all citizens may rise to supreme power.

Try to imagine, in the constitution of 1795, an inviolable Directory and an active and energetic ministry. Would we have put up for very long with five men who did nothing behind six who did all the work? A republican government needs to exercise upon its ministers a more absolute authority than a hereditary monarch: for it is exposed to the risk that its instruments may become its rivals. But, in order to exercise such an authority, it must take upon itself responsibility for its actions. For one cannot make oneself obeyed by men without guaranteeing them against the consequences of their obedience.

It follows that republics are forced to make the supreme power responsible. But then this responsibility becomes illusory.

A responsibility that can only be exercised upon men whose fall would interrupt foreign relations, and immobilize the internal machinery of the state, will never be exercised. Who will want to turn society upside down to avenge the rights of a single individual, of ten, of a hundred, of a thousand citizens scattered over an area of thirty thousand square leagues? Arbitrary power will remain without remedy because the remedy would always prove more repellent than a moderate evil. The culprits will escape, either thanks to the use which they make of their power to corrupt, or because those who would be ready to accuse them would shrink from the destruction of the constitutional structure that their denunciation would cause. For, to punish the violation of a single law, it would be necessary to jeopardize what serves as the guarantee of all laws. Thus the weak and reasonable, the mercenary and the scrupulous alike will, for different reasons, find themselves having to treat the untrustworthy custodians of the executive power with tact. Responsibility would be void, because it has been set too high. Finally, as it is in the nature of power, whenever it can commit abuses with impunity, to commit further abuses, if harassment continues to increase to the point of becoming intolerable, the responsibility will be exercised, but, being directed against the heads of the government, it will probably result in the destruction of the government itself.

I shall not consider here whether it would be possible, through a new organization, to remedy the defects connected with responsibility in a republican constitution. All I have wished to prove is that the first and indispensable condition for the exercise of responsibility is to separate executive power from supreme power. Constitutional monarchy attains this great aim. But this advantage would be lost if the two powers were confused.

So true is it that ministerial power is the only resort of the executive in a free constitution, that a monarch makes proposals only through the intermediary of his ministers. He never orders anything which they have not signed as a guarantee to the nation of their responsibility.

When it comes to nominations, the monarch alone decides: it is his incontrovertible right. But whenever it comes to direct action, or even simply to a proposal, the ministerial power is obliged to step forward, so that the discussion or resistance should not compromise the head of the state.

Some have claimed that in England royal power and ministerial power is by no means so clearly distinguished. They have cited an occasion in which the personal will of the sovereign prevailed over that of his ministers in refusing to allow Catholics to share the privileges of his other subjects. Here, however, two things are being confused: the right to maintain what is in existence, which belongs necessarily to royal power, and which makes of it, as I claim, the neutral and preserving authority; and the right to propose the establishment of what does not yet exist, a right which belongs to the ministerial power.

In such circumstances, it was only a question of maintaining what was already in existence, as the laws against the Catholics are fully in force, even though their execution has been mitigated. Now, no law can be abolished without the participation of royal power. I do not wish to discuss here whether, in this particular instance, the exercise of this power was good or bad. Indeed I regret that scruples, respectable because they spring from the conscience, but mistaken in principle and disastrous in their application, should have caused the King of England to employ harsh and intolerant measures. But all we are attempting to prove here is that, in maintaining them, the royal power did not exceed its own limits. To be still more thoroughly convinced of this, let us reverse the hypothesis: let us suppose that these laws against the Catholics had never existed. The personal will of the monarch could not have forced any minister to propose them, and I dare say that, in our day, the King of England would hardly find a minister ready to propose laws of this kind. Thus the difference between royal and ministerial power is proved by the same example which is generally put forward to obscure it. The neutral and purely preservative character of the former is apparent; it is also clear that, of the two, only the second is active: since, if the latter refused to act, the former would not find means of compelling it to do so, nor would it be able to act without it. Notice, too, that in this way, royal power offers only advantages and no drawbacks. In fact, while the King of England would find, in the refusal of his ministry to act, an insurmountable obstacle to proposing laws contrary to the spirit of the country and to religious freedom, the same ministerial opposition would be impotent if it attempted to prevent the royal power from proposing laws in accord with this spirit and favourable to that liberty. The King would only have to replace his ministers, and while no one would offer himself to challenge public opinion and promote a confrontation with enlightened views, a thousand will volunteer to become the instruments of popular measures, which the nation would support with her approval and her acknowledgement.[1]

I do not wish to deny that there is something seductive in the picture of a more animated and active monarchical power, but institutions depend on times much more than on men. The direct action of the monarch becomes inevitably weaker as a consequence of the progress of civilization. Many things which we admire and find moving in other ages would be simply unacceptable today. Try to imagine the kings of France administering justice to their subjects under an oak tree. You may be moved by that sight, and you may revere that august and naive exercise of paternal justice. But what would we see today in a judgement administered by the king without the participation of the courts?

---

[1] What I say here about the respect for, or regard of English ministers for national opinion, unfortunately only applies to their internal administration. The renewal of the war, without pretext, without excuse, in response to the most moderate demonstrations, to the most patently sincere of peaceful intentions, proves only too clearly that, with respect to continental affairs, this English ministry neither consults the inclination of the people, nor their reason or interests.

The violation of all principles, the confusion of all powers, the destruction of the juridical independence so energetically desired by all classes. One cannot make a constitutional monarchy out of memories and poetry.

Noble, beautiful, sublime prerogatives are left to monarchs under a free constitution. To them belongs the right of pardon, a right of an almost divine nature, which repairs the errors of human justice, or those too inflexible rigours which are also errors. To them belongs the right to invest prominent citizens with a lasting distinction by placing them in that hereditary magistrature which combines the glory of the past with the solemnity of the highest political functions. To them belongs the right to nominate the instruments of the law, to ensure that society enjoys public order, and innocent citizens security. To them belongs the right to dissolve the legislative assemblies and thus to preserve the nation from the aberrations of its representatives by summoning her to new choices. To them belongs the nomination of ministers, a nomination which directs towards the monarch the gratitude of the nation when the ministers acquit themselves worthily of the mission he entrusted to them. Finally to them belongs the distribution of graces, of favours, of rewards, the prerogative to repay by a look or a word a service rendered to the state, a prerogative which confers on monarchy an inexhaustible treasurehouse of knowledge, which turns all self-interest to his service, and profits from the ambitions of others.

This is certainly a great career, demanding remarkable gifts and a strong and noble sense of vocation. Only wicked and malicious counsellors could present to a constitutional monarch, as an object of desire or regret, that despotic power, without limits or rather without restraint, which would be ambiguous, because it would be unlimited, precarious because violent, and which would weigh in equally disastrous manner upon the prince, whom it could only mislead, and upon the people, whom it could only torment or corrupt.[1]

---

[1] It is quite remarkable that a rather confused instinct should always have alerted men to the truth which I have developed in this chapter, although this has never been expressed; but precisely because it had not been expressed, this confused instinct has been the cause of very dangerous errors.

Because many had the vague feeling that royal power was, by its nature, a neutral authority which, restricted within its own limits, had no unacceptable prerogatives, they concluded that there would be no disadvantage in investing it with those prerogatives, and neutrality has thus been destroyed.

If someone had proposed granting ministers arbitrary power over individual liberty,

CHAPTER 3

On the right to dissolve representative assemblies

There are questions which all enlightened men regard as long settled, and to which consequently they avoid returning. Yet, to their great surprise, as soon as it is necessary to pass from theory to practice, those questions are once again in dispute. One is almost tempted to suggested that the human mind can accept evidence only by shrinking from its application.

Some have protested against the right to dissolve representative assemblies, a right which, according to our Constitutional Act and to the English constitution, is given to the holder of the supreme power.[a] Nevertheless, any political organization which failed to entrust this right to the head of state would necessarily become an unbridled and turbulent demagogy, unless despotism, by replacing the legal prerogative with acts of authority, were to reduce the assemblies to the role of passive, dumb and blind instruments.

Undoubtedly no liberty can exist in a large country without strong, numerous and independent assemblies, but those assemblies are not free from dangers, and in the interests of liberty itself it is necessary to prepare infallible means of preventing their lapses.

The tendency of assemblies to multiply indefinitely the number of the laws is in itself an irremediable defect unless their immoderate dissolution, and their recomposition with new elements, are there to arrest their impetuous and irresistible march.

The multiplicity of laws flatters two natural inclinations in the

everybody would have rejected this proposition, because the nature of ministerial power, always in contact with all interests, would have immediately shown the danger of investing it with such an arbitrary authority. But the same authority has frequently been granted to kings, because they were considered disinterested and impartial; and through this concession they have destroyed the very impartiality which served as its pretext.

Any arbitrary power is opposed to the nature of royal power. Thus one of two things always occurs: either this power becomes the attribute of ministerial authority; or the king himself, ceasing to be neutral, becomes a sort of more formidable minister, because he associates with the inviolability which he possesses attributes which he should never possess. In this case such attributes destroy all possibility of peace, all hope of liberty.

---

[a] *Acte additionnel*, title 1, art. 21: 'L'Empereur peut proroger, ajourner et dissoudre la chambre des représentants'.

legislators,[a] the need to act, and the pleasure of believing themselves necessary. Every time you give to a man a special task, he will tend to do more rather than less. Those who are charged with arresting vagrants on the main roads are inclined to pick a quarrel with any travellers. When spies fail to discover anything, they invent. It is sufficient to create in a country a ministry that watches over conspirators, to hear incessant talk of conspiracy. Legislators share out amongst themselves human existence, by right of conquest, in the same way as Alexander's generals shared out the world. It may be suggested that the multiplicity of laws is the disease of representative governments, because in those states everything is done by means of the laws, while the absence of laws is the disease of unlimited monarchies, because in these monarchies everything is done through men.

It is the imprudent multiplication of laws which in some periods has thrown discredit upon the most noble of things, on liberty itself, and made men seek refuge in the most miserable and lowest of them, servitude.

The veto is precisely a direct means of repressing the indiscreet activity of representative assemblies but, when employed too often, it irritates without disarming them. Their dissolution is the only remedy whose effectiveness is assured.

When no limits are imposed upon the representative authority, the people's representatives are no longer the defenders of liberty, but rather candidates for tyranny: and once tyranny is constituted, it is likely to prove all the more terrible when tyrants are more numerous. Under a constitution which includes national representation, the nation is free only when its deputies are subject to restraint.

An assembly that can be neither repressed nor controlled is of all powers the blindest in its movements, the most unpredictable in its consequences, even for its own members. It rushes into excesses which at first would seem out of the question. We witness for example an intrusive activity in all domains, a multiplicity of immediate laws, the desire to please the most passionate part of the people by abandoning itself to impulse or even by anticipating it, the spite aroused in it by any resistance it encounters or by any censure it suspects; one moment opposition to the national spirit and persistence in its errors, sometimes the party spirit which leaves only a choice between extremes; some-

---

[a] The multiplicity of laws was the subject of Book 4 in the unfinished 1806 draft. For the surviving fragments, see E. Hofmann (ed.), *Les 'Principes de Politique'*, vol. 2, pp. 81–9.

times an *esprit de corps* which only bestows strength in order to usurp; by turns temerity or indecision, violence or exhaustion, complacency for a single individual or defiance against all; being carried away by purely physical sensations like enthusiasm or terror; the absence of all moral responsibility; the certainty of escaping, thanks to its numbers, from the shame of cowardice, or the perils of audacity: such are the vices of assemblies, when not restrained by limits which they cannot overstep.[1]

An assembly, the power of which is unlimited, is more dangerous than the people. Men assembled in large numbers have generous impulses. They are almost always won over by pity or restrained by justice. But this is because they act on their own behalf. The crowd may sacrifice its own interest to its emotions. But the representatives of the people are by no means authorized to impose such a sacrifice upon it. The nature of their mission prevents them. In them the violence of a popular gathering is combined with the impassivity of a tribunal and this combination allows no other excess than that of rigour. Those who are called traitors in front of an assembly are generally those who plead in favour of measures of indulgence. Implacable men, if they are sometimes blamed, are never suspected.

Aristides told the Athenians gathered on the public square that even their greeting would be bought at too high a price by an unjust or treacherous resolution. In professing such a doctrine our assembly would fear that those who have elected it, having failed to receive either a necessary explanation from reasoning, or a generous impulse from eloquence, might accuse it of sacrificing public to private interest.

It would be in vain to count upon the strength of a reasonable majority if that majority did not have the guarantee of a constitutional power outside the assembly. A closely united minority, with the advantages of attack, which by turns frightens or seduces, convinces or threatens, is bound sooner or later to dominate the majority. Violence unites men because it leaves their mind open to every partial consideration.

The Constituent Assembly was formed by the most esteemed and enlightened men in France. And yet how many times did it vote for laws condemned by its own reason! You could not have found in the

---

[1] I must observe that it is not merely as of today that I profess these principles about assemblies which unite all the powers. This whole passage is taken from my *Réflexions sur les constitutions et les garanties*, published in May 1814, when I was somewhat in opposition to the existing government and my only hopes for liberty lay in the chamber of deputies.

legislative assembly a hundred men who wished to overthrow the throne. Yet it was driven, from the beginning to the end of its short career, in a direction opposed to its own wishes. Three quarters of the Convention were horrified by the crimes that soiled the early days of the republic. Yet the authors of those crimes, even though they were a small number, soon contrived to subjugate it.

Anyone who has inspected the authentic acts of the English parliament, from 1640 to its dispersal by Colonel Pride, before Charles I's death, must be convinced that two thirds of its members fervently wished for that peace which their votes incessantly rejected, and regarded as nefarious the war which every day they unanimously proclaimed as a necessity.

Shall we conclude from these examples that there should be no representative assemblies? There would no longer be any bodies representing the people, the government would have no more support, public credit no guarantees. The nation would detach itself from its leaders, and individuals would become estranged from a nation which no longer had any identity. It is representative assemblies alone that can infuse life into the political body. This way of life undoubtedly has its dangers, and we have not attempted to minimize them. Yet whenever governments, in order to emancipate themselves from these dangers, wish to stifle the national spirit and to replace it with a mechanism, they learn to their cost that there are other dangers against which the national spirit is the sole defence, and which the best contrived mechanism cannot avert.

Thus the representative assemblies must be free, imposing and lively. But their vagaries must be repressed. Thus the repressive power must be placed outside them. The rules that an assembly imposes upon itself by its own will are illusory and impotent. The same majority that agrees to be tied by forms, breaks these forms at its convenience and resumes its power after having renounced it.

The dissolution of assemblies is by no means, as some have argued, an insult to the rights of the people. On the contrary, when elections are free, it is an appeal made to their rights in favour of their interests. I say when elections are free, since when they are not free there is no representative system.

Between an assembly which obstinately refused to make any law, to supply any need, and a government which had no right to dissolve it, what means of administration would be left? Yet, whenever such a means cannot be found within the political organization, sheer force of circumstance will bring about the same result. Force always comes to the rescue of necessity. Without the right to dissolve the representative assemblies, their inviolability is merely chimerical. Without the possibility of renewing their elements, their very existence will be threatened.

CHAPTER 4

On a hereditary assembly and on the importance of not limiting the number of its members

In a hereditary monarchy, the existence of a hereditary class is indispensable. It is impossible to conceive how, in a country where all distinctions of birth were rejected, such privilege could nevertheless be reserved for the most important transmission, that of the function which most essentially affects the peace and life of the citizens. For the government of one man to subsist without a hereditary class, it must indeed be pure despotism. Anything can last for a more or less lengthy period of time under a despotism which is pure force. But any system which is maintained through despotism takes its chances, or, in other words, is threatened by the risk of being overthrown. The elements of the government of one man, without a hereditary class are: a single man who rules, soldiers who execute and a people that obeys. In order to give further support to the monarchy, you need an intermediate body. Montesquieu insists on this, even in an elective monarchy. Whenever you place a single individual in such a high position it is necessary, unless you want to have him permanently sword in hand, to surround him with other men who have an interest in defending him. Here experience confirms reasoning. Writers of all parties had predicted, since 1791, the outcome of the abolition of the nobility in France, although the nobility was invested with no political prerogative; and no Englishman would believe for a moment in the stability of the English monarchy, if the House of Lords were abolished.

Would those who dispute the hereditary character of the first chamber wish to have the nobility subsisting alongside but apart from that chamber, and create the latter only for life? What would a hereditary nobility without functions be, alongside a life magistracy charged with important functions? This is exactly what the French nobility was in the last years before the revolution, and it was precisely this that prepared its ruin. Nobility was seen only as an elegant decoration, without any precise function; agreeable for those who possessed it, slightly humiliating for those who did not, but altogether without real means or strength. Its eminence had become almost negative, that is, it consisted more of exclusions for the commoners, than of positive advantages for the favoured class. It irritated without restraining. It was not an intermediary body, which kept the people in order, and watched over liberty. It was a corporation without foundation, and without a fixed place in the social body. Everything contributed to weakening it, even the enlightenment and the individual superiority of its own members. Separated from feudalism by the progress of ideas, it was the indefinable reminder of a half-destroyed system.

In our century the nobility needs to hang on to constitutional and well-determined prerogatives. These prerogatives are less injurious to those who are excluded from them, while they confer greater strength on those who possess them. The peerage, if we choose this name to indicate the first chamber, will be an office as well as honour. It will be less exposed to attacks and more susceptible to defence.

Notice in addition that, if this first chamber is not hereditary, it will be necessary to establish some procedure to renew its elements. Shall it be by nomination on the part of the king? Would a chamber, nominated by the king for life, prove sufficiently strong to counterbalance another assembly emanating from popular election? In hereditary peerage, the peers are strong from the independence which they acquire immediately after their nomination. In the eyes of the people they assume a character other than that of mere delegates of the crown. To wish for two chambers, one nominated by the king, the other by the people, without any fundamental difference (since elections for life are only too similar to any other kind of election) means setting one against the other the very powers between which an intermediary is really necessary: I mean the power of the king and that of the people.

Let us remain faithful to experience. We see that in Great Britain the hereditary peerage is compatible with a high degree of civil and political liberty. All those citizens who distinguish themselves may achieve it. It does not present the only genuinely odious character of heredity: its exclusiveness. The day following his nomination to the peerage, any citizen will enjoy the same rights as the most ancient of peers. The cadet branches of the first houses of England re-enter the mass of the people. They form a link between the peerage and the nation, as the peerage itself forms a link between the nation and the throne.

But, some argue, why not limit the number of the members of the hereditary chamber? None of those who have proposed this limitation have reflected upon its possible consequences.

This hereditary chamber is a body which the people has no right to elect, and which the government has no right to dissolve. If the number of members in that body is limited, a party may be formed within it, and that party, without being supported by the assent either of the government or of the people, cannot nevertheless be overturned without simultaneously overturning the constitution itself.

A remarkable period in the annals of the British parliament will serve to highlight the importance of this consideration. In 1783 the king of England dismissed from his counsel the coalition of Lord North and Fox. Almost the entire parliament belonged to the party of that coalition; while the English people held a different opinion. The king having appealed to the people by dissolving the House of Commons, an immense majority came to support the new ministry. But let us suppose that the coalition had in its favour the House of Lords, which the king could not dissolve. It is clear that, if the royal prerogative had not the power to create a sufficient number of new peers, the coalition, though rejected by both king and nation, would still have retained control of affairs.

To limit the number of peers or senators, would be to create a formidable aristocracy which could challenge prince and subjects alike. Any constitution which committed this mistake would soon be smashed to pieces. For it is assuredly necessary that the will of the prince and the will of the people, when they are in agreement, should not be disobeyed; and when something necessary cannot be effected by means of the constitution, it is bound to be effected in spite of it.

To those who object that the peerage is demeaned by the excessive multiplication of new peers, I shall answer that the only remedy in the interests of the prince is not lowering the dignity of the body which surrounds and sustains him. Should he deviate from this interest, experience will bring him back to it.

CHAPTER 5

On the election of representative assemblies

The present constitution has maintained the electoral colleges,[a] with only two improvements. The first consists in ordering that these colleges should be filled by annual elections;[b] the second in depriving the government of the right to nominate their presiding officer. The necessity of giving the nation its representative bodies promptly did not permit the revision and correction of this important part of our Constitutional Act. But it is unquestionably the most imperfect part of this. Electoral colleges, chosen for life, and yet threatened with dissolution, have all the disadvantages of the old electoral assemblies[c] and none of their advantages. These assemblies, emanating from a popular source, and created at the moment when the nominations were due to take place, could be regarded as representing, in a more or less faithful way, the opinion of those who elected them. This opinion, on the contrary, penetrates within the electoral colleges only slowly and partially. It is never in a majority, and by the time it becomes the opinion of the college it has generally ceased to be that of the people. Thus the small number of electors exercises a negative influence upon the nature of their choices. The assemblies charged with electing the representatives of the nation must be as numerous as is compatible with the maintenance of order. In England the candidates, from the top of a tribune, in the middle of a public square, or a plain covered by an immense crowd, harangue the electors who surround them. In our electoral colleges, the numbers are small and the forms severe. A rigorous silence is required.

---

[a] Created by the Constitution of the year VIII (title 1, arts. 7–10), and retained by the *Sénatus-consulte* of the Constitution of 16 Thermidor year X (4 August 1802) (title 3, arts. 18–20), the project of the electoral colleges had been designed by Sieyès. The election of representatives went through three successive stages: the electors chose one tenth of the general electorate to form the communal lists; the elected tenth on the communal lists again chose a tenth of its numbers for the departmental lists; and finally one tenth of the departmental lists to form the national lists.

[b] The constitution of 1802 (year X) had established the renewal of the lists only every three years.

[c] Created by the Constituent Assembly in 1791 on the model of the *assemblées des notables* of the *ancien régime*. With the system of indirect election the number of electors proper (electors in the second degree) was somewhat smaller than before the revolution: about 50,000 in 1791; about 60,000 (departmental lists) at the time when Constant was writing.

No question presents itself which might stir up the spirits and subjugate even for a moment individual egoism. No enthusiasm is possible. The problem is that vulgar men are just only when they are carried away; and they can hardly be carried away unless, gathered in a crowd, they act and react upon one another. One can only attract the attention of several thousands of citizens either by great wealth or by a wide reputation. A few domestic relations may gain a majority in a meeting of two or three hundred people. In order to be elected by the people, one must have partisans beyond one's ordinary surroundings. In order to be chosen by a few electors it is sufficient not to have enemies. The advantage is all on the side of negative qualities, and chance is even against talent. In this way national representation among us has often proved less advanced than public opinion upon a good many objects.[1]

If some day we want to enjoy fully the advantages of representative government in France, we must adopt direct election. It is this that, since 1788, brings to the British House of Commons all the most enlightened men. One could hardly mention a single Englishman, distinguished for his political talents, who has not been honoured by election, provided he canvassed for it.

Direct election alone can invest national representation with a real force, and give it deep roots in public opinion. The representative who is nominated by a different method cannot find anywhere a voice which recognizes his own. No section of the people acknowledges his courage, because all are discouraged by the long chain of events in the twist and turns of which their suffrage has been denatured or has disappeared.

To those who fear the French character, impetuous and impatient of the yoke of the law, I shall reply that we are like that simply because we have never formed the habit of controlling ourselves. It is with elections as it is with everything that concerns good order. By useless precautions, disorder is caused or increased. In France, our spectacles, our festivals, bristle with guards and bayonets. One would think that three citizens cannot meet without needing two soldiers to keep them apart. In England 20,000 men assemble and not a single soldier appears among them. The security of each of them is entrusted to the reason and interest of all, and that multitude which feels entrusted with both public and individual tranquillity watches with care over its charge.

---

[1] I do not mean here questions of party, on which, in the midst of upheavals, knowledge has no influence; I am talking of the objects of political economy.

Moreover, it is possible, through a more complex organization than that of British elections, to bring a greater calm into the exercise of this right of the people. An author, famous on more than one account, as eloquent writer, ingenious politician, and indefatigable friend of liberty and morality, M. Necker, has proposed, in one of his works[a] a system of election which seems to meet with general approval. One hundred property holders nominated by their equals, would, in each district, present five candidates to all the citizens who have the right to vote, from whom the citizens would choose. This method is to be preferred to those we have thus far tried. All the citizens would thus contribute directly to the nomination of their representatives.

Yet this system has a defect: if you give priority to a hundred men, some individual, who enjoys great popularity in his district, may find himself excluded from the list. This exclusion would be sufficient to discourage the voters, summoned to choose between five candidates among whom they would fail to find the object of their real desires and genuine preference.

I would wish, while leaving to the people the final choice, to give it also the first initiative. I would wish that, in each district, all the citizens who have the right to vote should make a first list of fifty, then form an assembly of a hundred, charged to present five out of the fifty, and that the choice between the five would then be made once more by all the citizens.

In this way, the hundred individuals to whom the presentation would be entrusted could not be led by their partiality for a candidate to present, along with him, only competitors whom it would be impossible to elect. Let us not hear that this danger is imaginary: we have seen the Council of the Five Hundred resorting to this expedient to force the composition of the Directory. The right to present is often equivalent to the right to exclude.

This inconvenience would be reduced by the modification I propose. (1) The assembly which presents the candidates would be forced to choose them from amongst men already designated by popular preferences, all of whom, consequently, enjoy a certain degree of credit and respect among their fellow citizens. (2) If in the first list there were a man whose vast reputation would gain him the majority of the votes, the hundred electors would hardly fail to present him; while on the other

[a] Jacques Necker, *De l'administration des finances de la France, Oeuvres complètes*, vol. 5, pp. 54–7: 'Sur l'élection des membres des assemblées provinciales'.

hand, if they were at liberty to form a list before the people's preference had manifested itself, motives of attachment or jealousy might lead them to exclude those whom this preference would designate, without, however, having the means to give legal force to the choice.

Moreover, it is only out of deference to prevailing opinion that I am prepared to compromise on direct election. Having witnessed the apparent disorders which trouble contested elections in England, I have seen to what extent the picture of these disorders is exaggerated. I have, it is true, seen elections accompanied by brawls, uproar, violent disputes; yet the choice fell upon men distinguished either by their fortune or their talents; once the election was over, all went back to normal. The electors of the lower orders, previously obstinate and unruly, returned to being industrious, docile and even respectful. Satisfied with having exercised their rights, they submitted the more readily to the authority and conventions of their social superiors as, in doing so, they were aware they were only acting in their own interest. The day following the election nothing remained of the excitement of the previous day. The people resumed their labours, but the public spirit had received the salutary shock, necessary to revive it.

Some enlightened men blame the maintenance of electoral colleges for motives directly opposed to those on which I base my views. They regret that elections are not made by a single body, and they support their regrets with arguments which it is helpful to refute, because they are to some extent plausible.

'The people', they claim, 'are totally incapable of assigning to the different parts of the public establishment those men whose character and talents are the most suitable. They must not be allowed to make any direct choice. The electoral bodies must be instituted not from the bottom, but from the top of the establishment. Choices must proceed not from below, where they are bound to be always bad, but from the top, where they are sure to be always good. The electors will in fact always have the greatest interest in maintaining order and public liberty, in the stability of institutions, the progress of ideas, the fixity of good principles and the gradual improvement of the laws and administration. When it falls to the people to nominate civil servants for certain tasks, the choices are generally essentially bad.[1] When it is a question of

---

[1] I cannot refrain from comparing this assertion with the sentiments of Machiavelli and Montesquieu. Men, says the first, though liable to be mistaken on general issues, are never wrong on particular ones. The people are admirable, says the second, at choosing those to

the highest magistracies, the subordinate electoral bodies themselves make rather a poor choice. It is in the end only by a sort of chance that men of merit are now and then called on to serve. The nominations to the legislative body can only be adequately made by men who know the object and general aim of all legislation well, who are well-informed about the present state of affairs and public opinion, who are able, by glancing over the different parts of the territory, to indicate confidently in it the elite of talents, of virtue and of knowledge. When a people nominates its main representatives without intermediary, and when it is numerous and disseminated over a large territory, that operation necessarily forces it to divide itself into sections: these sections are placed at a distance which does not permit them either communication or mutual accord. The result is sectional choices. It is necessary to find the unity of elections in the unity of the electoral power.'[a]

These reasonings rest upon a very exaggerated idea of the general interest, of the general aim, of the general legislation, of all the things to which this attribute is applied. What is after all the general interest if not the negotiation that takes place between particular interests? What is general representation but the representation of all partial interests which must reach a compromise on the objects they have in common? The general interest is certainly different from particular interests, but it is by no means opposed to them. People always speak as if one gains in so far as the others lose, yet it is only the result of the combination of those interests. It differs from them only in the same way as a body is different from its parts. Individual interests are what must interest individuals. Sectional interests are what must concern sections. It is these individuals, these sections, which form the political body. It is consequently the interests of these individuals and these sections which must be protected. If they are all protected, one will subtract by this very fact from each individual interest whatever can be damaging to the others. It is from this only that the true public interest can result.

whom they must commit part of their authority; and all the rest of the paragraph goes to show that Montesquieu has in mind a special designation, a definite function. [Niccolò Machiavelli, *Discorsi sopra la Prima Deca di Tito Livio*, Book 1, ch. 47: 'Gli uomini, come che s'ingannino ne' generali, ne' particulari non s'ingannino' in *Tutte le Opere*, p. 129; C. L. S. de Montesquieu, *Esprit des lois*, Book 2, ch. 2, *Oeuvres complètes*, vol. 2, pp. 240–1.]

[a] Pierre Jean Georges Cabanis, *Quelques considérations sur l'organisation sociale en général et particulièrement sur la nouvelle constitution*, Corps législatif, Commission du Conseil des Cinq-Cents, meeting of 25 Frimaire Year VIII (16 December 1799) (Paris, Imprimerie nationale, Year VIII–1799), pp. 25–6.

This public interest is nothing but the individual interests set reciprocally in a condition where they cannot harm each other. One hundred deputies, nominated by a hundred sections of a state, bring into the assembly the particular interests, the local preoccupations of their electors. This standpoint is useful to them. Forced to decide together, they soon become aware of the respective sacrifices which are indispensable. They attempt to reduce the extent of these sacrifices, and this is the advantage of their mode of nomination. Necessity always unites them in a common transaction, and the more sectional the choices, the more representation attains its general aim. If you reverse the natural order, if you place the electoral body at the top of the building, the men whom it nominates find themselves called upon to pronounce on matters of public interest of which they know nothing. You charge them with negotiating on behalf of parties whose needs they either do not know or despise. It is good that the representative of a section should be the instrument of that section; that he should not renounce any of their real or imaginary rights without first defending them; that he should be partial in favour of the section of which he is the delegate, because if everyone is partial towards his own electors, the partiality of each of them, united and reconciled, will have the advantage of being the impartiality of all.

Assemblies, however sectional their composition, are already far too inclined to develop a corporate spirit which isolates them from the nation. Living in the capital city, away from the section of the population that nominated them, the representatives lose touch with the customs, the needs, the way of life of the department they represent. They become disdainful and careless in relation to these things. What will happen if these instruments of the public are released from all local responsibility,[1] set forever above the votes of their fellow citizens and chosen by a body placed, as some would wish, at the top of the constitutional edifice?

The larger a state is, and the stronger its central authority, the more a single electoral body is inadmissible and direct elections indispensable. A tribe of a hundred thousand men could perhaps invest a senate with the right to nominate its deputies; federal republics may still do so; at least their internal administration would run no risks. But in any government that tends to unity, to deprive the different parts of the

---

[1] It is clear that by the word responsibility I do not mean here a legal responsibility, but one of opinion.

state of spokesmen nominated by them, means creating corporations who deliberate in the void and mistake their indifference towards individual interests for their devotion to the general interest. That is by no means the only disadvantage of the nomination of the representatives of the people by a senate.

This system destroys in the first place one of the greatest advantages of representative government, which is to establish frequent contact between the different classes of society. This advantage can only be the outcome of direct election. It is this election which requires, from the classes in power, a sustained level of consideration for the lower orders. It compels wealth to dissimulate its arrogance, and power to moderate its actions by placing, in the suffrage of the least prosperous part of the property holders, a reward for justice and generosity, and a punishment for oppression. We should not give up lightly this everyday source of happiness and harmony, nor disdain the motive behind the kindness which may initially be mere self-interest but in the end becomes a genuine virtue.

Some complain that riches are concentrated in the capital, while the rural districts are exhausted by the continual tribute which they bring to it and which never returns to them. Direct election drives the land-owners back to their estates, from which, without it, they tend to move away. Whenever they have no use for the suffrage of the people, their calculations are confined to extracting from their lands the highest possible revenue. Direct election suggests to them a somewhat nobler calculation, and one decidedly more useful to their dependants. Without popular election, all their need is credit, and this rallies them around the central authority. Popular election makes them need popularity, and drives them back to its source, by fixing the roots of their political existence in their possessions.

We sometimes hear the beneficial effects of feudalism praised because it kept the lord amongst his vassals and redistributed wealth equally throughout his territory. Popular election has the same advantages, without entailing the same abuses.

People are always talking about encouraging and honouring agriculture and labour. They try to do this through prizes distributed on a whim and by decorations which public opinion believes unjustified. It would be much simpler to give importance to the agricultural classes. But this importance cannot be created by decrees. It must be founded on the hopes and ambitions of the people who find in it their reward.

Secondly, the nomination to representative functions by a senate tends to corrupt, or at least to weaken the character of those who aspire to such eminent functions.

Whatever disgrace can be cast upon canvassing, and upon the efforts necessary to captivate a multitude, the effects are less pernicious than the extravagant attempts necessary to ingratiate oneself with a small number of men in power.

'Canvassing', says Montesquieu 'is dangerous in a senate; it is dangerous in a body of nobles; but it is not so in the people, whose nature is to act out of passion.'[1]

What one does to lead a large crowd must be done in broad daylight, and shame itself moderates public actions. But whenever we bow before a few men from each of whom we ask a favour, we prostrate ourselves in the shadows, while powerful individuals are only too ready to enjoy our humble prayers and obsequious supplications.

There are times when people fear everything which suggests energy. It is when tyranny is anxious to establish itself that servitude can still hope to take advantage of it. It is then that gentleness, docility, hidden talents, private qualities are praised. But those are in fact periods of moral enlightenment. Let the hidden talents become known, let private qualities find their reward in domestic affections, let gentleness and docility gain the favour of the great. It is to those men who attract attention and respect, who have acquired a right to the esteem, the truth, the gratitude of the people, that the choices of that people belong; and these more energetic men will also prove moderate.

People always imagine mediocrity as being peaceful. Yet it is peaceful only when it is impotent. When chance rallies a large number of mediocre men, and gives them a measure of strength, their mediocrity is more agitated, more envious, more violent in its course than talent itself even when it is carried away by passions. Enlightenment soothes the passions and moderates egotism by reassuring vanity.

Of the reasons which I put forward against elections, electoral colleges militate with equal strength against the process of renewal which was, until recently, employed in our assemblies and which our present constitution has fortunately just abolished. I am speaking of the periodical introduction of a third or a fifth in virtue of which the

---

[1] *Esprit des lois*, 2, 2.
  [*Oeuvres complètes*, vol. 2, pp. 239–44.]

newcomers in the representative bodies found themselves always in a minority.[a]

The renewal of the assemblies has as its aim not only preventing the representatives of the nation from forming a class apart, separated from the rest of the people, but also providing faithful interpreters of those changes in public opinion that might have occurred between one election and the next. Assuming that elections are well-organized, those elected recently will represent public opinion more faithfully than those elected in the previous elections.

Is it not absurd that the instruments of existing public opinion should be in a minority and those representing an outdated public opinion in the majority? Stability is no doubt desirable, and periods of renewal should never be excessively close in time to one another. For it is also absurd to make elections so frequent that public opinion has no time to become better informed in the interval between them. We have, moreover, a hereditary assembly which represents permanence. Let us not introduce elements of conflict into the elective assembly which represents improvement. The struggle between the conservative and the progressive spirit is more useful between two assemblies than within a single one. In this way there is no conquering minority. Its violences within the assembly of which it forms part collapse in the face of the calm of that other assembly which sanctions or rejects its resolutions. Irregular practices and threats are no longer suitable means of ruling over a majority which one intimidates, but causes of disrepute and discredit in the eyes of the judges who must express their verdict.

Renewal by a third or a fifth has serious drawbacks, both for the entire nation and for the assembly itself.

Even if a third or a fifth only can be named, all hopes are nonetheless set in motion. It is not the multiplicity of the chances, but the existence of a single one that stirs up all ambitions. Difficulty itself makes those ambitions even more jealous and hostile. The people are agitated by the election of a third or a fifth as much as by a total renewal. In the assemblies, newcomers were oppressed during the first year, and, soon

---

[a] The Constitution of 1795 (Year III) established that only one third of the legislative assemblies could be renewed at each election (title 5, art. 53); the Constitution of 1799 (Year VIII), (title 3, art. 27); and the Constitution of 1802 (Year X), (title 7, arts. 71–3) allowed the renewal of one fifth. The *Acte additionnel* established (title 1, art. 13) total re-election every five years.

after, they became oppressors. This truth has been proved by four successive experiences.[1]

The memory of our assemblies without a counterweight worries and bemuses us incessantly. We think we see in any assembly a cause for disorder, and that cause appears to us more powerful in any assembly which is renewed entirely. Yet the more real the danger, the more careful we must be as to the nature of the precautions we take. We must adopt only those of which the utility is proved, and the success certain.

The only advantage offered by a renewal of a third or a fifth can be found more fully, and free of all disadvantages, in the indefinite re-election which our present constitution permits, and which all our previous ones made the mistake of excluding.

The impossibility of re-election is, in all respects, a great mistake. The chance of uninterrupted re-election can alone offer to merit its deserved reward, and create in a people a mass of imposing and respected names. The influence of any individual cannot be destroyed by invidious institutions. Whatever survives of that influence in a given time is necessary to the time itself. Let us not dispossess talent by envious laws. There is nothing to be gained from alienating distinguished men in this way. Nature has wished them to take their place at the head of human institutions. The art of constitutions consists precisely in assigning them that place without their needing to disturb public peace in order to attain it.

Nothing is more opposed to liberty, and at the same time more favourable to disorder, than the forced exclusion of the representatives of the people after the expiry of their function. To have in assemblies men who cannot be re-elected means to fill them with as many weak men, who wish to make as few enemies as possible, in order to obtain some compensation or to live in peace during their retirement. If you set obstacles to indefinite re-election, you frustrate genius and courage of their due reward; you prepare consolation and triumph for cowardice and ineptitude; you place upon the same level the man who has spoken in accordance with his conscience, and one who has served factions by his audacity, or arbitrary power by his complaisance. Life

---

[1] The third of year IV (1796) were eliminated
The third of year V (1797) were expelled.
The third of year VI (1798) were rejected.
The third of year VII (1799) were victorious and destructive.

magistracies, Montesquieu observes,[1] have this advantages: they spare those who fill them those intervals of pusillanimity and weakness that precede, for the man destined to re-enter the class of simple citizens, the termination of their power. When re-election is not certain it offers the same advantage: it is in the politicians' interest to take a moral stance. Those calculations alone can achieve lasting success, but in order to do so, they need time.

Moreover, are men who are honest, courageous and experienced in public affairs really so numerous that we can voluntarily turn down those who have deserved general esteem? New talents will also arrive. The tendency of the people is to welcome them. Do not impose on it in this respect any constraint. Do not force it, at each election, to choose newcomers who will still have their fortune of self-regard to make, and fame to win. Follow the great examples: look at America, where the suffrage of the people has not ceased to flock around the founders of its independence; look at England, where names made illustrious by uninterrupted re-election have become a sort of popular property. Happy are the faithful nations, and those which are capable of lasting esteem.

Finally, our new constitution has come close to the true principles by replacing the salary granted thus far to the representatives of the nation with a more modest indemnity. It is by freeing those functions which demand greatest nobility of spirit from all calculation of self-interest, that the chamber of representatives will be elevated to the rank intended for it in our constitutional organization. Any salary attached to representative functions soon becomes their principal object. Candidates perceive in those august functions merely the occasion to increase or settle their fortune, facilities for manoeuvre, financial advantages. The electors themselves are carried away by a sort of party charity which engages them to favour the groom who wants to set up a household, the father of limited means who wants to educate his son or marry his daughters in the capital city. Creditors elect their debtors, the rich those of their relatives whom they prefer to assist at the expense of the state rather than themselves. Once the nomination has been made, one must preserve what one has obtained: the means resemble the end. Speculation ends in flexibility or in silence.

To pay the representatives of the people does not mean giving them

---

[1] *Esprit des lois*, 5, 7.
[*Oeuvres complètes*, vol. 2, pp. 281–3.]

an interest in exercising their functions scrupulously; it means simply giving them an interest in continuing to exercise those functions.

I am struck by other considerations.

I am not in favour of strong property qualifications for the exercise of public functions. Independence is in fact relative: as soon as a man has what is necessary, he needs only an elevated soul to do without the superfluous. However, it is desirable that representative offices should generally be occupied by men, if not from the wealthy classes at least in easy circumstances. Their starting point is more advantageous, their education more polished, their spirit freer, their intelligence better prepared for enlightenment. Poverty has its prejudices like ignorance. If your representatives receive no salary, you place power in property, while still leaving a fair chance for the legitimate exceptions.

Combine your institutions and your laws in such a way, says Aristotle, that offices could not be the object of interested calculation: otherwise the multitude, who are in any case hardly affected by exclusion from eminent posts, because they prefer to attend to their own business, will envy both the honour and the profit. All the preventative measures will work together if the magistracies do not tempt greed. The poor will prefer lucrative occupations to difficult and unpaid functions. The rich will take up the magistracies because they will have no need of material rewards.[1]

These principles are not applicable to all employments in modern states. Some of them demand a fortune above any private fortune; but nothing prevents their application to representative functions.

The Carthaginians had already drawn this distinction: all the magistracies elected by the people were exercised without reward. The others carried a salary.

In a constitution where the propertyless have no political rights, the absence of any salary for the representatives of the nation seems to me natural. Would it not be an outrageous and ridiculous contradiction to exclude the poor from national representation, as if the rich only had the right to represent him, and to make him pay for his representatives as if they were poor?

The corruption that originates from ambitious views is far less nefarious than that which results from ignoble self-interest. Ambition is compatible with a thousand ingenious qualities: honesty, courage,

---

[1] Aristotle, *Politics*, Book 5, ch. 7.

disinterestedness, independence. Avarice could not on the other hand coexist with any of these qualities. It is impossible to keep men of ambition out of office: let us at least eliminate from them those who are greedy. In this way we shall considerably diminish the number of competitors, and those who will be excluded will be precisely the least respectable.

However, one condition is necessary for the representative offices to be honorary: they must be important. No-one would wish to exercise unpaid functions which were puerile in their insignificance, and which would become shameful if they ceased to be puerile. Indeed in such a constitution it would be better if there were no representative functions at all.

CHAPTER 6

On the conditions of property

Our Constitution has made no pronouncement upon the property qualifications required for the exercise of political rights, because these rights, entrusted to the electoral colleges, are for this very reason in the hands of the property holders. However, if these colleges were replaced by direct election, some property qualifications would become indispensable.[a]

No people has ever considered as members of the state all the individuals residing, in whatever circumstances, within its territory. I am not talking here of the separation between slaves and free men in the ancient world, nor of the division between nobles and commoners in modern states. The most absolute democracy establishes two classes: the first includes the foreigners and those who have not reached the age established by law to exercise the rights of citizenship. The second is formed by the men who have reached that age and were born in the country itself. Accordingly, there is a principle which

---

[a] In the system of electoral colleges designed by Sieyès, the conditions for becoming an elector at the first (that is, communal) level were the ownership of a house or other property and the equivalent of the wages for 150 to 200 working days. But the property requirements at departmental level were very high, since the choice was made among the 600 citizens with the largest taxable income.

decides which of the individuals grouped in the same territory are and are not, members of the state.

This principle is clearly that, in order to be a member of the association, it is necessary to possess a certain degree of understanding and a common interest with the other members of the association. Men below the legal age are not deemed to possess that degree of understanding. Foreigners are not deemed to guide themselves by that interest. The proof is that the former, when they attain the age fixed by the law, do become members of the political association, while the latter may become such in virtue of residence, property or their relations. It is assumed that such things will give to the former the necessary understanding, to the latter the required interest.

Yet this principle requires a further extension. In our modern societies, to be born in the country and to have come of age is not sufficient reason to grant those qualities required for the exercise of the rights of citizenship. Those who are kept by poverty in eternal dependence, and who are condemned by it to daily labour, are neither more knowledgeable than children about public affairs, nor more interested than foreigners in national prosperity, of whose elements they are unaware, and in whose advantages they share only indirectly.

I do not wish in any way to wrong the labouring class. As a class it is by no means less patriotic than the others. It is often ready for the most heroic sacrifices and its devotion is the more admirable in so far as it is not rewarded by either fortune or glory. Yet the patriotism which gives one the courage to die for one's country is quite different, I believe, from the patriotism which enables one to fully understand its interests. There must be a further condition in addition to those prescribed by the law of birth and age. This condition is the leisure indispensable for the acquisition of understanding and soundness of judgement. Property alone makes men capable of exercising political rights.

It may be argued that the present state of society, by mixing up and confusing in a thousand different ways those with property and those without, gives to a part at least of the latter the same interests and means as to the former; that the working man is no less in need of peace and security than the man of property; that property holders are, by right and in practice, simply the distributors of the common riches amongst all individuals, and that it is to the advantage of all, that order and peace should favour the development of all talents and resources and of all individual means.

These reasonings have the defect of proving too much. If they were conclusive, there would be no reason to refuse to foreigners the rights of citizenship. The commercial relations of Europe make it the interest of the great majority of Europeans that peace and happiness should reign in all countries. The overthrow of an empire, however much it owes, is just as damaging to those foreigners who, through financial speculations, have bound their own fortune to that empire, as it could be to its own inhabitants, apart from the property holders. This is confirmed by facts. Amidst the most cruel wars, a country's shop-keepers often express their wish, and sometimes even make efforts towards this end, that the enemy nation should not be destroyed. Nonetheless such a vague consideration is hardly sufficient to elevate foreigners to the rank of citizens.

Notice that the necessary aim of those without property is to obtain some: all the means which you grant them are sure to be used for this purpose. If, to the freedom to use their talents and industry, which you owe them, you add political rights, which you do not owe them, these rights, in the hands of the greatest number, will inevitably serve to encroach upon property. They will pursue it by this irregular course instead of following the natural one: labour. It will become, for them, a source of corruption, for the state, a source of disorder. A famous writer[a] has most appropriately observed that, whenever the property-less enjoy political rights, three things may happen: they may exclusively follow their own impulse, and in this case they destroy society; they may be guided by the man or men in power, and in this case they become instruments of tyranny. Finally, they may be led by those who aspire to power, and become altogether the instruments of faction. Thus you need property qualifications and you need them both for the electors and for those who are eligible for election.

In all those countries which have representative assemblies it is essential that those assemblies, whatever their further organization, should be formed by property holders. A single individual, through his striking merit, may captivate the crowd; but political bodies, to sustain confidence in them, need to have interests which are clearly in accordance with their duties. A nation always expects that men grouped together will be guided by their own interests. It is certain that the love of order, justice and conservation will enjoy a majority among property

---

[a] Aristotle, *The Politics*, with an English trs. by H. Rackham, Loeb Classical Library (London, 1932), 4, 11.

holders. Consequently, these will be useful not only in virtue of those qualities which genuinely belong to them, but even more so for those qualities which are generally attributed to them, for the prudence which they are supposed to possess, and the favourable prejudices which they inspire. Place among the legislators those without property, however well-meaning, and the anxieties of the property holders will obstruct all their measures. The wisest of laws will be suspected and consquently disobeyed, while the contrasting system would have reconciled popular opinion even under a government which was in some respects defective.

During our revolution, it is true that property holders have collaborated with those without property in making absurd and ruinous laws. The reason was that the property holders were afraid of the propertyless being invested with power. They wanted to be forgiven for their property. The fear of losing what they have makes people cowardly, and in these cases they will imitate the fury of those who want to acquire what they do not have. The faults or crimes of the property holders were the consequence of the influence of the propertyless.

But what property qualifications is it equitable to establish?

Property can be so limited, that the owner is a property holder only in appearance. A writer who has treated this subject admirably[a] says that, whoever does not have, in land revenue, a sum sufficient to subsist for a year without being forced to work for others, is not fully a property holder. He finds himself, in relation to that portion of property which he lacks, in the class of those who live off their pay. The property holders are the masters of his existence, since they may refuse him work. Only he who possesses the necessary revenue to subsist independently of any external will can exercise the rights of citizenship. A lower condition of property would be illusory; a higher one would be unjust.

I think nonetheless that anyone owning a farm of sufficient revenue on a long lease must be regarded as a property holder. In the present state of property in France, the farmer who cannot be expelled is more of a true landowner than the citizen who is such only in appearance, in virtue of a benefit which he rents out. It is just to grant to the former the same rights as to the latter. To those who object that at the end of the lease the farmer loses his position as landowner, I shall reply that any property holder may, through a thousand accidents, lose his property from one day to the next.

[a] Cf. Jacques Necker, *Du pouvoir exécutif* in *Oeuvres complètes*, vol. 8, pp. 62–3.

Some will observe that I speak only of landed property, and they will perhaps argue that there are several classes of property, and that the ownership of land is only one of them. The constitution itself acknowledges this principle, since it grants representation not only to land but also to industry.

I must confess that, if the outcome of this clause had been to put on the same level landed and industrial property, I would not hesitate to condemn it.

Industrial property lacks several of the advantages of landed property, and these advantages are precisely those which form the conservative spirit which is necessary for political associations.

Land influences the character and the destiny of man by the very nature of the cares which it imposes.[a] The cultivator dedicates himself to constant and progressive occupations. In this way he acquires regularity in his habits. Chance, which is a great source of disorder in morals, never affects the life of the cultivator. Any interruption is damaging to him; any imprudence a certain loss; his achievements are slow. He cannot hasten or increase them by rash but fortunate actions. He depends on nature and is independent of men. All of these things endow him with a calm disposition, a feeling of security, a spirit of order, that attach him to the vocation to which he owes his peace as well as his subsistence.

Industrial property can influence man only by the positive gain which it brings or promises to bring him. It instills less regularity into his life. It is more artificial and less immutable than land. The operations of which it is composed consist often of fortuitous transactions. Its achievements are more rapid, but chance plays a much greater part in them. Industrial property does not have as a necessary component that slow, safe progress which creates the habit, and soon the need for uniformity. It does not make a man independent of other men. On the contrary, it places him in their dependence. Vanity, that fertile seed of political ferments, is frequently wounded in the industrialist almost never in the farmer.[1] The latter calculates in peace the order of seasons,

---

[1] '*Pius questus*', says Cato the elder, of agriculture, *stabilissimus minimeque invidiosus, minimeque male cogitantes qui in eo studio occupati sunt.*' (Those who are engaged in this activity are very pious, very stable, hardly envious or capable of any evil thought). [Constant obviously takes this quotation, which is slightly incorrect, from Adam Smith,

[a] Compare with Smith, *Wealth of Nations*, vol. 1, pp. 426–7.

the nature of the soil, the character of the climate. The former calculates the fantasies, the pride, the luxury of the rich. A farm is a fatherland in miniature. One is born there, raised there, brought up with the trees that surround it. In industrial property, nothing speaks to the imagination, to memory, to the moral part of man. One speaks of my ancestors' field, of my fathers' cabin. One never speaks of my fathers' shop or workshop. Improvements to land cannot be separated from the soil which receives them, and of which they become part. Industrial property is not susceptible of improvement but of growth, and that growth can be transferred at one's pleasure.

In relation to their intellectual qualities, the cultivator enjoys a great superiority over the artisan. Agriculture demands a series of observations and experiences which form man's judgement:[1] hence, in the peasant, that right and sound sense that so impresses us. The industrial professions are often confined by the division of labour to purely mechanical operations.

Land binds man to the country where he lives, surrounds his departure from it with obstacles, creates patriotism through interest. The advantages of land and the disadvantages of its industrial counterpart in political relations increase in so far as the value of the property decreases. The artisan has almost nothing to lose from emigrating. The owner of a small property in land would be ruined by expatriation. It is especially from the lower classes of property holders that the effects of the different types of property must be judged, because it is those classes which form the great majority.

Setting aside its moral pre-eminence, landed property is favourable to public order by the very position in which it places its owners. Artisans, crowded into the towns, are at the mercy of the factious, while it is almost impossible to collect farmers together and therefore to stir them up.

An Inquiry into the Nature and Causes of the Wealth of Nations, ed. by R. H. Campbell, A. S. Skinner, 2 vols, Oxford, 1976, vol. 2, p. 462.
    The original text says:
    'Ut ex agricolis et viri fortissimi et milites strenuissimi gignuntur, maximaeque pius questus stabilissimusque consequitur minimeque invidiosus, minimeque male cogitantes sunt qui in eo studio occupati sunt.'
    'On the other hand it is from the farming class that the bravest men and sturdiest soldiers come, their calling is most highly respected, their livelihood is most assured and it is looked on with the least hostility, and those who are engaged in that pursuit are least inclined to be disaffected.' Cato, *De Re Rustica*, Introduction and trs. by W. D. Hooper, The Loeb Classical Library (London and Cambridge, Mass., 1934), pp. 2–3.]

[1] Smith, *Wealth of Nations*, I, 10.

These truths were appreciated by Aristotle. He highlighted with great force the distinctive character of the agricultural and the mercantile classes, and opted in favour of the former.

Industrial property offers, no doubt, great advantages. Industry and commerce have created in credit a new means of defence for liberty. Landed property guarantees the stability of institutions, industrial property ensures the independence of individuals.

Thus, to refuse political rights to those merchants whose activity and wealth double the prosperity of the country which they inhabit, would be an injustice, and moreover an imprudence, because it would set wealth against power.

Yet, if we reflect upon it, we shall readily see that this exclusion would not affect those industrialists whom it would be awkward to exclude. Almost all of these are in fact also landowners. As to those who have no other property but their industry, bound as they are by a necessity that no institution will ever overcome, to mechanical occupations, they are deprived of any means of educating themselves, and can, with the purest of intentions, make the state bear the consequences of their inevitable errors. These men must be respected; they must be protected, guaranteed against all troubles on the part of the rich, freed from all the hindrances that weigh upon their labours, favoured as far as it is possible in their industrious careers. But they must not be carried into a new sphere, to which their destiny does not call them, where their participation is useless, where their passions would be threatening and their ignorance dangerous.

Yet our constitution decided to carry to excess its solicitude for industry. It has created for it a special representation. However, it has wisely confined the number of the representatives of that class to about one twenty-seventh of the general representation.[a]

Some writers have thought that they could identify a third kind of property. They have called it intellectual, and have defended this opinion with great ingenuity. A man distinguished in a liberal profession, they argued, for example a jurist, is no less strongly attached to the country which he inhabits than the landed proprietor. It is easier for the latter to alienate his patrimony than for the first to export his reputation. His fortune lies in the trust he inspires. That trust rests on several years of work, intelligence, ability, services rendered, on the

---

[a] The *Acte* (title 2, art. 30) created a special list in each department of representatives of industry, manufacture and trade.

habit which people have acquired of appealing to him in difficult circumstances, on the local acquaintances that his long experience has accumulated. Expatriation would deprive him of these advantages. He would be ruined by the very fact of presenting himself unknown in a foreign land.

However, the property which is called intellectual is only a matter of opinion. If it is permitted to anyone to assign it to himself, all will no doubt claim it, since political rights will become not only a social prerogative, but also an attestation of talent, and to deny them to oneself would indeed be a rare act both of disinterestedness and of modesty. If it is the opinion of others which must confer this intellectual property, this opinion manifests itself only by the success and fortune which are its necessary outcome. Property will be the natural lot of every kind of distinguished man.

Moreover, there are considerations of greater importance to take into account. The liberal professions require, possibly more than any other, to be connected with property, if their influence upon political discussion is not to prove destructive. These professions, so commendable in many respects, do not always include among their advantages that of incorporating into their ideas that practical justice necessary for assessing the positive interest of men. We have seen, in our revolution, literary men, mathematicians, chemists indulging in the most exaggerated opinions. One could scarcely claim that in other respects they were not knowledgeable and respectable. But they had lived far from other men. Some had become used to following their own imagination; others to taking into account only rigorous evidence; a third group through their observations of the natural laws of reproduction and death, to taking a detached view of things. They had arrived by different paths at the same result, that of disdaining considerations drawn from facts, of despising the real and tangible world and of reasoning about the social state as enthusiasts, about passions as geometers, about human sufferings as physicists.

If these errors were the lot of superior men, what aberrations should we not expect from subordinate candidates, from unsuccessful pretenders? How urgent it is to restrain wounded self-respect, embittered vanities, all those causes for resentment, for agitation, for discontent against a society in which one finds oneself displaced, for hatred against men who seem incapable of just appreciation! All intellectual activities are certainly honourable. All must be respected. Our first attribute, our distinctive quality, is thought. Whoever makes use of it is entitled to our esteem, quite independently of success. Whoever insults or rejects it renounces the name of man and places himself outside the human species. Nevertheless each science gives to the spirit of the person who cultivates it an exclusive direction, which proves dangerous in political affairs unless it is counterbalanced. But this counterbalance can only be found in property. Property alone establishes between men uniform ties. Property sets them on guard against the imprudent sacrifice of the happiness and tranquillity of others, by including in that sacrifice their own well-being, and by forcing them to calculate for themselves. It forces them to descend from the heights of chimerical theories and impracticable extravagances by re-establishing between them and the other members of the association numerous relations and common interests.

We must not believe that this precaution is useful only in maintaining order; it is in fact no less essential in the preservation of liberty. By a somewhat bizarre combination, those sciences that sometimes, during political troubles, dispose men towards impossible notions of liberty, make them, on other occasions, indifferent and servile beneath despotism. Savants are seldom troubled even by unjust power. It is only thought which power hates. It is fond enough of the sciences as instruments of government, and the fine arts as distractions for the governed. Thus the career of those men whose studies bear no direct relation on the active interests of life, protecting them from the oppressions of an authority that never sees them as rivals, such men are often all too little troubled by the abuses of power which weigh on other classes.

CHAPTER 7

On discussion in the representative assemblies

We owe to the present constitution one major improvement: the re-establishment of public discussion in the assemblies.

The constitution of the year VIII [1799] prohibited it; the Royal Charter permitted it only with many restrictions, for only one of the two chambers, while it surrounded all the deliberations of the other chamber with a mystery which could hardly be rationally explained. We have returned to simple ideas. We have grasped that we assemble merely to understand one another, that in order to understand one another it is necessary to speak, and that – with a few rare and brief exceptions – the representatives were not authorized to dispute with their electors the right to know how their interests are being treated.

An article which may at first appear painstakingly detailed, and which has been criticized in the constitution which is going to govern us, will contribute greatly to ensuring that such discussions prove useful. It is the article forbidding written speeches.[a] This is more regulatory than constitutional, I agree. Yet the abuse of those speeches has been so influential, and has so distorted the proceedings of our assemblies that it is fortunate that it should finally have been rectified.

It is only when orators are forced to speak extensively that a proper discussion is set in train. Everyone, struck by the arguments he has just heard, is naturally led to examine them. Those arguments impress his mind even if he does not realize it. He cannot banish them from his memory. The views he has encountered combine with and modify those he already holds, suggesting to him answers which present the same issue from different points of view.

When orators confine themselves to reading out what they have written in the silence of their study, they no longer discuss, they amplify. They do not listen, since what they hear must not in any way alter what they are going to say. They wait until the speaker whose place they must take has concluded. They do not examine the opinion he defends, they count the time he is taking and which they regard as a delay. In this way there is no discussion; everybody reproduces objections which have already been refuted. Everyone sets aside whatever he has not anticipated, all that might disrupt a case already completed in advance. Speakers follow one another without meeting; if they refute one another it is simply by chance. They are like two armies, marching in opposite directions, one next to the other, barely catching a glimpse of one another, avoiding even looking at one another for fear of deviating from a route which has already been irrevocably traced out.

This is neither the only, nor the most alarming defect of a discussion consisting exclusively of written speeches. There is another, still more serious.

What threatens most good order and liberty amongst us is not exaggeration or error, not even ignorance, although we lack none of

[a] *Acte additionnel* (title 1, art. 26).

these defects. It is rather the need to impress. This need, which degenerates into a kind of fury, is the more dangerous in so far as it does not originate in the nature of man, but is a social creation, the belated and artificial product of an ancient civilization and of an immense capital city. Consequently, it does not restrain itself, like those natural passions which are exhausted by their own duration. Sentiment does not stop it, as it has nothing in common with sentiment. Reason is impotent against it, for it is not a question of being convinced, but of convincing. Even fatigue does not calm it; as he who experiences it fails to note his own sensations, but observes only those it produces in other people. Opinions, eloquence, emotions, all become merely means, while man himself is transformed into the instrument of his own vanity.

In a nation so inclined it is necessary, as far as possible, to deprive mediocrity of the opportunity to produce any effect whatsoever, by the means within its reach. I say any effect, for our vanity is humble, as well as unrestrained: it aspires to everything but is contented with very little. By looking at the pretensions it displays, one would think it insatiable. But watching it clinging to the smallest achievements, one admires its frugality.

Let us now apply these truths to our subject. Do you wish our representative assemblies to be reasonable? Impose on those men who wish to shine in them the need for talent. The majority will seek refuge in reason as a lesser evil. But if you open up to that majority a career in which anyone can make a little progress, no-one will wish to renounce that advantage. Everyone will indulge in his moment of eloquence, his hour of fame. Anyone who can produce or commission a written speech will want to mark his legislative existence. The assemblies will become academies, with this difference, that academic harangues will decide there on the destiny, the property and even the life of the citizens.

I shall refrain from illustrating the unbelievable proof of this desire to impress which appeared in the most deplorable periods of our revolution. I have seen representatives looking for subjects on which to speak, so that their names should not remain unknown to the great movements which were taking place. The subject once found and the speech written, the result was for them a matter of indifference. By banishing written speeches, we shall create in our assemblies what they have always lacked, that silent majority which, disciplined, so to speak, by the superiority of the men of talent, is reduced to listening to them, in default of being able to talk in their place and becomes more enlightened because it is condemned to be modest, and more reasonable by being silent.[a]

The presence of the ministers in the assemblies will greatly contribute to impressing the right character upon their discussions.[b] Ministers themselves will discuss the decrees necessary for the administration. They will offer that knowledge of the facts which the exercise of government alone can give. Opposition will not seem a form of hostility, persistence will not degenerate into obstinacy. The government, yielding to reasonable objections, will amend sanctioned proposals and explain obscure formulations. Authority will be able to render a just homage to reason without compromising itself, and to defend itself with the weapons of reasoning.

However, our assemblies will only attain that degree of perfection of which the representative system is susceptible, when ministers, instead of taking part there as ministers, will be themselves members of the assemblies by national election. It was a great mistake of our previous constitutions to have established this incompatibility between ministry and representation.

When the representatives of the people are constantly excluded from participation in power, we have reason to fear that they will regard it as their natural enemy. If, on the contrary, the ministers could be received into the bosom of the assemblies, the ambitious will direct their efforts only against men and would respect the institutions. Because their attacks will be aimed at individuals, they will be less dangerous for the assembly as a whole. No-one will want to break an instrument the use of which he could hope to win, and the same individual who would attempt to diminish the strength of the executive power, if that strength were to remain forever inaccessible to him, will, if it could some day be his, treat it instead with care.

We can see an example of this in England. The enemies of the ministry see in its power their own future authority and strength: the opposition spares the prerogatives of the government as its own heritage, and respects its future means in its present enemies. It is a great vice for a constitution to be placed between parties in such a way that

---

[a] The prohibition of written speeches was modelled on the practice of the British House of Commons. See Thomas Erskine. *A practical treatise of the Law, Proceedings and Usage of Parliament* (London, 1859), ch. 11.

[b] *Acte additionnel*, title 1, art. 18: this article decreed that ministers and *conseillers d'état* should take part in the discussion of the Chambers, but could only vote when they were members of either Chamber in their own right (by election or because they belonged to the peerage) and not as ministers or *conseillers*.

each of them can reach the other only through the constitution. This is nevertheless what happens whenever the executive power, set beyond the reach of legislators, always represents for them an obstacle and never a hope.

We cannot flatter ourselves with the hope of excluding factions from a political organization in which we wish to preserve the advantages of liberty. Consequently it is important to work at making those factions as inoffensive as possible, and since they are bound sometimes to prove victorious, it is necessary to anticipate and mitigate the consequences of their victory in advance.

When the ministers are members of the assemblies, they are more easily attacked if they are guilty. It is hardly necessary to denounce them, it is sufficient to answer them. Similarly, it is much easier for them to justify themselves if they are innocent, because at any moment they can explain the reason for their conduct.

By uniting individuals without, however, uniting powers, we can form a harmonious government instead of creating two armed camps.

Another consequence is that an inept or suspect minister cannot retain his power. In England, the minister, in fact, loses his post if he finds himself in a minority.[1]

CHAPTER 8

On the right to initiate legislation

The meaning of the constitutional article on the right to initiate legislation[a] has been, I believe, generally misunderstood. The Royal Charter denied it almost entirely to the chambers which is had created.[b] It was only by a somewhat illegal extension that the deputies had arrogated to themselves the right to expound their proposals publicly, and the ministers announced their intention of contesting their entitlement to this privilege. When a proposal was accepted, slow and cumbersome rules hindered its progress. In a word, in the constitution of 1814, the

---

[1] Mr Pitt was the exception to this rule for two months in 1784. But the reason was that the whole nation was for his ministry, against the House of Commons.

[a] *Acte additionnel*, title 1, arts. 24–5.
[b] *Charte Constitutionnelle* of 4 June 1814, arts. 19–21. In the Charter any proposals for a new law had to be discussed by a secret committee of either Chamber, and again secretly, submitted to the king who could decide to pursue or ignore the matter without any public discussion.

right to make proposals was merely an inadequate resource, contrary to the intention of the constitution itself, and always in danger of being supplanted by some more rigorous interpretation of that constitution.

In our Constitutional Act, on the other hand, there is only one difference between the initiative of the chambers and that with which the British parliament is invested: the head of state is not obliged to pronounce his *veto*: silence replaces it. However, when public opinion demands the adoption of some popular measure, can a representative government respond to it for long merely by silence? Is it not precisely the character of such a government to be directed by public opinion? Therefore the initiative is, in practice, completely restored to the representatives of the nation, who can even renew their proposals as often as they judge it convenient, a right they had had been deprived of by article 21 of the Royal Charter.

My opinion on the right to initiate legislation has not in the least changed: it still seems to me – as it seemed to me a year ago – a necessary component of the powers of the national representation.[1] Undoubtedly it cannot be refused to the ministers. It is indeed their prerogative to express the desires of the government, as the deputies express the will of the people. But it will naturally happen that the government almost never exercises this prerogative. The ministers, sitting in the chambers, in the ranks of the representatives, will make in this capacity the proposals suggested by the circumstances or the needs of the state. The government will feel that it is more appropriate to its dignity to wait rather than to anticipate. Whenever it proposes a law it is in fact submitting itself to the judgement of the chambers. When it waits for the proposals of the chambers, it becomes their judge.

Let us, in these initial moments, allow our constitutional mechanism the opportunity to establish and simplify itself by custom and habit. Difficulties are often multiplied in the attempt to anticipate them; they are created whenever uncertainties due to inexperience are transformed into grievances. Let us set the constitution to work in good faith. Instead of destroying it by premature changes, let us see whether what is already there does not offer us the same advantages. Until a constitution has been tested in practice, its forms are a dead letter. Practice alone can demonstrate their effect and determine their meaning. We have only too often demolished the building on the pretext of reconstructing it. Let us take advantage henceforth of that knowledge

[1] *Réflexions sur les constitutions*, ch. IV, § 4.

which can be acquired only through practice, in order to provide gradually for all our partial needs, with moderation and wisdom, slowly, with the assistance of time, the gentlest and most powerful of allies.

CHAPTER 9

On the responsibility of ministers[a]

The present constitution is perhaps the only one to have established, on the responsibility of ministers, principles which are both perfectly applicable and sufficiently extensive.

Ministers can face accusation, and deserve to be prosecuted, in three different ways: 1. through the abuse or misuse of their legal power 2. through illegal acts prejudicial to the public interest, yet bearing no direct relation on particular individuals 3. through assaults upon the liberty, security and property of individuals.

In a work published three months ago[1] I have shown that, since this last sort of crime bears no relation whatsoever to the powers with which the ministers are legally invested, they ought to be treated in this respect like ordinary citizens, and subjected to the judgement of ordinary tribunals.

It is certain that if a minister, in an impulse of passion, were to carry off a woman or if, in a fit of rage, he were to kill a man, he ought not to be accused as minister in any special way, but undergo, as a violator of common laws, the penalties to which his crime would be subjected by the common laws, and in the forms prescribed by them.

The case of any act condemned by the law is in no way different from that of kidnapping or murder. A minister who commits illegal acts against the liberty or the property of a citizen does not err in his capacity as minister, since none of his powers gives him the right to act illegally against the liberty or property of any individual. He belongs to the class of all other offenders, and must be prosecuted and punished like them.

---

[1] *De la responsabilité des ministres* ch. 1.

---

[a] The issue of the responsibility of ministers and the procedures through which these may be brought under accusation is discussed in title 4 of the *Acte additionnel* ('Des ministres et de la responsabilité') in arts. 38–50, in much greater detail than by any previous French constitution.

It must be observed that any of us can act against individual liberty. I can, if I like, hire four men to wait for my enemy at the corner of the street and drag him into some obscure hiding place, where I may keep him a prisoner unknown to anyone else. The minister who has a citizen carried off without being authorized to do so by the law commits the same crime. His position as minister is foreign to this act and in no way alters its nature. Once again, since his position as minister does not give him the right to have citizens arrested in contempt of the law, and against its formal provisions, the crime he commits belongs in the same class as murder, kidnapping or any other private crime.

Undoubtedly the legitimate power of a minister gives him readier access to the means of committing illegitimate acts. But this use of his power is simply an additional crime. It is as if some individual were to forge a nomination as minister in order to impose his will upon the latter's agents. Such an individual would in fact simulate an assignment and assumed power with which he had never been invested. Similarly, the minister who orders an illegal act pretends to be invested with an authority which has not been conferred upon him. Consequently, for all those crimes the victims of which are private individuals, these must be able to bring a legal action directly against the ministers.

The right of ordinary courts to pronounce judgements on accusations of this nature has been called into question. Men have argued by turns about the weakness of the courts which would be afraid of threatening powerful men and about the inconvenience of entrusting to these courts so-called state secrets.

The last question stems from old-fashioned ideas. It is a survival from the system under which it was admitted that the security of the state could require arbitrary measures. As the arbitrary intervention of power cannot be justified, because it presupposes the absence of those facts and proofs which would make the law sufficient, it is alleged that secrecy is indispensable. When a minister has given the order to illegally arrest and detain a citizen, it is all too easy for his apologists to attribute this offence to secret reasons, which are known to the minister alone, and which he cannot reveal without endangering public security. For my part, I do not know of any public security without individual guarantee. I believe that public security is especially compromised when the citizens see in the authority a danger rather than a safeguard. I believe that arbitrary power is the real enemy of public security; that the obscurity with which arbitrary power shrouds itself can only increase this danger; that there can be public security only in justice, justice only in the law, and laws only in definite procedures. I believe that the liberty of any citizen is sufficiently important to the entire social body that the reason for any steps taken against him ought to be known to his natural judges. I believe that this is the chief purpose, indeed the sacred aim of all political institutions, and that because no constitution can find its full legitimacy elsewhere, it would be vain for it to look elsewhere for assured strength and permanence.

Whenever the courts are said to be too lenient on guilty parties, it is because these courts are imagined to be in that state of uncertainty, dependence and terror into which the revolution had plunged them. Governments uncertain of their rights, threatened in their interests, unhappy products of factions and deplorable heirs to the hatred which these factions had inspired, could neither create nor suffer independent tribunals.

Our constitution, by making irremovable from now on all those judges to be nominated in future*a* gives them an independence of which they have been deprived for too long. They will learn that, in judging ministers, as in judging other defendants, they cannot meet any constitutional obstacle, and that they are not exposed to any danger. And from their security will arise simultaneously impartiality, moderation and courage.

This does not mean that the representatives of the nation do not also have the right and the duty to respond to any attacks that the ministers might make against liberty, whenever the citizens, who are their victims, do not dare to make their complaints heard. The same article which permits the acccusation of the ministers for compromising the security or the honour of the state, grants to our representatives the power to accuse them if they introduce into the government what is most contrary to the security and the honour of any government, that is, arbitrariness. We cannot refuse the citizen the right to demand redress for the wrong of which he is the victim. But we must also see that the men invested with his trust should be able to take his cause into their hands. This double guarantee is both legitimate and indispensable.

Our constitution implicitly sanctions this. It only remains to reconcile it legally with that guarantee which is also due to the ministers themselves, who, more exposed than simple private citizens, and in

---

a Acte additionnel, title 5, art. 51.

spite of wounded passions, must find in the laws and in their forms an equitable and sufficient protection.

The case is quite different for illegal acts, prejudicial to the public interest, which bear no direct relation to private individuals, and for the misuse of the power with which the ministers are legally invested.

There are many illegal acts which jeopardize the general interest alone. It is clear that these acts can be denounced and prosecuted only by the legislative assemblies. No individual can derive any advantage from undertaking their prosecution nor has the right to do so.

As to the abuse of the legal power with which the ministers are invested, it is even more clear that the representatives of the people are alone in a position to judge whether there has been any abuse; while a special court, invested with a special authority, is alone entitled to pronounce on the gravity of the abuse.

Our constitution is, then, eminently wise when it allows to our representatives the amplest scope in their accusations, and when it gives discretionary power to the court that must pronounce the judgement.

There are a thousand ways in which a war may be unjustly or pointlessly undertaken; to direct it too precipitately, too lethargically or too negligently; to bring too much inflexibility or too much weakness to negotiations; to destroy credit through hazardous operations, ill-conceived economies or frauds disguised under different names. If each of these ways of harming the state had to be listed and specified by the law, the code of responsibility would become a treatise of history and politics, and even so its legal prescriptions would only cover the past. Ministers would easily find fresh ways to evade them for the future.

Do not even the English, so scrupulously faithful, in the domain of common law, to the literal interpretation of the law, indicate those crimes that impose responsibility upon ministers only by the vague terms, 'high crimes' or 'misdemeanours', words which neither specify the degree nor the nature of the crime?

We may think that this is to place the ministers in a very unfavourable and dangerous position indeed. While we demand for ordinary citizens the safeguard of the most accurate precision and the guarantee of the letter of the law, ministers are exposed to a sort of arbitrariness exercised upon them both by their accusers and by their judges. Yet this arbitrariness is in the nature of the case itself; its defects must be softened by the solemnity of the procedures, the august character of the judges and the moderation of the penalties. But the principle must be established: it is always better to acknowledge in theory what cannot be avoided in practice.

A minister has the power to cause such great evil, without deviating from the letter of any positive law, that unless you prepare constitutional means to repress this evil and to punish and remove the culprit (for it is much more important to deprive the offending ministers of their power than to punish them), necessity will find those means outside the constitution itself. Men reduced to quibbling over terms or flouting procedures will become malicious, treacherous and violent. Failing to see any course traced out for them, they will open another which will be shorter, but also more disorderly and dangerous. There is in reality a force which no amount of skill can long elude. If, by directing against the ministers only the specific laws, which can never cover the totality of their acts and the general tendency of their administration, you shield them in practice from all laws, they will no longer be judged on the basis of your punctilious and impracticable legal prescriptions. They will be ruthlessly dealt with, for the anxieties they will have caused, the evil they will have committed and the degree of resentment which will follow from this.

What proves I am by no means a friend to arbitrary power when I make it a principle that the law on responsibility cannot possibly be as detailed as the common laws, that it is a political law, the nature and application of which contains inevitably a discretionary element, is that I have on my side, as I just mentioned, the example of the English. Not only has liberty existed among them for 134 years, without troubles or storms, but of all their ministers, exposed to an indefinite responsibility, and perpetually denounced by the opposition, only a very small number indeed have ever been brought to trial, and none at all has ever been sentenced to any punishment.

Our memories must not mislead us. We have been as furious and turbulent as slaves who break their irons. But today we have become a free people. If we continue to be such, if we organize with courage and frankness the institutions of liberty, we shall soon be as calm and wise as a free people.

I will not pause here to prove that the prosecution of ministers must be entrusted, as the constitution demands, to the representatives of the nation. But I wish to stress an advantage of the present constitution over all those that have preceded it. Accusation, prosecution, hearing, and verdict can all be made in public, whereas in the past it was, if not prescribed, at least permitted, for these solemn procedures to take place in secret.

As we find in men invested with authority, a constant desire to surround themselves with a mystery which, in their view, adds to their importance, I shall reproduce here some arguments, which I have already presented in another work,[1] in favour of making accusations public.

Some claim that such openness leaves state secrets at the mercy of imprudent orators, that the honour of ministers would be incessantly compromised by reckless accusations, and finally that these accusations, even if they were proved to be false, would nevertheless have given a dangerous shock to public opinion.

Yet state secrets are not as plentiful as charlatans like to claim, and ignorance to believe. Secrecy is indispensable only in a few rare and temporary circumstances, for example, for a particular military expedition, or for some decisive alliance in a time of crisis. In all other cases, the authorities can only wish for secrecy in order to act without opposition, and in most cases, after taking action, it regrets the absence of an opposition which might have enlightened it.

In those cases where secrecy is really necessary, discussions concerning responsibility have no tendency to divulge it. They are in fact debated only after the object which has caused them has already become public.

The right of peace and war, the running of military operations, that of negotiations, the conclusion of treaties, belong to the executive power. It is only when a war has actually been undertaken that ministers can become responsible for the legitimacy of that war. It is only after the success or failure of some expedition that the ministers can be called on to answer for it. It is only after the conclusion of some treaty that its content may be examined.

Discussions can thus occur only on issues which are already public. They do not divulge any facts. They merely place public facts in a different perspective.

The honour of ministers, far from requiring that any accusation directed against them should be shrouded in mystery, on the contrary imperiously demands that its examination should be made in broad daylight. A minister vindicated in secret has never been fully vindi-

[1] *De la responsabilité des ministres*, ch. 9.

cated. Accusations will not have remained unknown. The impetus that dictates them inevitably leads those who formulate them to reveal them. But revealed in this way, in vague conversations, they are bound to assume all the gravity that passion seeks to give them. Truth has no opportunity to refute them. You will not prevent the accuser from speaking, you will only prevent him from being answered. The ministers' enemies take advantage of the veil of secrecy covering the case to make any untruthful accusations they wish. A full, public explanation, in which the representative bodies of the nation enlightened the entire nation on the conduct of the accused ministers, would prove perhaps both their moderation and his innocence. A secret discussion would leave hanging over him the accusation, which has been rejected only by some mysterious inquiry, and weighing upon them an appearance of connivance, weakness or complicity.

The same arguments apply to the shock which you fear to give to public opinion. A powerful man cannot be accused without awakening that opinion and stirring up curiosity. It is impossible to avoid this result. What is necessary is to reassure the former, and this cannot be done without satisfying the latter. One does not conjure away dangers by shielding them from the public eye. Far from it: they grow from the very night which surrounds them. Objects look larger in the darkness. In the shadow, everything appears gigantic and hostile.

Thoughtless declamations, unfounded accusations, wear themselves out; they discredit themselves and finally cease by the mere effect of that opinion which judges and withers them. They are dangerous only under despotism, or in demagogies with no constitutional counterweight. Under despotism, in spite of which they continue to circulate, they are taken up by everyone in opposition; in demagogies because, all powers being united and confused, as in a despotism, whoever dominates them by subjugating the crowd with his oratory, is the absolute master. It is despotism under another name. But when the powers are balanced and they restrain one another, words cannot have such a rapid and immoderate effect.

In England too there are, in the House of Commons, ranters and troublemakers. Yet what happens? They talk, no-one listens to them, and they fall silent. The same interest which makes an assembly attached to its own dignity teaches it to restrain its members without seeking to stifle their voices. The public itself learns to judge violent harangues and unfounded accusations. Let it get its own education. It must do so. To interrupt it is simply to retard its progress. Observe, if you must, the immediate results. Let the law prevent disorders. But be quite clear that openness is the most infallible means of preventing them. It wins over to your side the majority of the nation, which otherwise you would have to represss, perhaps even to fight. That majority will assist you. You have reason to help you, but in order to obtain this help you must not keep it in ignorance. You must instead enlighten it.

Do you wish to be sure that a people will remain peaceful? Tell it all you can about its own interests. The more it knows, the more it will judge healthily and calmly. It takes fright at what is kept concealed from it, and it is enraged by its own fear.

The constitution grants to the ministers a special court. It takes advantage of the institution of the peerage to make it the judge of ministers in all those cases where no injured individual presents himself as their accuser. Peers are in fact the only judges whose understanding is sufficient and whose impartiality can be relied on.

The prosecution of ministers is, in practice, a trial between the executive power and the power of the people. In order to settle it, it is necessary to resort to a tribunal whose interests are distinct from both the people and the government, while being united with both by other interests.

The peerage combines these two conditions. Its privileges set apart from the people the individuals who are invested with them. They no longer have to return to the common condition. Consequently their interests are different from those of the people. But because the number of peers presents a constant obstacle to the participation of most of them in the government, the majority of them have, in this respect, an interest different from that of the government itself. At the same time, the peers are interested in the liberty of the people, since, if this liberty were annihilated, their own liberty and dignity would disappear. They are likewise interested in the maintenance of the government since, if the government were overthrown, their own rank would collapse with it.

Because of the independence and neutrality which characterizes it, the chamber of peers is the appropriate judge for the ministers. Placed in a position which naturally inspires a conservative spirit in those who occupy it; educated in the knowledge of the great interests of the state; initiated through their offices into most of the secrets of the adminis-

tration, the peers derive in addition from their social position a serious-
ness which confers maturity on their inquiry and a mildness of manners
which, by predisposing them to care and attention, supplements the
positive law with the delicate scruples of equity.

The representatives of the nation, called to watch over the use of
power and the acts of public administration, more or less informed
about the details of negotiations since the ministers are obliged to
report to them about these when they are concluded, may appear as
well-qualified as the peers to decide whether the ministers deserve
approval or blame, indulgence or punishment. But the representatives
of the nation, elected for a limited span of time, and needing to please
their electors, always resent their popular origin and their precarious
position. This situation places them in a spate of double dependence on
popularity and on favour. Moreover, they are often called on to display
their opposition to the ministers, and for the very reason that they may
become their accusers, they would not know how to be their judges.

As to ordinary courts, they can and may judge the ministers guilty of
offences against individuals, but their members are hardly suited to
pronounce upon issues which are political rather than judicial. They
are more or less strangers to a knowledge of diplomacy, of military
alliances, of financial operations. They know only imperfectly conditions in Europe, they have studied exclusively the codes of positive
laws, they are forced by their habitual duties to consult only the dead
letter of these, and to demand only their strictest application. The
subtle spirit of jurisprudence is opposed to the nature of those great
questions which must be considered from the public, national, sometimes even European perspective, and upon which the peers must
pronounce their verdict as supreme judges, in accordance with their
enlightenment, their honour and their conscience.

For the constitution in fact invests the peers with a discretionary
power not only to establish crimes, but also to inflict punishments.

In fact, the crimes of which ministers may prove guilty do not consist
either of a single act, or of a series of positive acts, each of which might
require a precise law. Nuances which cannot be described in words, let
alone captured by the law, may aggravate or mitigate them. Any attempt
to formulate on the responsibility of ministers as precise and detailed a
code as the criminal law should be, is inevitably illusory. The peers'
conscience is a competent judge, and this conscience ought to be able
to pronounce freely on the punishment as well as on the crime.

I would only have wished that the constitution had ordered that no disgraceful punishment should ever fall upon the ministers. Punishments which carry disgrace have general defects, which become even more regrettable when they fall upon men who have previously been seen in a brilliant position. Whenever the law arrogates to itself the right to distribute honour and shame, it encroaches clumsily upon the domain of public opinion, and this latter is inclined to claim its own supremacy. A struggle follows which is always to the disadvantage of the law. This struggle is bound to take place especially in the case of political crimes, on which opinions are necessarily divided. Men's moral sense is weakened when we order them to display esteem or contempt in the name of authority. This sensitive and delicate feeling is hurt by the violence to which it is thus subjected, and the result is that, in the end, a people no longer knows what is contempt and what is esteem.

Disgraceful punishments directed against men whom it is useful, when in office, to surround with consideration and respect, in some measure degrade them in advance. The sight of a minister subjected to a degrading punishment would demean in the eyes of the people the minister still in power.

Finally, human nature is only too inclined to trample upon fallen greatness. Beware of encouraging this tendency! What, after a minister's fall, would be called hatred of his crime, would most often be only a remnant of envy and contempt for unhappiness.

The constitution has not limited the right of pardon which belongs to the head of state. He may then exercise it in favour of condemned ministers.

I know that this clause has raised alarm in more than one sensitive spirit. A monarch, it has been argued, can order his ministers to perform guilty acts, and subsequently pardon them for these. It is therefore to encourage, by the assurance of impunity, the zeal of servile ministers and the audacity of ambitious ones.

In order to assess this objection, it is necessary to return to the first principle of constitutional monarchy: inviolability. Inviolability presupposes that the monarch cannot act wrongly. It is evident that this hypothesis is a legal fiction, which does not really free from human affections and weaknesses the individual placed upon the throne. Yet it was felt that this legal fiction was necessary in the interests of order and of liberty itself, because, without it, there could be perennial disorder and warfare between the monarch and the factions. Thus one must respect this fiction in all its implications. If you abandon it for a moment, you plunge once more into all those dangers which you were attempting to avert. But you would certainly abandon it by restricting the prerogatives of the monarch on the pretext of his intentions. For this would be to admit that he is capable of wishing, and therefore of doing, something evil. From there on you have destroyed the hypothesis upon which his inviolability rests in the eyes of public opinion. The very principle of constitutional monarchy is under attack. According to this principle, we may envisage only the ministers themselves in the act of power. They are there to answer for it. The monarch is in a separate, sacred precinct. Your concerns, your suspicions, must never touch him. He has no intentions, no weaknesses, no connivance with his ministers, because he is not really a man[1] but an abstract and neutral power above the storms.

For the benefit of those who would stigmatize as metaphysical the constitutional perspective in which I consider this question, I shall willingly descend to the ground of practical application and morality, and I shall argue further that there would be another difficulty in refusing to the head of state the right to pardon the condemned ministers, a difficulty which would be all the graver the better founded the motive for limiting his prerogative.

It is indeed possible that a prince, seduced by the love of unlimited power, might instigate his ministers to plot culpably against the constitution or against liberty. These plots are uncovered. The criminal agents are accused and convicted. Their sentence is pronounced. What do you do if you dispute the prince's right to arrest the sword ready to strike the instruments of his secret ambitions, and if you force him to authorize their punishment? You force him to choose between his political duties and the most sacred duties of gratitude and affection. Zeal, although irregular, is still zeal, and no man could punish without ingratitude the devotion which he has accepted. In this way you force the prince to an act of cowardice and infamy. You abandon him to the remorse of his conscience, you debase him in his own eyes, and lower him in the eyes of his own people. This is what the English did when

---

[1] The partisans of despotism have also claimed that the king was not a mere man; but they have inferred from this that he could do anything and that his will replaced the laws. I argue that a constitutional king is not a mere man; but this is because he cannot do anything without his ministers, while his ministers cannot do anything except through the laws.

they forced Charles I to sign the execution of Strafford, and the degraded royal power was soon destroyed.

If you wish to preserve both monarchy and liberty, struggle with courage against the ministers to secure their dismissal. But in the prince, respect the man while honouring the monarch. Respect in him the feelings of the heart, because these feelings always deserve respect. Do not suspect mistakes which the constitution orders you to ignore. Especially, do not reduce the monarch to repair them through rigours which, directed against his too blindly faithful servants, would become crimes.

Notice that if we are a nation, if we have free elections, these mistakes will not be dangerous. The ministers, though unpunished, will nonetheless be disarmed. Let the prince exercise his prerogative in their favour. The pardon will be granted, but the crime will be acknowledged. The culprit will lose his authority, since he could hardly continue to govern the state when the majority accuse him, nor could he create for himself, through new elections, a new majority, because in those elections public opinion would replace within the assembly the accusing majority.

If, on the other hand, we were not a nation, if we were incapable of having free elections, all our precautions would be vain. We would never use the constitutional means which we prepare. We might, indeed, continue to triumph in horrible times through brutal violence. But we would never watch, accuse or judge our ministers. We would only hasten to proscribe them once they had been deposed.

Once a minister has been condemned, whether he has been subjected to the penalty established in his sentence, or whether he has benefited from the monarch's pardon, he must be preserved in future from all those various persecutions that the victorious parties direct, on different pretexts, against the vanquished. In order to justify their persecutory measures, these parties affect excessive anxieties. They know well enough that these anxieties are unfounded, and that one would honour man too much by imagining so warm an attachment to a fallen power. However, hatred hides beneath the appearance of cowardice, and, in order shamelessly to persecute a defenceless individual, he is presented as an object of terror. I should like the law to put up an insurmountable barrier to all these belated rigours, and that, after having condemned the culprit, it took him under its protection. I wish it were established that no minister, after being subjected to his punishment, could be exiled, imprisoned or removed from his home. I cannot think of anything more shameful than those prolonged proscriptions. They either degrade nations or they corrupt them. Anyone capable of noble and elevated feelings will sympathize with the victim. The minister, whose punishment had been applauded by public opinion, finds himself surrounded by public pity when his legal punishment is arbitrarily aggravated.

It follows from these arrangements that ministers will often be denounced, sometimes accused, rarely condemned, and almost never punished. At first sight this result might appear insufficient to those men who think that for the crimes of ministers, as for those of individuals, a positive and severe punishment represents an exact justice and an absolute necessity. I do not share this opinion. It seems to me that responsibility must, above all, secure two aims: that of depriving guilty ministers of their power, and that of keeping alive in the nation – through the watchfulness of her representatives, the openness of their debates and the exercise of freedom of the press applied to the analysis of all ministerial actions – a spirit of inquiry, a habitual interest in the maintenance of the constitution of the state, a constant participation in public affairs, in a word a vivid sense of political life.

On the question of responsibility, then, the problem is not, as it is in ordinary circumstances, to make sure that innocence should never be threatened and crime never go unpunished. In questions of this nature crime and innocence are seldom entirely evident. What is essential is that the conduct of ministers be readily subjected to scrupulous investigation and that, at the same time, they should be allowed ample resources for avoiding the consequences of such investigation, if their crime, were it proved, is not so odious as to deserve no mercy not only from the laws, but also in the eyes of universal conscience and equity, which are more indulgent than the written laws.

This mildness in the practical application of responsibility is merely a necessary and just consequence of the principle upon which my whole theory rests.

I have shown that responsibility can never be free from a certain degree of arbitrariness. But arbitrary power is, in all circumstances, a serious drawback.

If it affected simple citizens, nothing could legitimate it. The pact between citizens and society is clear and formal. They have promised to respect its laws, and society has promised to make these laws known to them. If they remain faithful to their commitment, society cannot exact anything more. They have the right to know clearly what will be the consequence of their actions, each of which must be taken separately and judged according to a precise text. The ministers have made a different pact with society. They have voluntarily accepted, in the hope of glory, power or fortune, vast and complicated functions, forming a compact and invisible unity. None of their ministerial actions can be taken in isolation. They have thus consented to their conduct being judged as a whole. Yet this cannot be done by any specific law. Hence there follows that discretionary power which must be exercised over them.

It is required by scrupulous equity, indeed, it is the strict duty of society, to bring to the exercise of this power all the mitigations compatible with the security of the state. Hence this particular tribunal, composed in such a way that its members may be preserved from all popular passions. Hence that power given to the tribunal of pronouncing itself only in accordance with its own conscience, and of choosing or mitigating the penalty. Hence finally the appeal to the clemency of the king, a recourse ensured to all subjects, but more favourable to the ministers than to anyone else, because of their personal relations.

Yes: the ministers will seldom be punished. But if the constitution is free and the nation energetic, of what importance is the punishment of a minister when, stricken by a solemn judgement, he re-enters the class of ordinary citizens, more impotent in fact than the lowest of citizens, because disapproval accompanies and pursues him? Liberty has nonetheless been preserved from his attacks, the public spirit has not failed to receive that salutary shock which enlivens and purifies it, social morality has not failed to obtain the dramatic homage of power called before its bar and smitten by its sentence.

Mr Hastings was not punished: but that oppressor of India appeared on his knees in front of the House of Lords while the voices of Fox, of Sheridan, of Burke, avenging a humanity long trampled under foot, awoke in the soul of the English people emotions of generosity and feelings of justice, and forced mercenary motives to disguise their greed and their violence.[a]

Lord Melville was not punished,[b] and I do not wish to question his

---

[a] T. B. Macaulay, *Warren Hastings* in *Critical and Historical Essays* (2 vols., London, 1856), vol. 2, pp. 181–243.
[b] Henry Dundas, Viscount Melville (1742–1811), tried for corruption, was absolved by the House of Lords in 1806.

innocence. But the example of a man, grown old in the habit of dexterity and the skill of speculation, yet denounced despite his adroitness, accused notwithstanding his many connections, has reminded those who followed the same career that there is value in disinterestedness and security in rectitude.

Not even Lord North was accused. But by threatening him with accusation his opponents renewed the principles of constitutional liberty, and claimed the right of each part of the state to bear the burdens to which it has consented.[a]

Finally, in even remoter times, the persecutors of Wilkes were punished only with fines, but their prosecution and judgement re-enforced the guarantees of individual liberty, and consecrated the axiom that an Englishman's home is his castle.[b]

Such are the advantages of responsibility, not merely a few imprisonments and executions.

The death, or even the imprisonment of a man have never been necessary for the security of the people, because that security must rest in the people itself. A nation which should fear for the life or liberty of a minister deprived of his power would be an unhappy nation indeed. It would resemble those slaves who killed their masters for fear that they might reappear with the whip in their hands.

If it is as an example for future ministers that we wish ministers declared guilty to be treated with rigour, I would say that the pain of an accusation resounding across Europe, the shame of a trial, being deprived of an eminent position, the isolation, troubled by remorse, which follows disgrace, are sufficiently severe punishments, sufficiently instructive lessons for ambition and pride.

It must be noted that this indulgence towards the ministers as regards their responsibility does not in any way compromise the rights and security of individuals, because the crimes which violate these rights and threaten this security are subjected to other procedures and judged by other judges. A minister may be wrong about the legitimacy or utility of a war; he may be wrong as to the necessity of a concession in

---

[a] Frederick Lord North, Earl of Guildford (1733–92). His responsibility for the successful revolt of the American colonies against Great Britain led to his resignation in 1782.

[b] John Wilkes (1727–97) was expelled from the House of Commons on 19 January 1764 and on 21 February was convicted by the Court of the King's Bench for republishing the 'North Briton' No. 45 and an 'Essay on Woman'. In November 1769, he brought his action against Lord Halifax, for false imprisonment and the seizure of his papers, and obtained an award of £4,000 in compensation.

a treaty; he may err in a financial operation. It is therefore necessary that his judges should be invested with the discretionary power to assess his motives, that is to say, to weigh up uncertain probabilities. But a minister cannot be mistaken when he illegally infringes the liberty of a citizen. He knows that he is committing a crime. He knows it as well as any individual who is guilty of the same violence. Thus the indulgence which is a form of justice in the examination of political questions must disappear when we deal with illegal or arbitrary acts. In such cases, the common laws resume all their strength, ordinary tribunals must pronounce their sentence, penalties must be precise and their application literal.

The king may, no doubt, remit the punishment. He may do it in this case as in any other. But his clemency towards the culprit does not deprive the individual who has been injured of the compensation which the tribunals have granted him.[1]

Chapter 10

On the declaration that ministers are unworthy of public trust

Among the projects presented last year on the issue of responsibility, there was a proposal to replace formal accusation with a procedure milder in appearance, whenever mismanagement on the part of the ministers had compromised the security of the state, the dignity of the crown or the liberty of the people without directly violating any positive law. This proposal was to invest the representative assemblies with the right to declare the ministers undeserving of public trust.

I shall first observe that this declaration against the ministers is, in fact, made every time they lose a majority in the assemblies. When we have what we still lack, and yet is an absolute necessity in any consti-

[1] I did not think it necessary here to reply to the reproach of slowness against those forms which the constitution has prescribed for the accusation and trial of ministers. One must indeed be in a hurry to find forty days too long a lapse of time to examine the most complex of questions, and to pronounce upon the destiny of men who have held in their hands the fortunes of the state.

tutional monarchy – I mean a ministry acting in accord, a stable majority and an opposition well separated from that majority – no minister will be able to keep his post if he does not have the greatest number of votes, unless the people are called to new elections. In that case, those new elections will be the touchstone of the trust enjoyed by that minister. I cannot therefore see in the declaration which is being proposed in place of the accusation, anything but the statement of a fact which proves itself without the need to proclaim it. Moreover, I believe that such a declaration, from the very fact that it will be less solemn and will appear less severe than a formal accusation, will be likely to be more frequently employed. If you fear that the accusation itself may be used too often, it is because you presume the assembly factious. But if the assembly is indeed factious, it will be readier to vilify the ministers than to accuse them, as it will be able to vilify them without compromising them with a declaration which does not commit it to anything, which does not call for any inquiry nor demand any proof, which is, in sum, a mere cry of vengeance. If the assembly is not factious, why should we invent such a formula, useless in this hypothesis, and dangerous in the other?

Secondly, when the ministers are accused, a tribunal is instructed to judge them. This tribunal, by its judgement, whatever this might be, re-establishes the harmony between the government and the representatives of the people. But there is no tribunal which can pronounce on the declaration in question. This declaration is an act of hostility, the more deplorable in its potential effects, in so far as it has no fixed and necessary outcome. The king and the representatives of the people are confronted with one another, and you lose the great advantage of having a neutral authority to arbitrate between them.

Moreover this declaration is a direct attack upon the royal prerogative. It questions the prince's freedom of choice. The same is not true of the accusation. The ministers may have become guilty, without the monarch having been wrong to nominate them before they were so. When you accuse the ministers, it is them alone whom you attack: while when you declare them undeserving of public trust, the prince is also under accusation, either for his intentions, or for his understanding; and this is something that must never happen in a constitutional government.

The essence of royalty in a representative monarchy is the independence of the nominations assigned to it. The king never acts in his own name. Placed at the summit of all powers, he creates some, moderates others, directs political life in this way, tempering it without taking part in it. It is from this that his inviolability derives. We must therefore leave this prerogative intact and respected. His right to choose must never be contested. The assemblies must never arrogate to themselves the right to exclude, a right which, obstinately exercised, implies the end of that of nomination.

I hope I shall not be accused of being too favourable towards absolute authority. I wish royalty to be invested with all the strength, surrounded by all the veneration, necessary for the safety of the people and the dignity of the throne.

Let the deliberations of the assemblies be perfectly free. Let the press, freed from all impediments, aid, encourage and enlighten them. Let the opposition enjoy the privileges of the most daring discussion. Deny it no constitutional resource to deprive the ministry of its majority. But do not trace out for it a course along which, once opened, it will always rush headlong. The declaration which is proposed will become, according to the circumstances, a formula without consequences or a weapon in the hands of factions.

I shall add that, for the ministers themselves, it is better to be sometimes accused, perhaps lightly, than to be exposed at any moment to a vague declaration, against which it would be much more difficult to guarantee them. It is a great argument in the mouth of the defenders of a minister this simple phrase: accuse him!

I have already said this, and I shall repeat it: the trust a minister enjoys or the suspicion he inspires are proved by the majority which either supports or deserts him. This is the legal course, the constitutional expression. It is superfluous to look for any other.

CHAPTER 11

On the responsibility of subordinates

It is not sufficient to have established the responsibility of ministers; this responsibility has no existence unless it begins with the immediate executor of the act which is its object.

It must weigh upon all the levels of the constitutional hierarchy.

When no legal route is laid out to subject all the officials to the accusation which they may all deserve, the mere appearance of responsibility is only a trap, ruinous for those who might be tempted to believe in it. If you punish only the minister who issues an illegal order, while leaving unpunished the instrument who executes it, you set reparation so high that it is often impossible to attain it. It would be as if you advised a man being attacked by another to direct his blows only to the head, but not to the arms of his aggressor, on the pretext that his arm is only a blind instrument, while it is in his head that the will, and consequently the crime, resides.

But, some will object, if subordinates can be punished, in whatever circumstances, for their obedience, you authorize them to judge the measures of the government before enforcing them. By this simple fact the whole action of the government is impeded. Where will you find officials, if obedience is dangerous? In what state of impotence will you place all those who are invested with authority! Into what uncertainty will you throw all those who are charged with its execution?

I shall answer in the first place that, if you prescribe for the officials of authority the absolute duty of an implicit and passive obedience, you let loose upon human society instruments of arbitrariness and oppression which any blind or furious power may unleash at will. Which of these two evils is greater?

But I believe I must, at this point, revert to some more general principles on the nature and possibility of passive obedience.

This obedience, as it is praised and recommended to us is, thank God, utterly impossible. Even in military discipline there are limits to this passive obedience, which, whatever abstract arguments are put forward, the nature of things established for it. It is wrong to maintain that armies must be like machines and that a soldier's intelligence lies in the commands of his corporal. Must a soldier, on the orders of his drunken corporal, shoot his captain? He must therefore recognize whether his corporal is drunk or not. He must reflect that the captain's authority is superior to the corporal's. We can see from this example that both intelligence and reflection are needed from the soldier. Must a captain, on the orders of his colonel, go along with his company, as obedient as himself, and arrest the minister of war? Here the captain too needs both intelligence and reflection. Must a colonel, on the orders of the minister of war, make a direct attempt on the life of the head of state? Again, intelligence and reflection are expected from the colonel.[1] Those who praise passive obedience do not take into account that over-docile instruments may be seized by any sort of hands, and turned against those who were originally their masters; that the same intelligence which predisposes man to inquiry helps him also to distinguish right from violence, to tell who really has the authority to give orders and who is usurping it.

[1] My opinion on passive obedience has been disputed by arguments which I think it useful to report, because they seem to me to add to the evidence of the principles which I have attempted to establish.

I asked 'whether a soldier must, on the order of his corporal, shoot his captain.' I was told: 'It is clear that the soldier, by the very principle of obedience, will have greater respect for his captain than for his corporal.' But I had said the same thing: 'The soldier must reflect that the captain's authority is superior to the corporal's.' Is this not exactly the same idea? Or are people worried by the word 'reflect'? But if the soldier does not reflect on the difference of rank which distinguishes these two men equally called to give him orders, how can the principle of obedience be applied? In order to know that one of them is entitled to a greater respect than the other, he must understand the distance between them.

I said 'that as a general principle, discipline was the indispensable basis of all military organization, and that if this rule had limits, these limits could not be described, they had to be felt.' What did my opponents reply? 'That cases like this are rare and indicated by one's inner feelings, and that they constitute no obstacle to the general rule.' Do we not find here not only conformity of principles, but even repetition of the same words? Are not the 'inner feelings' equivalent to 'limits which cannot be described, but can be felt?'. And is a 'general rule' different from a 'general principle'?

Again, I said that 'the guard or officer who had contributed to the illegal arrest of a citizen, would not be justified by the order of a minister.' Notice the word 'illegal arrest'. What has been the objection? 'That subordinates have only two things to consider.' Observe incidentally this expression 'two things to consider'. When I argue that inquiry is inevitable, I am not wrong, as the partisans of passive obedience are themselves forced to resort to it. The two things to consider are whether the order given them emanates from the authority on which they depend, and whether the request addressed to them falls within the authority of the agent who has issued it. This is all I ask. Some seem to confuse the arrest of an innocent person with an illegal arrest. An innocent person can be arrested very legally indeed if he is suspected. The executor of the order of arrest, military or civilian, does not need to inquire whether the object of the order he has received does or does not deserve to be arrested. What matters, is that the order should be legal, that is that it emanates from an authority who has the right to give it, and that it follows the prescribed forms. This is my doctrine, and it is also the doctrine of my alleged opponents. They say it in their own words: 'The guard or soldier . . . will only have to consider whether he has been charged with his mission by a competent or incompetent authority, and whether it is or is not in accord with the ordinary course of things and with the usual forms of justice and administration. If this is the case, he will execute the orders he has received blindly and he will be right.' No doubt he will be right. Who disputes it? But in order to know whether the authority who gives him orders is competent, and if the order is in or is not in accord with the ordinary course of things and the forms of justice, must he not examine, compare, judge? I do not add this note to answer an already forgotten newspaper article, but to show that the thesis of passive obedience cannot be sustained, that the same people who think they are defending it are forced to abandon it, and that, no matter how hard we try, we can never exclude human intelligence from human affairs.

Nobody doubts that, as a general principle, discipline is the basis of all military organization; that punctuality in the execution of received orders is the necessary resort of all civil administration. Yet this rule has its limits. These limits defy description since it is impossible to foresee all the cases which may arise. But they can be felt, everyone's reason makes him aware of them. He is their judge, and necessarily their only judge. He judges them at his own risk and danger. If he is wrong, he must bear the consequences. But man can never be made totally incapable of examination, and set aside that intelligence which he has been given by nature to guide him, and which no profession can prevent him from using.[1]

Undoubtedly the possibility of being punished for having obeyed will sometimes plunge subordinates into painful uncertainty. It would be more convenient for them to be either zealous automatons or intelligent mastiffs. Yet there is uncertainty in all human affairs. In order to free himself from all uncertainty, man would cease to be a moral being. Reasoning is simply a comparison of arguments, of possibilities and of chances. Where there is comparison there is the possibility of error, and consequently uncertainty. But for that uncertainty there is, in a well-constituted political organization, a remedy which not only makes up for the errors of individual judgement, but which shelters man from the too disastrous consequences of such errors when they are

---

[1] It is worth observing that in France we do not lack laws still in existence, which by decreeing penalties against the executors of illegal orders, without excepting, and indeed even formally including military personnel, oblige these personnel thereby to compare with these laws the orders they receive from their superiors. The law of 13 Germinal, year VI (2 April 1798) says, in article 165: 'Any officer, non-commissioned officer or gendarme who gives, signs, executes or who has executed the order to arrest some individual or who actually arrests him other than *in flagrante delicto*, or in the cases provided for by the law, to deliver him directly to the police authorities, will be prosecuted criminally and punished as guilty of the crime of arbitrary detention.' The guard or officer must therefore judge, before they obey, whether the individual whom they must arrest falls into the category of *flagrante delicto*, or one of the other cases provided for by the law. Following article 166, the same penalty will be applied for the detention of an individual in a place not legally and publicly designed to serve as place of arrest, trial or prison. Before they obey, the guard or officer must therefore judge, whether the place where they are to bring the person arrested is a legally and publicly designed place of detention. Article 169 says that, except in the cases of flagrant crime indicated by the laws, the *gendarmerie* will not have the power to arrest any individual except in virtue of a mandate to convey or to arrest following the prescribed forms, either an arrest warrant, a formal charge or a sentence. It is up to the guard or officer to decide all this before obeying. Here we have, I think, a sufficient number of cases in which the armed forces are called on to consult the laws; and in order to consult them, they will necessarily have to make use of their reason.

innocent ones. This remedy, of which the agents of the administration must be able to benefit like all other citizens, is trial by jury. In all questions of a moral nature and of a complex character trial by jury is indispensable. Freedom of the press, for example, could never exist without trial by jury. Only juries may decide if such and such a book, in such particular circumstances, is or is not a crime. The written law cannot be made to fit every nuance of every possible crime. Common reason, that good sense natural to all men, appreciates these nuances. The members of the jury represent just that common sense. Similarly, when it is necessary to decide whether a particular official under the authority of a minister, and who has either lent or refused his obedience, has acted rightly or wrongly, the written law is all too inadequate. It is once again for common reason to pronounce. It is therefore necessary in this case to have recourse to juries, its sole interpreters. They alone can evaluate the motives that guided those agents, and the degrees of innocence, of merit or of culpability of either their resistance or their collaboration.

We must not fear that the instruments of authority, relying upon the indulgence of the jurors to justify their disobedience, may prove too inclined to disobey. Their natural tendency, strengthened in addition by their interest and self-regard, is always to obey. That is the price of the favours of authority. It has so many secret means of rewarding them for the inconveniences of their zeal! If the counter-weight had a defect, it would be rather that of being ineffective. But this at least is no reason for suppressing it. The jurors themselves will not prove overindulgent in allowing the agents of power a free rein. The need for order is innate in man. Moreover, in all those who have a mission, this inclination is strengthened by the feeling of the importance and consideration with which they surround themselves by showing themselves scrupulous and severe. The good sense of the jurors will easily accept that, in general, subordination is necessary, and their decisions will generally be in its favour.

I am struck by one particular consideration: you will say that I confer arbitrary power upon jurors: but you confer it upon the ministers. It is impossible, I repeat, to regulate everything, to write everything and to transform the life and relations of men into minutes drafted in advance, where only the names remain blank, and which spare future generations all examination, all thought, all recourse to intelligence. If, no matter what we do, there always remains something discretionary in human affairs, I ask whether it is not preferable that the exercise of power required by that discretionary element should be committed to men who exercise it only on a single occasion, who are neither corrupted nor blinded by the routines of authority, and who are equally interested in liberty and good order, rather than that it should be entrusted to men who have as their permanent interest, their own particular prerogatives.

Once again, you cannot maintain unrestricted your principle of passive obedience. It would endanger all that you aim to preserve. It would threaten not only liberty, but also authority; not only those who must obey, but also those who rule; not only the people, but also the monarch. You would no longer be able to indicate precisely each circumstance in which obedience ceases to be a duty and becomes a crime. Would you say that any clause which goes against the written constitution must not be enforced? You would be driven back willy-nilly to examine what is contrary to the established constitution. This examination would be for you that palace of Strigiline, to which the knights returned incessantly in spite of their efforts to get away from it. And who, anyway, is going to be entrusted with this examination? Not, I believe, the same authority who issued the order which you wish to examine. You will have to find a way of pronouncing a judgement in each case, and the best method is precisely to confer the right to pronounce a judgement on those men who are the most impartial, the most identified with both private and public interest. These men are the jurors.

The responsibility of officials is recognized in England from the lowest to the highest level, in such a way as to leave no doubt. This is proved by a curious fact, that I cite the more willingly because the man who availed himself of this particular circumstance of the principle of responsibility of all officials was obviously wrong on the particular issue at stake, and consequently the tribute rendered to the general principle is even more patent.

At the time of the contested election of Wilkes, one of the London magistrates, convinced that the House of Commons had exceeded their powers in some of their resolutions, declared that, since there was no longer a legitimate House of Commons in England, the payment of taxes exacted on the strength of a law which had become illegal was no longer compulsory. Accordingly, he refused the payment of all taxes, allowed his furniture to be seized by the tax collector, and subsequently

prosecuted that same collector for forcible entry and illegal confiscation of goods. The issue was brought before the courts. No-one
questioned the fact that the collector would be punishable if the
authority in the name of which he acted was not a legal one. The
president of the tribunal, Lord Mansfield, confined himself to proving
to the jury that the House of Commons had not lost its legitimate
character. From this it follows that had the collector been found guilty
of carrying out illegal orders, or orders emanating from an illegitimate
source, he would have been punished, although he was an instrument
subject to the minister of finance, and liable to be removed from his
office by that minister.[1]

Until now our constitutions contained an article destructive of the
responsibility of officials, which the Royal Charter of Louis XVIII had
carefully preserved. According to this article, it was impossible to
obtain recourse for any crime committed by the holder of the most
subordinate power without the formal consent of the authority itself. If
a citizen was ill-treated, defamed, injured in whatever way by the mayor
of his village, the constitution stood between him and his aggressor. In
this way there were, in that particular class of officials alone, at least
forty-four thousand considered inviolable, and perhaps two hundred
thousand at the other levels of the hierarchy. These inviolable officials
could do anything, and no tribunal could bring proceedings against
them as long as the superior authority remained silent. The Constitutional Act which we now have has eliminated this monstrous pro-
vision. The same government which has consecrated the freedom of
the press which the ministers of Louis XVIII had attempted to snatch
from us, the same government which has formally renounced the
power of exile, which the ministers of Louis XVIII had demanded, this
same government has restored to the citizens their legitimate right to
act against all the agents of power.

[1] I could have cited another fact, even more decisive, in the same affair. As one of the chief
agents of the ministers who prosecuted Mr Wilkes had, together with four King's
messengers, seized his papers and arrested five or six people considered as his accomplices, Mr Wilkes obtained one thousand pound sterling in damages against that
agent, who after all had acted only in accordance with ministerial orders. That agent was
ordered to pay that sum privately. The four King's messengers were equally indicted by
the court of Common Pleas by the other arrested persons, and given a two thousand pound
fine. Moreover, I have already proved in the previous note that we have in France similar
laws against the executors of illegal orders, such as guards and gaolers, in questions of
personal liberty, and such as the collectors of public revenue in questions of taxation.
Those who thought they were attacking me in their writings were instead attacking our
code, as it is at present in force and as it ought to be daily observed.

CHAPTER 12

On municipal power, local authorities and a new kind of federalism

The constitution makes no pronouncements on municipal power, or on the composition of local authorities in the different parts of France. The representatives of the nation will have to see to it as soon as peace restores the calm which is necessary to improve our internal organization. Indeed, this is, after national defence, the most important subject to call to their attention. It is therefore not out of place to discuss it here.

The administration of our affairs is a matter for all of us, that is, for our representatives and delegates. What concerns only a few must be decided by that few; what concerns only the individual must be decided by that individual alone. We cannot repeat often enough that the general will is by no means due more respect than the individual will, whenever it strays from its own sphere.

Let us imagine a nation of a million individuals, divided into whatever number of communes. In each commune, every individual will have interests that concern him alone, and that consequently must not be subjected to the jurisdiction of the commune. There will be others that are of interest to the other inhabitants of the commune as well, and those will belong to the communal competence. Similarly these communes will have interests that concern only their internal organization, and others which may extend to a whole district. The former will be of purely communal concern, the latter will involve the district, and so on, up to those general interests common to each of the million individuals who compose its population. Clearly it is only interests of this last kind over which the whole population or its representatives have legitimate jurisdiction. If, instead, they interfere in the interests of districts, communes or individuals, they exceed their competence. Just the same would be true of a district which interfered with the particular interests of the commune or the commune which encroached upon the purely individual interests of one of its members.

National authority, the authority of the district, the authority of the commune, must remain, each of them, in its own sphere, and this leads us to establish a truth which we consider fundamental. Until now local power has been regarded as a dependent branch of executive power.

On the contrary, although it must never encroach upon the latter, it must by no means depend on it.

If we entrust to the same hands the interests of both small groups and the state, or if we make the custodians of the former the agents of the custodians of the latter, a number of different kinds of disadvantages will follow, and even those disadvantages which appear to be mutually exclusive will coexist with one another. The execution of the laws will often be hindered because the executors of those laws, being at the same time the custodians of the interests of those whom they administer, would attend to the interests which they are entrusted with protecting at the expense of the laws which they are entrusted with executing. Moreover, the interests of the administered too will often be injured because the administrators will be anxious to please a superior authority: and generally these two evils will occur simultaneously. The general laws will be badly executed, and the partial interests poorly protected. Whoever has reflected on the organization of municipal power in the different constitutions which we have experienced, must have convinced themselves that some effort on the part of executive power has always been necessary in order to get laws implemented, while there has always been a mute opposition, or at least an inert resistance, on the part of the municipal power. This constant pressure on the part of the first of these powers, this silent opposition of the second, were ever impending causes of dissolution. We still remember the complaints of the executive power, under the constitution of 1791, that municipal power was in constant opposition to it; and, under the constitution of the year III [1795], that the local administration was stagnant and impotent. The truth is that in the first of these constitutions there were, in the local administrations, no officials actually subject to the executive power; while in the second these administrations were so dependent, that the result was apathy and discouragement.

For as long as you make members of municipal power subordinate agents of the executive power, it will be necessary to give to this latter the right to dismiss them, so that your municipal power may be more than a mere ghost. If you have them elected by the people, this nomination will merely serve to lend it the appearance of a popular mission. This will set it in opposition to the superior authority, and will impose upon it duties which it will have no chance of fulfilling. The people will have elected their administrators only to see their choices annulled, and to be incessantly wounded by the exercise of an alien force that, under the pretext of the general interest, interferes with the particular interests which ought to be most independent of it.

The obligation to give grounds for dismissals is for executive power a derisory formality. As no-one can judge its motives, this obligation compels it only to discredit those whom it chooses to dismiss.

Municipal power must occupy, in the administration, the place of the justices of the peace in the judicial order. It is a power only in relation to those it administers, or rather it is their authorized representative for those affairs which concern themselves alone.

To those who object that the administered to will not wish to obey municipal power because it will be surrounded only by scanty forces, I shall answer that they will obey it because it is in their interest to do so. Men who are brought close to one another have a vested interest in not causing themselves mutual damage, in not alienating their mutual affections, and consequently in observing those domestic rules, one might almost say family rules, which they have imposed upon themselves. Finally, if the citizens' disobedience bore upon matters of public order, the executive power would intervene, as the custodian of public order, but it would intervene through direct agents, distinct from the municipal administrators.

For the rest, it is too readily assumed that men have a natural inclination to insubordination. Their natural disposition, when they are not either vexed or irritated, is rather to obey. At the beginning of the American revolution, from the month of September 1774 until the month of May 1775, the Congress was simply a deputation of legislators from the different provinces, and had no other authority than the one voluntarily accorded to it. It could neither dictate nor promulgate laws. It confined itself to issuing recommendations to the provincial assemblies, which were free not to follow them. Nothing coming from it was coercive. Yet it was more cordially obeyed than any other government in Europe. I do not cite this as a model, but as an example.

I do not hesitate to say: we must introduce into internal administration a great deal of federalism, but a federalism different from the one known up to now.

The name of federalism has been given to an association of governments which preserved their mutual independence, and were kept together merely by external political links. This institution is especially pernicious. On the one hand federal states claim over the individuals or portions of their territory a jurisdiction which they should not have; while on the other hand they pretend to maintain, in relation to municipal power, an independence which should not exist. Thus federalism is compatible both with internal despotism and external anarchy.

The internal constitution of a state and its external relations are intimately connected. It is absurd to wish to separate them and to submit the latter to the supremacy of the federal link, while leaving to the former full liberty. An individual ready to enter society with other individuals has the right, the interest and the duty to collect information about their private lives, because on their private lives depends the fulfilment of their obligations towards him. Similarly, a society that wishes to be united with another society has the right, the duty and the interest to inform itself about its internal constitution. Indeed a mutual influence must be established between them, because on the principle of their constitution may depend the execution of their respective commitments or the security of the country, for example, in the case of invasion. Each partial society, each group, must consequently be in a state of greater or lesser dependence, even for its internal organization, on the general association. But at the same time the internal arrangements of the particular groups, since they have no influence upon the general association, must remain in perfect independence, and just as in individual life that part which in no way threatens the social interest must remain free, similarly in the life of groups, all that does not damage the whole collectivity must enjoy the same liberty.

Such is the kind of federalism which seems to me useful and possible to establish among us. If we fail, we shall never achieve a peaceful and lasting patriotism. Love of one's birthplace, especially today, is the only true patriotism. We can find the pleasures of social life everywhere; it is habits and memories alone which cannot be recreated. Men must, therefore, be attached to those places which offer them memories and habits, and, in order to attain this aim, it is essential to grant them, in their homes, in their communes, as much political importance as possible without injuring the general good.

Nature would favour governments in this tendency if they did not resist it. Love of one's birthplace is reborn from its own ashes as soon as the hand of power for a moment loosens its grip. The magistrates of the smallest commune like to embellish it. They carefully maintain their ancient monuments. In almost every village there is a learned man who likes to recount its rustic annals, and who is listened to with respect. The inhabitants are pleased with all that gives them the impression, however illusory, of being constituted as a national body, and united by particular bonds. One feels that, were they not hindered in the development of this innocent and beneficial inclination, they would soon develop what we might call a communal honour, an honour of the town, an honour of the province, which would be a pleasure and a virtue at the same time. The attachment to local customs draws on all disinterested, noble and pious feelings. It is a deplorable policy which turns it into a form of rebellion. All the interests are grouped in the capital city; there, all ambitions go to exercise themselves; the rest is immobile. The individuals, lost in an unnatural isolation, strangers to the place of their birth, cut off from all contact with the past, forced to live in a hurried present, scattered like atoms over an immense, flat plain, detach themselves from a fatherland which they can nowhere perceive, and whose whole becomes indifferent to them because they cannot place their affections in any of its parts.[1]

CHAPTER 13

On the right to declare war and make peace

Those who have accused our constitution of failing to adequately limit the prerogative of the government on the right to make peace and declare war, have looked at this question very superficially indeed, allowing themselves to be dominated by their memories, instead of

[1] It is with the greatest pleasure that I find myself in agreement on this point with one of my most intimate colleagues and friends, whose knowledge is as extensive as his character is estimable, M. Degerando. People fear, he says in manuscript letters which he has sent to me, what is called the spirit of place. We also have our fears: we fear what is vague and so general as to be indefinite. Unlike the scholastics, we do not believe in the 'reality of universals' in themselves. We do not think that in a state there are any more real interests than local interests, united when they are the same, balanced when they are different, but known and felt in all cases . . . Particular ties rather than weakening the general tie, strengthen it. In the gradation of sentiments and ideas, we care first for our family, then for our town, for the province, and finally for the state. If you break the intermediate links, you will not shorten the chain, you will destroy it. The soldier carries in his heart the honour of his company, of his batallion, of his regiment, and in this way he contributes to the glory of the entire army. Multiply, multiply the bonds which unite men. Make the fatherland a part of everything, reflected in your local institutions as in so many faithful mirrors.

reasoning according to principles. Public opinion is almost never wrong about the legitimacy of wars undertaken by any government; yet it is impossible to establish precise maxims to that effect.

To say that one must keep on the defensive is to say nothing at all. It is easy for the head of a state, by means of insults, threats and warlike preparations, to force his neighbour to attack him. In this case it is not the aggressor who is responsible, but he who had reduced the other to seeking his safety in aggression. Thus sometimes defence is merely adroit hypocrisy, while the offensive may become a precaution of legitimate defence.

Similarly, to forbid governments to continue hostilities beyond their own frontiers is again a useless precaution. When enemies have attacked us gratuitously, and we drive them back outside our frontiers, ought we, by stopping at some ideal line, to give them time to recover from their losses and resume their efforts?

The only possible guarantee against useless or unjust wars is the energy of representative assemblies. They grant the conscription of men, they consent to the taxes. It is they and the national sentiment which must guide them, that we should trust, either to support the executive power when the war is a just one, whether it must be carried beyond the limits of the national territory, in order to render the enemy harmless; or to force the same executive power to make peace, when the object of defence has been achieved, and security is assured.

Our constitution contains on this point all the necessary clauses and, indeed, the only ones which are reasonable.

It does not submit the ratification of treaties to the representatives of the people, except in the case of the exchange of a portion of the territory, and this with good reason. This prerogative granted to the assemblies can only incur disfavour. To break a treaty once concluded is always an odious and violent resolution; it is in some way an infringement of the law of nations which communicate with each other only through their governments. An assembly is always bound to lack knowledge of the facts. Consequently, it cannot judge the need for a treaty of peace. When the constitution makes it the judge of this, the ministers could engulf the national representation in popular hatred. One article skilfully inserted amongst the conditions of a peace treaty could leave an assembly with the alternative of either continuing the war, or sanctioning clauses that violate liberty or honour.

England must once again serve us as a model. Treaties are examined by parliament, not, however, in order to determine whether to reject or accept them, but to establish whether the ministers have fulfilled their duty in the negotiations. The disapproval of the treaty has as its only consequence the dismissal or impeachment of the minister who has served his country badly. This question does not harm the mass of the people, greedy for repose, against an assembly which seems willing to dispute their enjoyment of this, and yet this power always restrains the ministers before the conclusion of a treaty.

CHAPTER 14

On the organization of armed forces in a constitutional state

There exists in all countries, and especially in the great modern states, a force that, although it is not a constitutional power, is in practice a most formidable one: the armed forces.

In treating the difficult issue of its organization, one is at first distracted by a thousand memories of glory which surround and dazzle us, by a thousand feelings of gratitude which carry us away and overwhelm us. Certainly, in recalling a mistrust that legislators have always felt towards military power, in proving that the present condition of Europe adds to the dangers that have always existed, in showing how difficult it is for armies, whatever their basic elements, not to acquire involuntarily a spirit different from that of the people, we do not wish to be unjust to those who have so gloriously defended our national independence, to those who, by so many immortal deeds, have laid the foundations of French liberty. When enemies dare to attack a people within its own territory, the citizens become soldiers to repel them. They were citizens, they were indeed the foremost of citizens, those who liberated our frontiers from the foreigner who had profaned them, those who have cast down into the dust the kings who had challenged us. The glory which they have acquired, they will crown once more with a new glory. An aggression, more unjust than the one which they chastised twenty years ago, summons them to new efforts and new triumphs.

Yet extraordinary circumstances bear no relation to the ordinary organization of the armed forces, and it is this latter stable and regular condition which we intend to discuss.

We shall begin by rejecting those chimerical plans for the dissolution of any standing army, plans which have often been offered to us in their writings by philanthropic dreamers. Even if this project were feasible, it would never be carried out. We are not writing in order to develop vain theories, but to establish, if possible, a number of practical truths. We take as our first assumption that the situation in the modern world, the relations between peoples, in short, the present nature of things, make it necessary for all governments and all nations to dispose of a paid standing army.

Because he did not formulate the question in these terms, the author of the *Spirit of the Laws* failed to resolve it. He first argues[1] that the army must come from the people, and share the same spirit as the people, and in order to give it this spirit he proposes that those who enroll in the army should be sufficiently well-off to answer for their conduct, and that they should be enlisted only for a year: two conditions which are quite impracticable for us. If there is a standing army, he wishes the legislative power to be able to dissolve it at will. But would this corps of troops, invested as it would be with all the material force of the state, submit without a murmur to a purely moral authority? Montesquieu explains how things ought to be very well, but offers no means of realizing this state of affairs.

If liberty has been maintained in England for a hundred years, it is because no military force is needed within the country itself. This circumstance, particular to an island, makes her example impracticable on the Continent. The Constituent Assembly struggled against this almost insoluble difficulty. It felt that entrusting the king with the command of a hundred thousand men of sworn obedience, under commanders named by him, would endanger any constitution. Consequently, it relaxed the rules of discipline to such an extent that any army organized according to those principles would have been less a military force than an anarchic assembly. Our initial defeats, the impossibility of the French being defeated for long, the need to sustain a struggle without precedent in history, have corrected the errors of the Constituent Assembly. But the armed forces have become more formidable than ever.

A citizens' army is possible only when a nation is confined within a narrow territory. In that case the soldiers of that nation can be obedient,

---

[1] *Esprit des lois*, 11, 6.
[*Oeuvres complètes*, vol. 2, pp. 396–407: 'De la Constitution de l'Angleterre'.]

and yet render their obedience reasonable. Stationed in the heart of their native country, in their own homes, amongst subjects and governors whom they know, their intelligence to some degree enters into their submission; but a vast empire makes this idea utterly unrealistic. The subordination it requires from its soldiers turns them into passive and unreflecting agents. As soon as they are transferred, they lose all those points of reference which could previously have enlightened their judgement. As soon as an army finds itself in the presence of foreigners, of whatever elements it is formed, it becomes a force that may equally well serve or destroy. Send the inhabitant of the Jura to the Pyrenees and the inhabitant of the Var to the Vosges, and those men, subject to a discipline which isolates them from the natives of the region, will only see their own commanders, and will recognize these alone. Citizens in their place of birth, they will be soldiers everywhere else.

Consequently, to employ them in the interior of a country means exposing the country itself to all the inconveniences by which a great military force threatens liberty, and it is precisely this which has ruined so many free peoples.

Their governments have applied to the maintenance of domestic order principles which are suitable only for external defence. Bringing back to their country victorious soldiers, from whom, outside their territory, they had with good reason demanded passive obedience, they continued to demand the same obedience from them against their fellow citizens. Yet the question at issue was completely different. Why are soldiers who march against a foreign army not required to use their reason? Because the very colour of the flags of that army proves its hostile intentions, and such proof dispenses with any examination. But in the case of citizens this difference no longer exists. The failure to reason here acquires a completely different character. There are certain weapons the usage of which is forbidden by the law of nations even to those countries which make war upon one another. What those forbidden weapons are between peoples, military force must be between the governors and the governed: an instrument capable of enslaving a whole nation is too dangerous to be employed against the crimes of individuals.

Armed force has three different objects: the first is to repel foreigners. Is it not natural to place troops intended for achieving this aim as close to these foreigners as possible, that is to say on the frontiers? We do not need any defence against the enemy where there is no enemy.

The second object of armed force is to repress private crimes committed in the country itself. The force designed to repress these crimes must be completely different from the frontier troops. The Americans have realized this. Not a single soldier appears in their vast territory to maintain public order. Every citizen is obliged to assist the magistrate in the exercise of his duties. But this obligation has the defect of imposing odious duties on the citizens.

In our populous cities, with our multiple relations, the activity of our life, our business, our occupations and our pleasures, carrying out such a law would be vexatious or, rather, impossible. Every day a hundred citizens would be arrested for having refused to assist in the arrest of a single individual. It is therefore necessary for salaried officers voluntarily to undertake these sad duties. It is undoubtedly a misfortune to create a class of men in order to devote them exclusively to the pursuit of their fellows. Yet this is a lesser evil than that of blighting the souls of all the members of society by forcing them to lend their assistance to measures, the justice of which they cannot appreciate.

Here we already have two sorts of armed force. The first one will be composed of soldiers stationed at the frontiers and ensuring external defence. These will be distributed in different units under commanders who depend only on a central authority and placed so as to be easily united under a single commander in case of attack. The other part of the armed force will be destined for policing. This second type of armed force will not present the dangers of a large military establishment. It will be dispersed throughout the land, as it could hardly be grouped at a single point without leaving criminals unpunished everywhere else. This body will itself know what its function is. Used to pursuing rather than to fighting, to supervising rather than to conquering, having never known the intoxication of victory, the name of its commanders will never carry it beyond its duties, and all the authorities of the state will be sacred in its eyes.

The third object of armed force is to suppress unrest and seditions. The body intended for the suppression of ordinary crimes is not sufficient for this. But why resort to the frontier troops? Do we not have the national guard, formed of property holders and citizens? I should have a very bad opinion indeed of the morality and happiness of a people if such a national guard were to show itself favourable to rebels or if it hesitated to recall them to their legitimate duties.

Notice that the same reason that makes it necessary to have a special force to deal with private crimes does not apply when it comes to public ones. What is painful in the suppression of crimes is not the attack, the fighting or the danger. It is the spying, the following, the having to be ten against one, the arresting and seizing of culprits when they are unarmed. But against more serious disorders, rebellions, riotous assemblies, the citizens who love the constitution of their country, as all will love it, since their property and liberty will be guaranteed by it, will hasten to offer their help.

Some will perhaps argue that the reduction in the army which would result from placing it only on the frontiers would encourage neighbouring peoples to attack us. This reduction, which must certainly not be exaggerated, will always leave an armed centre, around which the national guards, already trained, will rally against a foreign attack. If your institutions are free, you must not doubt their zeal. Citizens are not slow to defend their country when they really have one. They will hasten to defend their independence outside when, within it, they enjoy liberty.

Such are, it seems to me, the principles which ought to preside over the organization of the armed forces in a constitutional state. Let us welcome our defenders with gratitude and enthusiasm. But let them cease to be soldiers for us, and be our equals and our brothers. All military spirit, every theory of passive subordination, everything which makes warriors fearful to our enemies must be left behind at the frontier of every free state. These means are necessary against foreigners towards whom we are always, if not in a state of war, at least in one of mistrust. But citizens, even when they are guilty, have imprescriptible rights which foreigners do not possess.[1]

CHAPTER 15

On the inviolability of property

In the first chapter of this work I argued that the citizens have individual rights, independent from all social authority, and that these rights are personal liberty, religious liberty, liberty of opinion, a guarantee against arbitrary power and the enjoyment of property.

[1] See *Réflexions sur les constitutions*, ch. VI.

I nevertheless distinguish the right of property from the other rights of individuals.

Several of those who have defended property through abstract arguments seem to me to have fallen into a serious error: they have represented property as something mysterious, predating society and independent from it. None of these statements is true. Property is by no means prior to society, as without the security which gives it a guarantee, property would simply be the right of the first occupant, in other words, the right of force, that is to say a right which is not a right at all. Property is not independent from society, because a social condition, albeit a very miserable one, can be conceived without property, while it is impossible to imagine property without a social condition.

Property exists only through society. Society found that the best way of making its members enjoy the goods common to all, or disputed by all before its institution, was to give a part of them to each, or rather to maintain everyone in the part that he found himself occupying, guaranteeing him its enjoyment together with the changes which such enjoyment might undergo, either because of the multiple contingencies of chance, or because some worked harder than others.

Property is merely a social convention. But if we recognize it as such, it does not follow from this that we consider it as less sacred, less inviolable, less necessary, than those writers who subscribe to a different system. Some philosophers have regarded its establishment as an evil, and its abolition as possible.[a] But in order to support their theories, they had recourse to a mass of suppositions, some of which could never be realized, and the least realistic of which are relegated to a time that we will not live to see. What they imagined is a hypothetical increase in man's enlightenment upon which it would be absurd to found our present institutions. But they have also presumed a reduction of the labour presently required for the subsistence of mankind beyond any remotely imagined level of invention. Certainly each of our mechanical discoveries, which replace with instruments and machines man's physical strength, is a conquest for human thought. And, in accordance with the laws of nature, because these conquests become easier in so far as they multiply, they are also bound to follow one another at an increasing speed. But total exemption from manual labour is still far away from what we have thus far done, and even from what we can imagine doing

---

[a] We know that Constant was critical of Godwin's views on the subject. In his manuscripts he also refers to the ideas of Mably and Linguet.

in this respect. Yet this exemption would be necessary to make the abolition of property possible, unless we wished, as some of these writers require, to share this labour equally among all members of society. But this division, were it anything more than a dream, would go against its own purpose: it would take away from thought that leisure which makes it strong and deep, from industry that perseverance which carries it to perfection, from all classes the advantages of habit, of the unity of purpose and of the centralization of forces. Without property, mankind would not progress and would remain in the most primitive and savage state of its existence. Everyone, finding himself compelled to provide alone for all his needs, would have to distribute his energies in order to achieve this, and, bent under the weight of these multiple cares, would never advance a single step. The abolition of property would be destructive of the division of labour, the precondition for the improvement of all the arts and sciences. The tendency towards progress, the favourite hope of the writers against whom I am arguing, would perish for lack of time and independence, while the gross and forced equality which they recommend to us would form an invincible obstacle to the gradual establishment of true equality, that of happiness and enlightenment.

Property, as a social convention, belongs to the competence, and is under the jurisdiction, of society. Society possesses over it rights which it does not have over the liberty, life and opinions of its members.

But property is intimately bound up with other aspects of human existence, some of which are in no way subjected to collective jurisdiction, while others are subjected to it only to a limited extent. Consequently society must restrain its action over property because it could hardly exercise this to its full extent without encroaching upon objects which are by no means subordinate to it.

Arbitrary power over property is soon followed by arbitrary power over people; first, because arbitrary power is contagious; secondly, because violation of property necessarily provokes resistance. Authority in this case deals ruthlessly with the oppressed who resist; and because it has chosen to take away from him his possessions, it is led also to violate his liberty.

I shall not discuss in this chapter illegal confiscations and other political attacks upon property. Such violences cannot be considered the current practice of regular governments. They share the nature of all arbitrary measures. They are merely a component, and an inseparable component, of such measures. Contempt for the property of men is soon followed by contempt for their security and their lives.

I shall confine myself to observing that, by such measures, governments gain much less than they stand to lose.[a] 'Kings', – Louis XIV writes in his memoirs – 'are absolute lords and naturally enjoy the full and free disposal of all the possessions of their subjects.'[a] But when kings regard themselves as the absolute masters of what their subjects possess, the subjects either hide what they have, or fight for it. If they hide it, it is so much lost to agriculture, to commerce, to industry, to all kinds of prosperity. If they squander it in frivolous, gross and unproductive pleasures, it is again so much turned away from useful employments and beneficial speculations. Without security, economy becomes deception, and moderation imprudence. When everything can be taken away, one must spend as much as possible, in order to increase one's chances of saving something from spoliation. Again, when all can be taken away, one must spend as much as possible, because all that is spent is snatched away from arbitrary power. Louis XIV thought he was expressing a view very favourable to the wealth of kings. On the contrary, he was saying something destined to ruin kings and their peoples alike.

There are other, less direct forms of spoliation of which I think it useful to speak more extensively.[1] Governments allow themselves to resort to them to diminish their debts or to increase their resources, now on the pretext of necessity, now on that of justice, always putting forward the interest of the state: in the same way as the zealous apostles of popular sovereignty believe that public liberty gains from obstacles to individual liberty, many financiers of our days seem to believe that the state is enriched by the ruin of individuals. Honour to our government, that has rejected these sophisms, and has forbidden itself these errors through a positive article in our Constitutional Act![c]

---

[1] I must warn the reader that here and there in this chapter he will find phrases taken from the works of the best authors on political economy and public credit. I have sometimes transcribed their words, as I thought it pointless to change them to say less well what they

---

[a] The confiscation of property had been abolished by the Royal Charter of 1814, but reintroduced by the *Acte additionnel*. Constant described Napoleon's insistence on rejecting his views on the issue in the *Mémoires sur les Cent-Jours*, 2nd edn., Paris, 1829, 2 vols., vol. 2, pp. 47–9.

[b] *Mémoires de Louis XIV, écrits par lui-même*, vol. 1, p. 156.

[c] Title 6, art. 63: 'All properties owned or acquired by law, and all credits guaranteed by the state are inviolable.'

The indirect attacks upon property, which are to be the subject of the following considerations, are divided into two classes.

I shall put in the first class partial or total bankruptcies, the reduction of the national debt, either in capital or in interest, the payment of these debts in terms of value inferior to their nominal value, the alteration of the currency, deductions, etc. I include in the second the acts of authority against men who have negotiated with the governments to supply them with the objects necessary to their military or civil enterprises; retroactive laws or measures against the enriched, the *chambres ardentes,*[a] the annullment of contracts, of concessions, of sales made by the state to private individuals.

Some writers have regarded the establishment of public debts as a cause of prosperity; my opinion is radically different. Public debts have created a new sort of property which does not attach its owner to the land like agricultural property, which does not require either assiduous labour or difficult speculations like industrial property, and, finally, which does not demand distinguished talents like that property which we have called intellectual. The creditor of the state is interested in the prosperity of his country only in the same way as any creditor is interested in the prosperity of his debtor. Provided the latter pays, he is satisfied. Negotiations aiming at ensuring payment are always good for him, no matter how expensive. The power of alienating his credit makes him indifferent to the likely, but remote chance of national ruin. There is no corner of the land, no manufacture, no source of production of which he may not contemplate the impoverishment with indifference, so long as there are other resources to supply the payment of his revenues.[1]

Property in public funds is of an essentially selfish and solitary nature, which may easily become hostile, because it exists only at the expense of others. Through a remarkable effect of the complicated organization of modern societies, while the natural interest of every nation is that taxes should be reduced to the smallest possible sum, the

had said already. But I have not always been able to cite them, because I drafted this chapter from memory, without having my notes to hand.

[1] Smith, *Wealth of Nations*, 5, 3.
[Smith, *Wealth of Nations*, vol. 2, pp. 907–47.]

---

[a] Special tribunals instituted by the king of France Henri II on 8 October 1547 to prosecute heresy. Their name referred to the probability that those prosecuted before them would be burnt at the stake.

creation of a public debt makes it the interest of a part of every nation that taxes should be increased.[1]

But whatever the damaging effect of public debts, they now represent an inevitable evil for large states. Those who usually provide for the national expenses by means of taxation are almost always forced to advance the money, and their advances form a debt. Moreover, the first unexpected expenditure compels them to borrow. As to those who have adopted the system of borrowing rather than that of taxation, and who create taxes only to meet the interests of their loans (such is roughly the system adopted in England in our time) a public debt is inseparable from their existence. Thus to recommend to modern states giving up resources offered to them by credit would be utterly vain.

Once a national debt exists, there is only one way of mitigating its damaging effects, and that is to respect it scrupulously. This will give it a kind of stability which assimilates it, as much as its nature permits, to other kinds of property.

Bad faith can never be a remedy for anything. By failing to pay public debts you add to the immoral consequences of a property that gives to its owners interests different from those of the nation to which they belong, the even more disastrous consequences of uncertainty and arbitrariness. These are the first causes of what is called stockjobbing, which never flourishes more than when the state fails to meet its commitments. Then all the citizens are reduced to finding in the risks of speculation some compensation for the losses which the authority has caused them to suffer.

Any distinction between creditors, any inquiry into the transactions of individuals, any search of the course that the government securities have followed and of the hands through which they have passed until their extinction, is already bankruptcy. A state contracts debts and gives its securities in payment to those men to whom it owes money. These men are forced to sell the securities which it has given them. On what pretext will the government invoke that sale to contest the value of those securities? The more it contests their value, the more they will depreciate. It will rely upon this further depreciation to accept them at an even lower price. This double progression, by reacting upon itself, will soon reduce the credit to nothing, and private investors to ruin. The original creditor was in a position to do whatever he liked with his bond.

[1] Necker, *Administr. des Fin.*, II, 378–9.
[*De l'administration des finances de la France*, vol. 2, pp. 378–9.]

If he sold his credit, it was certainly not his fault, as he was driven by necessity, but the fault of the state, that paid him back only in securities which he was forced to sell. If he sold his credit at a negligible price, it is not the fault of the buyer, who bought it with unfavourable prospects; the fault is once again the state's, which has created those unfavourable chances, since the credit sold would not have fallen to such a low price had not the state inspired mistrust.

By establishing that any security will lower its value by passing into a second set of hands on conditions of which the government must be unaware, because they are free and independent stipulations, circulation, which has always been regarded as a source of wealth, is turned into a cause of impoverishment. How can we justify such a policy, that refuses to its creditors their due, and devalues what it pays them? On what basis can the courts condemn a debtor who is himself the creditor of a bankrupting authority? What: shall I be dragged into a dungeon and stripped of all I possess because I cannot satisfy debts contracted on public credit; shall I come in front of the same tribune from which emanate the ruinous laws? On the one side will sit the power which robs me, on the other the judges who punish me for having been robbed.

All nominal payment is a form of bankruptcy. All issuing of paper which cannot be converted into bullion at will is, says a commendable French author, spoliation.[1] That those who perpetrate it should be invested with public power can hardly change the nature of their act. The authorities which pay the citizens in imaginary values force them to make similar payments. To avoid blighting their own operations, and making these impossible, they are obliged to legitimize all similar operations. By creating the necessity for some, they offer an excuse to all. Egoism, far subtler, far more adroit, far prompter, far more differentiated than authority, hurls itself forward at the given signal. It overturns all precautions by the rapidity, the complication, the variety of its frauds. When corruption may be justified by necessity, it has no limits. If the state wants to establish a difference between its own transactions and those of private citizens, the injustice is merely the more scandalous.

The creditors of a nation are only a part of that nation. When taxes

---

[1] J. B. Say *Traité d'économie politique*, II, 5. Apply this to the present value of banknotes in England and reflect on the implications.
[(Book 2, ch. 5, 4th edn (Paris, 1819), vol. 2, pp. 67–81: 'Comment les revenus se distribuent dans la société').]

are introduced to discharge the interest on the public debt, these taxes weigh upon the entire nation: the creditors of the state in fact pay their part of these taxes as taxpayers. By reducing the debt, the charge falls on the creditors alone. This is to argue that, because a weight is too heavy to be sustained by the entire population, it will be more easily carried by the fourth, or by the eighth part of that same population.

Again, all forced reduction is a form of bankruptcy. A negotiation has been made with individuals according to conditions which have been freely offered. They have satisfied those conditions. They have surrendered their capital. They have withdrawn it from various branches of industry which promised them benefits. They are entitled to all that has been promised to them. The fulfilment of these promises is the legitimate compensation for the sacrifices they have made, the risks they have run. If a minister regrets having proposed onerous conditions, the fault is his alone, and not the fault of those who have simply accepted them. Indeed, it is doubly his own fault: because what has made his conditions especially onerous have been his previous breaches of faith. Had he inspired full confidence, he would have obtained better conditions.

If the debt is reduced by a fourth, what will prevent it from being reduced by a third, by nine tenths, or totally? What guarantee can we offer to our creditors, or indeed to ourselves? In all things the first step makes the second easier. If severe principles had compelled the authority to fulfil its promises, it would have sought the means to do so in order and economy. Instead it has chosen fraud, which it has admitted it finds congenial, for it exempts authority from any work, privation, or effort. And authority will keep resorting to fraud, since it no longer feels restrained by any sense of integrity.

Such is the blindness that follows the desertion of justice, that some have imagined that, by reducing debts by an act of authority, they could revive the credit which seemed to wane. They have started off from a principle which they misunderstood and misapplied. They thought that the less one owed, the more confidence one would inspire because one would be better placed to pay one's debts. But they have simply confused the effect of a legitimate discharge of debt with that of a bankruptcy. It is not sufficient for a debtor to be able to satisfy his commitments. It is also necessary that he should wish to do so, or that we should have the means to compel him to do so. A government which takes advantage of its authority to annul a part of its debt proves that it does not have the will to pay. Since its creditors cannot force it to do so, what do its resources in fact matter? The public debt is a different matter from the absolutely essential commodities: the fewer of these latter there are available, the more they are worth. This happens because these commodities have an intrinsic value, and their relative value increases with their scarcity. On the other hand, the value of a debt depends exclusively on the reliability of the debtor. Destroy this reliability, and you destroy the value. It is vain to reduce that debt to a half, to a quarter, to an eighth, what remains of it will simply be the more discredited. No-one wants or needs a debt which is not going to be paid. With individuals, the capacity to fulfil their commitments is the main condition, because the law is stronger than they are. But with governments, the main condition is their will.

There is another kind of bankruptcy in relation to which governments seem to act with even fewer scruples. Engaged, whether by ambition, by imprudence or even by necessity in expensive undertakings, they contract with tradesmen for the things necessary for those undertakings. True, their contracts are apt to be disadvantageous: the interests of a government can never be defended with the same zeal as the interests of individuals: it is the common and inevitable destiny of all those transactions which the principals cannot watch over personally. The authority then turns against those men who have profited from an advantage inherent in their position. It encourages declamations and calumnies against them. It cancels its contracts. It delays or refuses its promised payments. It takes general measures which, in order to strike at a handful of suspected individuals, indiscriminately involves an entire class. To disguise this iniquity, it takes care to represent these measures as directed exclusively against the men who are at the head of the enterprises, whose income is confiscated. It excites the hostility of the people against the few odious and corrupt names. Yet the men who are thus robbed are by no means isolated. They have not done everything themselves. They have employed artisans and manufacturers, who have supplied them with real goods. It is upon these latter that the spoliation, apparently directed solely against the former, in fact falls. The same people who, always credulous, applaud the destruction of a few fortunes, the alleged enormity of which they find infuriating, fail to realize that all those fortunes, built on their labours, tended to filter down to them, whilst the destruction of those fortunes robs them of their wages.

Governments are always in more or less acute need of men to do business with them. A government cannot buy in cash like a private individual. It must either pay in advance, which is impracticable, or obtain the things which it needs on credit. If it ill-treats or humiliates those who supply these, what will happen? Honest men withdraw, being unwilling to carry on a shameful business; corrupt men alone come forward. They calculate the price of their shame, and, foreseeing that, in addition, they will be poorly rewarded, they proceed to take things into their own hands and to pay themselves. The government is too slow, too confused in its movements, to follow the tangled and quick manouevres of individual interest. When it wants to compete in corruption with private individuals, the latter are always more skilful. The only effective policy is loyalty.

The immediate effect of disfavour thrown upon a branch of trade is to keep away from it all those merchants who are not seduced by greed. The immediate effect of a system of arbitrary power is to inspire in all honest men the desire to avoid meeting that arbitrary power, and to avoid any transactions which may force them to have anything to do with such a fearsome power.[1]

In all countries economies based upon the violation of public faith have, in the ensuing transactions, been duly punished. The interest on iniquity, despite its arbitrary reductions and its violent laws, has always proved a hundred times more expensive than that which good faith would have cost.

I should perhaps have included among the attacks levied upon property, the creation of any useless or excessive tax. Anything that exceeds real need – claims a writer whose authority on this subject will not be disputed[2] – ceases to be legitimate. The only difference between the abuses committed by private citizens and those of authority is that the injustice of the former involves simple ideas, which anyone can understand, while those of the latter, because they are linked to complicated schemes, can only be judged by conjecture.

Any useless tax is an assault against property, the more odious in that it is enacted with all the solemnity of the law, the more revolting

---

[1] See on the results of the revocation and annulment of treaties the excellent work on *Public revenue* by M. Ganilli, I, 303.

           [Charles Ganilh, *Essai politique.*]

[2] Necker, *Admin. des Finances*, I, 2.

        [*De l'administration des finances de la France*, vol. I, ch. 2.]

because it is the rich who levy it on the poor, the authority in arms against the unarmed individual.

Any tax, of whatever kind, always has a more or less pernicious influence:[1] it is a necessary evil, but like all necessary evils it must be made as negligible as possible. The more means are left for the use of private industry, the more a state prospers. Taxation, for the simple reason that it subtracts some portion of those means from that industry, is inevitably damaging.

Rousseau, who had no knowledge of financial questions, has repeated, together with many others, that in monarchical countries it is necessary, through the prince's wealth, to use up any excess wealth the subjects may have, because it is better that such a surplus should be absorbed by the government than dissipated by private citizens.[2] In this doctrine we can recognize an absurd mixture of monarchical prejudices and republican ideas. The prince's wealth, far from discouraging that of individuals, serves as an encouragement and example to them. We must not believe that, by despoiling the citizens, it will reform them. It may plunge them into poverty, but it cannot preserve their simplicity. The poverty of some is merely combined with the wealth of others, and this is the worst combination possible.

Excessive taxation leads to the subversion of justice, to a deterioration in morals, to the destruction of individual liberty. Neither the authority that takes away from the working classes their painfully acquired subsistence, nor those oppressed classes that see this subsistence torn from their own hands to enrich greedy masters, can remain faithful to the laws of equity, in this struggle between weakness and violence, poverty and avarice, destitution and spoliation.

We would be wrong to suppose that the drawbacks of excessive taxation are confined to the misery and hardship of the people. From it springs another, equally great evil, which thus has been rather neglected.

The possession of a very large fortune inspires, even amongst private individuals, desires, whims, disordered fantasies of which they would never normally conceive. The same thing is true of the men in power. What has suggested to the English ministers for the last fifty years such

---

[1] See Smith, book v, for the application of this general truth to each tax in particular.
[Smith, *Wealth of Nations*, vol. 2, pp. 817–906.]

[2] *Social Contract*, iii, 8.
[ed. by G. D. H. Cole, London, 1903, pp. 68–73: 'That all forms of government do not suit all countries.']

exaggerated and insolent pretensions, is the excessive ease with which they have been able to raise immense wealth through enormous taxes. Too much wealth, like too much power goes to one's head, because wealth is power, and the most real of all powers: hence the plans, ambitions, projects, that a ministry possessing only what it really needed would never have formed. Thus the people are not only miserable because they pay beyond their means, but also because of the use which is made of what they do pay. Its sacrifices turn against it. It no longer pays taxes in order to have its peace assured by a good system of defence. It pays them in order to have war, because authority, proud of its wealth, wishes to spend this gloriously. The people pay not to have public order maintained in the country, but on the contrary, to have favourites, enriched by its own spoils, disrupt public order by their misdemeanours and go unpunished for it. Thus, by depriving its people, a nation buys itself misery and danger. In this state of affairs the government is corrupted by its wealth and the people by its poverty.

CHAPTER 16

On the liberty of the press

The question of liberty of the press has been so well clarified recently that it requires only a few observations.

The first is that our present constitution differs from all the previous ones because it establishes the only effective means of repressing the crimes of the press while leaving it its full independence: I mean trial by jury. This is a great proof of both loyalty and enlightenment. The crimes of the press are different from other crimes in that they have less to do with positive facts than with intentions and results. Hence a jury alone, according to its moral conviction, can pronounce upon the former, and determine the latter through the examination and assessment of all the circumstances. Any court, in pronouncing its verdict according to precise laws, is necessarily faced with the alternative either of yielding to arbitrariness, or of sanctioning impunity.

I would further remark that a prediction which I ventured a year ago has been entirely fulfilled. 'Let us imagine', I wrote, 'a society prior to the invention of language, which substituted this rapid and easy means of communication by less easy and slower methods. The discovery of language would produce in such a society a sudden explosion. People would see enormous dangers in these still novel sounds, and many a wise and prudent spirit, solemn magistrates or ageing administrators, would regret the good old days of peaceful and utter silence. But the surprise and alarm would gradually subside. Language would become an instrument of limited effects. A salutary mistrust, the product of experience, would preserve the audience from any unthinking enthusiasm. Finally, everything would return to order, with this difference, that social communications, and consequently the improvement of all the arts, the perfecting of all ideas, would retain an additional instrument. The same thing will be true of the press whenever a just and moderate authority refrains from struggling against it.'[1]

Today we have unmistakable proof of the truth of this assertion. Never before has the liberty, or rather the licence, of the press been so unlimited; never before have pamphlets in every possible form been more numerous, and made more vigorously available to the curiosity of the public. Never before have these contemptible products received less attention. I seriously believe that today there are more pamphlets than readers.

I shall add that, despite the indifference and the disdain of the public, it will be necessary, in the interests of the press itself, that penal laws, drafted with moderation but also with justice, should soon distinguish what is innocent from what is harmful, and what is legitimate from what is prohibited. Incitements to murder, to civil war, invitations addressed to a foreign enemy, direct insults to the head of state, have never been allowed in any country. I am glad that experience should have proved the impotence of these provocations and insults. I am grateful to the man who is strong enough to maintain peace in France despite this unbridled exhibition by a party without other resources. I admire the man who is great enough to remain indifferent amidst so many personal attacks. Yet in England – and England is without a doubt the land of liberty – the king may not be insulted by any writing, and the mere reprinting of proclamations directed against him would be followed by severe punishment. This reservation imposed by the laws is motivated by a consideration of great importance.

The neutrality of the royal power, this indispensable condition for every constitutional monarchy, to which I keep returning, because the

---

[1] *Réflex. sur les const. et les garant.*, ch. VIII.

entire stability of the building rests upon this foundation, implies equally that this power should not act against the citizens, nor the citizens act against it. In England the king, in France the emperor, in all countries the holder of monarchical authority, are above the sphere of political agitations. They are not men; they are powers. Thus in the same way in which it is necessary that they must not revert to being men, or else their function would be perverted, they must also not be attacked like other men. The law guarantees all citizens from any aggression on their part; it must also protect them from any aggression on the part of the citizens. Insulted in his person, the head of state reverts to being a man: if you attack the man, he will defend himself, and the constitution will be destroyed.[1]

CHAPTER 17

On religious liberty[a]

The present constitution has returned to the only reasonable view on the subject of religion, that of sanctioning freedom of worship without restriction, without privilege, without even forcing individuals, provided they observe the purely legal forms, to declare their preference for a particular form of religion. We have avoided the stumbling block

---

[1] As I do not wish to be accused of having abjured my opinions, I shall recall here that, in defending the freedom of the press, I have always demanded the punishment of libels and subversive writings, and I transcribe here my own words:
'The principles which must guide a government on this question are simple and clear. Let authors be responsible for their writings when they are published, as any man is responsible for his own words when he has uttered them, and for his actions when he has committed them. The orator who preached theft, murder or pillage would be punished for his speeches. Thus the writer who preaches murder, pillage or theft must be punished.' *De la liberté des brochures, des pamphlets et des journaux*, 2nd edn, p. 72 (Paris, 1814). – Moreover I said: 'The Long Parliament invoked the principles of freedom of the press, giving them an excessively broad interpretation, and a totally false direction, as it used them to free some pamphleteers condemned by the courts, which is absolutely opposed to what we mean by freedom of the press; since everyone wants the courts to take severe action against pamphleteers.' *Observ. sur le discours de M. de Montesquiou*, p. 45 (Paris, 1814). In this case, as in the others, I think what I have always thought, and I demand merely what I used to demand.

---

[a] This chapter is largely based on the 1806 draft; see E. Hofmann (ed.), *Les 'Principes de Politique'*, vol. 2, pp. 155–78.

of that civil intolerance which some have sought to substitute for religious intolerance proper, now that the progress of ideas is opposed to the latter. To support this new kind of intolerance, many have cited Rousseau, who cherished all theories of liberty, while offering pretexts for every claim that tyranny makes.

'There is', he writes 'a purely civil profession of faith, of which it is the privilege of the sovereign to fix the articles, not exactly as dogmas of religion, but as feelings of sociability. If he cannot force anyone to believe in those dogmas, the sovereign can banish from the country whoever does not believe in them. He can banish them not as impious, but as unsociable.'[1] What is the state, then, for it to decide which feelings must be adopted? What good is it to me that the sovereign may not force me to believe, when he punishes me if I fail to do so? What is the advantage of not being punished as impious, if I am to be punished as unsociable? What does it matter if the authority abstains from meddling with the subtleties of theology, when it loses itself in this hypothetical morality, no less subtle and no less foreign to its natural jurisdiction?

I know of no system of servitude, which has sanctioned more nefarious errors than the eternal metaphysics of the *Social Contract*.

Civil intolerance is as dangerous, more absurd and above all more unjust than religious intolerance. It is as dangerous because it produces the same results under a different pretext. It is more absurd because it is not motivated by conviction. It is more unjust because the evil it causes is not the product of duty but of calculation.

Civil intolerance disguises itself in a thousand forms and takes refuge in one position after another to evade reasoning. Defeated on principle, it now fights over its application. We have seen men, who have been persecuted for almost thirty centuries, telling the government which relieved them from their long proscription that, if it was

---

[1] Rousseau, *Social Contract*, book IV, ch. VIII. He adds: 'that if someone, after having publicly recognized these same dogmas, behaves as if he did not believe in them, let him be punished with death; he has committed the greatest of crimes, he has lied before the laws'. [ed. by G. D. H. Cole, p. 121]

But whoever has the misfortune not to believe in these dogmas cannot confess his doubts without exposing himself to banishment; and if his affections restrain him, if he has a family, a wife, children whom he hesitates to leave, and throw himself into exile, is it not you and you alone who force him to what you call the greatest of crimes, to lying before the law? I shall say, moreover, that in these circumstances this lie seems to me far from being a crime. When alleged laws demand from us the truth only to proscribe us, we do not owe them the truth.

necessary to have several positive religions in a state, it was no less necessary to prevent the tolerated sects from producing new sects by subdividing themselves.[1] Yet is not any tolerated sect itself a sub-division of an ancient one? On what grounds can it deny to future generations the same rights which it has claimed against the past ones?

Some have even claimed that no recognized church could change its dogmas without the approval of authority. But if by any chance those dogmas came to be rejected by the majority of the religious community could the authorities force that majority to profess them? In matters of opinion the rights of the majority and those of the minority are the same.

One could understand intolerance when it imposes on everyone the same profession of faith: at least it is consistent. It may believe that it is retaining men within the sanctuary of truth. But when two opinions are permitted, one of which must necessarily be false, to let the government force the individuals belonging to one or other of those to remain attached to the opinion of their sect, or the sects themselves never to change their opinion, means giving it formal authorization to give its support to error.

The complete and utter freedom of all forms of worship is as favourable to religion, as it is in accordance with justice.

Had religion always been perfectly free, I believe it would never have been other than an object of respect and love. We would hardly be able to imagine that strange fanaticism which turns religion itself into an object of hatred or malevolence. It seems to me that this appeal from a miserable to a just being, from a weak to a good one, must arouse, even in those who regard it as unrealistic, only interest and sympathy. He who regards all the hopes of religion as mistakes must be moved more deeply than anyone else by this universal communion of all suffering beings, by those grief-stricken appeals raised to a sky of bronze, from all the corners of the earth, only to remain unanswered, and by that helpful illusion which takes as an answer the confused murmur of innumerable prayers repeated far off in the breezes.

The causes of our sufferings are numerous. Authority may proscribe us; falsehood may slander us. We are wounded by the bonds of an entirely artificial society; stricken by an inflexible nature in all that is

---

[1] *Discours des Juifs au gouvernement français.*

    [*Réponse d'Abraham Furtado, Président de l'Assemblée des Juifs, au discours des commissaires de S.M.I. et R.*, 18 September 1806, *Moniteur*, 22 September 1806, pp. 1171–2; repr. as a brochure (B.N., 4 Ld 184 225).]

dearest to us. Old age moves towards us, a dark and solemn time, in which objects become dim and seem to withdraw from us, and a chill and dreary pall spreads over all that surrounds us.

Against so many sorrows we look for consolation everywhere, and all our lasting consolations are religious. When men persecute us, we create for ourselves I do not know what sort of refuge beyond human reach. When we see our dearest hopes, justice, liberty, our country vanish, we have the illusion that somewhere a being exists who will reward us for having been faithful, in spite of the age we live in, to justice, to liberty, to our country. When we mourn a beloved being, we throw a bridge across the abyss, and traverse it with our thought. Finally when life deserts us, we launch ourselves towards another life. Religion is by its very essence the faithful companion, the ingenious and indefatigable friend of those in misfortune.

This is not all. Consoler of our misery, religion is at the same time the most natural of our emotions. Unknown to us, all our physical sensations, all our moral feelings, awake it in our hearts. All that appears to us without limits, and that generates the notion of immensity – the sight of the sky, the silence of the night, the vast extent of the seas – all that leads us to tenderness or to enthusiasm – the consciousness of a virtuous action, of a generous sacrifice, of a danger bravely confronted, of the pain of another aided or comforted – all that stirs up in the depths of our soul the primitive elements of our nature – the contempt for vice, the hatred of tyranny – feeds our religious feeling.

This feeling is intimately connected with all the noble, delicate, and deep passions. Like all these passions, it has something mysterious about it: for common reason cannot satisfactorily explain any of these passions. Love, that exclusive preference for an object towards which we could long have been indifferent and which is so similar to so many others; the need of glory, that thirst for a fame which should outlast us; the pleasure which we find in devotion, a pleasure opposed to the normal instinct of our egoism; melancholy, that sadness without a cause, at the bottom of which lies a pleasure which we do not know how to analyse, a thousand other sensations impossible to describe, which, however, fill us with vague impressions and confused emotions: all of these cannot be explained by the rigour of reasoning. They all share some affinity with religious sentiment. All these feelings are favourable to the development of morality: they stimulate man to step beyond the narrow circle of his interests. They restore to the soul that elasticity, that delicacy, that exaltation which stifles the habits of common life and the petty material interests that go with it. Love is the most mixed of these passions, because it has as its aim a specific enjoyment and because that aim is close to us and results in egoism. On the other hand religious sentiment is the purest of all these passions. It does not vanish together with youth. Sometimes in fact it is strengthened by old age, as if heaven had given it to us as a consolation in the most barren period of our life.

A man of genius used to say that the sight of the Apollo Belvedere or of a painting by Raphael made him a better man.[a] There is indeed in the contemplation of beauty of any kind, something which detaches us from ourselves by making us feel that perfection is worth more than we are; and that, through this conviction, by inspiring us with a momentary disinterestedness, awakens in us the power of sacrifice, which is the source of all virtues. There is in emotion, whatever its cause, something which makes our blood flow faster, which communicates to us a kind of wellbeing which doubles the sense of our existence and our powers, and that, by doing so, renders us capable of a greater generosity, courage, or sympathy, than we normally feel. Even a corrupt man is better when he is moved and as long as he is moved.

I do not with to argue that the absence of religious feeling proves in every individual the absence of morality. There are men who are predominantly ruled by their mind, and can surrender only to evidence. These men are generally dedicated to profound meditations, and are preserved from corrupting temptations by the pleasure of study and the habit of thought. They are capable, consequently, of a scrupulous morality. But in the crowd of vulgar men the absence of religious feeling, not proceeding from any such cause, more often announces, I believe, a barren heart, a frivolous spirit, a soul absorbed by petty and ignoble interests, a great sterility of imagination. I make an exception for the cases in which such men have been enraged by persecution. The effect of persecution is to excite people against what it orders, and it may happen that sensitive but proud men, outraged by a religion imposed upon them, may reject, without examining it, everything to do with religion. But this exception, which is purely circumstantial, does not in any way affect the general argument.

[a] Hofmann suggests that the 'man of genius' might be Schiller, Fauriel or Villiers. I find more persuasive Kloocke's belief that Constant was thinking of Goethe. See K. Kloocke, *Benjamin Constant, une biographie intellectuelle*, footnote 88, p. 140.

I would not form a bad opinion of an enlightened man if he were introduced to me as a stranger to religious feeling. But a people incapable of this sentiment would seem to me deprived of a precious faculty and disinherited by nature. If I were accused at this point of failing to offer a sufficiently precise definition of religious feeling I shall ask how we can define with precision that vague and profound part of our moral sense, which by its very nature defies all the efforts of language. How would you define the impression of a dark night, of an ancient forest, of the wind moaning through ruins or over graves, of the ocean stretching beyond our sight? How would you define the emotion caused by the songs of Ossian, the church of St Peter, meditation upon death, the harmony of sounds or forms? How would you define reverie, that intimate quivering of the soul, in which all the powers of the senses and thought come together and lose themselves in a mysterious confusion? There is religion at the bottom of all things. All that is beautiful, all that is intimate, all that is noble, partakes of the nature of religion.

Religion is the common centre in which all ideas of justice, love, liberty, pity, which in our ephemeral world form the dignity of the human species, unite themselves above the action of time and the reach of vice. It is the permanent tradition of everything that is beautiful, great and good across the degradation and iniquity of the ages, the eternal voice which answers virtue in its own language, the appeal from the present to the future, from the earth to heaven, the solemn recourse of all the oppressed, in all circumstances, the last hope of sacrificed innocence and of weakness trampled under foot.

Why has it come about then that this faithful ally, this necessary support, this unique light in the darkness surrounding us has, in every century, been the target of frequent and unremitting attacks? Why has it been the most enlightened, the most independent and the most learned class that has almost always been its sworn enemy? It is because religion has been distorted. Man has been pursued into this last refuge, into this intimate sanctuary of his existence. Religion has been transformed, in the hands of authority, into an institution of intimidation. Having been the cause of our cruellest sufferings, power has even tried to have control over our consolations. Dogmatic religion, that hostile and persecuting power, has sought to subject to its yoke the conjectures of the imagination and the needs of the heart. Religion has become a curse more terrible than those which it was destined to make us forget.

Consequently, in all those centuries in which men have claimed their moral independence, we find this resistance to religion, which has appeared to be directed against the sweetest of affections, while it was only in fact aimed at the most oppressive of tyrannies. Intolerance, by placing violence on the side of faith, placed courage on the side of doubt. The fury of the believers has exalted the vanity of those who could not believe, and in this way man has made a virtue of a system which he ought naturally to have considered as a misfortune. Persecution provokes resistance. Authority, by threatening any opinion whatsoever, provokes any courageous spirit to take up that very opinion. There is in man a principle of revolt against every form of intellectual constraint. This principle can be carried to the point of fury. It can cause many crimes; yet it issues from all that is most noble in our soul.

I have often felt myself stricken by sadness and astonishment while reading the famous *System of Nature*.[a] That lengthy frenzy of an old man to close off any future before him; that inexplicable thirst for destruction, that blind and almost cruel hatred for a gentle and consoling idea, seemed to me a bizarre delirium. But I could always understand it by recalling the dangers by which authority had surrounded that writer. In all ages the reflections of irreligious men have been harassed: they have never had the time or the liberty to consider at leisure their own opinion. It has always been for them a property of which men wished to rob them. They thought less of going deeper into it than of justifying or defending it. Only leave them in peace. They will be astonished at their own victory. The agitation of the struggle, the anxiety to reconquer, the right of inquiry, all these causes of exaltation, will no longer sustain them. Their imagination, thus far preoccupied with success, will return idle and deserted upon itself. They will see man alone upon an earth that must engulf him. The universe is lifeless: passing, casual, isolated generations appear upon it, suffer and die. No bond exists between these generations, whose lot here is one of pain and, hereafter, nothingness. All communication is severed between the past, the present and the future. No voice emanates from the races which are living no longer, while the voice of those still alive must soon sink into the same eternal silence. Who does not feel that, had not incredulity encountered intolerance, the discouragements of this

---

[a] Paul Henri Dietrich d'Holbach, *Système de la nature, ou des lois du monde physique et du monde moral* (London, 1770).

system would have acted upon the souls of its supporters, and kept them at least in apathy and silence.

I shall repeat the point. In so far as authority leaves religion perfectly independent, no-one will have any interest in attacking it. Thought itself will not even consider it. But if authority claims to defend it, especially if it attempts to turn it into its ally, intellectual independence will soon attack it.

Any government intervention in the domain of religion causes harm. It causes harm whenever it wishes to keep all spirit of inquiry out of religion, for authority cannot act out of conviction; it can only act out of self-interest. What can it gain from favouring men who profess the permitted opinions? To drive away those who freely express their own beliefs, those who, consequently, are at least frank. The rest may evade its precautions with a ready lie. These precautions affect scrupulous men; but they are powerless against those who are, or who become, corrupt.

What resources, moreover, does a government possess, to promote an opinion? Will it reserve the important functions of the state for its supporters? The individuals who have been excluded will be infuriated by this preference. Will it get people to write or speak in support of the opinion it is protecting? But others will write or speak against this. Will it limit freedom in writing, speaking, eloquence, reasoning, even irony or declamation? Here it is set on a completely new course: no longer favouring and persuading, but stifling and punishing. Does it believe that the laws will be able to capture every nuance, and adjust themselves accordingly? If its repressive measures are mild, people will defy them. Such measures will only embitter without intimidating. If they were severe, the government will find itself become a persecutor. Once on this slippery slope, it will be in vain to try to stop.

Moreover, what success could it hope to achieve even through its persecutions? No king, I believe, was surrounded with greater prestige than Louis XIV. Honour, vanity, fashion, all-powerful fashion itself were placed, in his reign, under obedience. He lent to religion the support of the throne and that of his own example. He attached the salvation of his own soul to the maintenance of the most rigid of practices, and he persuaded his courtiers that the salvation of the king's soul was of special importance. Yet, despite his ever increasing care, despite the austerity of an ancient court, despite the memory of fifty years of glory, doubts began to grow in men's spirits even before he was dead. We find in the memoirs of the age intercepted letters, written by assiduous flatterers of Louis XIV, and equally offensive, Madame de Maintenon tells us, to God and to the King. The King died. The philosophical impulse broke down all the dams; reasoning took its revenge for the constraint which it had suffered impatiently, and the result of lengthy recompression was incredulity carried to excess.

Authority causes no less harm, and proves no less impotent, when it seeks to re-establish religion in a sceptical century. Religion must establish itself only by the need that man feels for it. Whenever he is troubled by external considerations, he is, in fact, prevented from experiencing all the force of that need. They say, and I believe it myself, that religion is natural. Its voice must not therefore be covered by that of authority. The intervention of governments in defence of religion, when opinion is unfavourable to it, has this particular disadvantage, that religion is defended by men who do not believe in it. The governors are subjected, like the governed, to the progress of human ideas. Once doubt has penetrated the enlightened part of a nation, it worms its way into the government itself. In all ages opinions or vanity are stronger than interest. It is in vain that the holders of authority tell themselves that favouring religion is to their advantage. They may display their power on its behalf, but they will be unable to bring themselves to display their regard for it. They may find some pleasure in confiding their afterthoughts to the public. They will be afraid of looking convinced for fear of being taken for dupes. If their first expression is devoted to imposing credulity, the second is committed to reconquering for themselves the honours of doubt, and anyone is bound to be a bad missionary who tries to place himself above his own profession of faith.[1]

In this way is established the axiom that religion is essential for the people, an axiom which flatters the vanity of those who repeat it because, by repeating it, they distinguish themselves from the people.

This axiom is false in itself in so far as it implies that religion is more necessary to the labouring classes of society than to the idle and rich. If religion is necessary, it is equally so for all men at all levels of instruction. The crimes of the poor and uneducated classes are more violent and terrible in character, but at the same time they are easier to discover and to repress. The law surrounds them, it seizes them, it represses them easily, because these crimes clash directly with it. The

---

[1] This tendency was very noticeable in men in public positions, even in many of those who were at the head of the Church under Louis XV and Louis XVI.

corruption of the upper classes is subtle and varied. It evades the laws, mocks their spirit by eluding their form, and opposes them with money, influence and power.

Odd reasoning indeed! The poor man has no power. He is surrounded by impediments. He is tied down by all kind of bonds. He has neither protectors nor supporters. He may commit an isolated crime, but everything is armed against him as soon as he is found guilty. He can hardly expect the least consideration from his judges, who are always chosen from the class of his enemies. In his relations, as impotent as himself, he finds no chance of impunity. His behaviour never has the least influence upon the general destiny of the society to which he belongs. Yet it is for him alone that you wish the mysterious guarantee of religion! The rich man on the contrary, is judged by his peers, by his allies, by men upon whom the penalties they inflict inevitably to some degree rebound. Society lavishes support on him. All material and moral chances are in his favour, purely by reason of his wealth. He can exercise his influence from a distance, he can overthrow or corrupt. Yet it is this powerful and favoured being whom you wish to free from the yoke which you think must be placed around the neck of the poor defenceless creature.

I write all this on the conventional assumption that religion is especially precious as a re-enforcement of the penal laws. But this is by no means my own opinion. I place religion higher than this. I do not regard it as a supplement to power and to the wheel. There is a common morality founded upon calculation, interest and security, which can, strictly speaking, dispense with religion altogether. It can do without it in the case of the rich man, because he is capable of reflection; in the case of the poor man, because the law frightens him, and because, his work being cut out for him beforehand anyway, the habit of constant labour produces upon his life the same effect as reflection. But woe betide the people who possess only this common morality! It is to create a more elevated morality than religion seems desirable to me: I invoke it not to repress gross crimes, but to ennoble all the virtues.

The defenders of religion often believe that they have performed a wonderful service in representing it as essentially useful. What would they say if one were to show them that they are rendering to religion the worst of all possible services?

Just as in searching in all the beauties of nature for a positive goal, an immediate use, an application in daily life, we blight all the charm of its magnificent unity, similarly, by constantly treating religion as a useful tool, we make it dependent on that usefulness. It is relegated now to a secondary rank. It appears as no more than a means, and by this very fact it is demeaned.

Moreover, the axiom that religion is necessary for the people is the most appropriate way of destroying religion altogether. The people are alerted, by a fairly sure instinct, to what is happening over their heads. The cause of this instinct is the same as the insight of children and of all dependent classes. Their interest makes them alert to the secret thoughts of those who dispose of their destiny. To hope that the people should long continue to believe what its betters refuse to believe, is to overestimate their good nature. On the contrary, the sole fruit of their artifice is that the people, seeing them to be unbelievers, detach themselves from their own religion without knowing why. What they achieve by forbidding free enquiry is to prevent the people from being enlightened, but not to impede them from being irreligious. Indeed they become irreligious by imitation; they treat religion as a matter for simpletons and an exercise in deception and everyone reserves it for his inferiors who, for their part, hasten to push it even lower. In this way religion sinks, becoming more degraded every day. It is less threatened when it is attacked on all sides. Then at least it may seek refuge in the most sensitive souls. Vanity does not fear to show itself as stupid and to demean itself by respecting it.

Who would believe it! Political authority causes harm even when it wishes to bring within its jurisdiction the principles of tolerance: this is because it imposes upon tolerance positive and fixed forms which are opposed to the latter's own nature. Tolerance is nothing but the freedom of all present and future forms of worship. The emperor Joseph II wanted to establish tolerance, and, being a liberal, he began by ordering the compilation of a vast catalogue of all the religious opinions professed by his subjects. I do not know how many were registered as recipients of his protection. What happened? A sect which had been forgotten suddenly appeared, and Joseph II, the tolerant prince, said it had come too late. The deists of Bohemia were persecuted in view of the date of their application, and the philosopher king found himself simultaneously in conflict with Brabant, which demanded exclusive domination of Catholics, and with the unfortunate Bohemians, who demanded freedom of speech.

This limited tolerance implies a peculiar error. Imagination alone can satisfy the needs of imagination. When in some empire you have tolerated twenty religions, you have still done nothing for the devotees of the twenty-first. Governments which expect to leave their subjects enough latitude by allowing them to choose between a fixed number of religious beliefs, are like the Frenchman who, arriving in a German town where the inhabitants wanted to learn Italian, gave them the choice between Basque and Low Breton.

This multitude of sects, of which some are so frightened, is precisely what is most healthy for religion. Its effect is that religion remains a feeling and does not become a mere formality, an almost mechanical habit, which unites itself with every vice and sometimes even with every sort of crime.

When religion degenerates in this way it loses all its influence over morality. It lodges itself, so to speak, in a compartment of the human mind, where it remains in isolation from all the rest of life. In Italy we see the mass precede the murder, confession follow it, penitence absolve it, and man, thus liberated from remorse, prepare himself for fresh murders.

Nothing could be simpler: to prevent the subdivision of sects, you must prevent man from reflecting upon his religion; you must therefore prevent him from concerning himself with it; you must reduce it to symbols to repeat and practices to observe. It all becomes external, something to be done without reflection, and, consequently, with neither interest nor attention.

Certain Mongol peoples, obliged by their religion to say frequent prayers, convinced themselves that what pleased the gods in their prayers was the movement of the air which they took as a constant proof that men were attending to them. Consequently these peoples invented little prayer wheels, which, by disturbing the air in a certain way, perpetually maintained the desired movement. While those mills turn, everyone, convinced that the gods are satisfied, busies himself with a light heart about his own affairs or pleasures. Religion, in more than one European nation, often reminded me of the little prayer wheels of those Mongol peoples.[a]

The multiplication of sects has a great advantage for morality. All the new sects tend to distinguish themselves from those from which they break away by a more scrupulous morality, and often the sect that

---

[a] Constant's understanding of the liturgical significance of the Buddhist 'prayer wheel' may have been somewhat defective. See E. Hofmann (ed.), *Les 'Principes de Politique'*, vol. 2, pp. 165–6, footnote 15.

witnesses a new division at work within it, is inspired by a commendable desire to emulate them, not wanting to lag behind the innovators in this respect. Thus the appearance of Protestantism reformed the habits of the Catholic clergy. If the authority did not meddle with religion, sects would multiply themselves indefinitely; each new congregation would try to prove the goodness of its doctrine by the purity of its customs. Each deserted congregation would want to defend itself by the same weapons. Hence would result a happy struggle, in which success would consist in establishing a more austere morality. Customs would improve without effort, by a natural impulse and an honourable rivalry. This is what we may observe in America, or even in Scotland, where tolerance is far from being perfect but where nevertheless Presbyterianism has divided into numerous branches.

Up to now the birth of sects, far from being accompanied by such salutary effects, has almost always been marked by disruptions and misfortunes. It is because authority has meddled with it. Through its voice, by its indiscreet action, the most trivial of differences, until then innocent and even useful, have become seeds of discord.

Frederick William, the father of the Great Frederick, shocked to find that religion among his subjects was not ruled by the same discipline as in his barracks, decided one day to unite Lutherans and Reformed. He removed the causes of dissent from their respective formulae and ordered them to be in agreement. Up to then those two sects had lived separately, but in perfect understanding. Condemned to unity, they soon began a relentless war, attacked one another and resisted authority. At the death of his father, Frederick II came to the throne. He let them believe what they would. The two sects fought one another without attracting his attention. They spoke without being listened to. Soon they lost both the hope of success and the irritant of fear; they fell silent; their differences remained but their dissensions were appeased.

In opposing the multiplication of sects, governments misunderstand their own interests. When sects are very numerous in a country, they exercise mutual control and free the sovereign from the need to come to terms with any of them. When there is only a single dominant sect, power is forced to use a thousand stratagems in order to have nothing to fear from it. When there are only two or three of them, each sufficiently formidable to threaten the others, uninterrupted surveillance and repression become necessary. Strange expedient! You say that you want to maintain peace, and in order to secure this you prevent opinions from diverging in such a way as to divide men up into small, weak and virtually imperceptible groups. Instead you constitute three or four large hostile bodies, which you set before one another and which, thanks to the care that you take in maintaining them in these large and powerful groups, are ready to attack one another at the first signal.

Such are the consequences of religious intolerance. But irreligious intolerance is no less deadly.

Authority ought never to proscribe any religion, even when it believes it to be dangerous. Let it punish the guilty actions which a religion leads men to commit not as religious but as criminal acts. Then it will readily succeed in controlling them. If it attacked them as religious, it would turn them into a duty, and if it chose to go back as far as the opinion that first prompted them, it would engage itself in a labyrinth of endless oppressions and iniquities. The only means of undermining any opinion is to establish freedom of inquiry. Such freedom means detachment from every kind of authority, absence of all collective intervention: inquiry is essentially individual.

For persecution – which naturally revolts men's spirits and attaches them to the persecuted belief – to succeed, on the contrary, in destroying that belief, souls must be corrupted, and one must strike not merely the religion which one wishes to destroy, but all sense of morality and virtue. In order to persuade a man to despise or desert one of his fellows who is suffering on account of an opinion he holds, in order to force him to abandon today the doctrine which he professed yesterday, because this is suddenly under threat, it is necessary to stifle in him all justice and all pride.

To persecute only priests is an illusory way of mitigating persecution itself. Those measures soon affect all those who profess the same doctrine, and subsequently all those who sympathize with the misfortune of the oppressed. 'Do not tell me', M. de Clermont-Tonnerre said in 1791, and events have twice confirmed his predictions, 'that by persecuting to excess those priests who are called refractory, all opposition will be extinguished. I hope the contrary will be true, and I hope this out of esteem for the French nation. For any nation that yields to force, in a matter of conscience, is a nation so vile, so corrupt, that one can expect nothing of it as regards reason or liberty.'[a]

---

[a] Stanislas Marie de Clermont-Tonnerre, *Réflexions sur le fanatisme* in *Recueil des opinions de S. de Clermont-Tonnerre* vol. 4, pp. 98–9. The 'refractory priests' were those who had refused to swear obedience to the revolutionary government.

Superstition is nefarious only when it is either protected or menaced. Do not provoke it by injustices; merely deprive it of all the means to cause harm by its actions. It will first become an innocent passion, and will soon extinguish itself, unable to arouse concern through its sufferings, or to dominate through an alliance with authority.

Man's thoughts, true or false, are his most sacred property and tyrants are all equally guilty when they attack it. Whoever proscribes, in the name of philosophy, speculative superstition, whoever proscribes in the name of God, independent reason, deserves the execration of men of merit.

Let me cite once again, by way of conclusion, M. de Clermont-Tonnerre. He cannot be accused of extremist views. Although a friend of liberty, or perhaps because he was a friend of liberty, he was almost always rejected by the two parties in the Constituent Assembly. He died the victim of moderation. His opinion, I believe, will carry some weight. 'Religion and the state', he said, 'are two perfectly distinct, perfectly separate things, the union of which can only denature both of them. Man has relations with his creator; he forms or receives such and such a set of ideas about these relations; this system of ideas is called religion. Everyone's religion is therefore the opinion that everyone has of his relationship with God. Because every man's opinion is free, he may accept or not accept a given religion. The opinion of the minority can never be subjected to that of the majority. No opinion can therefore be commanded by the social pact. Religion belongs to all times, to all places, to all governments. Its sanctuary is in man's conscience, and conscience is the only faculty that man could never sacrifice to social convention. The social body must never impose any cult; it must never reject any.'[a]

Yet from the fact that authority must neither impose nor proscribe a cult it does not follow that it must not pay for any. Here again our constitution has remained faithful to the true principles. It is a mistake to have man's religion mixed up with his pecuniary interest. To force the citizens to pay the person who is in some sense his interpreter in the face of the God he adores, directly is to offer him the chance of an immediate profit if he gives up his belief. It is to make a burden of feelings against which the distractions of the world for some, its labours for others, are already militating only too effectively. Some have be-

---

[a] Clermont-Tonnerre, *Opinion sur la propriété des biens du clergé, Nov. 1789, ibid.* vol. 2, p. 71.

lieved that they were saying something philosophical in affirming that it was more worthwhile to clear a field than to pay a priest or to build a church. But what does building a church, or paying a priest mean, but acknowledging that there exists a good, just and powerful being with whom it would be desirable to be in communication? I would like the state to declare, in paying, I do not say a clergy, but the priests of all those communions which are at all numerous, I would like the state to declare that this communication has not been interrupted, and that the earth has not renounced heaven.

Nascent sects do not need society to undertake the maintenance of their priests. They are still in all the fervour of fresh ideas and deep convictions. But once a sect has come to gather around its altars a substantial number of the members of society at large, society itself ought to finance the new church. By paying for them all, the burden will be equal for all, and instead of representing a privilege it will be a common charge equally shared.

It is with religion as with main roads: I would like the state to maintain them, provided that it lets anyone free to choose the smaller paths.

CHAPTER 18

On the liberty of the individual

All the constitutions which have been given to France guaranteed the liberty of the individual, and yet, under the rule of these constitutions, it has been constantly violated. The fact is that a simple declaration is not sufficient; you need positive safeguards. You need bodies sufficiently powerful to be able to employ, in favour of the oppressed, the means of defence sanctioned by the written law. Our present constitution is the only one that has created these safeguards and invested the intermediary bodies with adequate power. Freedom of the press, placed beyond attack thanks to trial by jury; the responsibility of ministers, and especially that of subordinates; and, finally, the existence of a large and independent representation; such are the bastions by which the freedom of the individual is surrounded today.

This freedom is in fact the aim of all societies; upon it depend both public and private morality; upon it depend the expectations of industry; without it men can enjoy neither peace, nor dignity nor happiness.

Arbitrary power destroys morality, for there can be no morality without security; there are no gentle affections without the certainty that the objects of these affections rest safe under the shield of their innocence. When arbitrary power strikes without scruple those men who have awakened its suspicions, it is not only an individual whom it persecutes, it is the entire nation which it first humiliates and then degrades. Men always tend to avoid pain: when what they love is threatened, they either detach themselves from it, or defend it. Habitual ways of life, M. de Pauw says, are instantly corrupted in towns attacked by the plague. People rob one another as they die. Arbitrary power is for the moral what the plague is for the physical.[a]

It is the enemy of domestic bonds. For the sanction of these bonds is the well-founded hope of living free, under the shelter which justice grants to the citizens. Arbitrary power forces the son to see his father oppressed without defending him; the wife to suffer the arrest of her husband in silence; friends and relations to disown the holiest of affections.

Arbitrariness is the enemy of all the transactions that establish the prosperity of peoples. It disrupts credit, crushes commerce, strikes at all security. When an individual suffers without having been found guilty, anyone of any intelligence feels himself threatened, and with good reason. For security is destroyed; all transactions feel the impact; the earth trembles and it is only with fear that we go on our way.

When arbitrariness is tolerated, it spreads to such an extent that then the obscurest citizen can all of a sudden find it armed against himself. It is not sufficient to keep out of the way and to let others be struck. A thousand bonds unite us to our fellows, and the most anxious egoism could hardly succeed in severing them all. You believe yourself invulnerable in your deliberate obscurity. But you have a son, youth carries him away; a brother, less prudent than yourself, dares to express his disagreement; an old enemy, whom you have offended in the past, has succeeded in capturing some influence. What will you do then? After having bitterly stigmatized all protests, all complaints, will it be your turn to complain? You are condemned in advance, by your own conscience and by that debased public opinion which you have yourself contributed to form. Will you yield without resistance? Indeed, will you

---

[a] The same passage appears in the *Spirit of Conquest*: see above, footnote *a* p. 118.

be given the opportunity to yield? Will they not thrust aside, will they not persecute, an importunate object, a monument to an injustice? You have seen men oppressed; you have judged them guilty; you have opened up the route on which you yourself are now forced to march. Arbitrariness is incompatible with the existence of any government considered as a set of institutions. For political institutions are simply contracts; and it is in the nature of contracts to establish fixed limits. Hence arbitrariness, being precisely opposed to what constitutes a contract, undermines the foundation of all political institutions.

Arbitrariness is dangerous for a government in action: because, even though, in hastening its progress, it sometimes lends it an impression of power, it always deprives its action of regularity and permanence.

By telling a people: your laws are insufficient to govern you, we authorize that same people to answer: if our laws are insufficient, we want other laws. With these words all legitimate authority is put in doubt: force alone is left. For one would need to be too convinced of men's stupidity to tell them: 'You have agreed to impose upon yourself this or that inconvenience to ensure yourselves some protection. We are taking that protection away from you, but we are leaving you the inconvenience. On the one hand you will suffer all the constraints of the social state, while on the other hand you will be exposed to all the risks of the savage condition.'

Arbitrariness is of no help to a government in terms of its security. When a government uses the law against its enemies, those enemies cannot use the same precise and formal law against the government. But when a government takes arbitrary action against enemies, they can reply in kind because such action is vague and without fixed boundaries.[1]

When a regular government chooses to employ arbitrary power, it sacrifices the aim of its existence to the measures which it adopts to preserve this. Why do we wish authority to repress those who attack our property, our liberty or our life? Because we want to be assured of their enjoyment. But if our fortune can be destroyed, our liberty threatened, our life disturbed by arbitrary power, what good shall we derive from the protection of authority? Why do we wish it to punish those who plot against the constitution of the state? Because we fear the replacement of a legal organization by an oppressive power. But if the authority itself

---

[1] B. Constant, *Réactions politiques* (Paris, 1797), pp. 85–7.
[*Ecrits et discours politiques* vol. 1, p. 76.]

exercises this oppressive power, what advantage can it possibly offer? Perhaps for a while an advantage of fact. The arbitrary measures of established governments are always less numerous than those of factions which still have to establish their power. Yet even this advantage is lost in virtue of arbitrary power. Once its methods have been admitted at all, they are found so quick, so convenient, that it seems no longer worthwhile to use any other. Presented initially as a last resort to be used only in infinitely rare circumstances, arbitrariness becomes the solution for all problems and an everyday expedient.

What prevents arbitrary power is the observance of procedures. Procedures are the tutelary deities of societies: procedures alone protect innocence, they are the only means for men to relate to one another. Everything else is obscure: everything is handed over to solitary conscience and vacillating opinion. Procedures alone are fully in evidence; it is to them alone that the oppressed may appeal.

This remedy against arbitrary power is the responsibility of officials. The ancients believed that the places profaned by a crime must undergo an expiation, and I believe that, in the future, the ground blighted by an arbitrary act will need, in order to be purified, the exemplary punishment of the culprit. Every time I see in a country a citizen arbitrarily imprisoned, and do not see the prompt punishment of this violation of the procedures, I shall say: maybe this people wishes to be free; maybe it deserves to be; but it does not yet know the first elements of liberty.[a]

Many see in the exercise of arbitrary power simply a police measure. And since, apparently, they hope always to be those who administer it without ever becoming its objects, they find it exceedingly well adapted for public peace and good order. Others, less sanguine, nevertheless perceive in it only a passing vexation: but the danger is much greater.

Give to the holders of executive authority the power to infringe individual liberty, and you annihilate all those guarantees which are the first conditions and the unique aim of the union of men under the empire of the laws.

You want the independence of tribunals, of judges and of jurors. But if the members of the tribunals, the jurors and the judges could be arbitrarily arrested, what would be left of their independence? Or, indeed, what would happen if arbitrary measures were permitted against them not for their public conduct, but for secret reasons?

[a] B. Constant, *Discours au Cercle Constitutionnel*, 1798.

Ministerial authority, no doubt, would not notify them of their arrest while they were seated on their benches in that apparently inviolable precinct in which the law has placed them. It would not even dare, were they to go against it and obey their own conscience, to arrest or exile them in their capacity as jurors and as judges. But it would arrest and exile them as individuals under suspicion. At most it would wait until the judgement which constituted their crime in its eyes had been forgotten to attribute some other motive for the rigour exercised against them. It would not therefore be a handful of obscure citizens whom you would have delivered up to the arbitrariness of the police; it would be all the tribunals, all the judges, all the jurors, and consequently all the accused, that you would leave at its mercy.

In a country where ministers disposed indiscriminately of the power of arrest and exile, it would seem vain, for the sake of enlightened opinion, to grant some freedom or some security to the press. If a writer, while fully observing the laws, were to clash with the opinions or to criticize the acts of those in authority, he would not be arrested or exiled in his capacity as a writer; he would be arrested or exiled as a dangerous individual, without the reason being disclosed.

What is the point of giving more examples of the development of such a patent truth? All public functions, all private conditions, would be equally threatened. The importunate creditor who had as his debtor an agent of power, the intractable father who refused him his daughter's hand, the inconvenient husband, who defended against him the virtue of his wife, the competitor whose merit, or the supervisor whose vigilance gave him reason for alarm, would undoubtedly not be arrested as creditors, fathers, husbands, supervisors or rivals. For if authority can arrest or exile them for secret reasons, how can we be sure that those secret reasons will not be invented? What would the authority risk? It would plainly be impossible to call it to legal account; and as far as the explanation that, out of prudence, it would perhaps think it must accord with public opinion, since nothing could be looked into or verified, who would not foresee that calumny would be sufficient to motivate persecution?[1]

Nothing is safe from arbitrary power once this is tolerated. No institution can escape from it. It negates them all in their foundation. It deceives society by procedures that it renders powerless. All promises

---

[1] *De la Respons. des ministres*, ch. XIV.

become perjuries; all guarantees traps for the unfortunate who trust in them.

When men excuse arbitrary power, or wish to minimize its dangers, they always talk as if citizens had no relations except with the supreme holder of authority. But in fact they have inevitable and more direct relations with all its secondary agents. Whenever you permit exile, imprisonment or any oppression which is not sanctioned by any law, and which has not been preceded by any trial, it is not under the power of the monarch that you place the citizens, nor even under that of his ministers. It is beneath the rod of the most subordinate of authorities. It is this that can strike them down with an interim measure and justify the measure with a lie. It triumphs, provided that it deceives, and the power to deceive is assured to it. For the better the prince and his ministers are placed to direct affairs in general and to favour the increase and prosperity of the state, of its dignity, wealth and power, the more the very extent of these important functions makes it impossible for them to examine in detail the interests of individuals; minute and imperceptible interests, when compared to the whole, and yet no less sacred, since they include life, liberty and the security of innocence. The care of these interests must therefore be entrusted to those who can look after them, to tribunals exclusively charged with the examination of griev- ances, with the verification of complaints, and with the investigation of crimes; to tribunals which have the leisure, as well as the duty, to explore everything fairly; to tribunals, whose special mission it is, and which alone can accomplish it.

I do not distinguish in my reflections cases of exile from arrest and arbitrary imprisonments. It is a mistake to regard exile as a milder penalty. We are deceived by the traditions of the former monarchy. We are misled by the exile of a number of distinguished men. Our memory recalls M. de Choiseul,[a] surrounded by the respect of generous friends, and exile seems to us a triumphal progress. But let us descend to more obscure ranks, and let us travel to other epochs. We shall see in those lower ranks exile tearing the father away from his children, the husband from his wife, the merchant from his business, forcing parents to abandon the education of their family or to commit it to mercenary hands, separating friend from friend, taking the old man from his accustomed way of life, the industrious man from his speculations, and

[a] Minister of foreign affairs and of war from 1758 to 1770, exiled in 1770 through the intrigues of the Maréchal de Richelieu and the Duke of Aiguillon.

talent from its labours. We shall see exile combined with poverty, despoilment pursuing its victim into some unknown land, leaving the most elementary needs unsatisfied, and making the smallest of pleasures impossible. We shall see exile combined with disfavour, surrounding those it strikes with suspicion and mistrust, plunging them into an atmosphere of proscription, delivering them now to the coldness of the first stranger, now to the insolence of the last official. We shall see exile freezing all affections at their source, exhaustion depriving the exiled of the friend who followed him, oblivion disputing with him those other friends whose memory represented in his eyes his absent country, egoism adopting accusations and excuses for indifference, and the abandoned victim of the proscription attempting in vain to preserve, in his lonely soul, some imperfect vestige of his past life.

The present government is the first of all French governments to have formally renounced this terrible prerogative in the constitution it has proposed.[1] It is by consecrating in this way all rights and all liberties. It is by granting to the nation what it wished for in 1789, what it still wants today, what it has demanded with unflinching perseverance for twenty-five years every time it recaptures the power to make itself heard; it is thus that this government will each day put down deeper roots in the heart of the French.

CHAPTER 19

On judicial guarantees

The Charter of 1814 was very vague about the irremovability of judges. It declared irremovable only those names by the king, without establishing a fixed term for investing with a royal nomination those judges who were already in office by virtue of a previous appointment.[a] This dependence in which a large number of individuals found themselves was of considerable help to the ministry of that time.

---

[1] Art. 61. No-one can be pursued, arrested, detained or exiled except in the cases provided for by the law.

---

[a] *Charte Constitutionnelle* of 4 June 1814, arts. 57–62. Not only did the position of the judges already in charge remain ambiguous, but the *juges de paix*, named by the king, were not irremovable.

The present government, franker and firmer in its progress, has renounced in the new constitution all equivocal prerogatives. It has sanctioned the irremovability of judges starting from a fixed and recent date.[a]

In effect all temporary nominations, either by the government or by the people, all possibilities of dismissal, short of a positive judgement, are in fact so many attacks upon the independence of the judiciary power.

The venality of offices has met with violent criticism. It was an abuse, but this abuse had an advantage that the judicial order which has replaced it has often made us regret.

Throughout almost the whole revolution, tribunals, judges, trials, were none of them free. The different parties appropriated, one after the other, the instruments and forms of the law. The courage which makes one brave death on the battlefield is easier than the public profession of an independent opinion in the face of the threats of tyrants and factions. A judge who can be moved or dismissed is more dangerous than one who has purchased his post. To have bought one's post is less corrupting than having always to fear losing it. I assume also as established and consecrated the institution of juries, the openness of proceedings and the existence of severe laws against judges who prevaricate. But once these precautions have been taken, judicial power must be in a position of perfect independence; all authority must refrain even from insinuations against it. Nothing more effectively depraves public opinion and morals than those perpetual declamations, repeated amongst us in all directions, at different times, against men who either should have been inviolable, or who ought to have been brought to trial themselves.

It is a patent truth that in a constitutional monarchy the nomination of judges should be the prerogative of the prince. In such a government the royal power must be allowed all the influence, and even all the popularity, that is compatible with liberty. The people may often make mistakes in the election of judges. Mistakes by the royal power are necessarily more rare. It has no interest in making any, while it has a pressing one in avoiding them, since judges are irremovable and the commissions they hold are not temporary.

To achieve a full guarantee of the independence of judges, it will perhaps be necessary, some day, to increase their salaries. The general

---

[a] The date of the *Sénatus-consulte* of 12 October 1807.

rule is: give to public posts salaries which will surround those who hold them with respect and make them totally free. The representatives of the people, who are amply in evidence and may hope for glory, do not need to be paid. But the functions of the judges are not of a nature to be exercised without payment. And, any function that requires a salary is bound to be despised if the salary itself is particularly modest. Reduce the number of judges; allocate to them districts which they can inspect, and give them substantial salaries.[a]

The irremovability of judges would not be sufficient to surround innocence with the safeguards to which it is entitled if to those irremovable judges was not added the institution of juries, that institution so calumniated and yet so beneficial, despite the imperfections of which it has thus far been impossible entirely to free it.

I am aware that amongst us the institution of the jury is attacked because of the supposed lack of zeal, the ignorance, the carelessness and the frivolity of the French. It is not the institution, it is the nation which is being denounced. But who cannot see that an institution, if it is intrinsically good, while it may initially seem poorly suited to a nation unaccustomed to it, can still turn out to be both appropriate and beneficial, because the nation acquires through the institution itself that very capacity which it previously lacked? I shall always be reluctant to believe that a nation can fail to be concerned with the first of all its interests, the administration of justice and the guarantee due to the innocent in the face of accusation.

'The French', writes an opponent of the jury, whose work has, perhaps more than anyone else's, stirred up most feeling against the institution,[1] 'will never possess the education and the firmness which are necessary for the juror to discharge his duty. Such is our indifference to all that concerns public administration, such is the empire of egoism and individual interest, the lukewarmness, indeed the nullity of public spirit, that the law which establishes this kind of procedure cannot be enforced.

But a public spirit capable of overcoming that lukewarmness and that egoism is exactly what we need. Do you suppose that such a spirit

---

[1] M. Gach, president of a tribunal of first instance, in the department of the Lot.

---

[a] In his comment, Eduard Laboulaye observes that Constant clearly had in mind the English model, and cites the comparison between the English and French judicial system in Henry Brougham and Vaux, *The British Constitution* in *Works* (11 vols., London and Glasgow, 1855–61), vol. 11.

would exist amongst the English without the whole array of their political institutions? In a country in which the institution of juries has been suspended again and again, the freedom of tribunals violated, the accused dragged in front of commissions, this spirit cannot emerge. They criticize the institution of the juries, when it is the attackers who deserve criticism.

'The juror', we read 'will be unable to separate, as the institution requires, his own convictions from the documents, testimony, and other pieces of evidence: things that are unnecessary where conviction exists, and insufficient when it does not.' Yet there is no need to separate these things: indeed, they are essential elements in reaching a verdict. The spirit of the institution demands simply that the juror should not be forced to pronounce on the basis of a numerical calculation, but on the basis of the impression that the combination of documents, testimony and pieces of evidence has produced in him. Hence the light of ordinary common sense is sufficient to enable a juror to know and to declare whether, having heard the witnesses, read the documents and compared the pieces of evidence, he is or is not convinced.

'If the jurors', this author continues 'find a law too severe, they will absolve the accused, and declare the fact in question, against their own conscience,' and he imagines the case of a man accused of having sheltered his own brother and who, by that action, has incurred the death penalty. In my view this example, far from militating against the institution of the jury, constitutes its highest praise. It proves that this institution hinders the execution of laws that are contrary to humanity, to justice and to morality. One is a man before one is a juror. Far from blaming the juror who, in this particular case, should fail in his duty as a juror, I would praise him for discharging his duty as a man, and for rushing, by all the means in his power, to the aid of an accused person on the point of being punished for an action that, far from being a crime, is a virtue. This example does not prove that we do not need juries; it proves that we do not need laws that sentence to death someone who gives shelter to his own brother.

'But then', continues the author 'whenever the penalties are excessive or seem so to the juror, he will pronounce a sentence against his own beliefs.' I would reply that the juror, in his role as a citizen and property holder has an interest in not leaving unpunished those crimes which threaten the security, the property or the life of all the members of the social body. This interest will prevail over passing compassion: the example England offers us of this is, perhaps, an upsetting example. Rigorous penalties are applied to crimes that certainly do not deserve them, and the jurors do not deviate from their verdict even when they pity those whom their declaration sends to the scaffold.[1] There is in man a certain respect for the written law: he needs very powerful motives to overcome it. When such motives exist, it is the fault of the laws. If the penalties seem excessive to jurors, it is because they are excessive, since, once again, the jurors have no interest in finding them such. In extreme cases, that is to say when the jurors are placed between an irresistible feeling of justice and humanity and the letter of the law, I would dare to say that it is not an evil if they do depart from it. There must not be a law which revolts the common humanity of men to such a degree that jurors chosen from the bosom of the nation cannot bring themselves to enforce this law. The institution of permanent judges, reconciled by habit to such barbarous law, far from being an advantage, would be a curse.

'The jurors', argues the same writer 'will fail in their duty sometimes from fear, and sometimes from pity.'[a] If it is from fear it will be the fault of a negligent police force failing to shelter them from individual revenge; if it is from pity, it will be the fault of a too rigorous law.

The negligence, indifference and frivolity of the French are the result of their faulty institutions, and their effect is cited to perpetuate their cause. No people remains indifferent to its own interests when it is allowed to take care of them: whenever it is indifferent, it is because it has not been allowed to do so. The institution of the jury is, from this viewpoint, all the more necessary to the French people, in that it seems temporarily less capable of working it. In it the French people will find not only the particular advantages of that institution, but the general and more important advantage of remaking its own moral education.

To the irremovability of judges and the sanctity of juries it is also necessary to unite the constant and scrupulous respect of the judicial procedures.

By a peculiar begging of the question, during the revolution those

---

[1] In England I have seen juries declaring guilty a young girl who had stolen some muslin worth thirteen shillings. They knew that their declaration implied the death penalty against her.

[a] The quotations are from: Gach (forename unknown), *Des vices de l'institution du jury en France* (Paris, 1804).

who had still to be judged were incessantly declared guilty in advance.

Procedure constitutes a safeguard: to curtail it is to reduce or lose that safeguard, and is therefore in itself a penalty. If we inflict that penalty upon the accused, his crime has then been proved in advance. But, if his crime has been proved, what is the good of a tribunal, whatever it may be? But if his crime has not been proved, what right do you have to place him in a special and proscribed class and to deprive him, simply on suspicion, of the benefit common to all members of the social state?

This absurdity is by no means the only one. Procedure is either necessary or useless for conviction. If useless, why retain it at ordinary trials? If necessary, why suppress it in the most important ones? When a minor misdemeanour is in question, and neither the accused's life nor honour is at stake, his case is drawn up in the most solemn manner. But when it comes to some frightful crime, and is consequently a matter of infamy and death, all the protective precautions are suppressed with a simple word. The code of laws is shut, procedure is curtailed as if it were thought that the more serious the accusation, the less necessary it is to examine it!

It is only brigands, assassins, you say, conspirators, whom we deprive of the benefit of procedure. But before they are identified as such, is it not necessary to look at the evidence? Procedure is precisely the means for checking the evidence. If a better or quicker procedure exists, let us adopt it. But let us adopt it in all cases. Why should there be a class of facts in which unnecessary delays are observed or, alternatively, another class on which we decide with dangerous haste? The dilemma is clear. If haste is not dangerous, to proceed slowly is superfluous; if proceeding slowly is not superfluous, haste is dangerous. Will it not be argued that before the trial one can distinguish by infallible, external signs the innocent from the guilty, those who ought to enjoy the prerogative of legal forms and those who ought to be deprived of them? It is because such signs do not exist, that legal forms are indispensable. It is because legal procedure seemed the only way of distinguishing the innocent from the guilty, that all free and humane peoples have demanded its institution. However imperfect procedure may be, it has a power to protect of which it can only be deprived by its destruction. Procedure is the born enemy, the inflexible adversary of tyranny, popular or otherwise. While it survives, tribunals offer a more or less generous resistance to arbitrary power, sufficient to restrain it. Under

Charles I English tribunals absolved, despite the threats of the Court, several friends of liberty. Under Cromwell, though dominated by the Protector, they often absolved citizens accused of attachment to the monarchy. Under James II, Jefferies was forced to trample the legal forms under foot and to violate the independence of judges even those of his own creation, to ensure the numerous executions of the victims of his fury. There is in legal forms something imposing and specific which compels the judges to show respect for themselves, and to follow an equitable and regular course. The frightful law that under Robespierre, declared proof superfluous and suppressed advocates for the defence, is a tribute to the value of these forms.*ᵃ* That law showed that legal procedure, modified, mutilated, tortured in every sort of way by the ingenuity of factions, was still an embarrassment to men carefully selected from the whole population as the freest from all scruples of conscience, and all respect for opinion.[1]

Finally, I regard the right of pardon with which our constitution invests the emperor, as a final protection granted to the innocent.

Some have opposed to this right one of those trenchant dilemmas which seem to simplify questions because they misrepresent them. If the law is just, they have argued, no-one must have the right to prevent its execution; if it is unjust, it must be changed. This reasoning requires one condition only: that there should be one law for each particular fact.

The more general the law, the more it detaches itself from particular actions, upon which it is nevertheless called upon to pronounce. A law can only be perfectly just for one particular circumstance. As soon as it applies to two different circumstances, distinguished by the slightest of differences, it becomes more or less unjust in one or other of the cases. Facts present infinite nuances; the laws cannot follow all these nuances; the dilemma I have cited is consequently erroneous. The law may be just as a general law, that is to say it may be just to apply such a penalty to such and such an action; and yet the law may be unjust in its application to some other particular fact; that is to say, an action which

---

[1] An excellent article in the present constitution is the one limiting military jurisdiction exclusively to military crimes, rather than, as previously, to crimes committed by military personnel. On this pretext, either military personnel were deprived of civil procedures, or private citizens were subjected to military ones.
[*Acte additionnel*, title 5, art. 55.]

ᵃ The so-called 'Loi des suspects' of 17 September 1973.

is materially the same as that envisaged by the law, may be different in some real way, though it could hardly be legally defined. The right of pardon is nothing but the reconciliation of the general law with particular justice.

The necessity for this reconciliation is so pressing, that in all these countries in which the right of pardon is rejected, all sorts of expedients are substituted for it. In our country, in the past, the tribunal of Cassation was in some respects invested with it. In those judgements which seemed to inflict overly rigorous penalties, it sought some defect of form that authorized its annulment. In order to achieve this result, it often resorted to extremely pedantic formalities: but it was, of course, an abuse, even though its motivation made it excusable. The constitution of 1815 was right to revert from it to a simpler idea, and to restore to the supreme power one of its most touching and natural prerogatives.

CHAPTER 20

Final considerations

Our representatives will have to deal with several of the questions which I have discussed in this work. The government itself has taken care to announce, as I mentioned at the beginning, that the constitution will be open to improvement. We can only hope that such improvement will be effected slowly, at leisure, without impatience and without attempting to go beyond our own time. If this constitution has faults, it is a proof that the best-intentioned of men do not always foresee the consequences of each article of a constitution. The same thing could happen to those who might wish to recast it in order to correct it. It is easy to make one's home more comfortable by making only partial changes to it. These are the more gentle because they are almost imperceptible. But it is dangerous to knock down one's house to rebuild it, especially if, in between, one is left with no shelter.

Foreigners observe us. They know that we are a strong nation. If they see us enjoyng the benefits of a constitution, even if imperfect, they will see that we are a reasonable nation, and our reason will be for them more imposing than our force. Foreigners observe us. They know that at our head marches the greatest general of this century. If they see us rallied around him, they will believe themselves defeated in advance. But divided, we are bound to perish.

The magnanimity of our enemies has been greatly extolled. This magnanimity has not prevented them from compensating themselves for the expenses of war. They have taken from us Belgium and the Rhine, which long possession and solemn treaties had identified with France. Should they conquer today, they would take from us the Franche-Comté, Lorraine and Alsace. Why should the declarations of Brussels be better observed than those of Frankfurt?

The emperor has given the most indisputable pledge of the sincerity of his intentions: he has assembled around him six hundred and twenty-nine representatives of the nation, freely elected, and over whose choice the government has not been able to exercise any influence. At the moment of this solemn gathering he was exercising dictatorship. Had he simply wanted despotism, he could have made some attempt to preserve it.

We are told that it would have been against his own interests. No doubt, but does this not mean that his interests are in accord with liberty? Is this not a ground for trust?

He has been the first, since the Constituent Assembly, to convene an entirely national representation. He has respected, even before the constitution was yet in force, unlimited freedom of the press, the excesses of which are only a more striking tribute to the firmness of his noble resolution. He has restored to a large number of the people the right to choose their own magistrates.

As soon as he saw his goal, he recognized the route towards it. He has understood, better than anyone else, that once one has adopted a system, it must be adopted in full; that liberty must be complete; that it is the guarantee as well as the limit of power. The sense of his own strength has raised him above those equivocal and cowardly afterthoughts which seduce narrow minds and divide feeble spirits.

These are facts, and these facts explain the behaviour of those of us who have rallied around the present government in this moment of crisis, those who, although they remained strangers to the master of the earth, have now ranged themselves around the founder of a free constitution and the defender of our fatherland.

When his arrival resounded from one end of Europe to the other, we saw in him the conqueror of the world, and we wished for liberty. Who would not have said in fact that this would profit more from timidity and weakness than from an immense and almost miraculous force?

I believed it, I must confess, and in this hope, after having spent ten months without any communication with the fallen government, after having been in constant opposition to its measures, over the freedom of the press, over the responsibility of the ministers, over passive obedience, I got more involved when it collapsed. I told them again and again that it was liberty that must be saved, that they themselves could be saved only by liberty. But these powerless words frightened ears little used to hearing them.

A few words about a constitution were indeed uttered. But no national measure was taken, no open step came to reassure public opinion which was still undecided. All was chaos, stupor, confusion. It was time for those who had come to despair of the cause, to declare it hopeless. The truth is that liberty, the real means of salvation, was hateful to them.

This government fled. What were we supposed to do? Follow a party which was not our own, which we had fought when it had the appearance of strength, whose every intention and every idea were opposed to our opinions and to our wishes; a party which we had defended for a few days, only as a means, as a passage to liberty? But from then on the aim of all our efforts had failed. Was it a constitutional monarchy that we could anticipate from foreign powers? Certainly not. It had to be either the division of France, or a dependent administration, a docile executor of the orders which it received from them.

When James II left England, the English declared that this flight was an abdication: it is since then that they have been free.

No, I did not wish to join our enemies, and beg for the massacre of French men, in order to raise up for the second time what would fall down once again.

To make oneself defend a government which in fact abandons itself is not to promise to go into exile with it. To give proof of dedication to a weakness which has neither hopes nor resources is not to renounce the land of our fathers. To brave dangers for a cause which one hopes to render good after having rescued it, does not mean to devote oneself to that cause, when, utterly perverted and transformed, it adopts foreigners as its allies and massacre and fire as its method. To decide not to flee, finally, does not make one a renegade. Undoubtedly, in paying oneself a solemn testimonial, one is still displaying bitter feelings. One learns, not without surprise, and not without a pain which cannot be lessened by the novelty of the discovery, that respect is a heavy burden for human hearts, and how happy men are, when they believe that an irreproachable man has ceased to be so, to proceed to condemn him.

The future will give the answer. Liberty will emerge from that future, however stormy it may now look. Then, after twenty years of defending the rights of man, the safety of the individual and of land, freedom of thought, and the abolition of all arbitrary power, I shall dare to congratulate myself for joining, before the victory, those institutions which sanction all these rights. I shall have accomplished my life's work.

THE LIBERTY
OF THE ANCIENTS
COMPARED WITH THAT
OF THE MODERNS

SPEECH GIVEN AT
THE ATHÉNÉE ROYAL
IN PARIS

Bibliographical note

This translation of Constant's speech of 1819 on the liberty of the ancients and the moderns reproduces the text published in his *Collection complète des ouvrages publiés sur le gouvernement représentatif et la constitution actuelle, ou Cours de politique constitutionnelle*, 4 vols. (Paris and Rouen, 1820), vol. 4, pp. 238–74.

The speech contains numerous repetitions and reformulations of passages which appeared in the *Spirit of Conquest and Usurpation* and in the *Principles of Politics*. The general significance of these reformulations is discussed in the Introduction to this volume. It seemed too pedantic to indicate the repeated passages one by one in the annotation, as their presence does not affect the overall originality and interest of this text.

Gentlemen,

I wish to submit for your attention a few distinctions, still rather new, between two kinds of liberty: these differences have thus far remained unnoticed, or at least insufficiently remarked. The first is the liberty the exercise of which was so dear to the ancient peoples; the second the one the enjoyment of which is especially precious to the modern nations. If I am right, this investigation will prove interesting from two different angles.

Firstly, the confusion of these two kinds of liberty has been amongst us, in the all too famous days of our revolution, the cause of many an evil. France was exhausted by useless experiments, the authors of which, irritated by their poor success, sought to force her to enjoy the good she did not want, and denied her the good which she did want.

Secondly, called as we are by our happy revolution (I call it happy, despite its excesses, because I concentrate my attention on its results) to enjoy the benefits of representative government, it is curious and interesting to discover why this form of government, the only one in the shelter of which we could find some freedom and peace today, was totally unknown to the free nations of antiquity.

I know that there are writers who have claimed to distinguish traces of it among some ancient peoples, in the Lacedaemonian republic for example, or amongst our ancestors the Gauls; but they are mistaken.

The Lacedaemonian government was a monastic aristocracy, and in no way a representative government. The power of the kings was limited, but it was limited by the ephors, and not by men invested with a mission similar to that which election confers today on the defenders of our liberties. The ephors, no doubt, though originally created by the kings, were elected by the people. But there were only five of them. Their authority was as much religious as political; they even shared in the administration of government, that is, in the executive power. Thus their prerogative, like that of almost all popular magistrates in the ancient republics, far from being simply a barrier against tyranny, became sometimes itself an insufferable tyranny.

The regime of the Gauls, which quite resembled the one that a certain party would like to restore to us,[a] was at the same time theocratic and warlike. The priests enjoyed unlimited power. The military class or nobility had markedly insolent and oppressive privileges; the people had no rights and no safeguards.

In Rome the tribunes had, up to a point, a representative mission. They were the organs of those plebeians whom the oligarchy – which is the same in all ages – had submitted, in overthrowing the kings, to so harsh a slavery. The people, however, exercised a large part of the political rights directly. They met to vote on the laws and to judge the patricians against whom charges had been levelled: thus there were, in Rome, only feeble traces of a representative system.

This system is a discovery of the moderns, and you will see, Gentlemen, that the condition of the human race in antiquity did not allow for the introduction or establishment of an institution of this nature. The ancient peoples could neither feel the need for it, nor appreciate its advantages. Their social organization led them to desire an entirely different freedom from the one which this system grants to us.

Tonight's lecture will be devoted to demonstrating this truth to you.

First ask yourselves, Gentlemen, what an Englishman, a Frenchman, and a citizen of the United States of America understand today by the word 'liberty'.

For each of them it is the right to be subjected only to the laws, and to be neither arrested, detained, put to death or maltreated in any way by the arbitrary will of one or more individuals. It is the right of everyone to

---

[a] If the model of the ancient republics had dominated the politics of the Jacobins, during the Restoration the return to feudal liberty became the ideal of the monarchical 'reformers'. The most influential contemporary source is: Robert de Montlosier, *De la monarchie française.* For a survey of the political interpretations of France's feudal past, see: Stanley Mellon, *The Political Uses of History, a Study of Historians in the French Restoration* (Stanford, California, 1958); Shirley M. Gruner, 'Political Historiography in Restoration France', *History and Theory*, 8 (1969), 346–65.

express their opinion, choose a profession and practise it, to dispose of property, and even to abuse it; to come and go without permission, and without having to account for their motives or undertakings. It is everyone's right to associate with other individuals, either to discuss their interests, or to profess the religion which they and their associates prefer, or even simply to occupy their days or hours in a way which is most compatible with their inclinations or whims. Finally it is everyone's right to exercise some influence on the administration of the government, either by electing all or particular officials, or through representations, petitions, demands to which the authorities are more or less compelled to pay heed. Now compare this liberty with that of the ancients.

The latter consisted in exercising collectively, but directly, several parts of the complete sovereignty; in deliberating, in the public square, over war and peace; in forming alliances with foreign governments; in voting laws, in pronouncing judgements; in examining the accounts, the acts, the stewardship of the magistrates; in calling them to appear in front of the assembled people, in accusing, condemning or absolving them. But if this was what the ancients called liberty, they admitted as compatible with this collective freedom the complete subjection of the individual to the authority of the community. You find among them almost none of the enjoyments which we have just seen form part of the liberty of the moderns. All private actions were submitted to a severe surveillance. No importance was given to individual independence, neither in relation to opinions, nor to labour, nor, above all, to religion. The right to choose one's own religious affiliation, a right which we regard as one of the most precious, would have seemed to the ancients a crime and a sacrilege. In the domains which seem to us the most useful, the authority of the social body interposed itself and obstructed the will of individuals. Among the Spartans, Therpandrus could not add a string to his lyre without causing offence to the ephors. In the most domestic of relations the public authority again intervened. The young Lacedaemonian could not visit his new bride freely. In Rome, the censors cast a searching eye over family life. The laws regulated customs, and as customs touch on everything, there was hardly anything that the laws did not regulate.

Thus among the ancients the individual, almost always sovereign in public affairs, was a slave in all his private relations. As a citizen, he decided on peace and war; as a private individual, he was constrained, watched and repressed in all his movements; as a member of the collective body, he interrogated, dismissed, condemned, beggared, exiled, or sentenced to death his magistrates and superiors; as a subject of the collective body he could himself be deprived of his status, stripped of his privileges, banished, put to death, by the discretionary will of the whole to which he belonged. Among the moderns, on the contrary, the individual, independent in his private life, is, even in the freest of states, sovereign only in appearance. His sovereignty is restricted and almost always suspended. If, at fixed and rare intervals, in which he is again surrounded by precautions and obstacles, he exercises this sovereignty, it is always only to renounce it.

I must at this point, Gentlemen, pause for a moment to anticipate an objection which may be addressed to me. There was in antiquity a republic where the enslavement of individual existence to the collective body was not as complete as I have described it. This republic was the most famous of all: you will guess that I am speaking of Athens. I shall return to it later, and in subscribing to the truth of this fact, I shall also indicate its cause. We shall see why, of all the ancient states, Athens was the one which most resembles the modern ones. Everywhere else social jurisdiction was unlimited. The ancients, as Condorcet says, had no notion of individual rights.[a] Men were, so to speak, merely machines, whose gears and cog-wheels were regulated by the law. The same subjection characterized the golden centuries of the Roman republic; the individual was in some way lost in the nation, the citizen in the city.

We shall now trace this essential difference between the ancients and ourselves back to its source.

All ancient republics were restricted to a narrow territory. The most populous, the most powerful, the most substantial among them, was not equal in extension to the smallest of modern states. As an inevitable consequence of their narrow territory, the spirit of these republics was bellicose; each people incessantly attacked their neighbours or was attacked by them. Thus driven by necessity against one another, they fought or threatened each other constantly. Those who had no ambition to be conquerors, could still not lay down their weapons, lest they should themselves be conquered. All had to buy their security, their independence, their whole existence at the price of war. This was the constant interest, the almost habitual occupation of the free states of

[a] J. A. N. Caritat de Condorcet, *Sur l'instruction publique*, p. 47.

antiquity. Finally, by an equally necessary result of this way of being, all these states had slaves.[a] The mechanical professions and even, among some nations, the industrial ones, were committed to people in chains. The modern world offers us a completely opposing view. The smallest states of our day are incomparably larger than Sparta or than Rome was over five centuries. Even the division of Europe into several states is, thanks to the progress of enlightenment, more apparent than real. While each people, in the past, formed an isolated family, the born enemy of other families, a mass of human beings now exists, that under different names and under different forms of social organization are essentially homogeneous in their nature. This mass is strong enough to have nothing to fear from barbarian hordes. It is sufficiently civilized to find war a burden. Its uniform tendency is towards peace.

This difference leads to another one. War precedes commerce. War and commerce are only two different means of achieving the same end, that of getting what one wants. Commerce is simply a tribute paid to the strength of the possessor by the aspirant to possession. It is an attempt to conquer, by mutual agreement, what one can no longer hope to obtain through violence. A man who was always the stronger would never conceive the idea of commerce. It is experience, by proving to him that war, that is the use of his strength against the strength of others, exposes him to a variety of obstacles and defeats, that leads him to resort to commerce, that is to a milder and surer means of engaging the interest of others to agree to what suits his own. War is all impulse, commerce, calculation. Hence it follows that an age must come in which commerce replaces war. We have reached this age.

I do not mean that amongst the ancients there were no trading peoples. But these peoples were to some degree an exception to the general rule. The limits of this lecture do not allow me to illustrate all the obstacles which then opposed the progress of commerce; you know them as well as I do; I shall only mention one of them.

Their ignorance of the compass meant that the sailors of antiquity always had to keep close to the coast. To pass through the pillars of Hercules, that is, the straits of Gibraltar, was considered the most daring of enterprises. The Phoenicians and the Carthaginians, the

---

[a] In the 1806 draft, Constant observed: '. . . slavery, universally practised by the ancients gave to their mores a severe and cruel imprint, which made it easy for them to sacrifice gentle affections to political interests.' E. Hofmann (ed.), *Les 'Principes de Politique'*, vol. 2, p. 428.

most able of navigators, did not risk it until very late, and their example for long remained without imitators. In Athens, of which we shall talk soon, the interest on maritime enterprises was around 60%, while current interest was only 12%: that was how dangerous the idea of distant navigation seemed.

Moreover, if I could permit myself a digression which would unfortunately prove too long, I would show you, Gentlemen, through the details of the customs, habits, way of trading with others of the trading peoples of antiquity, that their commerce was itself impregnated by the spirit of the age, by the atmosphere of war and hostility which surrounded it. Commerce then was a lucky accident, today it is the normal state of things, the only aim, the universal tendency, the true life of nations. They want repose, and with repose comfort, and as a source of comfort, industry. Every day war becomes a more ineffective means of satisfying their wishes. Its hazards no longer offer to individuals benefits that match the results of peaceful work and regular exchanges. Among the ancients, a successful war increased both private and public wealth in slaves, tributes and lands shared out. For the moderns, even a successful war costs infallibly more than it is worth.

Finally, thanks to commerce, to religion, to the moral and intellectual progress of the human race, there are no longer slaves among the European nations. Free men must exercise all professions, provide for all the needs of society.

It is easy to see, Gentlemen, the inevitable outcome of these differences.

Firstly, the size of a country causes a corresponding decrease of the political importance allotted to each individual. The most obscure republican of Sparta or Rome had power. The same is not true of the simple citizen of Britain or of the United States. His personal influence is an imperceptible part of the social will which impresses on the government its direction.

Secondly, the abolition of slavery has deprived the free population of all the leisure which resulted from the fact that slaves took care of most of the work. Without the slave population of Athens, 20,000 Athenians could never have spent every day at the public square in discussions.

Thirdly, commerce does not, like war, leave in men's lives intervals of inactivity. The constant exercise of political rights, the daily discussion of the affairs of the state, disagreements, confabulations, the whole entourage and movement of factions, necessary agitations, the compulsory filling, if I may use the term, of the life of the peoples of antiquity, who, without this resource would have languished under the weight of painful inaction, would only cause trouble and fatigue to modern nations, where each individual, occupied with his speculations, his enterprises, the pleasures he obtains or hopes for, does not wish to be distracted from them other than momentarily, and as little as possible.

Finally, commerce inspires in men a vivid love of individual independence. Commerce supplies their needs, satisfies their desires, without the intervention of the authorities. This intervention is almost always – and I do not know why I say almost – this intervention is indeed always a trouble and an embarrassment. Every time collective power wishes to meddle with private speculations, it harasses the speculators. Every time governments pretend to do our own business, they do it more incompetently and expensively than we would.

I said, Gentlemen, that I would return to Athens, whose example might be opposed to some of my assertions, but which will in fact confirm all of them.

Athens, as I have already pointed out, was of all the Greek republics the most closely engaged in trade:[a] thus it allowed to its citizens an infinitely greater individual liberty than Sparta or Rome. If I could enter into historical details, I would show you that, among the Athenians, commerce had removed several of the differences which distinguished the ancient from the modern peoples. The spirit of the Athenian merchants was similar to that of the merchants of our days. Xenophon tells us that during the Peloponnesian war, they moved their capitals from the continent of Attica to place them on the islands of the archipelago. Commerce had created among them the circulation of money. In Isocrates there are signs that bills of exchange were used. Observe how their customs resemble our own. In their relations with women, you will see, again I cite Xenophon, husbands, satisfied when peace and a decorous friendship reigned in their households, make allowances for the wife who is too vulnerable before the tyranny of nature, close their eyes to the irresistible power of passions, forgive the first weakness and forget the second. In their relations with strangers, we shall see them extending the rights of citizenship to whoever would,

---

[a] Constant's notes to the 1806 draft show that he derived most of his illustrations and examples about Athens in this passage from Cornelius de Pauw, *Recherches philosophiques sur les Grecs*, vol. 1, pp. 93ff.

by moving among them with his family, establish some trade or industry. Finally, we shall be struck by their excessive love of individual independence. In Sparta, says a philosopher, the citizens quicken their step when they are called by a magistrate; but an Athenian would be desperate if he were thought to be dependent on a magistrate.[a]

However, as several of the other circumstances which determined the character of ancient nations existed in Athens as well; as there was a slave population and the territory was very restricted; we find there too the traces of the liberty proper to the ancients. The people made the laws, examined the behaviour of the magistrates, called Pericles to account for his conduct, sentenced to death the generals who had commanded the battle of the Arginusae. Similarly ostracism, that legal arbitrariness, extolled by all the legislators of the age; ostracism, which appears to us, and rightly so, a revolting iniquity, proves that the individual was much more subservient to the supremacy of the social body in Athens, than he is in any of the free states of Europe today.

It follows from what I have just indicated that we can no longer enjoy the liberty of the ancients, which consisted in an active and constant participation in collective power. Our freedom must consist of peaceful enjoyment and private independence. The share which in antiquity everyone held in national sovereignty was by no means an abstract presumption as it is in our own day. The will of each individual had real influence: the exercise of this will was a vivid and repeated pleasure. Consequently the ancients were ready to make many a sacrifice to preserve their political rights and their share in the administration of the state. Everybody, feeling with pride all that his suffrage was worth, found in this awareness of his personal importance a great compensation.

This compensation no longer exists for us today. Lost in the multitude, the individual can almost never perceive the influence he exercises. Never does his will impress itself upon the whole; nothing confirms in his eyes his own cooperation.

The exercise of political rights, therefore, offers us but a part of the pleasures that the ancients found in it, while at the same time the progress of civilization, the commercial tendency of the age, the communication amongst peoples, have infinitely multiplied and varied the means of personal happiness.

[a] Xenophon, *De Republica Lacedaemonium*, VIII, 2 in: J. M. Moore (ed.), *Aristotle and Xenophon on democracy and oligarchy* (London, 1975).

It follows that we must be far more attached than the ancients to our individual independence. For the ancients when they sacrificed that independence to their political rights, sacrificed less to obtain more; while in making the same sacrifice, we would give more to obtain less. The aim of the ancients was the sharing of social power among the citizens of the same fatherland: this is what they called liberty. The aim of the moderns is the enjoyment of security in private pleasures; and they call liberty the guarantees accorded by institutions to these pleasures.

I said at the beginning that, through their failure to perceive these differences, otherwise well-intentioned men caused infinite evils during our long and stormy revolution. God forbid that I should reproach them too harshly. Their error itself was excusable. One could not read the beautiful pages of antiquity, one could not recall the actions of its great men, without feeling an indefinable and special emotion, which nothing modern can possibly arouse. The old elements of a nature, one could almost say, earlier than our own, seem to awaken in us in the face of these memories. It is difficult not to regret the time when the faculties of man developed along an already trodden path, but in so wide a career, so strong in their own powers, with such a feeling of energy and dignity. Once we abandon ourselves to this regret, it is impossible not to wish to imitate what we regret. This impression was very deep, especially when we lived under vicious governments, which, without being strong, were repressive in their effects; absurd in their principles; wretched in action; governments which had as their strength arbitrary power; for their purpose the belittling of mankind; and which some individuals still dare to praise to us today, as if we could ever forget that we have been the witnesses and the victims of their obstinacy, of their impotence and of their overthrow. The aim of our reformers was noble and generous. Who among us did not feel his heart beat with hope at the outset of the course which they seemed to open up? And shame, even today, on whoever does not feel the need to declare that acknowledging a few errors committed by our first guides does not mean blighting their memory or disowning the opinions which the friends of mankind have professed throughout the ages.

But those men had derived several of their theories from the works of two philosophers who had themselves failed to recognize the changes brought by two thousand years in the dispositions of mankind. I shall perhaps at some point examine the system of the most illustrious of these philosophers, of Jean-Jacques Rousseau, and I shall show that, by transposing into our modern age an extent of social power, of collective sovereignty, which belonged to other centuries, this sublime genius, animated by the purest love of liberty, has nevertheless furnished deadly pretexts for more than one kind of tyranny. No doubt, in pointing out what I regard as a misunderstanding which it is important to uncover, I shall be careful in my refutation, and respectful in my criticism. I shall certainly refrain from joining myself to the detractors of a great man. When chance has it that I find myself apparently in agreement with them on some one particular point, I suspect myself; and to console myself for appearing for a moment in agreement with them on a single partial question, I need to disown and denounce with all my energies these pretended allies.

Nevertheless, the interests of truth must prevail over considerations which make the glory of a prodigious talent and the authority of an immense reputation so powerful. Moreover, as we shall see, it is not to Rousseau that we must chiefly attribute the error against which I am going to argue; this is to be imputed much more to one of his successors, less eloquent but no less austere and a hundred times more exaggerated. The latter, the abbé de Mably, can be regarded as the representative of the system which, according to the maxims of ancient liberty, demands that the citizens should be entirely subjected in order for the nation to be sovereign, and that the individual should be enslaved for the people to be free.

The abbé de Mably,[a] like Rousseau and many others, had mistaken, just as the ancients did, the authority of the social body for liberty; and to him any means seemed good if it extended his area of authority over that recalcitrant part of human existence whose independence he deplored. The regret he expresses everywhere in his works is that the law can only cover actions. He would have liked it to cover the most fleeting thoughts and impressions; to pursue man relentlessly, leaving him no refuge in which he might escape from its power. No sooner did he learn, among no matter what people, of some oppressive measure, than he thought he had made a discovery and proposed it as a model. He detested individual liberty like a personal enemy; and whenever in history he came across a nation totally deprived of it, even if it had no political liberty, he could not help admiring it. He went into ecstasies

---

[a] Gabriel Bonnot de Mably, *De la législation ou principes des lois.*

over the Egyptians, because, as he said, among them everything was prescribed by the law, down to relaxations and needs: everything was subjected to the empire of the legislator. Every moment of the day was filled by some duty; love itself was the object of this respected intervention, and it was the law that in turn opened and closed the curtains of the nuptial bed.

Sparta, which combined republican forms with the same enslavement of individuals, aroused in the spirit of that philosopher an even more vivid enthusiasm. That vast monastic barracks to him seemed the ideal of a perfect republic. He had a profound contempt for Athens, and would gladly have said of this nation, the first of Greece, what an academician and great nobleman said of the French Academy: 'What an appalling despotism! Everyone does what he likes there.'[a] I must add that this great nobleman was talking of the Academy as it was thirty years ago.

Montesquieu, who had a less excitable and therefore more observant mind, did not fall into quite the same errors. He was struck by the differences which I have related; but he did not discover their true cause. The Greek politicians who lived under the popular government did not recognize, he argues, any other power but virtue. Politicians of today talk only of manufactures, of commerce, of finances, of wealth and even of luxury.[b] He attributes this difference to the republic and the monarchy. It ought instead to be attributed to the opposed spirit of ancient and modern times. Citizens of republics, subjects of monarchies, all want pleasures, and indeed no-one, in the present condition of societies can help wanting them. The people most attached to their liberty in our own days, before the emancipation of France, was also the most attached to all the pleasures of life; and it valued its liberty especially because it saw in this the guarantee of the pleasures which it cherished. In the past, where there was liberty, people could bear hardship. Now, wherever there is hardship, despotism is necessary for people to resign themselves to it. It would be easier today to make Spartans of an enslaved people than to turn free men into Spartans.

The men who were brought by events to the head of our revolution were, by a necessary consequence of the education they had received, steeped in ancient views which are no longer valid, which the philosophers whom I mentioned above had made fashionable. The meta-

---

[a] The Duke of Richelieu.
[b] C. L. S. de Montesquieu, *Esprit des Lois*, Book 3.

physics of Rousseau, in the midst of which flashed the occasional sublime thought and passages of stirring eloquence; the austerity of Mably, his intolerance, his hatred of all human passions, his eagerness to enslave them all, his exaggerated principles on the competence of the law, the difference between what he recommended and what had ever previously existed, his declamations against wealth and even against property; all these things were bound to charm men heated by their recent victory, and who, having won power over the law, were only too keen to extend this power to all things. It was a source of invaluable support that two disinterested writers anathematizing human despotism, should have drawn up the text of the law in axioms. They wished to exercise public power as they had learnt from their guides it had once been exercised in the free states. They believed that everything should give way before collective will, and that all restrictions on individual rights would be amply compensated by participation in social power.

We all know, Gentlemen, what has come of it. Free institutions, resting upon the knowledge of the spirit of the age, could have survived. The restored edifice of the ancients collapsed, notwithstanding many efforts and many heroic acts which call for our admiration. The fact is that social power injured individual independence in every possible way, without destroying the need for it. The nation did not find that an ideal share in an abstract sovereignty was worth the sacrifices required from her.[a] She was vainly assured, on Rousseau's authority, that the laws of liberty are a thousand times more austere than the yoke of tyrants. She had no desire for those austere laws, and believed sometimes that the yoke of tyrants would be preferable to them. Experience has come to undeceive her. She has seen that the arbitrary power of men was even worse than the worst of laws. But laws too must have their limits.

If I have succeeded, Gentlemen, in making you share the persuasion which in my opinion these facts must produce, you will acknowledge with me the truth of the following principles.

---

[a] In the 1806 draft, Constant commented: 'All legislation which exacts the sacrifice of these enjoyments is incompatible with the present conditions of the human race. From this viewpoint, nothing is more curious to observe than the rhetoric of French demagogues. The most intelligent among them, St Just, made all his speeches in short sentences, calculated to arouse tired minds. Thus while he seemed to suppose the nation capable of the most painful sacrifices, he acknowledged her, by his style, incapable even of paying attention.' E. Hofmann (ed.), *Les 'Principes de Politique'*, vol. 2, p. 432.

Individual independence is the first need of the moderns: consequently one must never require from them any sacrifices to establish political liberty.

It follows that none of the numerous and too highly praised institutions which in the ancient republics hindered individual liberty is any longer admissible in the modern times.

You may, in the first place, think, Gentlemen, that it is superfluous to establish this truth. Several governments of our days do not seem in the least inclined to imitate the republics of antiquity. However, little as they may like republican institutions, there are certain republican usages for which they feel a certain affection. It is disturbing that they should be precisely those which allow them to banish, to exile, or to despoil. I remember that in 1802, they slipped into the law on special tribunals an article which introduced into France Greek ostracism;[a] and God knows how many eloquent speakers, in order to have this article approved, talked to us about the freedom of Athens and all the sacrifices that individuals must make to preserve this freedom! Similarly, in much more recent times, when fearful authorities attempted, with a timid hand, to rig the elections, a journal which can hardly be suspected of republicanism proposed to revive Roman censorship to eliminate all dangerous candidates.

I do not think therefore that I am engaging in a useless discussion if, to support my assertion, I say a few words about these two much vaunted institutions.

Ostracism in Athens rested upon the assumption that society had complete authority over its members. On this assumption it could be justified; and in a small state, where the influence of a single individual, strong in his credit, his clients, his glory, often balanced the power of the mass, ostracism may appear useful. But amongst us individuals have rights which society must respect, and individual interests are, as I have already observed, so lost in a multitude of equal or superior influences, that any oppression motivated by the need to diminish this influence is useless and consequently unjust.[b] No-one has the right to exile a citizen, if he is not condemned by a regular tribunal, according to a formal law which attaches the penalty of exile to the action of which

---

[a] The law of 23 Floréal, Year X (13 May 1802) which extended the functions and powers of special tribunals.

[b] 'The large states have created in our day a new guarantee: obscurity. This guarantee diminishes the dependence of individuals on the nation.' E. Hofmann (ed.), *Les 'Principes de Politique'*, vol. 2, p. 421.

he is guilty. No-one has the right to tear the citizen from his country, the owner away from his possessions, the merchant away from his trade, the husband from his wife, the father from his children, the writer from his studious meditations, the old man from his accustomed way of life.

All political exile is a political abuse. All exile pronounced by an assembly for alleged reasons of public safety is a crime which the assembly itself commits against public safety, which resides only in respect for the laws, in the observance of forms, and in the maintenance of safeguards.

Roman censorship implied, like ostracism, a discretionary power. In a republic where all the citizens, kept by poverty to an extremely simple moral code, lived in the same town, exercised no profession which might distract their attention from the affairs of the state, and thus constantly found themselves the spectators and judges of the usage of public power, censorship could on the one hand have greater influence: while on the other, the arbitrary power of the censors was restrained by a kind of moral surveillance exercised over them. But as soon as the size of the republic, the complexity of social relations and the refinements of civilization deprived this institution of what at the same time served as its basis and its limit, censorship degenerated even in Rome. It was not censorship which had created good morals; it was the simplicity of those morals which constituted the power and efficacy of censorship.

In France, an institution as arbitrary as censorship would be at once ineffective and intolerable. In the present conditions of society, morals are formed by subtle, fluctuating, elusive nuances, which would be distorted in a thousand ways if one attempted to define them more precisely. Public opinion alone can reach them; public opinion alone can judge them, because it is of the same nature. It would rebel against any positive authority which wanted to give it greater precision. If the government of a modern people wanted, like the censors in Rome, to censure a citizen arbitrarily, the entire nation would protest against this arrest by refusing to ratify the decisions of the authority.

What I have just said of the revival of censorship in modern times applies also to many other aspects of social organization, in relation to which antiquity is cited even more frequently and with greater emphasis. As for example, education; what do we not hear of the need to allow the government to take possession of new generations to shape them to its pleasure, and how many erudite quotations are employed to support this theory! The Persians, the Egyptians, Gaul, Greece and Italy are one after another set before us. Yet, Gentlemen, we are neither Persians subjected to a despot, nor Egyptians subjugated by priests, nor Gauls who can be sacrificed by their druids, nor, finally, Greeks or Romans, whose share in social authority consoled them for their private enslavement. We are modern men, who wish each to enjoy our own rights, each to develop our own faculties as we like best, without harming anyone; to watch over the development of these faculties in the children whom nature entrusts to our affection, the more enlightened as it is more vivid; and needing the authorities only to give us the general means of instruction which they can supply, as travellers accept from them the main roads without being told by them which route to take.

Religion is also exposed to these memories of bygone ages. Some brave defenders of the unity of doctrine cite the laws of the ancients against foreign gods, and sustain the rights of the Catholic church by the example of the Athenians, who killed Socrates for having undermined polytheism, and that of Augustus, who wanted the people to remain faithful to the cult of their fathers; with the result, shortly afterwards, that the first Christians were delivered to the lions.

Let us mistrust, Gentlemen, this admiration for certain ancient memories. Since we live in modern times, I want a liberty suited to modern times; and since we live under monarchies, I humbly beg these monarchies not to borrow from the ancient republics the means to oppress us.

Individual liberty, I repeat, is the true modern liberty. Political liberty is its guarantee, consequently political liberty is indispensable. But to ask the peoples of our day to sacrifice, like those of the past, the whole of their individual liberty to political liberty, is the surest means of detaching them from the former and, once this result has been achieved, it would be only too easy to deprive them of the latter.

As you see, Gentlemen, my observations do not in the least tend to diminish the value of political liberty. I do not draw from the evidence I have put before your eyes the same conclusions that some others have. From the fact that the ancients were free, and that we cannot any longer be free like them, they conclude that we are destined to be slaves. They would like to reconstitute the new social state with a small number of elements which, they say, are alone appropriate to the situation of the world today. These elements are prejudices to frighten men, egoism to corrupt them, frivolity to stupefy them, gross pleasures to degrade them, despotism to lead them; and, indispensably, constructive knowledge and exact sciences to serve despotism the more adroitly. It would be odd indeed if this were the outcome of forty centuries during which mankind has acquired greater moral and physical means: I cannot believe it. I derive from the differences which distinguish us from antiquity totally different conclusions. It is not security which we must weaken; it is enjoyment which we must extend. It is not political liberty which I wish to renounce; it is civil liberty which I claim, along with other forms of political liberty. Governments, no more than they did before, have the right to arrogate to themselves an illegitimate power. But the governments which emanate from a legitimate source have even less right than before to exercise an arbitrary supremacy over individuals. We still possess today the rights we have always had, those eternal rights to assent to the laws, to deliberate on our interests, to be an integral part of the social body of which we are members. But governments have new duties; the progress of civilization, the changes brought by the centuries require from the authorities greater respect for customs, for affections, for the independence of individuals. They must handle all these issues with a lighter and more prudent hand.

This reserve on the part of authority, which is one of its strictest duties, equally represents its well-conceived interest; since, if the liberty that suits the moderns is different from that which suited the ancients, the despotism which was possible amongst the ancients is no longer possible amongst the moderns. Because we are often less concerned with political liberty than they could be, and in ordinary circumstances less passionate about it, it may follow that we neglect, sometimes too much and always wrongly, the guarantees which this assures us. But at the same time, as we are much more preoccupied with individual liberty than the ancients, we shall defend it, if it is attacked, with much more skill and persistence; and we have means to defend it which the ancients did not.

Commerce makes the action of arbitrary power over our existence more oppressive than in the past, because, as our speculations are more varied, arbitrary power must multiply itself to reach them. But commerce also makes the action of arbitrary power easier to elude, because it changes the nature of property, which becomes, in virtue of this change, almost impossible to seize.

Commerce confers a new quality on property, circulation. Without circulation, property is merely a usufruct; political authority can always affect usufruct, because it can prevent its enjoyment; but circulation creates an invisible and invincible obstacle to the actions of social power.

The effects of commerce extend even further: not only does it emancipate individuals, but, by creating credit, it places authority itself in a position of dependence.

Money, says a French writer,[a] 'is the most dangerous weapon of despotism; yet it is at the same time its most powerful restraint; credit is subject to opinion; force is useless; money hides itself or flees; all the operations of the state are suspended'. Credit did not have the same influence amongst the ancients; their governments were stronger than individuals,[b] while in our time individuals are stronger than the political powers. Wealth is a power which is more readily available in all circumstances, more readily applicable to all interests, and consequently more real and better obeyed. Power threatens; wealth rewards: one eludes power by deceiving it; to obtain the favours of wealth one must serve it: the latter is therefore bound to win.

As a result, individual existence is less absorbed in political existence. Individuals carry their treasures far away; they take with them all the enjoyments of private life. Commerce has brought nations closer, it has given them customs and habits which are almost identical; the heads of states may be enemies: the peoples are compatriots.

Let power therefore resign itself: we must have liberty and we shall have it. But since the liberty we need is different from that of the ancients, it needs a different organization from the one which would suit ancient liberty. In the latter, the more time and energy man dedicated to the exercise of his political rights, the freer he thought himself; on the other hand, in the kind of liberty of which we are capable, the more the exercise of political rights leaves us the time for our private interests, the more precious will liberty be to us.

Hence, Sirs, the need for the representative system. The representative system is nothing but an organization by means of which a nation charges a few individuals to do what it cannot or does not wish to do herself. Poor men look after their own business; rich men hire

---

[a] Charles Ganilh, *Essai politique*, vol. 1, pp. 64–5.
[b] 'A deficit of 60 million caused the French revolution. Under Vespasian, a deficit of 600 million did not produce the slightest unrest in the empire.' E. Hofmann (ed.), *Les 'Principes de Politique'*, vol. 2, p. 426.

stewards.[a] This is the history of ancient and modern nations. The representative system is a proxy given to a certain number of men by the mass of the people who wish their interests to be defended and who nevertheless do not have the time to defend them themselves. But, unless they are idiots, rich men who employ stewards keep a close watch on whether these stewards are doing their duty, lest they should prove negligent, corruptible, or incapable; and, in order to judge the management of these proxies, the landowners, if they are prudent, keep themselves well-informed about affairs, the management of which they entrust to them. Similarly, the people who, in order to enjoy the liberty which suits them, resort to the representative system, must exercise an active and constant surveillance over their representatives, and reserve for themselves, at times which should not be separated by too lengthy intervals, the right to discard them if they betray their trust, and to revoke the powers which they might have abused.

For from the fact that modern liberty differs from ancient liberty, it follows that it is also threatened by a different sort of danger.

The danger of ancient liberty was that men, exclusively concerned with securing their share of social power, might attach too little value to individual rights and enjoyments.

The danger of modern liberty is that, absorbed in the enjoyment of our private independence, and in the pursuit of our particular interests, we should surrender our right to share in political power too easily.

The holders of authority are only too anxious to encourage us to do so. They are so ready to spare us all sort of troubles, except those of obeying and paying! They will say to us: what, in the end, is the aim of your efforts, the motive of your labours, the object of all your hopes? Is it not happiness? Well, leave this happiness to us and we shall give it to you. No, Sirs, we must not leave it to them. No matter how touching such a tender commitment may be, let us ask the authorities to keep within their limits. Let them confine themselves to being just. We shall assume the responsibility of being happy for ourselves.

Could we be made happy by diversions, if these diversions were without guarantees? And where should we find guarantees, without political liberty? To renounce it, Gentlemen, would be a folly like that of a man who, because he only lives on the first floor, does not care if the house itself is built on sand.

---

[a] This concept is derived from Sieyès: see footnote *a*, p. 23.

Moreover, Gentlemen, is it so evident that happiness, of whatever kind, is the only aim of mankind? If it were so, our course would be narrow indeed, and our destination far from elevated. There is not one single one of us who, if he wished to abase himself, restrain his moral faculties, lower his desires, abjure activity, glory, deep and generous emotions, could not demean himself and be happy. No, Sirs, I bear witness to the better part of our nature, that noble disquiet which pursues and torments us, that desire to broaden our knowledge and develop our faculties. It is not to happiness alone, it is to self-development that our destiny calls us; and political liberty is the most powerful, the most effective means of self-development that heaven has given us.

Political liberty, by submitting to all the citizens, without exception, the care and assessment of their most sacred interests, enlarges their spirit, ennobles their thoughts, and establishes among them a kind of intellectual equality which forms the glory and power of a people.

Thus, see how a nation grows with the first institution which restores to her the regular exercise of political liberty. See our countrymen of all classes, of all professions, emerge from the sphere of their usual labours and private industry, find themselves suddenly at the level of important functions which the constitutions confers upon them, choose with discernment, resist with energy, brave threats, nobly withstand seduction. See a pure, deep and sincere patriotism triumph in our towns, revive even our smallest villages, permeate our workshops, enliven our countryside, penetrate the just and honest spirits of the useful farmer and the industrious tradesman with a sense of our rights and the need for safeguards; they, learned in the history of the evils they have suffered, and no less enlightened as to the remedies which these evils demand, take in with a glance the whole of France and, bestowing a national gratitude, repay with their suffrage, after thirty years, the fidelity to principles embodied in the most illustrious of the defenders of liberty.[1]

Therefore, Sirs, far from renouncing either of the two sorts of freedom which I have described to you, it is necessary, as I have shown, to learn to combine the two together. Institutions, says the famous author of the history of the republics in the Middle Ages,[a] must

[1] M. de Lafayette, deputy of the department of the Sarthe.

[a] J. C. Simonde de Sismondi.

accomplish the destiny of the human race; they can best achieve their aim if they elevate the largest possible number of citizens to the highest moral position.

The work of the legislator is not complete when he has simply brought peace to the people. Even when the people are satisfied, there is much left to do. Institutions must achieve the moral education of the citizens. By respecting their individual rights, securing their independence, refraining from troubling their work, they must nevertheless consecrate their influence over public affairs, call them to contribute by their votes to the exercise of power, grant them a right of control and supervision by expressing their opinions; and, by forming them through practice for these elevated functions, give them both the desire and the right to discharge these.

Bibliography

This bibliography presents a selection of Constant's published writings and correspondence, and a necessarily limited choice of the existing studies on Constant. For a complete list of his published works, see:

Rudler, Gustave. *Bibliographie critique des oeuvres de Benjamin Constant*, Paris, 1909.

Courtney, Cecil Patrick. *A checklist of the published works of Benjamin Constant to 1833*, Cambridge, 1979.

A fuller account of the secondary literature can be found in:

Lowe, David K. *Benjamin Constant, an annotated bibliography of critical editions and studies, 1946–1978*, London, 1979.

Waridel, B., Tiercy, J. F., Furrer, N., Amoos, A. M. *Bibliographie analytique des écrits sur Benjamin Constant (1796–1980)*, Voltaire Foundation, Lausanne and Oxford, 1980.

The bibliography does not include all the works which appear in the annotation to this volume, but only those which are relevant to the study of Constant's life and thought. Thus it omits a few classical and literary sources cited by Constant in his writings which do not bear on the content of his arguments.

1. Selected works of Constant

Essai sur les moeurs héroiques de la Grèce – Tiré de *l'Histoire grecque* de J. Gillies, London and Paris, 1787.

De la force du Gouvernement actuel et de la nécessité de s'y rallier, Year IV, Paris, 1796.

Des réactions politiques, Year V, Paris, 1797.

Des effets de la Terreur, Year V, Paris, 1797.

Wallstein, tragédie en cinq actes et en vers, précédée de Quelques réflexions sur le théâtre allemand, Geneva and Paris, 1809; repr. ed. by Jean-René Derré, Paris, 1965.

De l'esprit de conquête et de l'usurpation, dans leurs rapports avec la civilisation européenne, Hanover, 1814.

De la liberté des brochures, des pamphlets et des journaux, considerée sous le rapport de l'intérêt du Gouvernement, Paris, 1814.

Réflexions sur les constitutions, la distribution et les garanties dans une monarchie constitutionnelle, Paris, 1814.

Observations sur le discours de S. E. le Ministre de l'Intérieur en faveur d'un projet de loi sur la liberté de la presse, Paris, 1814.

Principes de politique applicables à tous les Gouvernements – et particulièrement à la constitution actuelle de la France, Paris, 1815.

De la responsabilité des ministres, Paris, 1815.

The Responsibility of Ministers, London, 1815, The Pamphleteer, vol. 5.

On the Liberty of the Press, London, 1815 The Pamphleteer, vol. 6.

Adolphe – Anecdote trouvée dans les papiers d'un inconnu et publiée par M. Benjamin de Constant, London–Paris, 1816.

Adolphe: an anecdote found among the papers of an unknown person, and published by M. Benjamin de Constant, English trs. by Alexander Walker, London, 1816.

De la doctrine politique qui peut réunir les partis en France, Paris, 1816.

Des élections prochaines, Paris, 1817.

Collection complète des ouvrages publiés sur le Gouvernement représentatif et la Constitution actuelle de la France, formant une espèce de Cours de politique constitutionnelle, 4 vols., Paris, 1818–19 and Paris and Rouen, 1820; 3rd edn, ed. by Eduard Laboulaye, 2 vols., Paris, 1861.

De la liberté des anciens comparée à celle des modernes, Paris, 1819.

Eloge de Sir Samuel Romilly, prononcé à l'Athenée Royal le 2 Decembre, Paris, 1819.

Mémoires sur les Cent-Jours, en forme de lettres, Paris, 1820–22; and ed. by O. Pozzo di Borgo, Paris, 1961.

De la dissolution de la Chambre des députés et des résultats que cette dissolution peut avoir pour la nation, Paris, 1820.

On the dissolution of the Chamber of deputies, London, 1821, The Pamphleteer, vol. 18.

Commentaire sur l'ouvrage de Filangieri, 4 vols., Paris, 1822–4.

De la religion considérée dans sa source, ses formes et ses développements, 4 vols., Paris, 1824–31; and ed. by Pierre Deguise, Lausanne, 1971.

Appel aux nations chrétiennes en faveur des Grecs, Paris, 1825.

Discours à la Chambre des députés, Paris, 1827–8.

Mélanges de littérature et de politique, Paris, 1829.

Du polythéisme roman consideré dans ses rapports avec la philosophie grecque et la religion chrétienne, ed. by M. J. Matter, 2 vols., Paris, 1833.

Le Siège de Soisson, ed. by V. Waille, Poligny, 1892.

Les Chevaliers – Roman héroïque, Brussels, 1779, first published ed. by M. G. Rudler, Paris, 1932.

Cécile, ed. by A. Roulin, Paris, 1951.

Journaux intimes, Edition intégrale des manuscrits, ed. by A. Roulin and Charles Roth, Paris, 1952.

Oeuvres, ed. by A. Roulin, Paris, 1957.

'Les Mémoires de Juliette', *Revue de Paris*, 64 (September 1957), 46–62.
Conquista e usurpazione, trs. by Carlo Dionisotti, Preface by Franco Venturi, Turin, 1944; repr. 1983.
Adolphe and the Red Notebook (Adolphe trs. by Carl Wildman, the *Red Notebook* trs. by Norman Cameron), ed. by Harold Nicolson, London, 1948.
Adolphe, English trs. L. Tancock, Harmondsworth, 1964.
Ecrits et discours politiques, ed. by O. Pozzo di Borgo, 2 vols., Paris, 1964.
De la perfectibilité de l'espèce humaine, ed. by Pierre Deguise, Lausanne, 1967.
'Esquisse d'un essai sur la littérature du 18e siècle,' *Europe*, 467 (1968), 18–21 (written on 24 July 1807); repr. in R. Mortier. *Clartés et ombres du siècle des lumières: études sur le XVIIIe siècle littéraire*, Geneva, 1969.
Deux chapitres inédits de "l'Esprit des religions", 1803–1804, ed. by Patrice Thompson, Geneva, 1970.
Werke, ed. by A. Blaeschke and L. Gall, trs. by E. Rechel Mertens, 4 vols., Berlin, 1970–2.
De la religion, Livre Premier, ed. by Pierre Deguise, Lausanne, 1971.
De la justice politique, traduction inédite de l'ouvrage de William Godwin, ed. by Burton R. Pollin, Québec, 1972.
Recueil d'articles: 'Le Mercure', 'La Minerve' et 'La Renommé', ed. by Ephraim Harpaz, 2 vols., Geneva, 1972.
Recueil d'articles, 1795–1817, ed. by Ephraim Harpaz, Geneva, 1978.
De la liberté chez les modernes, ed. by Marcel Gauchet, Paris, 1980.
Les 'Principes de Politique' de Benjamin Constant (1806), ed. by Etienne Hofmann, 2 vols., Geneva, 1980.
Recueil d'articles 1820–1824, ed. by Ephraim Harpaz, Geneva, 1981.

2. Correspondence and biographical materials

Augustin-Thierry, A. 'Les funérailles d'Adolphe', *Le Temps*, Paris, 19 December 1830, p. 2.
Barras, Paul-Jean-François-Nicolas. *Mémoires de Barras, membre du Directoire*, ed. by George Durny, 4 vols., Paris, 1895–6.
Blanqui, Louis Auguste. 'Aux étudiants en médecine et en droit', Paris, 1830.
Blennerhasset, Charlotte. *Mme de Staël et son temps (1766–1817)*, avec des documents inédits, 3 vols., Paris, 1890.
Chateaubriand, François René de. *Mémoires d'outre-tombe*, ed. by M. Levaillant and G. Moulinier, 2 vols., 3rd edn, Paris, 1969–72.
Constant de Rebecque, Baronne. (ed.), *Correspondence de Benjamin Constant et d'Anna Lindsay*, Paris, 1933.
Cordey, Pierre (ed.), *Benjamin Constant, Cent Lettres*, Lausanne, 1974.
Garat, D. J. *Mémoires historiques sur la vie de M. Suard, sur ses écrits et sur le XVIIIe siècle*, Paris, 1820.
Harpaz, Ephraim. (ed.), *Benjamin Constant et Goyet de la Sarthe, correspondence 1818–1822*, Geneva, 1973.
Benjamin Constant, *Lettres à Mme Récamier, 1807–1830*, Paris, 1977.

Hasselrot, Bengt. *Nouveaux documents sur Benjamin Constant et Mme de Staël*, Copenhagen, 1952.

Lettres à Bernadotte. Sources et origine de 'l'esprit de conquête et de l'usurpation', Geneva, 1952.

Herriot, Edouard. *Souvenirs et correspondence de Mme Récamier*, 2 vols., Paris, 1859.

Mme Récamier, les amis de sa jeunesse et sa correspondence intime, Paris, 1872.

Leon, P. (ed.) *Lettres de Mme de Staël à Benjamin Constant*, Paris, 1928.

Mackintosh, James. (ed.), *Memoirs of the Life of the Rt. Hon. Sir James Mackintosh*, 2 vols., London, 1835.

Mistler, Jean. (ed.), *Lettres à un ami (de Benjamin Constant et Mme de Staël): cent onze lettres inédites à Claude Hochet*, Neuchâtel, 1949.

Pasquier, Etienne Denis. *Mémoires du Chancellier Pasquier*, 6 vols., Paris, 1895.

Rémusat, François Marie Charles de. *Mémoires de ma vie*, ed. by Charles H. Ponthas, 3 vols., Paris, 1958–60.

Robinson, Henry Crabb. *Diary, reminiscences and correspondence*, ed. by Thomas Sadler, 2nd edn, 3 vols., London 1869.

Roulin, Alfred and Suzanne. (eds.), *Correspondence (de Benjamin et Rosalie de Constant), 1786–1830*, Paris, 1955.

Saint-Beuve, Charles Augustin. 'Benjamin Constant et Belle de Charrière, Lettres inédites', *Revue des deux mondes*, 14 NS, vol. 6 (15 April 1844), 193–264.

'M. Coulmann, Réminiscences', *Nouveaux lundis*, 13 vols., Paris, 1863, vol. 9, pp. 135–60.

Staël, Anne Louise Germaine de. *Lettres à Mme Récamier*, ed. by E. Beau de Loménie, Domat, 1952.

Suard, Mme. *Essais de mémoires sur M. Suard*, Paris, 1820.

Talleyrand, Prince of. *Memoirs*, trs. by Ledos de Beaufort, 5 vols., London, 1891.

3. Works discussed or cited by Constant

Aristotle, *The Politics*, with an English trs. by H. Rackham, The Loeb Classical Library, London, 1932.

Bentham, Jeremy. *Traité de législation civile et pénale, précédé de principes généraux de législation et d'une vue d'un corps complet de droit*, ed. by E. Dumont, Paris, Year X, 1802.

Blackstone, William. *Commentaries on the Laws of England*, 4 vols., Oxford, 1765–9; French trs. *Commentaires sur les lois anglaises*, 6 vols., Paris, 1822–3.

Burke, Edmund. *Reflections on the Revolution in France*, ed. by C. Cruise O'Brien, Harmondsworth, 1969.

Cabanis, Pierre Jean Georges. *Quelques considérations sur l'organisation sociale en général et particulièrement sur la nouvelle constitution*, Paris, 1799.

Carvalho e Mello, Sébastien Joseph de. Marquês de Pombal. *Mémoires de*

Sébastien Joseph de Carvalho et Mélo, Comte d'Oeyras, Marquis de Pombal, 4 vols., Lyons, 1784.

Chamfort, Nicolas-Sébastien Roch, dit de. *Oeuvres complètes*, ed. by P. R. Auguis, Paris, 1824; English trs. by W. G. Hutchison, *The Cynic's Breviary: Maxims and Anecdotes from Nicolas de Chamfort*, London, 1902.

Charrière, Isabelle-Belle de Zuylen de. *Oeuvres complètes*, ed. by D. Candaux and others, Amsterdam and Geneva, 1979–.

Clermont-Tonnerre, Stanislas-Marie de. *Recueil des opinions de Stanislas de Clermont-Tonnerre*, 4 vols., Paris, 1791.

Condillac, Etienne Bonnot de. *Cours d'études pour l'instruction du Prince de Parme*, 12 vols., Geneva, 1780.

Condorcet, J. A. N. Caritat de. *Sur l'instruction publique*, offprint from the Bibliothèque de l'homme public, second year, vol. I, Paris, 1791.

Crébillon, fils. *Les égarements du coeur et de l'esprit* (1736–8), ed. by Etiemble, Paris, 1977.

Destutt de Tracy, Antoine Louis Claude. *Commentaire sur l'Esprit des lois de Montesquieu*, Liège, 1817; repr. Geneva, 1970.

Dunoyer, Charles. *L'industrie et la morale considerées dans leur rapports avec la liberté*, Paris, 1825.

Ferrand, Antoine François Claude de. *L'esprit de l'histoire, ou lettres d'un père à son fils sur la manière d'étudier l'histoire en général et particulièrement l'histoire de la France*, 4 vols., Paris, 1802.

Fichte, Johann Gottlieb. *Der Geschlossene Handelsstaat*, repr. of the original of 1800, Introduction by H. Waentig, Jena, 1920.

Filangieri, Gaetano. *Scienza della legislazione*, 8 vols., Napoli, 1780–8. French trs. by J. A. G. Gallois, *La science de la législation*, 5 vols., Paris, 1786–8.

Gain-Montagnac, J. L. M. de. (ed.), *Mémoires de Louis XIV, écrits par lui-même, composés pour le Grand Dauphin, son fils et addressés à ce Prince*, 2 vols., Paris, 1806.

Ganilh, Charles. *Essai politique sur le revenu public des peuples de l'antiquité, du moyen-âge, des siècles modernes, et specialement de la France et de l'Angleterre depuis le milieu du quinzième siècle*, 2 vols., Paris, 1806.

Gérando, Joseph Marie de. *Histoire comparée des systèmes de philosophie*, 3 vols., Paris, 1804.

Rapport historique sur le progrès de la philosophie, Paris, 1808.

Gillies, John. *The History of Ancient Greece, its colonies and conquests, from the earliest accounts till the division of the Macedonian empire in the East*, London, 1786.

Godwin, William. *Enquiry concerning Political Justice* (1793) ed. by I. Kramnick, Harmondsworth, 1976.

Goethe, Wolfgang. *Werke*, ed. by Eric Schmidt, 6 vols., Leipzig, 1909.

Wilhelm Meister's apprenticeship and travels, trs. by Thomas Carlyle, 3 vols., London, 1842.

d'Holbach, Paul Henri Dietrich. *Système de la nature, ou des lois du monde physique et du monde moral*, London, 1770.

Hume, David. *Essays, Moral, Political, Literary*, London, 1903.

Laclos, Choderlos de. *Oeuvres complètes*, ed. by Laurent Versini, Paris, 1979.

Lévis, Pierre Marc Gaston, duc de. *L'Angleterre au commencement du dix-neuvième siècle*, Paris, 1814.

Mably, Gabriel Bonnot de. *Parallèle des Romains et des François par rapport au gouvernement*, 2 vols., Paris, 1740.

Entretiens de Phocion, sur le rapport de la morale avec la politique, translated from the Greek of Nicocles, Amsterdam, 1763.

De la législation, ou principes des lois, Paris, 1776.

Machiavelli, Niccolò. *Tutte le opere*, ed. by M. Martelli, Firenze, 1971.

Mackintosh, Sir James. *The Miscellaneous Works of the Rt. Hon. Sir James Mackintosh*, ed. by R. J. Mackintosh, 3 vols., London, 1846.

'France', *Edinburgh Review*, 24 (November 1814), 505–37.

de Maistre, Joseph. *Considerations on France*, trs. by Richard A. Lebrun, Montreal and London, 1974.

Mirabeau, Victor Riqueti, Marquis de. *L'ami des hommes, ou traité de la population*, 6 vols., La Haye, 1758–62.

Molé, Louis Matthieu. *Essais de morale et de politique*, Paris, 1806.

Montesquieu, Charles Louis de Secondat de. *Oeuvres complètes*, ed. by R. Caillois, 2 vols., Paris, 1951.

Montlosier, Robert de. *De la monarchie française*, Paris, 1814.

Necker, Jacques. *Oeuvres complètes*, ed. by A. de Staël, 15 vols., Paris, 1820.

Du pouvoir exécutif dans les grands états, 2 vols., Paris, 1792.

An essay on the true principles of executive power in great states, 2 vols., London, 1792.

De l'administration des finances de la France, 3 vols., 1784.

Pauw, Cornelius Johannes de. *Recherches philosophiques sur les Grecs*, 2 vols., Berlin, 1788.

Rehberg, August Wilhelm. *Über den Code Napoléon und dessen Einführung in Deutschland*, Hanover, 1813.

Rhulières, Claude Carloman de. *Éclaircissements historiques sur les causes de la Révocation de l'Édit de Nantes et sur l'état des protestants en France depuis le commencement du règne de Louis XIV*, 2 vols., Paris, 1788.

Robespierre, Maximilien. *Discours et rapports à la Convention*, Paris, 1965.

Rousseau, Jean Jacques. *The Social Contract*, ed. by G. D. H. Cole, London, 1903.

Say, Jean Baptiste. *Traité d'économie politique*, 2 vols., Paris, 1803.

Sieyès, Emmanuel Joseph. *Qu'est-ce que le Tiers État?*, ed. by Roberto Zapperi, Geneva, 1970.

Sismondi, J. C. L. Simonde de. *Histoire de républiques italiennes du moyen âge*, 16 vols., Paris, 1807–24.

De la littérature dans le Midi de l'Europe, 4 vols., Paris, 1813.

Historical View of the Literature of the South of Europe, English trs. by Thomas Roscoe, 4 vols., London, 1823.

Recherches sur les Constitutions des peuples libres, ed. by Marco Minerbi, Geneva, 1963.

Smith, Adam. *An Inquiry into the Nature and Causes of the Wealth of Nations*, ed. by R. H. Campbell, A. S. Skinner, 2 vols., Oxford, 1976.

Spinoza, Benedict de. *The Political Works – The Tractatus Theologico-Politicus in part, and the Tractatus politicus in full*, ed. by A. G. Wernham, Oxford, 1958.

Staël, Anne Louise Germaine de. *Oeuvres complètes*, ed. by A. de Staël, 17 vols., Paris, 1820.

De l'Allemagne, ed. by S. Balaye and J. de Pange, Paris, 1958–60.

De la littérature considerée dans ses rapports avec les institutions sociales, ed. by P. van Tieghen, 2 vols., Paris, 1959.

Des circonstances actuelles qui peuvent terminer la révolution et des principes qui doivent fonder la république en France, ed. by Lucia Omacini, Geneva, 1979.

Considérations sur la révolution française, ed. by J. Godechot, Paris, 1983.

Villiers, Charles de. *Philosophie de Kant, ou principes fondamentaux de la philosophie transcendentale*, Metz, 1801.

Essai sur l'esprit et l'influence de la Réformation de Luther, Metz, 1803.

"De l'esprit de conquête et de l'usurpation" de Benjamin Constant de Rebecque', *Göttingische gelehrte Anzeigen*, 65 (23 April 1814), 641–45.

4. Secondary literature

(a) *Biographical studies*

d'Andlau, Beatrice. *La jeunesse de Mme de Staël*, Geneva, 1970.

Cordey, Pierre. *Mme de Staël et Benjamin Constant sur les bords du Léman*, Lausanne, 1966.

Cruickshank, John. *Benjamin Constant*, New York, 1974.

de Diesbach, Ghislain. *Madame de Staël*, Paris, 1983.

Farnum, Dorothy. *The Dutch divinity: a biography of Mme de Charrière, 1740–1805*, London, 1959.

Glachant, Victor. *Benjamin Constant sous l'oeil du guet: d'après des documents inédits*, Paris, 1906.

Guillemin, Henri. *Benjamin Constant muscadin, 1795–99*, Paris, 1958.

Mme de Staël, Benjamin Constant et Napoléon, Paris, 1959.

Henriot, Émile. 'Une amie de Benjamin Constant: Mme de Charrière' in: *Romanesques et romantiques*, Paris, 1930, pp. 10–17.

Herold, Christopher J. *Mistress to an Age: a life of Mme de Staël*, Indianapolis, 1958.

Holdheim, William W. *Benjamin Constant*, London, 1961.

Jasinski, Beatrice W. *L'engagement de Benjamin Constant: amour et politique (1794–1796)*, Paris, 1971.

Kerchove, Arnold de. *Benjamin Constant ou le libertin sentimental*, Paris, 1950.

Kloocke, Kurt. *Benjamin Constant: une biographie intellectuelle*, Geneva, 1984.

Mortier, Roland. 'Isabelle de Charrière, mentor de Benjamin Constant', Documentatieblad, Werkgroep 18e Eeuw, 27–9 (1975), pp. 101–40 (Colloque: 'Actualité d'Isabelle de Charrière', 12–14 September 1974).

Nicolson, Harold. *Benjamin Constant*, London, 1949.

Poulet, George. *Benjamin Constant par lui-même*, 'Les écrivains de toujours,', Paris, 1968.

Rudler, Gustave. *La jeunesse de Benjamin Constant: 1767–94; le disciple du XVIIIe siècle; utilitarisme et pessimisme; Mme de Charrière*, Paris, 1909.

Schermerhorn, Elisabeth W. *Benjamin Constant: his private life and his contribution to the cause of liberal government in France 1767–1830*, London, 1924.

Winegarten, Renée. *Madame de Staël*, Leamington Spa, 1985.

Zampogna, Domenico. *Benjamin Constant et Belle de Charrière*, Preface by Pierre Cordey, Messina, 1969.

(b) *On Constant's political thought*

Baelen, Jean. 'Benjamin Constant et la cause des Grecs', *France-Grèce* 10 (1954), 5–9.

'Benjamin Constant et la question sociale', *Bulletin de l'Association Guillaume Budé*, Paris, 13 (1954), 125–36.

Balaye, S. *Mme de Staël, lumières et liberté*, Paris, 1979.

Bastid, Paul. *Benjamin Constant et sa doctrine*, 2 vols., Paris, 1966.

'Benjamin Constant et le Saint-Simonisme', *Économies et Sociétés*, 4 (1970), 285–9/1149–53 (two sequences of pagination)

Bédé, Jean-Albert. 'Chateaubriand, Benjamin Constant et la question constitutionnelle, (1814–1816)', *Revue d'histoire littéraire de la France*, 68 (1968), 981–94.

Bourgeois, René. 'Jeu et politique: le cas de Benjamin Constant' in *Romantisme et politique 1815–1851*: Colloque de l'École Normale Supérieure de Saint-Cloud, 1966 (Paris, 1969) 55–61 and 129–30.

Dumont-Wilden, Louis. 'Benjamin Constant et la Révolution française de 1830', *Flambeau* (Brussels) 13 (1930), 343–8.

Fink, Beatrice C. 'Benjamin Constant on Equality', *Journal of the History of Ideas*, 33 (1972), 307–14.

'Benjamin Constant and the Enlightenment' in *Studies in Eighteenth-Century Culture*, vol. 3: *Racism in the Eighteenth Century*, Cleveland, 1973.

Fontana, Biancamaria. 'The shaping of modern liberty: commerce and civilization in the writings of Benjamin Constant', *Annales Benjamin Constant*, 5 (1985), 5–15.

Frosini, Vittorio. 'Constant e Action: libertarismo antico e liberalismo moderno', *Rivista Internazionale di Filosofia del Diritto*, ser. 3, 37 (1960), 409–19; repr. *La Ragione dello Stato*, Milano, 1963.

Gall, Lothar. *Benjamin Constant: seine politische Ideenwelt und der deutsche Vormärz*, Wiesbaden, 1963.

Gougelot, Henri. *L'idée de liberté dans la pensée de Benjamin Constant: essai de critique historique*, Melun, 1942.

Goyard-Fabre, S. 'L'idée de souveraineté du peuple et le "libéralisme pur" de Benjamin Constant', *Revue de Métaphysique et de Morale*, 71 (1976), 289–327.

Guillemin, Henri. 'Benjamin Constant sous la Révolution', *Pensée française*, 16 (December 1957), 24–8.

Gwynne, G. E. *Mme de Staël et la révolution française*, Paris, 1969.

Hartman, Mary S. 'Benjamin Constant and the Question of Ministerial Responsibility in France, 1814–15', *Journal of European Studies*, 6 (1976), 248–61.

Holmes, Stephen. *Benjamin Constant and the Making of Modern Liberalism*, New Haven, 1984.

Lauris, George de. *Benjamin Constant et les idées libérales*, Paris, 1904.

Loirette, Gabriel. 'Montesquieu et son influence sur la doctrine politique de Benjamin Constant', *Actes de l'Académie Nationale des Sciences, Belles-Lettres et Arts de Bordeaux*, 13 (1944–50), 61–79.

Mistler, Jean. '1767–1967: Benjamin Constant, prophète du libéralisme', *Les Annales-Conférencia*, 75 (February 1968), 3–16.

Mortier, Roland. 'Constant et les lumières', *Europe*, 467 (1968), 5–18.

Passerin, Ettore. 'Gaetano Filangieri e Benjamin Constant', *Humanitas*, 7 (1952), 1110–22.

Pizzorno, Alessandro. 'Benjamin Constant: diario intimo e liberalismo', *Itinerari*, 4 (1956), 167–77.

Romieu, André. *Benjamin Constant et l'esprit européen*, Paris, 1933.

Rudler, Gustave. 'Robespierre et les Jacobins dans la correspondence de Benjamin Constant' in *Annales révolutionnaires*, vol. 3, N° 1 (January–March 1910), 92–103.

Sainte-Beuve, Charles Augustin. 'Benjamin Constant, son *Cours de politique constitutionnelle*', *Nouveaux lundis*, 13 vols., Paris, 1863, vol. 1, pp. 408–34.

Siedentop, Larry. 'Two liberal traditions' in A. Ryan (ed.), *The Idea of Freedom, Essays in Honour of Isaiah Berlin*, Oxford, 1979, pp. 153–74.

Suter, Jean-François. 'L'idée de légitimité chez Benjamin Constant' in *L'idée de légitimité*, Paris, 1967, pp. 181–93.

Zanfarino, Antonio. *La libertà dei moderni nel costituzionalismo di Benjamin Constant*, Milano, 1961.

(c) On *Adolphe, Wallstein*, and literature.

Baldensperger, Fernand. *Goethe en France. Étude de littérature comparée*, Paris, 1904.

Cordié, Carlo. 'Il Wallstein di Benjamin Constant nelle testimonianze dell'autore e di alcuni suoi contemporanei' in *Studi in onore di Carlo Pellegrini*, Turin, 1963, pp. 411–54.

Courtney, C. P. 'Alexander Walker and Benjamin Constant: a note on the English translator of *Adolphe*', *French Studies*, 29 (1975), 137–50.

Delbouille, Paul. *Genèse, structure et destin d' 'Adolphe'*, Paris, 1971.

Elsen, Claude. 'Benjamin Constant ou l'impuissance d'aimer', *Table Ronde*, 43 (July, 1951), 146–9.

Fairlie, Alison. 'L'individu et l'ordre social dans *Adolphe*', *Europe*, 467 (1968), 30–8.

Heisig, Karl. 'L'art pour l'art. Über den Ursprung dieser Kunstauffassung' in *Zeitschrift für Religions und Geistesgeschichte*, 14 (1962), N° 3–4, 201–29, 334–52.

Martin du Gard, Maurice. 'L'actualité de Benjamin Constant', *Les nouvelles littéraires, artistiques et scientifiques*, 318 (17 November 1928), 1–2.

Mattucci, Mario. 'Sainte-Beuve critico di Constant', *Saggi e ricerche di letteratura francese*, 12 (1973), 353–78.

Murry, John Middleton. *The Conquest of Death*, London, 1951.

Olivier, A. *Benjamin Constant: écriture et conquête du moi*, Paris, 1970.

'*Cécile* et la genèse d'*Adolphe*', *Revue de sciences humaines*, 32 (1967), 5–27.

Papst, W. '*Cécile* de Benjamin Constant', *Actes du Congrès de Lausanne, 1967*, Geneva, 1968, 145–52.

Pourtalès, Guy de. *De Hamlet à Swann*, Paris, 1924.

Riggan, William. '*Werther, Adolphe* and *Eugene Onegin*: the decline of the new hero of sensibility', *Research Studies of Washington State University*, 41 (1973), 252–67.

Roulin, Alfred. 'Benjamin Constant et la publication d'*Adolphe*', *Mercure de France*, 314 (1952), 469–78.

Rudler G. '*Adolphe*' de Benjamin Constant, Paris, 1935.

Stendhal (Henri Beyle). 'À propos d'*Adolphe*' in Geoffrey Strickland (ed.), *Selected Journalism from English Reviews by Stendhal*, London, 1959, pp. 70–2.

Todorov, Tzvetan. 'The discovery of language: *Les liaisons dangereuses* and *Adolphe*', *Yale French Studies*, 45 (1970), 113–26.

(d) *On the history of religion*

Deguise, Pierre. *Benjamin Constant méconnu: le livre 'De la religion' avec des documents inédits*, Geneva, 1966.

Gouhier, Henri. *Benjamin Constant*, Paris, 1967.

Hogue, Helen H. S. *On changes in Benjamin Constant's Books on Religions, with notes concerning an unpublished version of 'Florestan, ou le Siège de Soissons, poème' and other works*, Geneva, 1964.

Rochat, Ernest. 'Benjamin Constant' in *Le développement de la théologie protestante française au XIXe siècle*, Geneva, 1942, pp. 147–58.

Stendhal (Henri Beyle). 'Benjamin Constant. De la religion' in Geoffrey Strickland (ed.), *Selected Journalism from English Reviews by Stendhal*, London, 1959, pp. 167–80.

Thompson, Patrice. *La religion de Benjamin Constant: les pouvoirs de l'image*, Pisa, 1978.

(e) *Miscellaneous*

Acomb, Frances D. *Anglophobia in France, 1763–89: an essay on the history of constitutionalism and nationalism*, Durham, NC, 1950.

Alatri, Paolo. *Parlamenti e lotta politica nella Francia del settecento*, Bari, 1977.

Alengry, Frank. *Condorcet, guide de la révolution française*, 2 vols., Paris, 1904.

Ameline, A. *L'idée de souveraineté d'après les écrivains français du XVIIIe siècle*, Paris, 1904.

Bagge, Dominique. *Les idées politiques en France sous la Restauration*, Paris, 1952.

Baldensperger, Fernand. *Le mouvement des idées dans l'Émigration française 1789–1815*, 2 vols., Paris, 1924.

Barbey, Jean. *Le conseil des ministres sous la Restauration*, Paris, 1936.

Barthélemy, Joseph. *L'introduction du régime parlementaire en France sous Louis XVIII et Charles X*, Paris, 1904.

Bastid, Paul. *Emmanuel Joseph Sieyès et sa pensée*, Paris, 1970.

Beer, S. H. 'The representation of interests in British Government', *American Political Science Review*, 51 (September 1957), 619–30.

Berlin, Isaiah. *Four Essays on Liberty*, Oxford, 1969.

Bertier de Sauvigny, Guillaume de. *The Bourbon Restoration*, Pennsylvania, 1966.

Bonnefon, Joseph. *Le régime parlementaire sous la Restauration*, Paris, 1902.

Bosher, J. F. *French Finances, 1770–1795: from business to bureaucracy*, Cambridge, 1970.

Bourdon, J. *La Constitution de l'an VIII*, Rodez, 1941.

Burrow, John W. *Gibbon*, Oxford, 1985.

Cahen, Léon. *Condorcet et la révolution française*, Paris, 1904.

Cannon, John. *Parliamentary Reform, 1640–1832*, Cambridge, 1973.

Capitant, René. *Ecrits constitutionnels*, Paris, CNRS 1982.

Carré, Henri. *La fin des parlements*, Paris, 1912.

Challamel, Augustin. *Les clubs contre-révolutionnaires: cercles, comités sociétés, salons, réunions, cafés, restaurants et librairies*, Paris, 1895; on the Club de Salm: pp. 507–11.

Charlton, D. G. (ed.), *The French Romantics*, 2 vols., Cambridge, 1984.

Chevallier, J. J. *Histoire des institutions et des régimes politiques de la France de 1789 à nos jours*, Paris, 1977.

Clark, J. C. D. *English Society 1688–1832*, Cambridge, 1986.

Cobb, Richard. *The Police and the People: French Popular Protest 1780–1820*, Oxford, 1970.

Cobban, A. *A History of Modern France*, 2 vols., Harmondsworth, 1981.

Collins, Irene. *The Government and the Newspaper Press in France 1814–1881*, Oxford, 1959.

Cordié, Carlo. *Ideali e figure d'Europa*, Pisa, 1954: 'Studi sul gruppo di Coppet', pp. 97–411; 'L'appello di Constant in favore dei Greci', pp. 319–31.

Darnton, Robert. *The Literary Underground of the Old Régime*, Cambridge, Mass., 1982.

Dedeyan, Charles. *Le cosmopolitisme européen sous la Révolution et l'Empire*, 2 vols., Paris, 1976.

Derathé, Robert. *Jean Jacques Rousseau et la science politique de son temps*, Paris, 1970.

Diaz, Furio. *Filosofia e politica nel 700 francese*, Turin, 1973.

Dickson, W. K. *The History of the Speculative Society, 1764–1904*, Edinburgh, 1905.

Dodge, Guy. *Benjamin Constant's Philosophy of Liberalism: a Study in Politics and Religion*, Chapel Hill, NC 1980.

Doyle, W. 'Was there an aristocratic reaction in pre-revolutionary France?' *Past and Present*, 57 (November 1972), 97–122.

Droz, Jacques. *Histoire des doctrines politiques en France*, Paris, 1956.

Dunn, John. *Western Political Theory in the Face of the Future*, Cambridge, 1979.

Durand, Charles. *L'exercice de la fonction législative de 1800 à 1814*, Aix-en-Provence, 1955.

Duvergier de Hauranne, Prosper. *Histoire du gouvernement parlementaire en France: 1814–1848*, 10 vols., Paris, 1857; esp. vols. 1 and 2.

Egret, Jean. *La révolution des notables: Mounier et les monarchiens*, Paris, 1950.

Bibliography

La pré-révolution française, 1787–88, Paris, 1962.

Necker ministre de Louis XVI: 1776–1790, Paris, 1975.

Escarpit, Robert. *L'Angleterre dans l'oeuvre de Mme de Staël*, Paris, 1955.

Fontana, Biancamaria. *Rethinking the Politics of Commercial Society: the 'Edinburgh Review', 1802–1832*, Cambridge, 1985.

Forbes, Duncan. *Hume's Philosophical Politics*, Cambridge, 1975.

Furet, François. *Penser la révolution française*, Paris, 1978; English trs. *Interpreting the French Revolution*, Cambridge, 1981.

'Une polémique thermidorienne sur la terreur', *Passé Présent*, 2 (1983), 44–55.

Furet, F. and Richet, D. *La révolution française*, Paris, 1965; repr. Vervier, 1973.

Gibbons, P. A. *Ideas of Political Representation in Parliament, 1651–1832*, Oxford, 1914.

Girard, Louis. *Les libéraux français, 1814–1875*, Paris, 1985.

Godechot, Jacques. *Les institutions de la France sous la révolution et l'empire*, Paris, 1968.

La vie quotidienne en France sous le Directoire, Paris, 1977.

(ed.), *Les Constitutions de la France depuis 1789*, Paris, 1979.

Godet, Philippe. *Histoire littéraire de la Suisse française*, Geneva, 1890.

Madame de Charrière et ses amis, d'après des nombreux documents inédits (1740–1805), 2 vols., Geneva, 1906.

Gomel, Charles. *Les causes financières de la révolution française*, 2 vols., Paris, 1892–3.

Gooch, R. K. *Parliamentary Government in France – The Revolutionary Origins 1789–91*, New York, 1960.

Grange, Henri. *Les idées de Necker*, Lille, 1973.

'On negative and positive liberty', *Political Studies*, 28 (1980), 507–26.

Gray, John, *Mill on Liberty: a defence*, London, 1983.

Guerchi, Luciano. *Libertà degli antichi e libertà dei moderni: Sparta, Atene e i 'Philosophes' nella Francia del settecento*, Napoli, 1979.

Haag, Eugène and Émile. *La France protestante, ou vies des protestants français*, 10 vols., Paris, 1847–58.

Hampson, Norman. *Will and Circumstance: Montesquieu, Rousseau and the French Revolution*, London, 1983.

Harpaz, Ephraim. *L'école libérale sous la restauration*, Geneva, 1968.

Harris, E. *The Assignats*, Harvard, 1932.

Harris, R. D. *Necker, Reform Statesman of the Ancien Régime*, Berkeley, 1979.

Herold, Christopher J. *Bonaparte in Egypt*, New York, 1962.

History of the Speculative Society of Edinburgh, from its institution in 1764, Edinburgh, 1845.

Hont, I. and Ignatieff, M. (eds.), *Wealth and Virtue: Political Economy in the Scottish Enlightenment*, Cambridge, 1983.

Jardin, André. *Histoire du libéralisme politique, de la crise de l'absolutisme à la Constitution de 1875*, Paris, 1985.

Kelly, George A. 'Liberalism and aristocracy in the French Restoration', *Journal of the History of Ideas*, 26 (October–December 1965), 509–30.

King, Norman. 'La candidature de Bernadotte', *Europe*, 467 (March 1968), 85–92.

Kloocke, Kurt Viredaz, Christian. 'Les *livres de dépenses* de Benjamin Constant', *Annales Benjamin Constant*, 4 (1984), 115–63; 5 (1985), 105–79.

Lajoux, Charles. *Les rapports du gouvernement et des Chambres dans l'Acte Additionnel aux Constitutions de l'Empire du 1815*, Paris, 1902.

Laski, H. J. 'The English Constitution and French public opinion, 1789–1794', *Politica*, 3 (1938), 27–42.

Lefebvre, G. *Les Thermidoriens*, Paris, 1937.

Lough, John. *The 'Philosophes' and Post-Revolutionary France*, Oxford, 1982.

Lyons, M. *France under the Directory*, London, 1975.

McAdam, James I. 'Rousseau and the Friends of Despotism', *Ethics*, 74 (1963), 34–43.

MacCallum, Gerard. 'Negative and Positive Freedom', *The Philosophical Review*, 76 (July 1967), 312–34.

Manuel, Frank E. *The Eighteenth Century Confronts the Gods*, Harvard, 1959.

Meinecke, Friedrich. *Cosmopolitanism and the National State*, Princeton, 1970.

Mellon, Stanley. *The Political Uses of History, a Study of Historians in the French Restoration*, Stanford, California, 1958.

Meynier, A. *Les coups d'état du Directoire*, 3 vols., Paris, 1928.

Michel, Henri. *L'idée de l'État: essai critique sur l'histoire des théories sociales et politiques en France depuis la Révolution*, Paris, 1895.

Michou, Louis. *Le gouvernement parlementaire sous la Restauration*, Paris, 1905.

Miginiac, Louis. *Le régime censitaire en France, spécialement sous la monarchie de Juillet*, Paris, 1900.

Moore, D. C. *The Politics of Deference – a Study of the Mid-Nineteenth Century English Political System*, New York, 1976.

Moraud, Marcel. *Le romantisme français en Angleterre de 1814 à 1848: contribution à l'étude des relations littéraires entre la France et l'Angleterre dans la première moitié du XIXe siècle*, Paris, 1933.

Moravia, Sergio. *Il tramonto dell'illuminismo: filosofia e politica nella società francese (1770–1810)*, Bari, 1968.

Mousnier, Roland. 'Comment les français du XVIIe siècle voyaient la constitution', *XVIIe Siècle* 256 (1955), 9–36.

Munteanu, Basil. 'Episodes Kantiens en Suisse et en France sous le Directoire', *Revue de littérature comparée*, 15 (1935), 387–454.

Namier, Sir Lewis. *The Structure of Politics at the Accession of George III*, 2nd edn., London, 1957.

Ollivier, A. *Le dix-huit Brumaire*, Paris, 1959.

Parker, Harold T. *The Cult of Antiquity and the French Revolutionaries: a Study in the Development of the Revolutionary Spirit*, Chicago, 1937.

Picavet, François. *Les idéologues: essai sur l'histoire des idées et des théories scientifiques, philosophiques, religieuses etc. en France depuis 1789*, Paris, 1891.

Pingaud, Léonce. *Bernadotte, Napoléon et les Bourbons (1797–1844)*, Paris, 1901.

Pocock, J. G. A. *The Machiavellian Moment*, Princeton, 1975.

Porritt, Edward and Anne. *The Unreformed House of Commons: Parliamentary Representation before 1832*, Cambridge, 1903.

Porter, Roy, Teich, M. (eds.), *The Enlightenment in National Context*, Cambridge, 1981.

Radiguet, Léon. *L'Acte Additionnel aux Constitutions de l'Empire du 22 avril 1815*, Caen, 1911.

Reboul, Pierre. *Le mythe anglais dans la littérature française sous la Restauration*, Lille, 1962.

Reiss, Hans. (ed.), *The Political Thought of the German Romantics, 1793–1815*, Oxford, 1955.

Renouvin, P. *Les assemblées provinciales de 1787: origines, devéloppements, résultats*, Paris, 1921.

Richard, Guy. *Les institutions politiques de la France de Louis XV à Giscard d'Estaing*, Paris, 1979.

Rosanvallon, Pierre. *Le moment Guizot*, Paris, 1985.

Roussel, Jean. *Jean Jacques Rousseau en France après la Révolution, 1795–1830: lectures et légendes*, Paris, 1972.

Salis, Jean René de. *Sismondi, 1773–1842: la vie et l'oeuvre d'un cosmopolite philosophe*, Paris, 1932.

Schatz, Albert. *L'individualisme économique et social: ses origines, son évolution, ses formes contemporaines*, Paris, 1907.

Scott, Franklin. 'Bernadotte and the throne of France, 1814', *Journal of Modern History*, 5 (1933), 465–78.

'Benjamin Constant's "Project" for France in 1814', *Journal of Modern History*, 7 (1935), 41–4.

'Propaganda activities of Bernadotte, 1813–1814' in D. McKay, (ed.), *Essays in the History of Modern Europe*, New York, 1936, pp. 16–30.

Sée, Henri. *L'évolution de la pensée politique en France au XVIIIe siècle*, Paris, 1925.

Sévery, William de Charrière de. *La vie de société dans le pays de Vaud à la fin du dix-huitième siècle*, 2 vols., Lausanne and Paris, 1911–12.

Sherwig, John M. *Guineas and Gunpowder, British Foreign Aid in the Wars with France, 1793–1815*, Harvard, 1969.

Shklar, Judith N. *Men and Citizens: a Study of Rousseau's Social Theory*, Cambridge, 1969.

'D'Alembert and the Rehabilitation of History', *Journal of the History of Ideas*, 42, Nº 4 (October–December 1981), 643–64.

Skinner, A. S., Wilson, T. (eds.), *Essays on Adam Smith*, Oxford, 1975.

Skinner, Quentin. 'The idea of negative liberty: philosophical and historical perspectives' in Rorty, R., Schneewind, J. B., Skinner, Q. (eds.), *Philosophy in History – Essays on the Historiography of Philosophy*, Cambridge, 1984, pp. 193–221.

Smitson, Rulon Nephu. *Augustin-Thierry, Social and Political Consciousness in the evolution of a historical method*, Geneva, 1973.

Stendhal (Henri Beyle). 'Mémoires sur les Cent-Jours' in *Courier Anglais*, ed. by Henri Martineau, *Le Divan* (1936), vol. 1, pp. 54–6.

'Discours de Benjamin Constant sur la liberté de la presse', *ibid.* vol. 3, 383–5.

Stone, Bailey. *The 'Parlement' of Paris, 1774–1789*, Chapel Hill, NC, 1981.

Stourm, René. *Les finances de l'ancien régime et de la révolution*, 2 vols., Paris, 1885.

Talmon, J. L. *Romanticism and Revolt: Europe 1814–1848*, New York, 1967.

Bibliography

Tambour, Ernest. *Études sur la Révolution dans le Département de Seine-et-Oise*, Paris, 1913.

Taylor, Charles. 'What's wrong with negative liberty' in A. Ryan (ed.), *The Idea of Freedom*, Oxford, 1979, pp. 175–93.

Ten, C. L. *Mill on Liberty*, Oxford, 1980.

Tönnesson, K. D. *La défaite des sans-culottes: mouvement populaire et réaction bourgeoise en l'an III*, Paris, 1959.

Ullmann, Helene. *Benjamin Constant und seine Beziehungen zum deutschen Geistesleben*, Marburg, 1915.

Veitch, G. S. *The Genesis of Parliamentary Reform*, London, 1913.

Vermale, François. 'Les origines des "Considérations sur la France" de Joseph de Maistre', *Revue d'histoire littéraire de la France*, 33 (1926), 521–9.

Vile, M. J. C. *Constitutionalism and the separation of powers*, Oxford, 1967.

Villefosse, Louis de. *L'opposition à Napoléon*, Paris, 1969.

Vovelle, Michel. *La chute de la monarchie, 1787–92*, Paris, 1972.

Warlomont, R. 'La réprésentation économique dans l'Acte Additionnel aux Constitutions de l'Empire (1815)', *Revue internationale d'histoire politique et constitutionnelle*, 15 (1954), 244–56; *Revue du Nord* (Lille), 37, Nᵒ 145 (1955), 81–2.

Weiss, Charles. *Histoire des refugiés protestants en France*, 2 vols., Paris, 1853.

Welch, Cheryl B. *Liberty and Utility, the French Idéologues and the Transformation of Liberalism*, New York, 1984.

Weulersse, George. *La physiocratie sous les ministères de Turgot et Necker, 1774–1781*, Paris, 1950.

Wittmer, Louis, *Charles de Villiers, 1765–1815: un intermédiaire entre la France et l'Allemagne*, Geneva, 1908.

Wolock, I. *Jacobin Legacy: the Democratic Movement and the Directory*, Princeton, 1970.

Woronoff, Denis. *La république bourgeoise de Thermidor à Brumaire, 1794–99* ('Nouvelle Histoire de la France contemporaine', vol. 3), Paris, 1972.

(f) Conference papers

Actes du Colloque Saint-Just, Sorbonne, 25 June 1967, Paris, 1968.

'Benjamin Constant', *Actes du Congrès Benjamin Constant*, Lausanne, October 1967, ed. by Pierre Cordey and Jean Luc Seylaz, Geneva, 1968.

'Mme de Staël et l'Europe', *Actes du Colloque de Coppet*, 18–24 July 1966, Paris, 1970.

'Le Groupe de Coppet', *Actes et documents du deuxième Colloque de Coppet*, Geneva–Paris, 1977.

Actes du troisième Colloque Coppet, 1980, Oxford, Voltaire Foundation, 1982.

343

Index

Index

Index

Index